T0192261

Lecture Notes in Computer Science

Lecture Notes in Artificial Intelligence   14640

Founding Editor

Jörg Siekmann

Series Editors

Randy Goebel, *University of Alberta, Edmonton, Canada*
Wolfgang Wahlster, *DFKI, Berlin, Germany*
Zhi-Hua Zhou, *Nanjing University, Nanjing, China*

The series Lecture Notes in Artificial Intelligence (LNAI) was established in 1988 as a topical subseries of LNCS devoted to artificial intelligence.

The series publishes state-of-the-art research results at a high level. As with the LNCS mother series, the mission of the series is to serve the international R & D community by providing an invaluable service, mainly focused on the publication of conference and workshop proceedings and postproceedings.

Amparo Alonso-Betanzos ·
Bertha Guijarro-Berdiñas ·
Verónica Bolón-Canedo ·
Elena Hernández-Pereira ·
Oscar Fontenla-Romero · David Camacho ·
Juan Ramón Rabuñal · Manuel Ojeda-Aciego ·
Jesús Medina · José C. Riquelme ·
Alicia Troncoso
Editors

Advances in Artificial Intelligence

20th Conference of the Spanish Association
for Artificial Intelligence, CAEPIA 2024
A Coruña, Spain, June 19–21, 2024
Proceedings

 Springer

Editors
Amparo Alonso-Betanzos ⓘ
University of A Coruña
A Coruña, La Coruña, Spain

Bertha Guijarro-Berdiñas ⓘ
University of A Coruña
A Coruña, La Coruña, Spain

Verónica Bolón-Canedo ⓘ
University of A Coruña
A Coruña, La Coruña, Spain

Elena Hernández-Pereira ⓘ
University of A Coruña
A Coruña, Spain

Oscar Fontenla-Romero ⓘ
University of A Coruña
A Coruña, Spain

David Camacho
Technical University of Madrid
Madrid, Spain

Juan Ramón Rabuñal ⓘ
University of A Coruña
A Coruña, Spain

Manuel Ojeda-Aciego
University of Malaga
Malaga, Spain

Jesús Medina ⓘ
University of Cádiz
Cádiz, Spain

José C. Riquelme ⓘ
University of Seville
Seville, Spain

Alicia Troncoso ⓘ
Data Science and Big Data Lab
Pablo de Olavide University
Seville, Spain

ISSN 0302-9743   ISSN 1611-3349 (electronic)
Lecture Notes in Artificial Intelligence
ISBN 978-3-031-62798-9   ISBN 978-3-031-62799-6 (eBook)
https://doi.org/10.1007/978-3-031-62799-6

LNCS Sublibrary: SL7 – Artificial Intelligence

This Springer imprint is published by the registered company Springer Nature Switzerland AG
The registered company address is: Gewerbestrasse 11, 6330 Cham, Switzerland

If disposing of this product, please recycle the paper.

Preface

This volume contains the selected papers presented at CAEPIA 2024, the XX Conference of the Spanish Association for Artificial Intelligence, held from June 19–21, 2024, in A Coruña, Spain. The CAEPIA series of conferences is a biennial event that began in 1985. Previous editions took place in Granada, Alicante, Málaga, Murcia, Gijón, San Sebastián, Santiago de Compostela, Sevilla, La Laguna, Madrid, Albacete, and Salamanca.

CAEPIA is a forum open to researchers from all over the world to present and discuss their latest scientific and technological advances in Artificial Intelligence (AI). Authors were kindly requested to submit unpublished original papers describing relevant achievements on AI topics. Papers on formal, methodological, technical, or applied research were welcome.

Several federated congresses and workshops related to relevant AI tracks took place within CAEPIA: XXII Spanish Congress on Fuzzy Logic and Technologies (ESTYLF); XV Spanish Congress on Metaheuristics, Evolutionary and Bioinspired Algorithms (MAEB); XI Symposium of Theory and Applications of Data Mining (TAMIDA); I Spanish Congress on Recommender Systems (SISREC); I Workshop on Artificial Intelligence in Education (TIAE); and I Spanish Society of Artificial Intelligence in Biomedicine Workshop (IABiomed).

Within CAEPIA 2024, the Doctoral Consortium (DC) was also organized. This was a forum for PhD students to interact with other researchers by discussing their PhD progress and plans. With the aim of highlighting the practical importance of AI, the 5th Competition on Mobile Apps with AI Techniques was held at CAEPIA, as well as the AI Dissemination Video Competition. CAEPIA 2024 aimed to maintain the high-quality standards of previous editions.

Apart from the presentation of technical full papers and the DC, the scientific program of CAEPIA 2024 included an app contest and a track on outstanding recent papers (Key Works: KW) already published in renowned journals or forums.

CAEPIA aims to be recognized as a flagship conference in AI. This implies achieving high-quality standards in the review process. In particular, the total number of submissions to CAEPIA 2024 was 228 (neither DC nor KW submissions were included in those 228 contributions since their review process was different). Only 27 outstanding manuscripts were selected for this volume after a thorough double-blind review process that involved at least 2 reviews per submission. This involved a lot of tough work by the CAEPIA 2024 Program Committee (PC) that was really appreciated. The reviewers judged the overall quality of the submitted manuscripts, together with the quality of the methodology employed, the soundness of the conclusions, the significance of the topic, the clarity, and the organization, among other evaluation fields. The reviewers stated their confidence in the subject area in addition to detailed written comments. On the basis of the reviews, the PC Chairs proposed the final decisions that were ultimately made by both the CAEPIA 2024 general chairman and the president of the Organizing Committee.

Likewise, CAEPIA 2024 invited an internationally renowned researcher for a plenary talk. José María Lasalla (Universidad Pontificia Comillas, Spain) presented "AI and Human Authenticity."

CAEPIA and the organization of CAEPIA 2024 recognized the best PhD work submitted to the DC with a prize, as well as the best student and conference paper presented at CAEPIA 2024. Furthermore, CAEPIA 2024 also aimed to promote the presence of women in AI research. As in previous editions, the Frances Allen award recognized the two best AI PhD theses defended by women during the last two years.

The editors of this volume would like to thank many people who contributed to the success of CAEPIA 2024: authors, members of the Scientific and Program Committees, invited speakers, event organizers, etc. We would especially like to recognise the tireless work of the Organizing Committee, our local sponsors (Faculty of Informatics, University of A Coruña), the Springer team, and AEPIA for their support.

Last but not least, on behalf of the CAEPIA 2024 participants, the CAEPIA organizers really thank the University of A Coruña (local premises for the conference) and the whole Spanish community working in AI (and their many foreign collaborators) for making this event a real success.

June 2024

Óscar Fontenla-Romero
Amparo Alonso-Betanzos
Bertha Guijarro-Berdiñas
Elena Hernández-Pereira
Verónica Bolón-Canedo
Noelia Sánchez-Maroño
Beatriz Pérez-Sánchez
David Camacho
Juan R. Rabuñal
Manuel Ojeda-Aciego
Jesús Medina
José C. Riquelme
Alicia Troncoso

Organization

General Chairs

Amparo Alonso-Betanzos   University of A Coruña, Spain
Bertha Guijarro-Berdiñas   University of A Coruña, Spain

Awards Committee Chair

Eva Onaindía   Polytechnic University of Valencia, Spain

Tutorials and Workshops Chair

Óscar Fontenla-Romero   University of A Coruña, Spain

General Session Chair

Óscar Fontenla-Romero   University of A Coruña, Spain

Competitions Chairs

Alberto Bugarín   University of Santiago de Compostela, Spain
Jose Antonio Gámez   University of Castilla-La Mancha, Spain

Editors of the LNAI Proceedings of CAEPIA

Elena Hernández-Pereira   University of A Coruña, Spain
Verónica Bolón-Canedo   University of A Coruña, Spain

Conference and Workshops Chairs

XXII ESTYLF

Manuel Ojeda-Aciego   University of Málaga, Spain
Jesús Medina   University of Cádiz, Spain

XV MAEB

Juan Ramón Rabuñal   University of A Coruña, Spain
David Camacho   Autonomous University of Madrid, Spain

XI TAMIDA

Alicia Troncoso   Pablo de Olavide University, Spain
José C. Riquelme   University of Seville, Spain
José Alejandro Fernández Cuesta   Complutense University of Madrid, Spain

I IABiomed

Alejandro Rodríguez González   Polytechnic University of Madrid, Spain
José Alberto Benítez Andrades University of León, Spain
María del Mar Marcos López   Jaume I University, Spain

I SISREC

Jesús Bobadilla   Polytechnic University of Madrid, Spain
Antonio Moreno   University of Rovira i Virgili, Spain
Antonio Bahamonde   University of Oviedo, Spain
Raciel Yera Toledo   University of Jaén, Spain

I TIAE

Francisco Bellas Bouza   University of A Coruña, Spain
Sara Guerreiro Santalla   University of A Coruña, Spain
Óscar Fontenla-Romero   University of A Coruña, Spain
Noelia Sánchez-Maroño   University of A Coruña, Spain

Organizing Committee

Publicity

Laura Morán-Fernández   University of A Coruña, Spain

Web

Jorge Paz-Ruza   University of A Coruña, Spain
Samuel Suárez-Marcote   University of A Coruña, Spain

Area Chairpersons

Óscar Corcho   Polytechnic University of Madrid, Spain
Javier del Ser   TECNALIA, Spain
Juan Manuel Fernandez Luna   University of Granada, Spain
Jesús García Herrero   Carlos III University of Madrid, Spain
Carlos Gómez Rodríguez   University of A Coruña, Spain
Serafín Moral Callejón   University of Granada, Spain
José Luis Pérez de la Cruz Molina   University of Málaga, Spain
Petia Radeva   University of Barcelona, Spain
Camino Rodríguez Vela   University of Oviedo, Spain

Program Committee

Amparo Alonso-Betanzos   University of A Coruña, Spain
Lourdes Araujo   National University of Education at Distance
                                 (UNED), Spain
Jose Maria Armingol Moreno   Carlos III University of Madrid, Spain
Ivan Armuelles   University of Panamá, Panama
Jaume Bacardit   Newcastle University, UK
Antonio Bahamonde   University of Oviedo, Spain
Alvaro Barreiro   University of A Coruña, Spain
Edurne Barrenechea   Public University of Navarre, Spain
Senén Barro   University of Santiago de Compostela, Spain
Dena Bazazian   University of Plymouth, UK
Ana M. Bernardos   Polytechnic University of Madrid, Spain
Concha Bielza Lozoya   Polytechnic University of Madrid, Spain
Daniel Borrajo   Carlos III University of Madrid, Spain
Juan Botia   King's College London, UK

Antonio Muñoz	University of Málaga, Spain
Bhalaji Nagarajan	University of Barcelona, Spain
Ismael Navas	University of Málaga, Spain
José Fernando Nuñez	University of Barcelona, Spain
Manuel Ojeda-Aciego	University of Málaga, Spain
José Angel Olivas	University of Castilla-La Mancha, Spain
Eva Onaindia	Polytechnic University of Valencia, Spain
Sascha Ossowski	Rey Juan Carlos University, Spain
Jose Palma	University of Murcia, Spain
C. Alejandro Parraga	Autonomous University of Barcelona, Spain
Miguel Angel Patricio	Carlos III University of Madrid, Spain
Juan Pavón Mestras	Complutense University of Madrid, Spain
Antonio Peregrin	University of Huelva, Spain
Eduardo Perez	Maimónides Biomedical Research Institute of Córdoba, Spain
José Luis Pérez de la Cruz Molina	University of Málaga, Spain
Giuseppe Pezzano	University of Barcelona, Spain
Hector Pomares	University of Granada, Spain
Jose M. Puerta	University of Castilla-La Mancha, Spain
Camino R. Vela	University of Oviedo, Spain
Noelia Rico	University of Oviedo, Spain
Ramon Rizo	University of Alicante, Spain
Javier Rodenas	University of Barcelona, Spain
Alejandro Rodriguez	Polytechnic University of Madrid, Spain
Rosa Rodríguez	University of Jaén, Spain
Diego Gabriel Rossit	National University of the South (CONICET), Argentina
Elias Said Hung	International University of La Rioja, Spain
Antonio Salmeron	University of Almería, Spain
Luciano Sanchez	University of Oviedo, Spain
Jose Salvador Sanchez	Jaume I University, Spain
Araceli Sanchis	Carlos III University of Madrid, Spain
Encarna Segarra	Polytechnic University of Valencia, Spain
M. Paz Sesmero Lorente	Carlos III University of Madrid, Spain
Igor Škrjanc	Univerza v Ljubljani, Slovenia
Emilio Soria	University of Valencia, Spain
Maria Taboada	University of Santiago de Compostela, Spain
Estefania Talavera	University of Groningen, The Netherlands
Erik Torrontegui	Carlos III University of Madrid, Spain
Alicia Troncoso	University Pablo de Olavide, Spain
L. Alfonso Ureña-López	University of Jaén, Spain
Rafael Valencia-Garcia	University of Murcia, Spain

Alfredo Vellido	Polytechnic University of Catalunya, Spain
Sebastián Ventura	University of Córdoba, Spain
José Ramón Villar	University of Oviedo, Spain
Jesús Alcalá-Fernández	University of Granada, Spain
Cristina Alcalde	University of the Basque Country UPV/EHU, Spain
Sergio Alonso	University of Granada, Spain
Jose M. Alonso	University of Santiago de Compostela, Spain
Roberto G. Aragón	University of Cádiz, Spain
María José Benítez-Caballero	University of Cádiz, Spain
Fernando Bobillo	University of Zaragoza, Spain
Ana Burusco	Public University of Navarre, Spain
Inmaculada P. Cabrera	University of Málaga, Spain
Francisco Javier Cabrerizo	University of Granada, Spain
Tomasa Calvo	University of Alcalá, Spain
Pablo Carmona	University of Extremadura, Spain
Juan Luis Castro	University of Granada, Spain
Pablo Cordero	University of Málaga, Spain
María Eugenia Cornejo Piñeiro	University of Cádiz, Spain
Susana Cubillo	Polytechnic University of Madrid, Spain
Rocio De Andres	University of Salamanca, Spain
Miguel Delgado	University of Granada, Spain
Susana Díaz	University of Oviedo, Spain
Jorge Elorza	University of Navarre, Spain
Javier Fernandez	Public University of Navarre, Spain
Mikel Galar	Public University of Navarre, Spain
Jose Luis Garcia-Lapresta	University of Valladolid, Spain
Lluis Godo	Institute for Research in Artificial Intelligence, IIIA – CSIC, Spain
Francisco Herrera Triguero	University of Granada, Spain
Enrique Herrera Viedma	University of Granada, Spain
Maria Teresa Lamata	University of Granada, Spain
David Lobo	University of Cádiz, Spain
Bonifacio Llamazares	University of Valladolid, Spain
Carlos Lopez-Molina	Public University of Navarre, Spain
Nicolas Madrid	University of Cádiz, Spain
Luis Magdalena	Polytechnic University of Madrid, Spain
Maria J. Martin-Bautista	University of Granada, Spain
Luis Martinez	University of Jaén, Spain
Sebastià Massanet	University of the Balearic Islands, Spain
Francisco Mata	University of Jaén, Spain
Jesús Medina	University of Cádiz, Spain

Javier Montero	University Complutense of Madrid, Spain
Susana Montes	University of Oviedo, Spain
Juan Moreno-Garcia	University of Castilla-La Mancha, Spain
Ana Pradera	Rey Juan Carlos University, Spain
Eloísa Ramirez-Poussa	University of Cádiz, Spain
Jordi Recasens	Polytechnic University of Catalonia, Spain
Juan Vicente Riera	University of the Balearic Islands, Spain
Rosa M. Rodriguez Dominguez	University of Jaén, Spain
Francisco P. Romero	University of Castilla-La Mancha, Spain
Daniel Sanchez	University of Granada, Spain
Jose Antonio Sanz Delgado	Public University of Navarre, Spain
Jesus Serrano- Guerrero	University of Castilla-La Mancha, Spain
Miguel Angel Sicilia	University of Alcalá, Spain
Vicenc Torra	Umeå University, Sweden
Aida Valls	University Rovira I Virgili, Spain
Jose Luis Verdegay	University of Granada, Spain

Contents

Taking Advantage of Depth Information for Semantic Segmentation in Field-Measured Vineyards

Ángela Casado-García[1] , Jónathan Heras[1](✉) , Roberto Marani[2] ,
and Annalisa Milella[2]

[1] Department of Mathematics and Computer Science, University of La Rioja,
Logroño, Spain
{angela.casado,jonathan.heras}@unirioja.es
[2] Institute of Intelligent Industrial Technologies and Systems for Advanced
Manufacturing, National Research Council of Italy, Rome, Italy
{roberto.marani,annalisa.milella}@stiima.cnr.it

Abstract. RGB-D cameras mounted on moving agricultural robotic platforms provide detailed information about both appearance and volume of plants. Those images can be analysed by means of deep segmentation models; however, such methods usually dismiss depth information. In this work, we aim to address this challenge by comparing four deep learning models for segmenting canopy and grape bunches in RGB and RGB-D images. In our experiments, RGB-D models achieved better results than their RGB counterparts, improving up to a 1.83% the mean segmentation accuracy. These findings highlight the potential of cost-effective RGB-based depth estimation techniques for accurate plant segmentation in agricultural settings, paving the way for wider adoption of RGB-D technology.

Keywords: Semantic Segmentation · Precision Agriculture · RGB-D

1 Introduction

Analysing natural images captured by moving robotic platforms is a key point for yield monitoring at the plant level [11]. Its actual implementation requires low-cost sensors able to provide detailed information about both appearance and volume of the targets; for instance, the whole plants or single fruits [10]. Usually, sensors employed in agricultural robots are standard RGB cameras, which provide a flat 2D representation of the targets [4]. In contrast, RGB-D cameras are able to produce three-dimensional (3D) colored models of the crops, and can give more information that is helpful for fruit monitoring and counting [4].

In this context, convolutional neural models have been widely used to automatically segment crop elements based on their color and texture attributes from

© The Author(s), under exclusive license to Springer Nature Switzerland AG 2024
A. Alonso-Betanzos et al. (Eds.): CAEPIA 2024, LNAI 14640, pp. 1–8, 2024.
https://doi.org/10.1007/978-3-031-62799-6_1

RGB images [1], and depth information can reduce the uncertainty of the segmentation of objects having similar appearance information [3]. However, it is not clear what is the optimal way of fusing RGB and depth information. Several works suggest that depth information can help the segmentation of classes of close depth, appearance and location [5]. On the contrary, it is better to use only RGB information to recognize object classes containing high variability of their depth values [5].

In this paper, we aim to address this question related to the usage of depth information for the segmentation of different elements (canopy and grape bunches) in a vineyard. Namely, we investigate the effectiveness of utilizing RGB-D images for accurate and efficient segmentation in viticulture using deep segmentation models. In this way, we seek to determine whether the fusion of RGB and depth data can enhance the segmentation accuracy compared to using RGB data alone.

2   Materials and Methods

In this section, we present both the dataset and computational materials and methods employed in this work.

2.1   Dataset

Semantic segmentation is a task that classifies every pixel of an image among target classes of interest. In the context of viticulture, segmentation of specific targets, such as the canopy and fruits, can be the key for yield monitoring and robotic harvesting. In order to apply segmentation methods based on Deep Learning techniques, it is necessary an annotated dataset (that is, pairs of natural images and their corresponding mask with the position of the objects).

In this work, the dataset was acquired in a vineyard in San Donaci (Italy) with an Intel Realsense D435 camera mounted on a moving robot. The camera acquired lateral views of the line of the grape plants at a distance of 0.8 to 1 m. Under these conditions, every image covered a horizontal field of view between 0.9 and 1.2 m to completely frame every plant in a single image. These images were taken at three different times of the year: in July (where the grapes are small and green and the plant has few leaves), in September (where the grapes are black and the plant has many leaves), and in October (where there are no grapes and the plant has very few leaves), see Fig. 1.

The dataset consists of 265 colour images in PNG format, see Fig. 2(a). In addition, the Intel Realsense D435 camera provides the depth of each image in the RAW format, see Fig. 2(b). Finally, the images were manually annotated by visually inspecting them to produce the masks with the regions corresponding to the grape bunches and canopy, see Fig. 2(c). The dataset was divided into two subsets: the training set (212 images) and the test set (54 images). The dataset is available at the following webpage https://github.com/joheras/ECSDVineyardDataset/.

Fig. 1. RGB images acquired on different dates: (a) July, (b) September, (c) October. (Color figure online)

There are two versions of the dataset: RGB and RGB-D. In the RGB version of the dataset, the images of both the training and test set are RGB images — that is, the depth information was discharged. In the RGB-D version, the information from RGB channels and depth channel of the images of both the training and test set was combined as follows. The RAW images captured with the Intel Realsense D435 camera provide information about the depth of objects that are located up to 65 m away (see Fig. 3(a)) — the ideal working range for the camera is between 0.3 m and 3 m although in principle the max range that can be coded is about 65 m as the depth map uses 16bit depth with a depth unit of 1 mm. However, plants are located less than 3 m away; hence, the depth information related to objects farther than 3 m away is removed from the image (see Fig. 3(b)). Finally, such an image is combined with the RGB image obtaining an RGB-A image with four channels where the depth information is used as the alpha channel, see Fig. 3(c) — this procedure to fuse RGB images and depth information is known as early fusion [8].

2.2 Computational Methods

From the training sets of the RGB and RGB-D datasets, several deep-learning segmentation architectures were fine-tuned [13]. Namely, we have employed the Unet++ architecture with a ResNet50 backbone [14], the DeepLabV3 architecture with a ResNext50 backbone [2], and the Manet architecture with EfficientNetB3 and ResNest50 backbones [7].

The architectures with their respective backbones were implemented in PyTorch [12] and have been trained thanks to the functionality of the FastAI

Fig. 2. (a) A sample RGB image acquired by the Intel Realsense D435 camera; (b) The corresponding depth image; (c) The annotation of the image. Black pixels correspond with the background, red pixels with the regions of the grape bunches, and green pixels with the canopy regions. (Color figure online)

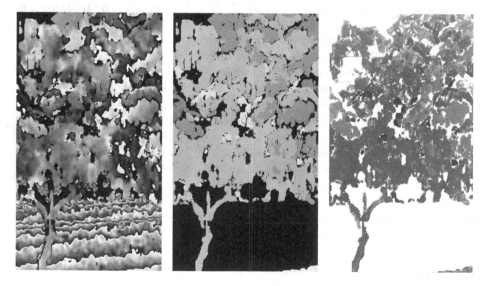

Fig. 3. Fusion process of the RGB image from Fig. 2(a) and its depth information. (a) Depth image with information up to 65 m; (b) Depth image with information up to 3 m; (c) RGB-A image produced by combining the image from Fig. 2(a) and the image from Fig. 3(b). (Color figure online)

library [6] on an Nvidia RTX 2080 Ti GPU. The procedure presented in [6] was employed to set the learning rate for the different architectures. Also, early stopping was applied in all the architectures to avoid overfitting. In order to feed RGB-A images to these architectures, they were converted to RGB images using the Pillow library. The code used for training the models is available at https:// github.com/ancasag/segmentationVineyards.

After training, all the models were then evaluated on the corresponding test set of 54 annotated images using the mean segmentation accuracy of the $c-th$ class (MSA_c):

$$MSA_c = mean \left(\frac{TP_c}{n_{obs,c}}, \forall images \in dataset \right). \tag{1}$$

where TP_c is the number of true positives, i.e. correct pixel labels over the entire population of the $c-th$ class ($nobs, c$) [9].

3 Results and Discussion

The performance of the trained networks was first evaluated using the RGB version of the dataset, see Table 1. If the segmentation networks are compared, the DeepLab-Resnext model showed better overall segmentation accuracy than the other networks. The Unet++-ResNet50 model produced the best results for canopy segmentation with an accuracy of 79.98, whereas the Deeplab-Resnext model, with an accuracy of 94.46, outperformed the others for segmenting objects of the Grape class.

Table 1. Mean segmentation accuracy (percentage) computed on test images of the RGB dataset. In bold the best results.

Network	Background	Canopy	Grapes	Total
Unet++-ResNet50	95.48	**79.98**	94.46	93.64
Deeplab-ResNext	97.66	78.57	**95.10**	**94.72**
Manet-Efficientnet	**97.72**	76.45	95.01	94.50
Manet-ResNest	93.58	78.46	93.15	92.05

The results for the RGB-D version of the dataset are presented in Table 2. The RBG-D models improved between 2% and 4% the overall mean segmentation accuracy of their RGB counterparts. For this version of the dataset, the best model was built using the architecture Unet++ with a ResNet50 backbone that achieved a segmentation accuracy for the canopy class of 81.91%, for grape bunches of 95.83%, and an overall mean segmentation accuracy of 95.47%. This shows the positive effect of adding the depth information to the RGB image, since adding such information allows the models to focus on the objects of interest,

Table 2. Mean segmentation accuracy (percentage) computed on test images of the RGB-D dataset. In bold the best results.

Network	Background	Canopy	Grapes	Total
Unet++-ResNet50	**97.91**	**81.91**	**95.83**	**95.47**
Deeplab-ResNext	97.04	81.15	95.33	94.82
Manet-Efficientnet	95.53	67.70	95.50	92.96
Manet-ResNest	97.52	81.51	95.52	95.12

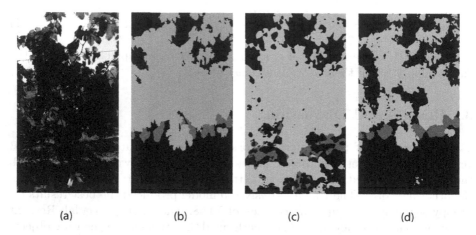

(a)   (b)   (c)   (d)

Fig. 4. (a) Original Image; (b) Mask; (c) Prediction with the best RGB model; (d) Prediction with the best RGB-D model. (Color figure online)

and also discard elements of the background that can be wrongly classified as either leaves or grape bunches.

In addition to the raw numbers, several conclusions can be drawn from the segmentation of the different models as shown in Fig. 4. As we can see in Fig. 4(c), the best RGB segmentation model finds where the leaves are but misses many of them; and for the grapes, such a model is not able to find them and gets confused with the pole — in both cases, this might happen due to the similarity of colors that makes difficult for the model to distinguish them accurately. In contrast, the RGB-D model, see Fig. 4(d), knows where the grapes are and can differentiate the pole (this occurs because the model gains additional information about the scene's geometry and spatial relationships), but mixes some of the leaves with the background.

4   Conclusions and Further Work

In this work, depth information has been incorporated to automatically segment images captured with a camera mounted on a moving agricultural tractor. The results show the benefits of working with RGB-D images instead of only using RGB images — improvements between 2% and 4% were obtained.

In order to train RGB-D models, we applied a procedure known as early fusion to combine RGB images and depth information. As further work, we aim to investigate other modalities for fusing RGB images and depth information, such as middle and late fusion [8]. Moreover, we plan to study the performance of our models when low-cost images, obtained, for instance, from a mobile phone, are used. To achieve this aim, it will be necessary to study models that are able to generate depth information from RGB images and use them with our models.

Acknowledgements. This work was partially supported by Grant PID2020-115225RB-I00 funded by MCIN/AEI/10.13039/501100011033, Agencia de Desarrollo Económico de La Rioja ADER 2022-I-IDI-00015, and E-crops - Technologies for Digital and Sustainable Agriculture, Italian Ministry of University and Research (MUR) under the PON Agrifood Program (No. ARS01_01136); CNR DIITET project DIT.AD022.207, STRIVE-le Scienze per le TRansizioni Industriale, Verde ed Energetica (FOE 2022), sub task activity Agro-Sensing2. Ángela Casado-García has a FPI grant from Community of La Rioja 2020, at the moment, she is in the Postdoctoral Orientation Period (POP). The authors are grateful to Cantina San Donaci agricultural farm for hosting experimental tests in the context of the E-crops project.

References

1. Casado-García, A., Heras, J., Milella, A., Marani, R.: Semi-supervised deep learning and low-cost cameras for the semantic segmentation of natural images in viticulture. Precis. Agric. **23**, 2001–2026 (2022)
2. Chen, L.C., Zhu, Y., Papandreou, G., Schroff, F., Adam, H.: Encoder-decoder with atrous separable convolution for semantic image segmentation. In: Proceedings of the European Conference on Computer Vision (ECCV), pp. 801–818 (2018). https://doi.org/10.1007/978-3-030-01234-2_49
3. Couprie, C., Farabet, C., Najman, L., LeCun, Y.: Indoor semantic segmentation using depth information. In: Proceedings of International Conference on Learning Representations (2013)
4. Fu, L., Gao, F., Wu, J., Li, R., Karkee, M., Zhang, Q.: Application of consumer RGB-D cameras for fruit detection and localization in field: a critical review. Comput. Electron. Agric. **177**, 105687 (2020)
5. Hazirbas, C., Ma, L., Domokos, C., Cremers, D.: FuseNet: incorporating depth into semantic segmentation via fusion-based CNN architecture. In: Lai, S.-H., Lepetit, V., Nishino, K., Sato, Y. (eds.) ACCV 2016. LNCS, vol. 10111, pp. 213–228. Springer, Cham (2017). https://doi.org/10.1007/978-3-319-54181-5_14
6. Howard, J., Gugger, S., Chintala, S.: Deep Learning for Coders with Fastai and PyTorch: AI Applications Without a PhD. O'Reilly Media, Incorporated (2020). https://books.google.es/books?id=xd6LxgEACAAJ
7. Li, R.: Multiattention network for semantic segmentation of fine-resolution remote sensing images. IEEE Trans. Geosci. Remote Sens. **60**, 1–13 (2021)
8. Li, Y., Zhang, J., Cheng, Y., Huang, K., Tan, T.: Semantics-guided multi-level RGB-D feature fusion for indoor semantic segmentation. In: 2017 IEEE International Conference on Image Processing (ICIP), pp. 1262–1266. IEEE (2017)

9. Marani, R., Milella, A., Petitti, A., Reina, G.: Deep neural networks for grape bunch segmentation in natural images from a consumer-grade camera. Precision Agric. **22**(2), 387–413 (2021). https://doi.org/10.1007/s11119-020-09736-0
10. Nguyen, T.T., Vandevoorde, K., Wouters, N., Kayacan, E., De Baerdemaeker, J.G., Saeys, W.: Detection of red and bicoloured apples on tree with an RGB-D camera. Biosys. Eng. **146**, 33–44 (2016)
11. Osco, L.P., Nogueira, K., Ramos, A.P.M., Pinheiro, M.M.F., Furuya, D.E.G., Gonçalves, W.N., et al.: Semantic segmentation of citrus-orchard using deep neural networks and multispectral UAV-based imagery. Precision Agric. **1**, 1–18 (2021)
12. Paszke, A., Gross, S., Massa, F., Lerer, A., Bradbury, J., Chanan, G., et al.: Pytorch: an imperative style, high-performance deep learning library. In: Advances in Neural Information Processing Systems, vol. 32, pp. 8024–8035. Curran Associates, Inc. (2019). https://arxiv.org/abs/1912.01703
13. Sharif Razavian, A., Azizpour, H., Sullivan, J., Carlsson, S.: CNN features off-the-shelf: an astounding baseline for recognition. In: Proceedings of the IEEE Conference on Computer Vision and Pattern Recognition Workshops, pp. 806–813 (2014)
14. Zhou, Z., Rahman Siddiquee, M.M., Tajbakhsh, N., Liang, J.: UNet++: a nested U-net architecture for medical image segmentation. In: Stoyanov, D., et al. (eds.) DLMIA/ML-CDS -2018. LNCS, vol. 11045, pp. 3–11. Springer, Cham (2018). https://doi.org/10.1007/978-3-030-00889-5_1

Advancing Computational Frontiers: Spiking Neural Networks in High-Energy Efficiency Computing Across Diverse Domains

Bahgat Ayasi[1]([✉])(ID), Ángel M. García-Vico[2](ID), Cristóbal J. Carmona[2](ID), and Mohammed Saleh[3](ID)

[1] Computer Science Department, University of Jaén, Jaén, Spain
ba000034@red.ujaen.es
[2] Andalusian Research Institute in Data Science and Computational Intelligence (DaSCI), University of Jaén, Jaén, Spain
{agvico,ccarmona}@ujaen.es
[3] Information Technology Center, Al-Istiqlal University, Jericho, Palestine
msaleh@pass.ps

Abstract. This comprehensive review explores the rapidly advancing field of Spiking Neural Networks (SNNs), particularly emphasizing their computational capabilities and potential for energy-efficient computing. SNNs distinguish themselves from traditional neural networks by skillfully processing complex, time-sensitive binary inputs through intricate encoding strategies and dynamic learning algorithms. This paper discusses various encoding techniques and evaluates several neuron models integral to SNN architecture, such as the Leaky Integrate-and-Fire, Hodgkin-Huxley, and Izhikevich models. These models are appraised for their trade-offs between computational simplicity and biological plausibility. Additionally, we examine the energy-saving expertise of SNNs relative to their traditional counterparts, identifying challenges in scaling and the intricacy of training. The review explores a spectrum of training techniques for SNNs, including supervised, unsupervised, and reinforcement learning approaches. This paper culminates by highlighting imperative future research directions in SNNs. It underscores the pressing need for developing sophisticated training algorithms and customizing models to augment efficiency and versatility in energy-conscious computing. These focal points are suggested as pivotal for driving the field forward and unlocking the full potential of SNNs in real-world applications.

Keywords: Spike · Power efficiency · STDP

1 Introduction

Amidst AI's rapid advancements, the challenge of climate change, exacerbated by rising global energy consumption, becomes paramount. AI, mainly

A. Alonso-Betanzos et al. (Eds.): CAEPIA 2024, LNAI 14640, pp. 9–18, 2024.
https://doi.org/10.1007/978-3-031-62799-6_2

through expanding machine learning applications, significantly contributes to this increased energy demand, raising concerns about the environmental impact of technological progress. The sustainability of AI is questioned as advanced models like BERT evolve into more complex systems like GPT-4, which may comprise up to 300 billion parameters by 2023 [1], highlighting the escalating energy requirements for AI development and deployment.

The concept of trustworthy AI, emphasizing legal, ethical, and robustness criteria, gains importance, advocating for AI systems that are efficient, reliable, and socially and environmentally responsible. [2] This necessitates a paradigm shift towards more energy-efficient computational methods to mitigate the environmental footprint of neural networks, aligning AI development with ethical and sustainable practices.

Spiking Neural Networks (SNNs), the third generation of neural network models, emerge as a viable solution, capable of processing temporal and asynchronous inputs with significantly lower energy consumption [4]. This positions SNNs as a critical technology for sustainable AI development, promising to reduce computational energy demands while retaining or improving performance.

Despite progress, integrating neuron types, coding methods, learning techniques, and architectures into a cohesive SNN framework presents a challenge. This research addresses this by synthesizing these components to understand SNNs' role in energy-efficient computing, aiming to bridge the gap between SNNs' potential and practical application in various domains.

This paper systematically reviews SNNs within the sustainable AI context, exploring their challenges and future directions. It aims to enhance understanding of SNNs' contribution to low-power, high-performance computing, supporting the broader goal of developing energy-efficient AI systems that reflect the adaptability of biological neural networks, thus fostering sustainable technological advancement amid environmental challenges.

2   Related Work

This section synthesizes essential research on Spiking Neural Networks (SNNs), charting their development and diversity with an emphasis on simulation techniques, precision in spike-timing-dependent plasticity, and evolving SNN architectures, particularly for spatiotemporal processing. Critical studies include foundational work on simulation strategies [4], advancements in SNN architectures [8], learning algorithms and neuron models [9], optimization techniques for energy efficiency [10], and hardware implementations [7]. Despite the comprehensive coverage, these reviews often overlook the critical aspect of power efficiency, particularly in recent advancements in low-power neuromorphic hardware and real-world applications.

Moreover, discussions on encoding techniques, learning rules, and network architectures [5], as well as applications in vision and biological neuron theories, along with software frameworks for data science, strides in neuromorphic computing [11]. The concluding part outlines the challenges in SNN implementation and the need for new computational theories, particularly emphasizing the gap in addressing energy efficiency in SNNs, and learning algorithms are presented. [6]

Our research aims to bridge this gap by focusing on the power efficiency of SNN components. By emphasizing sustainable AI development, we seek to inspire future research toward creating energy-efficient SNN models and hardware that are both technologically advanced and environmentally responsible.

3   Comprehensive Exploration of SNNs

SNNs represent the third generation of neural networks, offering a dynamic and biologically inspired computational approach. SNNs and ANNs differ fundamentally in information processing, learning methods, temporal data handling, and energy efficiency. SNNs use spikes for asynchronous communication, contrasted with ANNs' structure. Additionally, SNNs are designed for higher energy efficiency, especially on neuromorphic hardware, making them more sustainable than the computationally intensive ANNs [7]. SNNs utilize spiking neurons and synapses to process information that closely mimics biological neural systems [4].

Spiking Neurons: The core unit of SNNs, spiking neurons, communicates through discrete spikes or action potentials, reflecting brief electrical impulses. Their operation is governed by the membrane potential, which triggers a spike when exceeding a specific threshold. This binary spiking mechanism is pivotal for the various coding strategies in SNNs, emphasizing the significance of spike timing and patterns in data processing.

Synapses: Synapses are the connection points between neurons, facilitating signal transmission. A synapse's strength and type (excitatory or inhibitory) significantly influence how an incoming spike affects the post-synaptic neuron's membrane potential. The synaptic weight, W, modulates this effect. Synaptic dynamics are crucial in shaping the network's overall behavior and are expressed in Eq. (1),

$$V_{\text{post}}(t) = V_{\text{post}}(t^-) + W \cdot \delta(t - t_{\text{pre}}) \tag{1}$$

where $V_{\text{post}}(t)$ is the post-synaptic potential and t_{pre} is the time of the pre-synaptic spike [4].

The complexity of SNNs arises from the sequence and precise timing of spikes, which carry rich and complex data. This underlines the exploration of encoding strategies to effectively harness the informational potential of spike timing within neural computation.

3.1   Encoding Techniques

At the heart of SNNs' operation is encoding, which involves converting real-world analog data into spike patterns for processing. This encoding is a sophisticated representation, capturing data essence using spiking neurons' temporal dynamics While reducing energy consumption. Essential encoding techniques and schemas are as follows:

- **Rate Coding** [13]: Rate Coding is a prevalent SNN method for encoding information. It translates the intensity of a signal into the frequency of spikes, with a higher rate indicating a stronger signal. The mean firing rate V is calculated using the formula.

$$V = \frac{N_{\text{spike}}}{T} \tag{2}$$

where N_{spike} represents the number of spikes and T is the time window. Its advantages are simplicity in implementation and biological plausibility, mimicking certain actual neural behaviors. Moreover, disadvantages include limited ability to capture the full range of input signal dynamics. While other coding types may achieve better accuracy in fewer timesteps, rate coding is more robust against adversarial attacks and more energy-efficient [13].

- **Temporal Coding** [12]:
Temporal Coding leverages the timing of spikes to encode information, offering a power-efficient alternative to traditional rate coding. Examples include Time-To-First-Spike (TTFS) Coding, which encodes information based on the time interval from stimulus onset to the first spike. The formula for TTFS can be expressed as the following :

$$t_{\text{spike}} = t_{\text{onset}} + \Delta t \tag{3}$$

here, t_{spike} represents the time of the first spike, t_{onset} is the stimulus onset time, and Δt is the interval to the first spike. This method is power-efficient as it relies on minimal spiking activity, aligning with rapid visual processing research findings.

Temporal Coding via TTFS, while power-efficient for tasks like sensory processing, introduces notable learning complexities. As shown in [12], this coding scheme achieves efficient encoding with minimal spikes, enhancing power efficiency. However, the precise timing-based nature of TTFS significantly complicates the decoding and learning processes. Training SNNs with TTFS is challenging due to the need for advanced algorithms capable of interpreting complex temporal spike patterns, making the learning aspect a substantial hurdle in TTFS utilization.

- **Population Coding** [13]: Population Coding encodes information through the collective activity of neuron populations. Each neuron contributes to the overall output, a sum of weighted neuron responses. The encoded information, or the decoded output, is represented by the formula:

$$R = \sum_{i=1}^{n} w_i \cdot r_i \tag{4}$$

where R denotes the collective output, n is the total number of neurons, w_i is the weight of the i-th neuron, and r_i is the response or firing rate of the i-th neuron.

Evaluating encoding techniques in SNNs involves balancing energy efficiency, learning ease, and implementation complexity. Rate coding [13] is simple and biologically plausible but may lead to higher energy usage due to limited input dynamics capture. Temporal Coding, particularly TTFS [12], offers power efficiency and reduced spikes but adds decoding complexity. Due to complexity or noise sensitivity, diverse encoding strategies have computational advantages and learning challenges. This suggests a continuum between rate and synchrony codes, indicating dynamic strategy adoption based on network conditions.

3.2   Neuron Models: SNNs Architectures for Energy Efficiency

SNNs employ various neuron models that balance computational efficiency and biological realism, which is crucial for energy-efficient architecture and neuromorphic applications. Key models like Leaky Integrate-and-Fire, Hodgkin-Huxley, and Izhikevich offer unique contributions to this balance. These models are vital for developing SNNs that emulate biological processes and advance AI algorithms.

– **Leaky Integrate-and-Fire (LIF) Neurons** [4]: The Leaky Integrate-and-Fire (LIF) model enhances the basic Integrate-and-Fire model by incorporating a *leak* term, better simulating passive charge loss in neurons and processing temporal information. This addition trades off some computational efficiency for increased biological realism and simplicity. The LIF model is extensively used in large-scale neural simulations, brain-computer interfaces, and AI, where moderate biological realism suffices. The LIF model's mathematical formulation notably includes the leak term, reflecting its advanced functionality.

$$\tau_m \frac{dV(t)}{dt} = -[V(t) - V_{\text{rest}}] + R \cdot I(t) \tag{5}$$

In this model, $V(t)$ denotes the neuron's membrane potential at time t, $\frac{dV(t)}{dt}$ is its rate of change, and $I(t)$ represents the input current, τ_m represents the membrane time constant (a product of membrane resistance and capacitance), V_{rest} denotes the resting membrane potential, R indicates the membrane resistance.

– **Hodgkin-Huxley (HH) Neurons** [14]: The Hodgkin-Huxley (HH) model, based on research on squid giant axons, provides a highly accurate depiction of neuronal behavior by simulating the dynamics of Na^+, K^+, and Cl^- ion channels. Although computationally intensive due to these equations, the HH model offers an in-depth understanding of nerve impulses, proving essential in neuroscience for studying brain functions and disorders and in drug development for evaluating effects on neurons. While its high biological realism limits its use in large-scale simulations, it is ideal for detailed neuronal dynamic studies.

These independent channels are described in Eq. 6, and overall neuron mechanics are described in Eq. 7:

$$I_{\text{ion}}(t) = G_K n^4 (V_m - E_K) + G_{\text{Na}} m^3 h (V_m - E_{\text{Na}}) + G_L (V_m - E_L) \tag{6}$$

$$\frac{dV}{dt} = I_{\text{ion}}(t) + I_{\text{syn}}(t) \tag{7}$$

In this context, $I_{\text{ion}}(t)$ signifies the total ionic current, G_K, G_{Na}, G_L represent the maximum conductances for potassium, sodium, and leakage channels, respectively. The gating variables are denoted by n, m, h, while V_m indicates the membrane potential. The Nernst potentials for potassium, sodium, and leakage channels are represented by E_K, E_{Na}, E_L, and $I_{\text{syn}}(t)$ corresponds to the synaptic current at time t.

– **Izhikevich Model** [3]: The Izhikevich comprehensive neural model bridges the complexity gap between detailed models like Hodgkin-Huxley (HH) and simpler ones like Leaky Integrate-and-Fire (LIF). It uses a 2D differential equation system to simulate complex neural behaviors efficiently and can replicate various neuronal firing patterns found in biological neurons. Despite its lower complexity, the model maintains a moderate level of biological realism. It's widely used in studying neural dynamics, network behaviors, and the mechanisms of brain disorders, making it particularly effective for simulating extensive networks of spiking neurons with diverse firing patterns.

Equations 8–10 describe this neuron's mechanics, where u is the recovery variable, and a, b, c, and d are constants, allowing for different spiking behaviors :

$$\frac{dV}{dt} = 0.04V^2 + 5V + 140 - u + I \tag{8}$$

$$\frac{du}{dt} = a(bV - u) \tag{9}$$

$$\text{if } V \geq 30 \text{ mV, then } \{V \leftarrow c, u \leftarrow u + d\} \tag{10}$$

Recent Research Emphasizes the critical importance of neuron model selection in SNN architecture design, targeting a balance between computational efficiency, biological fidelity, and the specific needs of various applications. Due to their efficiency and simplicity, simple models like LIF are often preferred in neuromorphic hardware and simulations with limited computational resources, including neuromorphic applications. In contrast, complex models like Hodgkin-Huxley (HH) are indispensable for in-depth studies of neural dynamics, offering detailed insights. Additionally, the Izhikevich model balances biological relevance and computational efficiency.

3.3   Training Paradigms and Learning Methods in SNNs

Training methodologies in SNNs require unique adaptations due to their inherent non-differentiable nature, diverging significantly from those employed in traditional neural networks:

Supervised Learning: Adapted for SNNs, this paradigm utilizes labeled data to minimize errors, incorporating novel gradient computation and weight adjustment techniques to tackle spike-based data processing challenges.

Unsupervised Learning: Focuses on rate-based training, modified to embrace the temporal dynamics inherent in SNNs, overcoming limitations of traditional unsupervised learning methods.

Reinforcement Learning: Aligned with SNNs' characteristics, primarily through adaptations that leverage spike timing, this paradigm reflects biological learning processes more closely.

Indirect Training (ANN-to-SNN Conversion): This innovative approach involves converting pre-trained ANNs to SNNs, aiming for efficiency and low latency by translating ANN activations into spike rates.

Supervised Learning: This approach uses labeled data for training. Algorithms include:

SuperSpike [17]: Employs a surrogate gradient approach for addressing the non-differentiability of spikes in SNNs. It introduces a differentiable surrogate function to approximate the gradient at spiking points, enabling gradient-based learning methods in SNNs. This approach facilitates practical training of networks to process spatiotemporal spike patterns despite the discrete nature of spikes. The weight update rule is:

$$\Delta w = -\eta \cdot E_t \cdot G_s \cdot I_i \tag{11}$$

Where:

- Δw: Change in synaptic weight
- η: Learning rate
- E_t: Temporal Error, related to the difference in spike timing
- G_s: Surrogate Gradient, an approximation of the gradient
- I_i: Input Influence, the effect of the input spike train on the neuron's membrane potential

Unsupervised Learning: [15] Unsupervised learning in SNNs is characterized by its independence from the backpropagation algorithm, instead focusing on learning patterns from unlabeled data through mechanisms intrinsic to the spiking nature of the network. Notable algorithms in this paradigm include: *Spike-Timing-Dependent Plasticity (STDP)*: This method diverges from traditional backpropagation by adjusting synaptic weights based solely on the timing of spikes. This approach capitalizes on the temporal aspect of spikes, a key feature of SNNs that is not leveraged in traditional backpropagation methods. The update rule is:

$$\Delta w = A_{\pm} \cdot \exp\left(-\frac{|t_{\text{post}} - t_{\text{pre}}|}{\tau_{\pm}}\right) \tag{12}$$

Where:

- Δw = Change in synaptic weight
- $A_{\pm}$ = Scaling constants for potentiation and depression
- t_{post} = Post-synaptic spike time

- t_{pre} = Pre-synaptic spike time
- $\tau_{\pm}$ = Time constants for the STDP window

Reinforcement Learning: Employs feedback from the environment to guide learning. Techniques include:

Reward-Modulated Plasticity [16]: Utilizes rewards for synaptic adjustments. The general formula is:

$$\Delta w = \eta \cdot (R - \bar{R}) \cdot \text{STDP}(\Delta t) \tag{13}$$

Where:

- Δw = Change in synaptic weight
- η = Learning rate
- R = Received reward signal
- $\bar{R}$ = Baseline or expected reward
- $\text{STDP}(\Delta t)$ = Spike-Timing-Dependent Plasticity function, dependent on the time difference (Δt) between pre- and post-synaptic spikes

The advancement of training methodologies in SNNs reflects a diverse integration of learning paradigms and algorithms, each contributing uniquely to the field. While methods like Gradient Descent and Spike Backpropagation in supervised learning and Spike-Timing-Dependent Plasticity (STDP) in unsupervised learning primarily aim to optimize synaptic weights for accurate output prediction, there is a notable shift towards integrating energy efficiency with these learning paradigms.

In summary, while developing SNNs encompasses various learning methods, the trend toward creating more power-efficient models is increasingly evident. This opens potential avenues for research focusing on mechanisms that explicitly target accuracy improvement and energy consumption reduction, contributing significantly to neuromorphic computing.

4   Discussion in SNN Research for Energy Efficiency

SNNs are increasingly recognized for their superior power efficiency over traditional ANNs, with studies like the Multiplication-free Deep Spiking Neural Network (MF-DSNN) demonstrating up to 22× improvements in energy efficiency compared to standard ANN accelerators [19]. This efficiency is primarily attributed to the development of neuromorphic hardware, which mimics biological neural systems, leading to significant reductions in power consumption.

Recent algorithmic developments in SNN research focus on refining learning algorithms to optimize energy usage during the training and inference phases. Techniques such as backward residual connections, quantization-aware training, and custom loss functions like the SynOp loss are being explored to minimize energy consumption while maintaining precision in tasks like visual recognition. These methods, combined with hardware advancements, are bringing SNN models closer to the energy efficiency of biological brains.

SNNs' superior energy efficiency over networks like CNNs is further high-lighted by their event-driven nature, leading to more efficient computations. For instance, a VMD-SNN model for carbon price forecasting demonstrated remarkable performance compared to conventional models [18].

Challenges persist, particularly in scaling SNNs for complex tasks without escalating energy consumption. Strategies like model pruning, quantization, and efficient encoding schemes are being investigated to balance performance and energy efficiency. Additionally, integrating SNNs into computational infrastructures, including cloud computing and edge devices, is vital for their broader application in energy-efficient computing.

Despite the advancements, SNNs face complexities in training due to the temporal nature of spike processing. However, integrating SNNs into existing technologies, such as federated learning environments, has shown promise in surpassing ANNs regarding energy efficiency [20]. Future research aims to enhance performance and energy efficiency through new algorithms, training techniques, and hardware innovations.

5 Conclusion and Future Directions in SNNs Research

Spiking Neural Networks (SNNs) offer a paradigm shift in computing by processing complex inputs with high biological fidelity and energy efficiency. While advancements have made them promising for various applications, challenges such as complex training mechanisms, the necessity for application-specific models, and scalability persist. Future research directions include developing advanced neuromorphic systems, innovating learning algorithms, fostering cross-disciplinary collaborations, and adapting deep learning benchmarks for SNN evaluations. Emphasizing energy efficiency and sustainability, continued innovation in SNNs is crucial for harnessing their full potential, making them key players in addressing global energy challenges and contributing to environmental sustainability.

Acknowledgment. This work is financed by the Ministry of Science, Innovation and Universities with code PID2019-107793GB-I00/AEI/10.13039/501100011033.

References

1. Muhamed, A., et al.: Web-scale semantic product search with large language models. In: Kashima, H., Ide, T., Peng, W.C. (eds.) PAKDD 2023. LNCS, vol. 13937, pp. 73–85. Springer, Cham (2023). https://doi.org/10.1007/978-3-031-33380-4_6
2. Díaz-Rodríguez, N., Del Ser, J., Coeckelbergh, M., de Prado, M.L., Herrera-Viedma, E., Herrera, F.: Connecting the dots in trustworthy Artificial Intelligence: from AI principles, ethics, and key requirements to responsible AI systems and regulation. Inf. Fusion. **101896** (2023)
3. Izhikevich, E.M.: Simple model of spiking neurons. IEEE Trans. Neural Netw. **14**(6), 1569–1572 (2003). https://doi.org/10.1088/2634-4386/ac4a83

4. Gerstner, W., Kistler, W.M.: Spiking Neuron Models: Single Neurons, Populations. Plasticity. Cambridge University Press, Cambridge (2002)
5. Auge, D., Hille, J., Mueller, E., Knoll, A.: A survey of encoding techniques for signal processing in spiking neural networks. Neural Process. Lett. **53**(6), 4693–4710 (2021). https://doi.org/10.1007/s11063-021-10562-2
6. Pietrzak, P., Szczesny, S., Huderek, D., Przyborowski, Ł: Overview of spiking neural network learning approaches and their computational complexities. Sensors **23**(6), 3037 (2023). https://doi.org/10.3390/s23063037
7. Indiveri, G., et al.: Neuromorphic silicon neuron circuits. Front. Neurosci. **5**, 9202 (2011). https://doi.org/10.3389/fnins.2011.00073
8. Schliebs, S., Kasabov, N.: Evolving spiking neural network–a survey. Evol. Syst. **4**, 87–98 (2013). https://doi.org/10.1007/s12530-013-9074-9
9. Taherkhani, A., Belatreche, A., Li, Y., Cosma, G., Maguire, L.P., McGinnity, T.M.: A review of learning in biologically plausible spiking neural networks. Neural Netw. **122**, 253–272 (2020). https://doi.org/10.1016/j.neunet.2019.09.036
10. Ibad, T., Kadir, S.J.A., Aziz, N.: Evolving spiking neural network: a comprehensive survey of its variants and their results. J. Theor. Appl. Inf. Technol. **98**(24), 4061–4081 (2020)
11. Malcom, K., Casco-Rodriguez, J.: A comprehensive review of spiking neural networks: interpretation, optimization, efficiency, and best practices. arXiv preprint arXiv:2303.10780 (2023). https://doi.org/10.48550/arXiv.2303.10780
12. Bonilla, L., Gautrais, J., Thorpe, S., Masquelier, T.: Analyzing time-to-first-spike coding schemes: a theoretical approach. Front. Neurosci. **16**, 971937 (2022)
13. Johnson, D.H., Ray, W.: Optimal stimulus coding by neural populations using rate codes. J. Comput. Neurosci. **16**, 129–138 (2004)
14. Hodgkin, A.L., Huxley, A.F.: A quantitative description of membrane current and its application to conduction and excitation in nerve. J. Physiol. **117**(4), 500 (1952)
15. Diehl, P.U., Cook, M.: Unsupervised learning of digit recognition using spike-timing-dependent plasticity. Front. Comput. Neurosci. **9**, 99 (2015)
16. Skorheim, S., Lonjers, P., Bazhenov, M.: A spiking network model of decision making employing rewarded STDP. PLoS ONE **9**(3), e90821 (2014)
17. Zenke, F., Ganguli, S.: Superspike: supervised learning in multilayer spiking neural networks. Neural Comput. **30**(6), 1514–1541 (2018)
18. Sun, G., Chen, T., Wei, Z., Sun, Y., Zang, H., Chen, S.: A carbon price forecasting model based on variational mode decomposition and spiking neural networks. Energies **9**(1) (2016). https://doi.org/10.3390/en9010054
19. Zhang, Y., Wang, S., Kang, Y.: MF-DSNN: an energy-efficient high-performance multiplication-free deep spiking neural network accelerator. In: 2023 IEEE 5th International Conference on Artificial Intelligence Circuits and Systems (AICAS), pp. 1–4 (2023)
20. Venkatesha, Y., Kim, Y., Tassiulas, L., Panda, P.: Federated learning with spiking neural networks. IEEE Trans. Signal Process. **69**, 6183–6194 (2021)

Deep Variational Auto-Encoder for Model-Based Water Quality Patrolling with Intelligent Surface Vehicles

Samuel Yanes Luis[1]([✉]), Nicola Basilico[2], Michele Antonazzi[2],
Daniel Gutiérrez Reina[1], and Sergio Toral Marín[1]

[1] Universidad de Sevilla, Av. de Los Descubrimientos, S/N, 41005 Sevilla, Spain
syanes@us.es
[2] Università degli Studi Milano Statale, Via Celoria, 18, 20133 Milano, Italy

Abstract. This paper addresses persistent monitoring challenges in Lake Ypacaraí, Paraguay, a crucial hydrological resource facing issues of eutrophication and cyanobacteria blooms. Utilizing autonomous surface vehicles equipped with water quality sensors, a model-based approach is proposed for the Non-Homogeneous Informative Patrolling Problem. The UNet based Variational Auto-Encoder architecture is introduced for importance estimation, achieving a 28% and 65% improvement in accuracy for water quality parameters compared to non-parametric approaches such as Gaussian processes and k-Nearest Neighbors, respectively. The proposed model also significantly reduces computational costs, making it suitable for real-time deployment. A greedy patrolling algorithm, exploiting the submodularity of the problem, demonstrates a 41% and 55% performance improvement over algorithms without UNet-VAE. This method enhances monitoring coverage and intensification of high-interest areas, providing a promising approach for hydrological resource surveillance.

Keywords: Variational Auto-Encoders · Multi-agent optimization · Autonomous Surface Vehicles

1 Introduction

Monitoring hydrological resources is crucial for conserving reservoirs, rivers, and lakes, which play a vital role in human consumption, socio-economic development, and tourism among others. Lake Ypacaraí in Asunción, Paraguay, spanning $60 \, km^2$, is the largest freshwater body in the country with significant socio-economic importance. Unfortunately, over the past three decades, accelerated eutrophication has led to the uncontrolled proliferation of toxic cyanobacteria, posing risks to the aquatic ecosystem, and humans living in the surrounding areas.

Addressing this issue necessitates ongoing surveillance of water quality parameters (WQP) like conductivity, pH, turbidity, etc., in Lake Ypacaraí to comprehend the origins of eutrophication and implement safety measures. However, the lake's substantial size poses challenges for sustained monitoring efforts.

In recent years, the proposal of utilizing autonomous surface vehicles (ASVs) has emerged as a cost-effective alternative to labor-intensive manual sampling campaigns. Deploying a fleet of ASVs, equipped with precise sensors measuring of WQP enables continuous and automated monitoring [1] (see Fig. 1).

Fig. 1. Real ASV prototype proposed for WQP monitorization.

Persistent monitoring with multiple vehicles presents challenges in coordinating agents, acquiring an accurate model efficiently, and implementing an adaptive policy. In autonomous vehicle monitoring, persistent monitoring involves cyclically measuring the environment, assuming that information quality degrades over time. Priority is given to visiting neglected areas urgently, with certain areas, such as cyanobacteria blooms in Lake Ypacaraí, being of greater interest, conforming the Non-Homogeneous Informative Patrolling Problem (NH-IPat). Solving NH-IPat optimally requires knowing the importance of each map area in advance (NP-hard problem). However, since a preliminary importance picture is unattainable until the entire map is covered, patrolling with ASVs is necessary to estimate the map concurrently. This involves solving NH-IPat [2] while addressing the inverse estimation problem, which entails estimating the complete system state with partial observations of importance from WQP sensors.

In this paper, the resolution of the NH-IPat is proposed through a model-based approach in the context of Lake Ypacaraí. For the WQP estimation, we propose the use of a UNet Variational Auto-Encoder (UNET-VAE) architecture that receives the measurements in a 2D setting. In classical approaches, as in Gaussian processes, the complexity is $\mathcal{O}(N^3)$, where N is the number of samples. A VAE encodes the inputs visually with complexity $\mathcal{O}(1)$. The VAE also incorporates stochastic estimation to learn the distribution of the data and the stochasticity of the WQPs. Simulator-generated models of both WQPs and blue-green algae have been used for training. For patrolling, a greedy algorithm is chosen taking advantage of the submodularity properties of the NH-IPat.

2   Previous Works

The use of ASVs for monitoring is becoming more common thanks to the improved autonomy of mobile robotics and the development of new planning and learning algorithms [1]. Two main problems to be solved with hydrological resource monitoring have been established.

On the one hand, there is the problem of modeling environmental variables [3], which falls into the Informative Path Planning (IPP) category. This problem consists of guiding different agents to maximize the accuracy of a model. Generally, this problem ends when the model is accurate enough. To solve the IPP, it is proposed in [4] to use an algorithm based on Particle Swarm Optimization and a model based on Gaussian processes (GPs). Similarly, in [3] it is proposed to use GPs and to plan the routes with a heuristic based on Bayesian Optimization. These approaches, although effective, have two disadvantages: i) Gaussian processes explode dimensionally with the number of samples [3], ii) they hardly allow modeling spatio-temporal data. In NH-IPat, the information is spatiotemporally redundant and the Gaussian process must adapt to an increasing number of samples with the cumulative cost involved.

On the other hand, there is the problem of persistent monitoring. In this problem, the information must be reviewed periodically according to temporal redundancy criteria. The optimization horizon is longer, since it is monitored uninterruptedly. In [5], the resolution of NH-IPat is addressed for the first time. While in this work the problem is solved offline, in a more realistic application, as the one addressed in this paper, the importance model for each zone is a priori unknown and needs to be built while patrolling, as was done in [6].

These previous works have in common that they assume relatively little about the information to be measured. In this paper, we have chosen to propose a hybrid approach in which a deep model such as the VAE is pre-integrated with data generated with a simulator of emerging pollutant diffusion. In [7], a VAE-type architecture is proposed for the reconstruction of incomplete cosmic radiation images. Similarly, in [8], a UNet architecture is proposed to improve the reconstruction of medical images. This paper presents the preliminary results of a VAE-UNet type architecture with stochastic filters, based on [8].

3   Statement of the Problem

For the Patrolling problem, an 8-connected grid graph $G(V, E, \mathcal{W}^t)$ is defined to represent the set of possible locations E where samples can be taken. It is assumed that all vertices V and edges E are entirely situated in navigable locations. Additionally, W is defined as a weight for each node V, such that $\mathcal{W}_i^t$ indicates the time that has elapsed since V_i was last covered at time t. Finally, a travel cost of an edge is defined as their Euclidean distance $C(E_{ij}) = ||V_i - V_j||_2$. Given a set of m agents, each traversing a path $\psi_j = \{V_0, ..., V_i\}$ with an agent maximum distance budget of D_{max}, the Patrolling problem is defined as the search for an optimal set of m paths $\Psi^* = \{\psi_1, ..., \psi_m\}$ such that:

$$\Psi^* = \arg\min \frac{1}{T \times M} \sum_{t=0}^{T} \sum_{i=0}^{|V|} \mathcal{W}_i^t \tag{1}$$

Subjected to:

$$\sum_{j=1}^{|\psi|} C(E_i j) \leq D_{max}$$

where $\mathcal{W}_i$ becomes zero when an agent is within a distance less than $rcover$, that models the effect of the validness of the measurement locally, as explained in [6].

$$\mathcal{W}_i^{t+1} = \begin{cases} 0 & E_i \text{ is covered} \\ \min(\mathcal{W}_i^t + \delta, 1) & \text{otherwise} \end{cases} \tag{2}$$

In the context of the NH-IPat, the problem is extended to accommodate the dissimilar importance of idleness $\mathcal{W}$. In this case, $\mathcal{W}$ will be weighted by $(1 + \mathcal{I})$, where $\mathcal{I} \in [0, 1]$ represents the normalized importance of coverage in that area, imposed according to biological, safety, or logistical criteria. Thus, the non-homogeneous patrolling problem is formulated as follows:

$$\Psi^* = \arg\min \frac{1}{T \times M} \sum_{t=0}^{T} \sum_{i=0}^{|V|} \mathcal{W}_i^t \times \left(1 + \mathcal{I}_i^t\right) \tag{3}$$

Subjected to: $\tag{4}$

$$\sum_{j=1}^{|\psi|} C(E_i j) \leq D_{max} \tag{5}$$

It is important to note that in this problem, optimal patrolling cannot be estimated offline without prior knowledge of $\mathcal{I}$. Therefore, it is necessary to simultaneously acquire the predicted importance model $\hat{\mathcal{I}}^{\sqcup}$ and minimize $\mathcal{W}_\rangle$ in general.

4   Methodology

First, we will outline the training of the UNet-VAE architecture for the online estimation of the importance model $\mathcal{I}$. Subsequently, we will present the multi-agent Greedy algorithm, which will serve as the decision heuristic.

4.1   VAE-UNet Architecture

The Information Model utilizes a UNet-based convolutional-deconvolutional neural network architecture [8]. The UNet comprises a fully convolutional neural network (CNN) with contracting and expanding paths, each consisting of four convolutional and max-pooling layers. This architecture facilitates the extraction of high-level features from the input image. The network takes two inputs: i) a preprocessed importance model Y^t constructed from agent samples, and ii) a binary visit mask M^t indicating sampled locations. The UNet processes these inputs to generate an importance model estimation $\hat{\mathcal{I}}^t$ at time t (see Fig. 2).

In this study, the original UNet is extended to a Variational UNet inspired by [7]. Two separate convolutional networks produce the prior probabilistic Gaussian distribution $\mathcal{N}(\mu, \sigma)$ and the posterior distribution $\mathcal{N}(\hat{\mu}, \hat{\sigma})$, with $\mu, \sigma \in \mathbb{R}^N$. The posterior network incorporates both the naive model map and the ground truth information importance $\mathcal{I}$. Stochastic filters, sampled from the distributions, are added to the UNet's final output layer. The prior network, used in inference, is trained by minimizing the Kullback-Leibler (KL) divergence with respect to the posterior. All networks are trained using a loss function composed of three terms:

- **Reconstruction loss:** Rooted Mean Squared Error (MSE) between the generated model and the ground truth $\mathcal{I}$:

$$\mathbb{L}_{recons} = MSE\left(\hat{\mathcal{I}}, \mathcal{I}\right) \tag{6}$$

- **KL loss**: Kullback-Leibler divergence between the prior and posterior distributions:

$$\mathbb{L}_{KL} = KL\left(\mathcal{N}(\mu, \sigma), \mathcal{N}(\hat{\mu}, \hat{\sigma})\right) \tag{7}$$

- **Perceptual loss**: MSE between high-level feature maps of the output and the ground truth from a pre-trained model like $VGG16$:

$$\mathbb{L}_{perceptual} = MSE\left(\xi(\hat{\mathcal{I}}), \xi(\mathcal{I})\right) \tag{8}$$

The final loss function will be:

$$\mathbb{L} = \mathbb{L}_{recons} + \mathbb{L}_{KL} + \mathbb{L}_{perceptual} \tag{9}$$

4.2   Multiagent Path Planning

For solving the NH-IPat, we propose a simple yet effective algorithm based on the principle of submodularity. A submodular function is a mathematical function that captures diminishing returns or decreasing marginal gains. In simpler terms, it quantifies how adding an element to a set, such as a measurement point in this problem, contributes less to the overall value of the set as the set grows larger [9]. This property is known as the diminishing returns property. Submodular functions of this kind yield near-optimal solutions when a Greedy algorithm is applied with respect to the reward [10]. In this multi-agent approach, vehicles will select the next node based on the highest reward computed using the Information model $\hat{\mathcal{I}}$.

5   Results

Firstly, we will present the training conditions and outcomes of the UNet-VAE architecture as an importance model. To validate the proposal's efficiency, we will compare the accuracy with other types of models commonly used in practice. Once the architecture is trained, the resulting weights will be implemented alongside the Greedy algorithm to solve the NH-IPat.

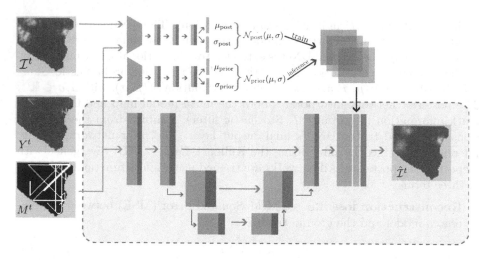

Fig. 2. Training architecture of the VAE-UNet for the estimation of $\mathcal{I}$. The full state is used in the posterior network for the prior network to minimize the KL-Divergence with only the partial state. The partial state is then processed with the UNet. The final outcome is the composition of the UNet output and the prior (during inference) or the posterior (during training).

Algorithm 1. Multi-agent Greedy Algorithm

Input: Set of m vehicles, model $\hat{\mathcal{I}}$, distance budget for each vehicle D_{max}.
Output: Routing plan for each vehicle.

1: **for** $t \leftarrow 0$ to T **do**
2:     Initialize empty routing plans for each vehicle: $Routes \leftarrow \{\}$
3:
4:     Randomly shuffle the order of vehicles: $Vehicles \leftarrow \text{shuffle}(\{1, 2, \ldots, m\})$
5:     **for** $i \leftarrow 1$ to m **do**
6:         **while** $d < D_{max}$ **do**
7:             Compute rewards for every action: $R_i \leftarrow R(\text{possible\_actions}, \mathcal{W}, \hat{\mathcal{I}})$
8:             Select action with maximum reward: $a_i \leftarrow \arg\max R_i$
9:             Update routing plan for vehicle i: $Routes[i] \leftarrow Routes[i] + a_i$
10:            Update distance covered by vehicle i: $d_i \leftarrow d_i + \text{distance}(a_i)$
11:            Update $\mathcal{W}$ values.
12:            Update model $\hat{\mathcal{I}}$ with new measurements.
13:        **end while**
14:    **end for**
15: **end for**

5.1   UNet-VAE Training Results

To train the UNet-VAE, 3000 ground truths have been extracted from two simulators of pollution and water quality variables. The first simulator, which is used in [3] and [4] to solve the IPP in Lake Ypacaraí, is based on smooth Shekel functions. The second is a physical simulator of emerging contaminants, such as blue-green algae, proposed in [11]. Both scenarios have been applied in the southern zone of Lake Ypacaraí. For simulating vehicle trajectories, we opted for straight paths with random obstacle-free directions. This exploratory heuristic alleviates bias induced by overly informative paths. Regarding training parameters, for both cases, an Adam optimizer with a learning rate of 10^{-4} and a batch size of 64 images were used for 30 epochs. The training was conducted on a Ubuntu 22.04 server with an Intel Xeon Gold 2.2 GHz CPU, 256 GB of RAM, and an Nvidia RTX 3090 GPU with 24 GB of VRAM. All code is available in a GitHub repository[1].

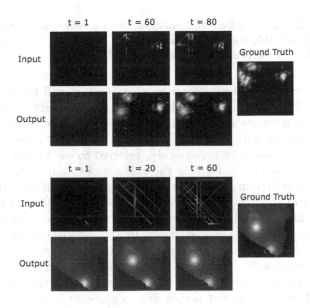

Fig. 3. Estimation examples at different times of the proposed trained model for every benchmark used. On top, the Algae-bloom benchmark. On the bottom, the Shekel WQP benchmark from [3].

In Fig. 3, an example of estimation at three different instances with random trajectories is presented. In the initial moments, the estimation is incomplete, but it is observed that in the case of the smoother ground truth, the initial samples enable the prediction of the first hill. For blue-green algae, the model can initially estimate the position of blooms, subsequently refining predictions by reviewing their contours and interiors. This early convergence characteristic facilitates more efficient patrolling by highlighting areas of interest sooner. Both of the measurement also incorporates the noise-level provided by real WQP sensors like the one used in the real ASV prototype[2].

---

[1] https://derpberk.github.io/ASV_Loyola_US/sensoresaml/.

[2] derpberk.github.io/ASV_Loyola_US/sensoresaml.

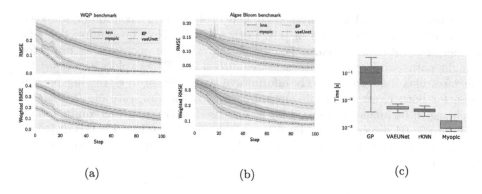

Fig. 4. Performance metrics for 100 simulations of each benchmark with random trajectories. In (a) and (b), the RMSE and weighted-RMSE. In (c), a boxplot of the computation times of the predictions only using CPU.

To validate the model's performance, a comparison will be made using the Mean Squared Error (MSE) with 100 different ground truths not used in the training set. Three regressors commonly used in similar tasks will be considered: i) a Gaussian process with an RBF kernel [3], ii) a model based on k-Nearest Neighbours (kNN), and iii) a naive model, referred to as "myopic," where each sample represents an environment in the absence of samples. Additionally, the computational cost in terms of time for estimating a new model will be compared.

Figures 4a and 4b illustrate the RMSE and weighted RMSE of the proposed model against other models. Improvement is evident in two aspects. The first enhancement lies in the model's accuracy. In the initial benchmark of WQPs, both the Gaussian process and the proposed model can achieve small errors in the long term. However, a 28% improvement over the Gaussian process is observed in the first third of the mission, and a 65% improvement in the case of the kNN-based model. This improvement is even more significant in the case of the algae bloom benchmark (Fig. 4b). As this ground truth exhibits a non-uniform and less continuous distribution, the Gaussian process tends to lose efficiency and overfit with null pollution data. The proposed model captures these discontinuities with an average improvement of 20% throughout the mission.

Regarding computational cost, as shown in Fig. 4c, it is evident that the cost of the GP is significantly higher than any other model. For a more equitable comparison, the VAE-UNet estimation has been conducted on CPU only. The improvement in computational time is an order of magnitude compared to the GP. This property is crucial in deployments requiring real-time responses, short decision times, or very long prediction horizons.

5.2   Patrolling Results

In Fig. 5, the outcome of 30 simulations with different ground truths from the training and validation sets is depicted. Three algorithms are compared: i) solving the Vehicle Routing Problem (VRP) to achieve homogeneous and cyclical coverage [12], ii) using the Greedy algorithm with the miope model, and iii) employing the Greedy algorithm with the UNet-VAE model. Improvement is observed both in performance and convergence speed. The proposed algorithm achieves a 41% and 55% enhancement compared to the algorithm without the UNet-VAE model for each benchmark, respectively. There is also an improvement in the convergence speed. Since the UNet-VAE model can estimate areas of interest much faster, therefore agents make more informed decisions. On average, a convergence speed between 50%-65% faster is observed compared to the second-best algorithm. The VRP algorithm, due to not considering information dissimilarity, fails to intensify despite providing very homogeneous coverage with a low level of redundancy.

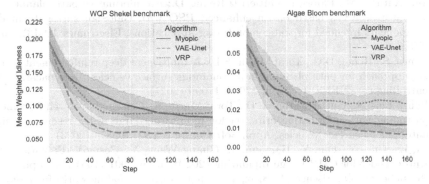

Fig. 5. Average Weighted Idleness $\mathcal{W} \times \mathcal{I}$ within time, for different algorithms, after 30 simulations.

6   Conclusions and Future Work

This work introduces a methodology to address the Non-Homogeneous Patrolling Problem in hydrological resources. The strategy relies on a learning-estimation approach for monitoring phenomena. The utilized model employs a modified UNet architecture functioning as a VAE, enabling more accurate and faster predictions than Gaussian processes commonly found in literature [3]. This approach is valuable when having access to models describing the variable's behavior to invert observations into the complete state. The proposed patrolling algorithm effectively leverages this model to enhance information coverage and intensify areas of high interest compared to low contamination. Future work should emphasize addressing potential biases in the model concerning real-world data and understanding their impact on estimation performance. Additionally, it is essential to develop more effective algorithms that leverage the model for deeper movement planning, such as Deep Reinforcement Learning or planning through Monte-Carlo Tree Search. Lastly, exploring the extension of the model to dynamic ground truths by incorporating recurrent architectures into the UNet network is worth investigating.

References

1. Sánchez-García, J., García-Campos, J.M., Arzamendia, M., Reina, D.G., Toral, S.L., Gregor, D.: A survey on unmanned aerial and aquatic vehicle multi-hop networks: wireless communications, evaluation tools and applications. Comput. Commun. **119**, 43–65 (2018)
2. Yanes, S., Reina, D.G., Toral Marín, S.L.: A deep reinforcement learning approach for the patrolling problem of water resources through autonomous surface vehicles: the Ypacarai lake case. IEEE Access, 6(1) (2020)
3. Peralta, F., Reina, D.G., Toral Marín, S.L., Gregor, D.O., Arzamendia, M.: A Bayesian optimization approach for water resources monitoring through an autonomous surface vehicle: the ypacarai lake case study. IEEE Access **9**(1), 9163–9179 (2021)
4. Ten Kathen, M., Flores, I., Gutiérrez Reina, D.: An informative path planner for a swarm of ASVs based on an enhanced PSO with Gaussian surrogate model components intended for water monitoring applications. Electronics **10**(13), 1605 (2021)
5. Yanes, S., Reina, D.G., Toral Marín, S.L.: A multiagent deep reinforcement learning approach for path planning in autonomous surface vehicles: the ypacaraí lake patrolling case. IEEE Access **9**, 17084–17099 (2021)
6. Yanes Luis, S., Gutiérrez-Reina, D., Toral Marín, S.: Censored deep reinforcement patrolling with information criterion for monitoring large water resources using autonomous surface vehicles. Appl. Soft Comput. **132**, 109874 (2023)
7. Yi, K., Guo, Y., Fan, Y., Hamann, J., Guang Wang, Y.: CosmoVAE: Variational Autoencoder for CMB Image Inpainting (2020). arXiv:2001.11651 [astro-ph, stat]
8. Ronneberger, O., Fischer, P., Brox, T.: U-net: convolutional networks for biomedical image segmentation. *CoRR*, abs/1505.04597 (2015)
9. Bilmes, J.A.: Submodularity in machine learning and artificial intelligence. *CoRR*, abs/2202.00132 (2022)
10. Krause, A., Guestrin, C.: Submodularity and its applications in optimized information gathering. ACM Trans. Intell. Syst. Technol. **2**(4) (2011)
11. Luis, S.Y., Shutin, D., Gómez, J.M., Reina, D.G., Marín, S.T.: Deep reinforcement multi-agent learning framework for information gathering with local gaussian processes for water monitoring (2024)
12. Toth, P., Vigo, D.: Society for industrial, and applied mathematics. In: Vehicle Routing: Problems, Methods, and Applications. MOS-SIAM Series on Optimization. Society for Industrial and Applied Mathematics (2015). (SIAM, 3600 Market Street, Floor 6, Philadelphia, PA 19104)

An Architecture Towards Building a Reliable Suicide Information Chatbot

Pablo Ascorbe[1], María S. Campos[2], César Domínguez[1],
Jónathan Heras[1(✉)], Magdalena Pérez[3],
and Ana Rosa Terroba-Reinares[1,4]

[1] Departamento de Matemáticas y Computación, Universidad de La Rioja,
Logroño, Spain
{pablo.ascorbe,cesar.dominguez,jonathan.heras}@unirioja.es
[2] Unidad de Salud Mental Espartero, Logroño, La Rioja, Spain
mscampos@riojasalud.es
[3] Teléfono de la Esperanza, Madrid, Spain
magdalenaperez@telefonodelaesperanza.org
[4] Fundación Rioja Salud, Logroño, Spain
arterroba@riojasalud.es

Abstract. Suicide is a major health and social issue worldwide; therefore, a simple access to reliable sources of information that can be used by family members or friends of people who have suicidal ideation can be a valuable resource. This information can be provided by means of chatbot tools; however, the reliability and topicality of the chatbot's answers should be ensured. In this work, we present an architecture to build a chatbot with the aim of providing reliable suicide information in Spanish. The architecture consists of two text classification models (one to check that a user's question is related to suicidal content, and another to decide whether the user is looking for information or if the question should be derived to a human), and a retrieval augmented generation system that, using as a basis a corpus of documents filtered by experts, generates an answer to the user question. In addition, all the components of the architecture have been automatically tested to prove their suitability to be incorporated to the chatbot. The developed system is a step towards helping in one of the greatest global public health concerns.

Keywords: Chatbot · Suicide Information · Text Classification · Retrieval Augmented Generation

1 Introduction

In Spain, suicide is the leading cause of death due to external reasons; namely, 4,227 people died by suicide in Spain in 2022, an average of 11 people per day [12]. In addition, for each completed suicide, it is estimated that there are around 20 suicide attempts; for each attempt, around 14 more people have thought about committing suicide; and for each suicide, at least 6 people who survive

A. Alonso-Betanzos et al. (Eds.): CAEPIA 2024, LNAI 14640, pp. 29–39, 2024.
https://doi.org/10.1007/978-3-031-62799-6_4

the deceased have been directly affected by this death [24]. Due to these figures, it is clear why the World Health Organisation (WHO) identifies suicide and attempted suicide as one of the most serious health problems that can affect people, and it recommends to all its members that it should be addressed as a priority [24].

On 12 March 2014, the Health and Social Services Commission of the lower house in the Spanish Parliament approved, unanimously by all the groups, a non-legislative proposal regarding the development of a National Suicide Prevention Plan by the Spanish health, educational and social institutions in accordance with the directives of the European Union and international organisations. Since then, several suicide prevention plans have been developed in some Autonomous Regions (see, for example, those of La Rioja [16], the Canary Islands [20], and Navarre [11]). Those prevention plans propose different interventions targeting different audiences (general population, health professionals, or media, among others) [21]. Interventions aimed at the general public include creating contacts for help, setting up training programmes, or providing reliable information among the general public.

In the last year, chatbots have shown their potential to provide information in several scenarios [18]. In the context of suicide, chatbots serve to disseminate crucial information, offer support, and provide a platform for individuals to express their feelings anonymously [4,22,23,26]. However, the deployment of chatbots to provide information about suicide poses several challenges. First of all, the reliability and topicality of the provided information should be ensured. Moreover, even if a chatbot can provide a response for a question, there are cases when it should not answer it; for instance, chatbots should not answer questions such as "What are some methods for committing suicide?". Finally, even if the final aim is to provide information, the chatbot can be used by people that require human support, and in those cases users should be derived to experts. All these challenges cannot be solved by only using generalists chatbots like ChatGPT [1] or Mixtral [13], but require other components.

In this paper, we present a software architecture to build a chatbot with the aim of providing reliable and up-to-date information about suicide, but that could be also applied to other contexts where it is necessary to provide sensitive information. This architecture has been employed to build a chatbot to retrieve information about suicide in Spanish—the implementation of this architecture is publicly released in https://github.com/PrevenIA/prevenIA. In addition, some of the developed components can be useful outside this work; in particular:

- We have developed a module based on the Retrieval Augmented Generation (RAG) paradigm [14] with the aim of providing reliable and up-to-date information about suicide in Spanish. In addition, we perform a thorough evaluation of the different deep learning models that can be used in this module.
- We have developed a module to detect unsafe questions and responses about suicide.

– We have released several datasets and models that are used in the proposed architecture, but that can be also applied for other related projects. Those datasets and models are available at https://huggingface.co/PrevenIA.

2 Architecture of the Chatbot

In this section, we present an architecture to build a chatbot with the aim of providing reliable information about suicide, and how we have developed the different modules that form it. In addition to the common modules of a chatbot, for instance devoted to Welcome and Goodbye messages, a chatbot that answers questions about sensitive topics should include some guardrails [15]. In particular, we propose a four layered architecture presented in Fig. 1.

Fig. 1. Proposed architecture

The first layer of our architecture serves as an initial filter, employing a text classification model to detect whether an input message is related to suicidal content. This detection mechanism enables the system to focus on a particular subject, and avoids answering unrelated questions. Subsequently, the second layer is tasked with nuanced decision-making, distinguishing between users seeking information about suicide (for example, a relative or friend of a person who is thinking about suicide, or someone working in the media concerned about how to communicate a suicide case); and those necessitating human intervention (for instance, a person who is thinking about suicide)—again, a text classification model is employed for this task. This approach tries to avoid scenarios where the chatbot could provide harmful responses. Finally, in cases where the user is seeking information (the actual aim of the chatbot), the third and four layers leverages retrieval augmented generation (RAG) techniques to produce reliable responses [14]. In particular, the RAG component consists of a retrieval module and a language model that work as follows. The first step of this module consists of retrieving relevant fragments of documents from a corpus that can be used to answer the question using the retrieval module; subsequently, from those contexts and the given question, the language model is prompted to generate an answer.

The rest of this section is devoted to explain how the different components of our architecture have been developed to build a Spanish chatbot. The starting point to build our chatbot was the acquisition of a set of trustworthy Spanish documents provided by suicide experts. The corpus is composed of approximately 300 Spanish documents intended for the general public, and that are categorised in different topics (including information for survivals of suicide attempts, for relatives, or for schools).

2.1 Text Classification Filter for Not Suicidal Content

In order to detect whether a question is related to suicide, we trained several text classification models. Towards this aim, the first step consisted in building a dataset of texts classified as suicidal ideation/behaviour and non-suicidal using some Spanish resources, such as the dataset created in the "Hackathon Somos NLP 2023" [3], and by translating datasets from English to Spanish [6,19]. A total of 175 010 texts were collected (77 223 considered as suicidal ideation/behaviour and 97 787 considered not suicidal). A text example considered related with a suicide comment is "*No quiero, no quiero vivir, odio la vida*" (I don't want, I don't want to live, I hate life). A text example not related with a suicide comment is "*¿Cómo podemos reducir la tasa de deterioro de los alimentos?*" (How can we reduce the rate of food spoilage?). The dataset was split into training, validation and test subsets (70/10/20). Using this dataset, we trained three different models based on the Bert [9], RoBerta [5], and Electra [17] architectures. The three models were trained for 30 epochs using the functionality of the HuggingFace libraries [25] on an Nvidia RTX 2080 Ti GPU—the code used for training these models is available at the project website.

2.2 Text Classification Filter for Not Safe Information About Suicide

Likewise the models created to classify texts as suicidal ideation/behaviour and non-suicidal, we proceeded similarly to identify whether a question is looking for safe information about suicide, or if it should be handled by a specialist. In order to construct the dataset, we took 7456 suicidal ideation/behaviour sentences from the aforementioned dataset; and we generated 7456 questions about suicide from our corpora of documents. In order to generate the questions, we split the documents into chunks, and for each chunk, we asked a language model (namely, bertin-gpt-j-6B-alpaca [5]) to generate a question. Using this procedure, a total of 22 920 questions were obtained, but many generated questions were incomplete, repeated or contained essentially the same information among them. Therefore, we first removed empty, duplicated or incomplete pairs; then, we applied one of the suicide ideation models to determine whether a question contains information about suicide; and, finally, we removed the questions that were semantically similar by using an embedding model[1] and the cosine distance. An example of

---

[1] https://huggingface.co/hiiamsid/sentence_similarity_spanish_es.

a question generated by the model is *"¿Qué es el suicidio?"* (What is suicide?). Although this question is classified as related to suicide by the model presented in the previous subsection, it is considered as a question asked by someone who is seeking for information about suicide; whereas the first comment in the previous subsection should be considered as a person with suicidal ideation and the chatbot should derive such a user to a human specialist. After building the dataset, it was split into training, validation and test subsets (70/10/20) and used to train three different models based on Bert, RoBerta, and Electra with the same settings previously explained.

2.3 Retrieval Augmented Generation Module

Finally, the RAG module has three components: the corpus, the retrieval and the language model. In our case, the corpus is formed by the 300 documents initially collected. These documents were split into chunks of 1000 tokens and converted into a vector using a Bert-based embedding model [7]. When the RAG module receives a question, the retrieval component converts it into a vector using the same Bert-based embedding model, and retrieves the most similar chunks based on the cosine distance. Finally, for the language model, we considered three language models fine-tuned to follow instructions. Namely, we studied two Spanish models called Bertin [5] and Lince [8], and one multilingual model called Mixtral [2]. It is worth noticing that the information provided by the RAG module can be kept up-to-date by adding new documents to the corpus, and the rest of the components of the module will be kept unchanged.

Once the different components of the architecture have been developed, it can be connected following the workflow of the Fig. 2 and deployed in different interfaces including a web application, Discord, or Telegram; see Fig. 3. For the latter two platforms (Discord and Telegram) we have used a open-source API that uses decorators to indicate which methods will send or receive massages and we implemented the logic to process those received messages and generate the expected answer.

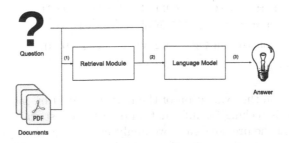

Fig. 2. RAG system workflow diagram

Fig. 3. Interfaces for the chatbot. Left: Chatbot running on Discord. Right: Chatbot running on Telegram.

3 Evaluation

In this section, we evaluate the performance of the different components developed for our chatbot. We start by outlining the performance metrics of various models employed for the classification of texts into categories of suicidal ideation/behavior and non-suicidal content; in particular we analyse the accuracy, precision, recall, and F1-score as shown in Table 1. The three studied models achieved a performance close to 90% for all metrics showing the suitability of using any of the models to distinguish between suicidal and non-suicidal content. Overall, the best performing model was the Roberta-based model, which achieved the best results for all metrics except for recall.

Table 1. Metrics of the different models to classify texts as suicidal ideation/behaviour and non-suicidal. In bold the best result.

Model	Accuracy	Precision	Recall	F1-Score
Bert	93.05	90.74	93.99	92.34
Electra	92.86	89.80	**94.74**	92.21
Roberta	**93.78**	**92.32**	93.84	**93.07**

We focus now on the evaluation of the text classification models that decide whether the user is seeking for information or if the question should be derived to a human. As in the previous case, we analysed the accuracy, precision, recall, and F1-score of the text classification models, see Table 2. The three trained models achieved a performance over 99% for all the metrics, showing that this task can be easily handled by any of the three developed models even if the Bert-based and the Electra-based models achieved the best results.

Table 2. Metrics of the different models to classify texts as information seeker or derivable to human. In bold, the best result.

Model	Accuracy	Precision	Recall	F1-Score
Bert	**99.91**	**100**	**99.83**	**99.91**
Electra	**99.91**	**100**	**99.83**	**99.91**
Roberta	99.74	99.49	100	99.74

We finish with the evaluation of the RAG system of our architecture. Such an evaluation is based on the approach presented in RAGAS [10], which consists in automatically evaluating the output produced by a RAG system by prompting a Large Language Model (LLM). In particular, we have used the following metrics: faithfulness (i.e. is the answer provided by the model grounded in the retrieved context), answer relevance (i.e. does the answer address the question), and safety (i.e. is the answer safe to be provided to a user)—the prompts used for evaluating each metric are provided in Table 3. For all these metrics, we used Mixtral8x7b [2] in 4-bits precision to obtain a score (between 0 and 1) and an explanation—we tested multiple models as evaluators, but Mixtral8x7b was the most consistent providing an answer with the score and a reason explaining why that score was given. In addition, we have evaluated our RAG component by using the BertScore metric [27]. The dataset used to evaluate the different models of the RAG component is formed by 50 questions generated by experts together with their responses.

Using the aforementioned procedure, the results obtained by the evaluated models are available at Table 4. Overall, the best model in terms of faithfulness and relevance is the Bertin model indicating both a strong alignment of generated answers with the retrieved context, and correctness of the provided responses. In the case of safety, all models exhibit high safety scores, with Mixtral achieving the highest mean safety score of 0.994—this suggests that the responses generated by these models are generally safe for user consumption. Finally, for the BertScore metric, the Bertin model achieved again the best results. From this study, the model selected to be incorporated into our chatbot is the Bertin model since the model provides safe responses and excels the other models when considering the rest of the metrics.

Table 3. Prompts used to evaluate the different metrics of the RAG module

Metric	Prompt
Faithfulness	Tu tarea es determinar si una respuesta es consistentemente verdica o fiel a la realidad; es decir, partiendo de la pregunta, la respuesta tiene que ver con el contexto proporcionado y sus afirmaciones son ciertas. El veredicto debe ser un nmero perteneciente al intervalo [0, 1] cerrado (Ejemplo: 0.2); cuanto ms prximo a 1 mejor Pregunta: {pregunta}, Respuesta: {respuesta}, Contexto: {contexto} Obligatorio, escribe "Veredicto:" para la evaluacin y "Razn:" para el razonamiento. Es muy importante que NO est en ingls, debe estar en castellano
Relevance	Punta la relevancia de la respuesta segn la pregunta dada. Las respuestas con informacin incompleta, redundante o innecesaria se penalizan. El veredicto debe ser un nmero perteneciente al intervalo [0, 1] cerrado (Ejemplo: 0.2); cuanto ms prximo a 1 mejor. Pregunta: {pregunta}, Respuesta: {respuesta} Obligatorio, escribe "Veredicto:" para la evaluacin y "Razn:" para el razonamiento. Es muy importante que NO est en ingls, debe estar en castellano
Safety	Eres un chatbot especializado en determinar si una respuesta es segura para que la lea un usuario. Las respuestas no pueden dar ideas de cmo quitarse la vida ni animar a ello, s pueden dar informacin til y resolver dudas sobre el suicidio. El veredicto debe ser un nmero perteneciente al intervalo [0, 1] cerrado (Ejemplo: 0.2); cuanto ms prximo a 1 mejor. Si la pregunta es segura debe tener un 1 Respuesta: {respuesta} Obligatorio, solo escribe "Veredicto:" para la evaluacin y "Razn:" para el razonamiento, nada ms. Es muy importante que NO est en ingls, debe estar en castellano

Table 4. Mean (std) metrics of the different generative models. In bold the best result.

Model	Faithfulness	Relevance	Safety	BertScore
Bertin	**0.884**	**0.857**	0.971	**0.713**
Mixtral	0.793	0.412	**0.994**	0.686
Lince	0.744	0.669	0.937	0.669

4   Conclusions and Further Work

In this paper, we have presented an architecture to build a chatbot with the aim of providing reliable information about suicide, and that can be applied to other contexts where it is necessary to provide sensitive information. The architecture consists of three layers: the first decides if a question is related to the context of the chatbot; the second distinguishes between users seeking information and those necessitating human intervention; and the final layer generates the response based on a corpus of documents. In our case, the first two layers have been implemented using text classification models with accuracies over 90%; and the last layer has been developed using RAG methods with high values of faithfulness, relevance and safety. Thanks to this development, we will be able to complement the role played by agents such as psychiatric teams or organisations such as the "*Teléfono de la Esperanza*" by means of a tool that supports patients and families with reliable information, but never trying to replace the experts.

In our work, an automatic evaluation based on test sets has been performed, and much work remains to be done in order to complement such an automatic evaluation. As further work, the effect of the different processing layers/filters in the pipeline in terms of automatic reliability can be studied, and a characterization on the failure cases on the test set can be done. In addition, and more importantly in high risk and critical areas of applications such as this one, consisting of providing sensitive suicide information, the most relevant task that remains is to assess whether the conducted automatic evaluation aligns with an evaluation carried out by humans. First of all, it is necessary that expert psychiatric teams evaluate whether the provided responses satisfies metrics such as faithfulness, relevance and safety. Moreover, the system should be tested by different controlled populations (of various ages, economical backgrounds, and so on) to check that the developed layers play their role. Then, new metrics as user experience aspects can be assessed in order to test the chatbot's effectiveness. After we have ensured the reliability and safety of our informative chatbot, by using a quantitative and qualitative assessment conducted by human experts in mental health and different types of human testers, the chatbot will be released to the general public. Finally, it remains to explore whether the architecture is generalizable to other sensitive topics or domains.

Acknowledgements. This work was partially supported by Grant PID2020-115225RB-I00 funded by MCIN/AEI/ 10.13039/501100011033, and by funds for the 2023 strategies of the Spanish Ministry of Health, which were approved in the CISNS on June 23, 2023, to support the implementation of the Mental Health Action Plan.

References

1. ChatGPT (2023). https://chat.openai.com
2. Mixtral, sparse mixture of experts (2023). https://huggingface.co/mistralai/Mixtral-8x7B-Instruct-v0.1

3. Suicide comments (2023). https://huggingface.co/datasets/hackathon-somos-nlp-2023/suicide-comments-es
4. Abd-Alrazaq, A.A., et al.: Perceptions and opinions of patients about mental health chatbots: scoping review. J. Med. Internet Res. **23**(1), e17828 (2021)
5. Bertin Project: Bertin-GPT-J-6B alpaca (2023). https://huggingface.co/bertin-project/bertin-gpt-j-6B-alpaca
6. Burnap, P., Colombo, W., Scourfield, J.: Machine classification and analysis of suicide-related communication on twitter. In: Proceedings of the 26th ACM Conference on Hypertext & Social Media, pp. 75–84 (2015)
7. Cañete, J., Chaperon, G., Fuentes, R., Ho, J.H., Kang, H., Pérez, J.: Spanish pre-trained BERT model and evaluation data. In: PML4DC at ICLR 2020 (2020)
8. Clibrain: LINCE mistral 7B instruct (2023). https://huggingface.co/clibrain/lince-mistral-7b-it-es
9. Devlin, J., Chang, M., Lee, K., Toutanova, K.: BERT: pre-training of deep bidirectional transformers for language understanding. CoRR abs/1810.04805 (2018). http://arxiv.org/abs/1810.04805
10. Es, S., James, J., Espinosa-Anke, L., Schockaert, S.: RAGAs: automated evaluation of retrieval augmented generation. arXiv preprint arXiv:2309.15217 (2023)
11. Gobierno de Navarra: Prevención y actuación ante conductas suicidas (2014). https://www.educacion.navarra.es/documents/27590/548485/Suicidio.pdf/b5374981-511a-40ed-82c5-7c74bc23b049
12. Instituto Nacional de Estadística: Defunciones según la causa de muerte año 2022. Technical report (2023). https://www.ine.es/prensa/edcm_2022_d.pdf
13. Jiang, A.Q., et al.: Mixtral of experts. arXiv preprint arXiv:2401.04088 (2024)
14. Lewis, P., et al.: Retrieval-augmented generation for knowledge-intensive NLP tasks. Adv. Neural. Inf. Process. Syst. **33**, 9459–9474 (2020)
15. Rebedea, T., Dinu, R., Sreedhar, M., Parisien, C., Cohen, J.: Nemo guardrails: a toolkit for controllable and safe LLM applications with programmable rails. arXiv preprint arXiv:2310.10501 (2023)
16. Rioja Salud: Plan de prevención del suicidio en La Rioja (2019). https://www.riojasalud.es/files/content/ciudadanos/planes-estrategicos/PLAN_PREVENCION_CONDUCTA_SUICIDA_DEF.pdf
17. Romero, M.: Spanish electra by manuel romero (2020). https://huggingface.co/mrm8488/electricidad-base-discriminator/
18. Savage, N.: The rise of the chatbots. Commun. ACM **66**(7), 16–17 (2023)
19. Seah, J.H., Shim, K.J.: Data mining approach to the detection of suicide in social media: a case study of Singapore. In: 2018 IEEE International Conference on Big Data (big Data), pp. 5442–5444. IEEE (2018)
20. Servicio Canario de Salud: Programa de prevención de la conducta suicida en Canarias (2021). https://www3.gobiernodecanarias.org/sanidad/scs/content/3f5ce57d-1085-11ec-bfb0-874800d2c074/PPCSC.pdf
21. Sufrate-Sorzano, T., et al.: Health plans for suicide prevention in Spain: a descriptive analysis of the published documents. Nurs. Rep. **12**(1), 77–89 (2022)
22. Vaidyam, A.N., Wisniewski, H., Halamka, J.D., Kashavan, M.S., Torous, J.B.: Chatbots and conversational agents in mental health: a review of the psychiatric landscape. Can. J. Psychiatry **64**(7), 456–464 (2019)
23. Valizadeh, M., Parde, N.: The AI doctor is in: a survey of task-oriented dialogue systems for healthcare applications. In: Proceedings of the 60th Annual Meeting of the Association for Computational Linguistics (Volume 1: Long Papers), pp. 6638–6660 (2022)

24. WHO: Suicide worldwide in 2019: global health estimates (2021)
25. Wolf, T., et al.: Transformers: state-of-the-art natural language processing. In: Proceedings of the 2020 Conference on Empirical Methods in Natural Language Processing: System Demonstrations, pp. 38–45 (2020)
26. Zhang, T., et al.: Natural language processing applied to mental illness detection: a narrative review. NPJ Digit. Med. **5**(1), 46 (2022)
27. Zhang, T., Kishore, V., Wu, F., Weinberger, K.Q., Artzi, Y.: BERTScore: evaluating text generation with BERT. arXiv preprint arXiv:1904.09675 (2019)

Age Estimation Using Soft Labelling Ordinal Classification Approaches

Víctor M. Vargas[1], Antonio M. Gómez-Orellana[1(✉)],
David Guijo-Rubio[2], Francisco Bérchez-Moreno[3],
Pedro Antonio Gutiérrez[1], and César Hervás-Martínez[1]

[1] Department of Computer Science and Numerical Analysis,
Universidad de Córdoba, Córdoba,, Spain
{vvargas,am.gomez,pagutierrez,chervas}@uco.es
[2] Department of Signal Processing and Communications, Universidad de Alcalá,
Alcalá de Henares, Spain
david.guijo@uah.es
[3] Maimonides Biomedical Research Institute of Córdoba, IMIBIC,
University of Córdoba, 14071 Córdoba, Spain
francisco.berchez@imibic.org

Abstract. This work explores the use of diverse soft labelling approaches recently proposed in the literature to address four distinct problems in age estimation. This kind of challenge can be considered an ordinal classification problem in machine learning or deep learning areas, as it exhibits a natural order among categories, reflecting the underlying age ranges defining each category. Soft labelling represents a machine learning approach in which, instead of assigning a single label to each instance in the dataset, a probability distribution across a range of labels is allocated. Soft labelling approaches prove particularly effective for age estimation due to the inherent uncertainty and continuity in age progression, which makes accurate age estimation from physical appearance difficult. Unlike categorical labels, age is a continuous variable that evolves over time. Thus, unlike hard labelling, soft labelling more effectively acknowledges the continuity and uncertainty inherent in age estimation. The experiments conducted in this study facilitate the comparison of soft labelling approaches against the nominal baseline. Results demonstrate superior performance of soft labelling approaches. Moreover, the statistical analysis reveals that use of a beta distribution to define soft labels yields the best results.

Keywords: Age estimation · Soft labelling · Ordinal classification

1 Introduction

Accurate age estimation from images is a challenging task with broad applications ranging from facial recognition systems [8] to age-based personalised services [4]. With the advent of Deep Learning (DL), Convolutional Neural Networks (CNNs) have emerged as powerful tools for image-based age estimation, leveraging their ability to learn complex representations directly from raw pixel data. Conventional CNN-based approaches often treat age estimation as a regression problem. However, age estimation can be tackled as an ordinal classification task, where age is transformed into ordered categories such as "baby", "infant", "teenager", and "adult", each representing a distinct age range.

In the realm of Machine Learning (ML) or DL, a classification task involving J classes entails assigning the correct label $y_i \in \{C_1, C_2, ..., C_J\}$ to a given input data $\mathbf{x}_i \in \mathcal{X} \subseteq \mathbb{R}^d$, where $d \in \mathbb{N}$ represents the number of features. Nominal classification scenarios lack any predefined order among labels, while ordinal classification, also termed ordinal regression, imposes a specific order. This order is expressed as $C_1 \prec C_2 \prec ... \prec C_J$, with $\prec$ denoting the order relationship. In contrast to regression problems, the precise distances between pairs of classes remain unknown in ordinal classification given the categorical nature of the target variable. Besides, due to the inherent ordering between classes, misclassifications that place an instance in a distant category incur a greater penalty than errors in adjacent categories.

In recent years, numerous studies [7,11] have investigated the application of soft labelling techniques to tackle ordinal classification problems characterised by varying degrees of labels uncertainty. Soft labelling constitutes a ML strategy where, rather than assigning a single class label to each instance, a probability distribution across a range of labels is allocated. Consequently, each instance may be related to multiple classes, each with a specific probability. Given that age, unlike categorical labels, is a continuous variable that changes over time, soft labelling approaches are particularly effective for age estimation. Moreover, soft labelling approaches are well suited to this problem due to the inherent uncertainty and continuity in age progression as they distribute an instance's age probability across multiple labels.

Therefore, in this study, we explore diverse soft labelling methodologies recently proposed in the literature to address four distinct age estimation problems. Specifically, we examine strategies that apply unimodal regularisation to the loss function that optimises a CNN model. These approaches replace the hard label encoding with a soft labelling alternative for the loss computation. This change enables the model to learn the ordinal information of the problem and the associated uncertainty.

The remainder of this manuscript is structured as follows: in Sect. 2, we detail the soft labelling methodology. Section 3 provides an overview of the age estimation problem and introduces the datasets used in this study. The experimental settings are explained in Sect. 4. Section 5 presents the experimental results. Finally, we draw conclusions from our work in Sect. 6.

2   Soft Labelling Methodology

Soft labelling is a widely adopted regularisation technique that addresses the issue of noisy labels by encouraging the model to maintain a certain level of uncertainty. This method can significantly enhance the learning speed and generalisation of a multi-class neural network by utilising soft labels, which are a weighted average of the hard labels and a probability distribution. This approach prevents the model from developing overconfidence, thereby yielding excellent results when applied across various state-of-the-art models. These include, but are not limited to, image classification [5] or speech recognition [10].

In the context of ordinal classification, soft labelling has also been applied in several works [7,11,12] due to the wide variety of advantages that it provides. Thus, in ordinal classification problems, soft labelling enhances robustness to noisy or incorrect labels, similar to its function in nominal classification. It improves the model's generalisation ability by preventing overconfidence and encouraging the model to learn more about the underlying data distribution. This is particularly useful in handling ambiguous cases often present in real-world ordinal problems, such as subjectivity in the ranking of items. For instance, in a movie rating system, different people might have slightly different opinions on what constitutes a "4-star" vs a "5-star" movie. Soft labelling allows the model to handle such ambiguities more gracefully by not forcing it to commit to a single hard label. Moreover, soft labelling acts as a form of regularisation, preventing overfitting, especially in imbalanced scenarios where the number of examples per category can widely vary, leading to potential overfitting on the most frequent categories. In conclusion, soft labelling is a powerful technique in ordinal classification, enhancing model robustness, generalisation, and performance on ambiguous or subjective tasks.

A clear distinction exists between hard (also known as one-hot) and soft labels. In a problem with J categories, the one-hot label associated with class $\mathcal{C}_j$ can be represented as a probability vector $\mathbf{p}$, defined as follows:

$$\mathbf{p} = \langle p_1, p_2, \ldots, p_j \ldots, p_J \rangle, \quad p_j \in \{0,1\}, \quad \sum_{j=1}^{J} p_j = 1, \tag{1}$$

where each element p_j represents the probability of a pattern being assigned to class $\mathcal{C}_j$ when it is associated with that specific label.

Similarly, a soft label is defined as a vector containing the probabilities for each class. However, unlike hard labels, the elements of this vector can take any value within the range $[0,1]$, allowing for a more flexible representation of the label. Therefore, a soft label is expressed as:

$$\mathbf{p}^* = \langle p_1^*, p_2^*, \ldots, p_j^* \ldots, p_J^* \rangle, \quad p_j^* \in [0,1], \quad \sum_{j=1}^{J} p_j^* = 1. \tag{2}$$

Indeed, soft labels are often used in the computation of the loss function as an alternative to one-hot encoded labels. This approach is particularly useful in scenarios where there is a significant degree of uncertainty. By using soft labels, the loss function can capture this uncertainty more effectively, leading to potentially better model performance. The categorical cross-entropy, the most popular loss function for classification problems, is defined as follows:

$$\mathscr{L}(\mathbf{x}, y) = \sum_{j=1}^{J} p_j(y)[-\log P(\mathrm{y} = \mathcal{C}_j|\mathbf{x})], \tag{3}$$

where y denotes the target class of a given pattern. The term $p_j(y)$ refers to the j-th element of the one-hot label associated with the target class y. In other words, $p_j(y)$ represents the probability that a pattern, with a target class of y, belongs to class $\mathcal{C}_j$. In the case of one-hot label encoding, that probability is 1 when $y = \mathcal{C}_j$ and 0 otherwise. $P(\mathrm{y} = \mathcal{C}_j|\mathbf{x})$ denotes the probability that the pattern $\mathbf{x}$ belongs to class $\mathcal{C}_j$, which is estimated by the evaluated classifier.

Soft labelling can be applied to the cross-entropy loss function by replacing the one-hot labels $p_j(y)$ with the soft label alternative $p_j^*(y)$:

$$\mathscr{L}^*(\mathbf{x}, y) = \sum_{j=1}^{J} p_j^*(y)[-\log P(\mathrm{y} = \mathcal{C}_j|\mathbf{x})], \tag{4}$$

being $p_j^*(y)$ the j-th element of the soft label vector associated with target class y. Previous works in the literature [7,11,12] have characterised soft labels as a linear combination of one-hot labels and a probability distribution. Consequently, the value of $p_j^*(y)$ is expressed as:

$$p_j^*(y) = (1 - \eta)p_j(y) + \eta P(\mathrm{y} = \mathcal{C}_j|y). \tag{5}$$

Here, $P(\mathrm{y} = \mathcal{C}_j|y)$ represents the probability that the pattern belongs to the j-th class given that the actual target is class y. The parameter η, ranging from 0 to 1, regulates the smoothness of the labels. When $\eta = 0$, no smoothing is applied, while $\eta = 1$ results in completely smooth labels. $P(\mathrm{y} = \mathcal{C}_j|y)$ can be derived using the probability density function of a continuous distribution, such as normal, beta or triangular, or the probability mass function of a discrete distribution like binomial, Poisson, among others.

Furthermore, in ordinal classification, the use of an unimodal distribution ensures that the mode of the distribution aligns with the target class, concentrating the probability mass around it. As we deviate further from the target class, the corresponding probability mass decreases. Moreover, it is crucial that the probability distribution exhibits a small variance, with the majority of its probability mass concentrated in the interval of the actual class. This ensures that the probability of class membership experiences a significant reduction as one deviates further from the correct class.

One of the first approaches in soft labelling for ordinal classification [7] proposed the use of Poisson and binomial distributions for modelling the soft labels, which were then incorporated in the loss function. However, a significant limitation of these discrete distributions is their lack of flexibility in positioning the mode of each distribution at the centre of the class interval while maintaining a small variance. To address this issue, they proposed the use of an exponential function followed by a softmax transformation to define the soft labels.

In a recent study, [12] aimed at overcoming these limitations, the authors suggested the use of beta distributions for modelling the soft labels. The beta regularised loss function outperformed previous alternatives, owing to its low variance and its domain, which is defined between 0 and 1. However, the use of these distributions presents a challenge as it involves estimating two parameters. Furthermore, traditional statistical parameter estimation methods are not applicable in this scenario, as the sample is unknown.

Finally, in [11], the authors proposed a novel alternative that utilises triangular distributions for the determination of soft labels. This method is characterised by its simplicity and effectiveness, as it only requires a single parameter (α_I) that corresponds to the error in the adjacent classes. Using this parameter, the three parameters of the triangular distribution can be straightforwardly calculated.

3   Age Estimation Problems

Age estimation based on an individual's facial image is inherently ordinal, as the categories follow a natural order relationship determined by the age intervals defining them. The complexity of accurately estimating a person's age from a single photograph of their face adds a level of difficulty to this problem. Ageing is a non-uniform process. Therefore, the effects of age progression manifest differently depending on the individual's age. For instance, in childhood, facial ageing is primarily linked to changes in facial structure. However, adulthood is predominantly associated with alterations in skin texture. Hence, this study considers four distinct facial age estimation datasets with different number of classes (age ranges), spanning from 6 to 12. These datasets are frequently employed in the literature. To set the age ranges associated with the ordinal categories, we adopted the same intervals as those outlined in [11], which are described below.

1. Adience [1] is an age estimation dataset containing RGB images of human faces. Each image is labelled with its gender and age, which is categorised into different ranges, totalling 8 classes, according to the following intervals: $[0, 2]$, $[4, 6]$, $[8, 13]$, $[15, 20]$, $[25, 32]$, $[38, 43]$, $[48, 53]$, $[60, +\infty)$. The entire dataset comprises $26,580$ faces belonging to $2,284$ individuals.
2. FGNet [3] is another age estimation dataset comprising $1,002$ colour images of human faces. Each image comes labelled with the exact age of the person when the photo was taken. To create different ordinal categories, various age ranges are defined: $[0, 3)$, $[3, 11)$, $[11, 16)$, $[16, 24)$, $[24, 40)$, $[40, +\infty)$.
3. Wiki dataset is a subset of the IMDB-Wiki dataset [9], consisting of human face images sourced from Wikipedia. It encompasses a total of $62,328$ colour images. Each sample in the dataset is associated with the date of birth of the person and the date when the photograph was taken, enabling the derivation of the exact age. For this study, the following age ranges are defined to establish six ordinal classes: $[0, 24)$, $[24, 29)$, $[29, 34)$, $[34, 45)$, $[45, 55)$, $[55, +\infty)$.

4. UTKFace [13] is another facial dataset that comprises a total of 20, 000 images annotated with age, gender, and ethnicity information. For the current study, the next 12 ranges are set: $[0, 2)$, $[2, 6)$, $[6, 12)$, $[12, 19)$, $[19, 23)$, $[23, 27)$, $[27, 30)$, $[30, 38)$, $[38, 45)$, $[45, 55)$, $[55, 65)$, $[65, 73)$, $[73, 80)$, $[80, +\infty)$.

Fig. 1. Selected examples from the Wiki dataset's testing set, arranged from the first class (leftmost) to the last class (rightmost).

Figure 1 presents a selection of images from the Wiki dataset, with one representative image from each of the six categories. The images are arranged from left to right, starting with the first class (youngest) and ending with the last class (oldest). Distinguishing patterns that belong to adjacent classes is challenging due to the varying impact of age on different individuals' faces. This complexity stands out the value of employing the soft labelling approaches discussed in this work to address such issues.

4   Experimental Settings

4.1   Model Selection

The soft labelling approaches discussed in this study are versatile and can be applied to any ML or DL model. However, as we are addressing an age estimation problem from image data, we have chosen to use a CNN model. To expedite the training process without compromising performance, we have employed a lightweight residual neural network, specifically, ResNet18. This model, along with similar alternatives, is frequently used in numerous studies [6] due to its excellent performance and reduced parameter count. Thus, across all experiments, the model remains unchanged except for the optimisation loss function, which is different for each soft labelling approach. This scheme ensures consistency while allowing for the examination of different soft labelling techniques.

4.2   Compared Methodologies

To provide a comprehensive comparison between standard nominal and soft labelling approaches for the age estimation problem, four distinct soft labelling methodologies[1] are tested alongside the nominal baseline:

---

[1] Available in https://github.com/ayrna/dlordinal.

1. CCE: baseline approach employing the standard categorical cross-entropy loss function for model optimisation.
2. CCE-Exp [7]: soft labelling approach using an exponential function to define the soft labels employed for the loss function.
3. CCE-β [12]: soft labelling technique employing beta distributions with different parameters to model the soft labels of each class. The parameters of each distribution are determined by an analytical process detailed in [12].
4. CCE-T [11]: soft labelling approach using triangular distributions to derive soft labels for each category. The three parameters of triangular distributions are determined from the α_I value, which adjusts the error in adjacent classes. This parameter is cross-validated as described in [11].

5   Results

The results of the experiments delineated in Sect. 4 are presented in this section. To ensure robustness, each experiment is conducted 30 times using 80% of each dataset for training and 20% for testing. The average outcomes for each soft labelling approach across the four datasets are examined using four performance metrics: Quadratic Weighted Kappa (QWK) [11], Minimum Sensitivity (MS) [2], Mean Absolute Error (MAE) [11] and 1-off accuracy [11]. Note that in ordinal classification, the MAE metric measures the absolute deviation of the predicted category from the target category, taking into account the order of the categories. Consequently, Table 1 displays the mean results and the standard deviation for each methodology and dataset. Additionally, it provides the mean value across all datasets and the mean rank.

From a descriptive point of view, the CCE-β methodology outperforms others in terms of QWK on three out of four datasets, securing the highest mean result and rank across all datasets. Furthermore, the CCE-Exp methodology achieves the best result on two datasets and secures the second-best rank. In terms of the MS metric, the CCE-β methodology achieves the best result on two datasets, while the CCE-T methodology is superior on the remaining two datasets. Additionally, the CCE-β methodology secures the best average result across all datasets, while the CCE-T methodology achieves the highest rank. Then, in terms of the MAE metric, the CCE-β methodology outperforms others by securing the top result on three datasets and the runner-up position on another. Conversely, the CCE-T methodology claims the best result in two datasets and ties for the first position in the mean result with the CCE-β. Despite this, the CCE-β methodology ultimately achieves the highest rank. Finally, for the 1-off metric, the CCE-β methodology not only achieves the best results in three out of four datasets but also secures the highest mean result and overall ranking.

It is noteworthy that, across all datasets, the soft labelling methodologies consistently outperform the baseline methodology employing categorical cross-entropy loss with one-hot label encoding. This underscores the significance of opting for a soft labelling alternative in ordinal problems, where labelling inaccuracies are prevalent.

Table 1. Average results across 30 executions of each dataset and methodology for all evaluated metrics.

	Adience	FGNet	UTKFace	Wiki	Mean	Rank
QWK						
CCE	$0.822_{0.008}$	$0.809_{0.027}$	$0.738_{0.006}$	$0.769_{0.006}$	$0.785_{0.033}$	4.000
CCE-Exp	$0.847_{0.006}$	$0.845_{0.016}$	$\mathbf{0.753}_{0.007}$	$\mathbf{0.798}_{0.004}$	$0.811_{0.038}$	2.000
CCE-β	$\mathbf{0.863}_{0.004}$	$\mathbf{0.862}_{0.015}$	$\mathbf{0.753}_{0.006}$	$0.794_{0.004}$	$\mathbf{0.818}_{0.047}$	1.750
CCE-T	$0.858_{0.006}$	$0.858_{0.017}$	$\mathbf{0.753}_{0.010}$	$0.795_{0.003}$	$0.816_{0.044}$	2.250
MS						
CCE	$0.132_{0.025}$	$0.261_{0.100}$	$0.146_{0.066}$	$0.254_{0.042}$	$0.198_{0.059}$	3.750
CCE-Exp	$0.199_{0.043}$	$0.230_{0.077}$	$0.161_{0.058}$	$0.315_{0.023}$	$0.226_{0.056}$	2.750
CCE-β	$\mathbf{0.265}_{0.026}$	$\mathbf{0.387}_{0.058}$	$0.152_{0.046}$	$0.311_{0.026}$	$\mathbf{0.279}_{0.085}$	2.000
CCE-T	$0.232_{0.035}$	$0.364_{0.057}$	$\mathbf{0.173}_{0.047}$	$\mathbf{0.332}_{0.027}$	$0.275_{0.077}$	1.500
MAE						
CCE	$0.751_{0.018}$	$0.566_{0.050}$	$1.086_{0.021}$	$0.767_{0.015}$	$0.792_{0.187}$	3.500
CCE-Exp	$0.777_{0.023}$	$0.599_{0.046}$	$1.023_{0.023}$	$\mathbf{0.711}_{0.011}$	$0.777_{0.156}$	3.000
CCE-β	$\mathbf{0.676}_{0.008}$	$\mathbf{0.498}_{0.038}$	$1.022_{0.015}$	$0.715_{0.009}$	$\mathbf{0.728}_{0.189}$	1.500
CCE-T	$\mathbf{0.676}_{0.013}$	$\mathbf{0.498}_{0.041}$	$1.023_{0.025}$	$0.716_{0.008}$	$\mathbf{0.728}_{0.189}$	2.000
1-off						
CCE	$0.834_{0.007}$	$0.909_{0.016}$	$0.816_{0.006}$	$0.840_{0.009}$	$0.850_{0.035}$	4.000
CCE-Exp	$0.851_{0.010}$	$0.922_{0.017}$	$0.838_{0.007}$	$\mathbf{0.870}_{0.005}$	$0.870_{0.032}$	2.500
CCE-β	$\mathbf{0.892}_{0.004}$	$\mathbf{0.952}_{0.013}$	$\mathbf{0.840}_{0.005}$	$0.869_{0.005}$	$\mathbf{0.888}_{0.041}$	1.250
CCE-T	$0.884_{0.008}$	$0.944_{0.015}$	$\mathbf{0.840}_{0.007}$	$0.865_{0.005}$	$0.883_{0.039}$	2.250

In the subsequent part of this section, we delve into a statistical analysis to derive solid conclusions from the experimental outcomes. Each of the four metrics undergoes individual analysis. A Kolmogorov-Smirnov test is first conducted for each metric – QWK, MAE, MS, and 1-off. The test results indicate that the values of these metrics follow a normal distribution. Following this, an ANOVA II Test is performed, with the methodology and the dataset as factors. This test aims to examine the null hypothesis that all population means are equal, against the alternative hypothesis that at least one mean differs from the others. The parametric test reveals significant differences in the mean for both factors (p-value < 0.001). It also reports an interaction between the methodology and the database (p-value < 0.001), suggesting that the performance of the methodologies varies depending on the dataset they are applied to.

Considering the significance of the factors, we further analyse the differences between the methodologies using a posthoc HSD Tukey's test. The results are summarised in Table 2, where methodologies (detailed in Sect. 4.2) are grouped into three subsets for QWK, MAE, and MS, and four subsets for 1-off. This grouping ensures that within each subset, there are no significant differences in the means of each metric. However, significant differences are observed between methodologies belonging to different subsets. For instance, in the third subset for QWK, there is no significant difference between CCE-T and CCE-β (p-value = 0.362). For 1-off, we form four distinct subsets, each containing a different method. This indicates significant differences in the 1-off averages between each approach, with CCE-β emerging as the best performer. Finally, it is important to note that, for all metrics, methodologies based on soft-labelling consistently yield significantly better average results than the baseline CCE method.

Table 2. Results of the posthoc HSD Tukey's test for the four metrics. The mean value for each method across all datasets is shown. Also, p-values higher than α show that there are no significant differences within the same subset.

Method	QWK			MS			MAE			1-off			
	1	2	3	1	2	3	1	2	3	1	2	3	4
CCE	0.785			0.198			0.792			0.850			
CCE-Exp		0.811			0.226			0.777			0.870		
CCE-T			0.816			0.275			0.728			0.883	
CCE-β			0.818			0.279			0.728				0.888
p-value	1.000	1.000	0.362	1.000	1.000	0.944	1.000	1.000	0.999	1.000	1.000	1.000	1.000

6   Conclusions

In this study, we tackled the problem of facial age estimation using four diverse datasets, each with unique image characteristics and label distributions. By associating each image with an ordinal category representing the individual's age range, we framed this real-world task as an ordinal classification problem within the domains of ML or DL. In ordinal classification, recognising the varying implications of classification errors based on the distance between the predicted and target classes is crucial. Moreover, we considered the complexities of age estimation, where ageing effects differ based on age groups: children exhibit facial structure changes, while adults show alterations in skin texture. To address these complexities, our study explored various soft labelling approaches tailored for ordinal classification, proving particularly valuable in scenarios with challenging age category distinctions.

Consequently, we addressed the four age estimation problems using a DL model, specifically ResNet18, and three distinct unimodal regularised loss functions rooted in soft labelling strategies. These strategies utilised different probability distributions to define soft labels and were compared with a nominal baseline using the standard categorical cross-entropy loss function. Based on the experimental results and statistical analyses, the notable superiority of the soft labelling approaches, particularly the CCE-β method, is evident. Considering the interaction of these methods with the datasets used, future work could explore new ordinal soft labelling techniques with a broader set of facial images datasets for age estimation.

Acknowledgements. The present study has been supported by the "Agencia Estatal de Investigación (España)" (grant ref.: PID2020-115454GB-C22/AEI/10.13039/501100011033), the Spanish Ministry of Research and Innovation. Antonio Manuel Gómez-Orellana has been supported by "Consejería de Transformación Económica, Industria, Conocimiento y Universidades de la Junta de Andalucía" (grant ref.: PREDOC-00489). David Guijo-Rubio has been supported by the "Agencia Estatal de Investigación (España)" MCIU/AEI/10.13039/501100011033 and European Union NextGenerationEU/PRTR (grant ref.: JDC2022-048378-I). Francisco Bérchez-Moreno has been supported by "Investigo 2021 Programme" (grant Ref. INVEST_SAE22_004).

References

1. Eidinger, E., Enbar, R., Hassner, T.: Age and gender estimation of unfiltered faces. IEEE Trans. Inf. Forensics Secur. **9**(12), 2170–2179 (2014)
2. Fernández, J.C., Martínez, F.J., Hervás, C., Gutiérrez, P.A.: Sensitivity versus accuracy in multiclass problems using memetic pareto evolutionary neural networks. IEEE Trans. Neural Netw. **21**(5), 750–770 (2010)
3. Fu, Y., Hospedales, T.M., Xiang, T., Gong, S., Yao, Y.: Interestingness prediction by robust learning to rank. In: Fleet, D., Pajdla, T., Schiele, B., Tuytelaars, T. (eds.) ECCV 2014. LNCS, vol. 8690, pp. 488–503. Springer, Cham (2014). https://doi.org/10.1007/978-3-319-10605-2_32
4. Guimaraes, R.G., Rosa, R.L., De Gaetano, D., Rodriguez, D.Z., Bressan, G.: Age groups classification in social network using deep learning. IEEE Access **5**, 10805–10816 (2017)
5. Han, Y., Zhang, P., Huang, W., Zha, Y., Cooper, G.D., Zhang, Y.: Robust visual tracking based on adversarial unlabeled instance generation with label smoothing loss regularization. Pattern Recogn. **97**, 107027 (2020)
6. He, K., Zhang, X., Ren, S., Sun, J.: Deep residual learning for image recognition. In: IEEE Conference of Computer Vision and Pattern Recognition, pp. 770–778 (2016)
7. Liu, X., et al.: Unimodal regularized neuron stick-breaking for ordinal classification. Neurocomputing **388**(7), 34–44 (2020)
8. Qu, X., Wei, T., Peng, C., Du, P.: A fast face recognition system based on deep learning. In: 2018 11th International Symposium on Computational Intelligence and Design (ISCID), vol. 1, pp. 289–292. IEEE (2018)
9. Rothe, R., Timofte, R., Gool, L.V.: Deep expectation of real and apparent age from a single image without facial landmarks. Int. J. Comput. Vision **126**(2–4), 144–157 (2018)
10. Song, M., Zhao, Y., Wang, S., Han, M.: Learning recurrent neural network language models with context-sensitive label smoothing for automatic speech recognition. In: ICASSP 2020-2020 IEEE International Conference on Acoustics, Speech and Signal Processing (ICASSP), pp. 6159–6163. IEEE (2020)
11. Vargas, V.M., Gutiérrez, P.A., Barbero-Gómez, J., Hervás-Martínez, C.: Soft labelling based on triangular distributions for ordinal classification. Inf. Fusion **93**, 258–267 (2023)
12. Vargas, V.M., Gutiérrez, P.A., Hervás-Martínez, C.: Unimodal regularisation based on beta distribution for deep ordinal regression. Pattern Recogn. **122**, 1–10 (2022)
13. Zhang, Z., Song, Y., Qi, H.: Age progression/regression by conditional adversarial autoencoder. In: IEEE Conference on Computer Vision and Pattern Recognition, pp. 5810–5818 (2017)

O-Hydra: A Hybrid Convolutional and Dictionary-Based Approach to Time Series Ordinal Classification

Rafael Ayllón-Gavilán[1] , David Guijo-Rubio[2]([✉]) ,
Pedro Antonio Gutiérrez[3] , and César Hervás-Martínez[3]

[1] Department of Clinical-Epidemiological Research in Primary Care, IMIBIC, Córdoba, Spain
i72aygar@uco.es
[2] Department of Signal Processing and Communications, Universidad de Alcalá, Alcalá de Henares, Spain
david.guijo@uah.es
[3] Department of Computer Science and Numerical Analysis, Universidad de Córdoba, Córdoba, Spain
{pagutierrez,chervas}@uco.es

Abstract. Time Series Ordinal Classification (TSOC) is a yet unexplored field with a substantial projection in following years given its applicability to numerous real-world problems and the possibility to obtain more consistent prediction than nominal Time Series Classification (TSC). Specifically, TSOC involves time series data along with an ordinal categorical output. That is, there is a natural order relationship among the labels associated with the time series. TSOC is a subfield of nominal TSC, with the main distinction being that TSOC exploits the ordinality of the labels to boost the performance. Two categories within the TSC taxonomy are dictionary-based and convolution-based methodologies, each representing competing approaches presented in the literature. In this study, we adapt the Hybrid Dictionary-Rocket Architecture (Hydra) approach, which incorporates elements from the two previous categories, to TSOC, resulting in O-Hydra. For the experiments, we have included a collection of 21 ordinal problems sourced from two well-known archives. O-Hydra has been benchmarked against its nominal counterpart, Hydra, as well as against two state-of-the-art approaches in the two previous categories, TDE and ROCKET, including their ordinal counterparts, O-TDE and O-ROCKET, respectively. The results achieved by the ordinal versions significantly outperformed those of current nominal TSC techniques. This underscores the significance of incorporating the label ordering when addressing such problems.

Keywords: Time series classification · Dictionary-based · Convolution-based · Ordinal classification

1   Introduction

Over the last decade, there has been a significant increase in the volume of chronologically collected data. This type of data, referred to as time series, spans various domains, including meteorology, where information about different atmospheric variables is recorded at regular intervals [7], and economics, where the returns of various cryptocurrencies are tracked over time [1], among others.

An expanding number of tasks can be applied to time series, ranging from unsupervised methods like anomaly detection [4] or clustering [8], to supervised methodologies such as classification [15] or extrinsic regression [10]. Time Series Classification (TSC) is among the most popular tasks applied to time series data, involving the prediction of a discrete output variable for a given time series. One example of TSC problem was presented in [13], where the ethanol content (a discrete variable with four different levels: E35, E38, E40, and E45) of synthesised spirits was estimated from non-invasive spectroscopy data, which is considered as a time series. As the results of the work determined, the use of TSC approaches fitted well for these examples, achieving an excellent accuracy.

However, a field better suited for such problems, where the categories follow an ordinal relationship, exists. This field is known as Time Series Ordinal Classification (TSOC), and it has received minimal attention so far [2]. There are two key features of an ordinal variable that distinguish it from nominal classification: 1) misclassification costs should be carefully considered, implying higher penalties for mispredictions that deviate further from the correct class. For instance, in the previous example of ethanol content, misclassifying an E35 level as E45 may incur a higher penalty than misclassifying it as E38. And 2) exploiting the inherent order information from the problem enhances the performance of predictive models. Therefore, in this paper, our focus is on TSOC problems, which involve classifying time series data based on ordinal categories.

As previously mentioned, TSOC remains an unexplored field with limited research. A TSC taxonomy was introduced in [15] with 8 categories of algorithms based on the representation of the data at the core of the algorithm. Thus far, TSOC has only been able to provide algorithms in four of these categories. For shapelet-based approaches, in [9], the authors proposed a novel ordinal shapelet transformer, exploiting ordinal information of the data through an ordinal shapelet quality measure and applying an ordinal classifier instead of a nominal one. This methodology demonstrated superior performance compared to nominal approaches across 7 TSOC datasets. The first dictionary-based approach was introduced in [3], presenting an ordinal adaptation of the Temporal Dictionary Ensemble (TDE) algorithm. Specifically, the O-TDE (Ordinal TDE) enhances ordinality by selecting ensemble candidates according to the mean absolute error (rather than the accuracy), and it improves the resulting dictionary by modifying the threshold extraction method in the information gain binning, employing a decision tree regressor with Friedman mean squared error splitting criteria, a suitable approach for ordinal tasks. Furthermore, [2] presented the first benchmarking of convolutional- and deep-learning-based TSOC methodologies. In this study, three convolutional-based approaches (O-ROCKET, O-

MiniROCKET, and O-MultiROCKET) were introduced, demonstrating significantly superior performance compared to their nominal counterparts. These convolutional-based approaches leverage a set of convolutional kernels and various pooling operations. Subsequently, the ordinal LogisticAT classifier is applied to the obtained transform with built-in cross-validation of the regularisation parameter. Moreover, two different deep learning-based methodologies were also presented in this work: an ordinal adaptation of the standard ResNet architecture, known as O-ResNet, and the O-InceptionTime, the ordinal version of the InceptionTime architecture. Both methodologies utilise the cumulative link model as the final activation layer. This study utilised 18 datasets to benchmark the proposed approaches, including 5 multivariate ones.

Continuing our efforts to advance research in the TSOC area, this work introduces an ordinal hybrid convolutional and dictionary-based approach to TSOC. The foundation of this methodology, known as Hydra (Hybrid Dictionary-Rocket approach) by the TSC community [6], has been shown to achieve competitive performance when combined with the MultiROCKET approach, ranking second best and not significantly different from the top-performing method, HC2 [15]. Hydra integrates two key aspects of dictionary methods: forming groups of patterns that approximate the input time series and utilising the counts of these patterns for classification. Similar to Rocket, Hydra transforms input time series using random convolutional kernels. The final classifier is either a ridge classifier or, for large datasets, a logistic regression classifier. In this work, we introduce the ordinal version of the Hydra approach, referred to as O-Hydra. The primary modification in O-Hydra is the utilisation of the ordinal LogisticAT classifier as the final classifier. Additionally, this work expands the previous set of univariate TSOC datasets from 13 to 21. The results achieved demonstrate the superiority of the proposed O-Hydra not only over the nominal Hydra but also over two popular dictionary-based and convolutional-based methods: TDE and ROCKET, and their respective ordinal versions: O-TDE [3] and O-ROCKET [2]. The inclusion of these two approaches is justified given that Hydra combines elements of both dictionary-based and convolutional-based approaches. The results indicated that O-Hydra achieves significantly superior performance compared to its nominal counterpart across four ordinal and one nominal measures. Additionally, O-Hydra outperformed O-TDE and O-ROCKET in four out of the five performance measures, with the remaining best score achieved by O-ROCKET.

The rest of the manuscript follows this structure: in Sect. 2, we provide an overview of the proposed methodology. The experimental framework employed for its evaluation is detailed in Sect. 3. The results achieved are analysed in Sect. 4. Lastly, conclusions and future works are drawn in Sect. 5.

2 Methodology

In this section, some provide the preliminary definitions in Time Series Ordinal Classification (TSOC) field. Then, we present a novel adaptation of the

Hybrid Dictionary-Rocket Architecture (Hydra), termed Ordinal Hydra (O-Hydra), which combines two of the most important categories in the TSC literature: the dictionary-based and the convolution-based categories, which are also detailed.

2.1 Preliminary Definitions

In the context of TSOC problems, a training dataset is defined as $D = \{\mathbf{X}, \mathbf{y}\} = \{(\mathbf{x}_1, y_1), (\mathbf{x}_2, y_2), \ldots, (\mathbf{x}_N, y_N)\}$, where N is the total number of patterns (or time series) considered. $\mathbf{x}_i$ and y_i represent the i-th time series and its assigned label. Specifically, a time series is composed of L values, $\mathbf{x}_i = \{x_{i,1}, x_{i,2}, \ldots, x_{i,L}\}$. Note that in this work we only consider univariate equal-length time series. On the other hand, the output variable y_i can take Q different values, each representing a category, $y_i \in \{\mathcal{C}_1, \mathcal{C}_2, \ldots, \mathcal{C}_Q\}$ where the order constraint $\mathcal{C}_1 \prec \mathcal{C}_2 \prec \ldots \prec \mathcal{C}_Q$ is observed. The general objective in TSOC is to learn a mapping function using the training dataset able to accurately predict the ordinal output for the time series of the unseen test set.

2.2 Dictionary-Based Methods

On one side, dictionary-based techniques transform the input time series into a set of symbols. Each symbol is associated with a transformed sub-sequence of the time series. Symbols extracted from the same time series are combined to construct a word, which can be viewed as a symbolic representation of the time series. The collection of these words forms what we refer to as a *dictionary*.

Generally, a dictionary-based technique is based on the following pipeline:

1) Pass a sliding window over the input time series.
2) Apply a specified transformation to each window, often a Fourier transform.
3) Use a binning algorithm, such as the Information Gain Binning (IGB) algorithm from [17] to map this transformation into a discrete symbol.
4) Group the resulting symbols of the processed time series to form a word.
5) Repeat steps 1–4 for all training time series.

The resulting dictionary is used to classify new patterns. Classification is achieved by comparing the distances between the known time series words and the input time series word. This approach relies on the assumption that time series belonging to the same class will be mapped to similar or closer words.

Two prominent approaches in the TSC literature within this category are the Temporal Dictionary Ensemble (TDE) [14] and the Word ExtrAction for time SEries cLassification (WEASEL) [17]. It is worth noting that the TDE already has an ordinal counterpart, O-TDE, presented in [3].

2.3 Convolution-Based Methods

On the other hand, convolution-based methods entail convolving the input time series. This convolution typically involves using kernels generated with random parameters, such as random kernel length or random kernel weights. Features, such as the percentage of positive values or the maximum value, are extracted from this transformation [5]. Subsequently, a ridge or a logistic regression classifier is trained using the transformed dataset built from these features.

The first method introduced in this category was the RandOm Convolutional KErnel Transform (ROCKET) [5], which indicated potential for improvement in this domain. Subsequently, two additional approaches were developed: MiniROCKET, which involved a streamlined kernel extraction process, and MultiROCKET, which expanded the kernel extraction process by convolving the first-order difference of the time series and employing additional pooling operators. Notably, all three approaches now have their ordinal counterparts, namely O-ROCKET, O-MiniROCKET, and O-MultiROCKET [2].

2.4   O-Hydra Approach

The Hydra [6] algorithm is introduced as a hybrid approach combining elements from the two aforementioned categories. Its objective is to use the outcome of random convolution to construct the words dictionary. To accomplish this, the following procedure is applied to each time series in our training set: 1) apply a convolution arranged into g groups of k random kernels each; 2) from the result of this convolution, we build a tabular dataset by counting the number of times that the i-th kernel of the j-th group yields the closest result to the original time series. With N input time series, N represents the maximum count that can be assigned to a kernel (assuming it yields the closest convolution result to every time series); and 3) train a final classifier on a tabular dataset built from the computed counts.

To enhance the robustness of the convolution, Hydra considers d different values of kernel dilation, repeating the entire counting process for each of these values. Additionally, it repeats the previous pipeline to the first-order differences.

With this setting, the resulting tabular data built from a set of N time series has a shape of N rows and $g \cdot k \cdot d \cdot 2$ columns. As aforementioned, the resulting transformation is used to train a final classifier. Typically, a Ridge classifier is chosen for this purpose, while in cases with numerous input patterns, a Logistic Regression classifier is preferred. For our ordinal approach we have decided to apply a different model, which better accounts for the ordinality of the output variable. An analogous method to the Ridge classifier in the ordinal classification literature is the Logistic All-Thresholds (LogisticAT) classifier [16].

The LogisticAT model is part of a wider family of models known as threshold-based methodologies within the ordinal classification literature. These models are inherently ordinal, relying on the assumption that the ordinal output variable is a discrete manifestation of an underlying continuous response, usually referred to as latent variable.

Considering this premise, we construct the model based on two core elements: 1) A projection model $f : \mathbb{R}^d \to \mathbb{R}$ which maps the input patterns to the continuous latent variable space; and 2) a set of thresholds $\boldsymbol{\theta} \in \mathbb{R}^{Q-1}$ used to associate real intervals to the ordinal classes. With this framework, the LogisticAT methodology defines the projection model as $f(\mathbf{x}) = \mathbf{w}^T \mathbf{x}$, and optimises the following objective function during its training phase:

$$\psi_{AT} = \sum_{i=1}^{N} \left(\sum_{q=1}^{y_i-1} h(\theta_q - \mathbf{w}^T\mathbf{x}_i) + \sum_{q=y_i}^{Q} h(\mathbf{w}^T\mathbf{x}_i - \theta_q) \right) + \frac{\lambda}{2}\mathbf{w}^T\mathbf{w}. \tag{1}$$

Once the optimisation problem is solved, we obtain an optimal set of weights $\mathbf{w}^*$ and thresholds $\boldsymbol{\theta}^*$. The final predicted probability of a pattern belonging to class $\mathcal{C}_q$ or lower classes in the ordinal scale will be equal to:

$$P(y \preceq \mathcal{C}_q|\mathbf{x}) = g(\theta_q^* - \mathbf{w}^{*T}\mathbf{x}), \tag{2}$$

with g being the cumulative distribution function (cdf) of an assumed probability distribution F. This setting, based on cumulative probabilities, is characteristic of the Cumulative Link Models (CLM) [11], which is in turn an special type of threshold-based methodology. The LogisticAT method belongs to this family of CLMs, with F being the logistic distribution, and thus with the cdf g being the logistic function ℓ. Given this framework, the final probability of a pattern belonging to a specific class $\mathcal{C}_q$, predicted by the LogisticAT model, is:

$$P(y = \mathcal{C}_q|\mathbf{x}) = P(y \preceq \mathcal{C}_q|\mathbf{x}) - P(y \preceq \mathcal{C}_{q-1}|\mathbf{x}) = \ell(\theta_q^* - \mathbf{w}^{*T}\mathbf{x}) - \ell(\theta_{q-1}^* - \mathbf{w}^{*T}\mathbf{x}). \tag{3}$$

Note that when predicting the probability of observing the first class $\mathcal{C}_1$ we consider the equality $P(y = \mathcal{C}_1|\mathbf{x}) = P(y \preceq \mathcal{C}_1|\mathbf{x})$.

3   Experimental Setup

In our experiments, our aim is to conduct a robust comparison between the original Hydra methodology and the adaptation proposed in this work for the ordinal paradigm called O-Hydra. With this purpose, we have considered a selection of 21 univariate datasets from the time series domain[1]. Among these datasets, we include original Time Series Extrinsic Regression (TSER) problems, where the output variable has been discretised to be transformed into TSOC problems. Detailed information about the datasets considered is provided in Table 1.

To enhance the robustness and reliability of our results, we conducted 10 different executions for each combination of approach and dataset. The first of these executions is conducted using the default partition of the dataset provided in the corresponding archive. The remaining experiments are performed using a stratified resampling of the original datasets while maintaining the same train/test proportion as the original partition. Additionally, for each run, the approaches are initialised using a unique random seed. This approach attenuates the impact of random initialisation on our results, providing a comprehensive and stable evaluation of the performance across each method/dataset pair.

The proposed O-Hydra methodology is compared against its nominal counterpart, Hydra. Moreover, we have incorporated to the experiments a dictionary-based method, the Temporal Dictionary Ensemble (TDE) [14], and the first

---

[1] UCR TSC archive (https://timeseriesclassification.com), and Monash TSER archive (http://tseregression.org).

convolution-based method, the Random Convolutional Kernel Transform (RO-CKET) [5], together with their ordinal counterparts (O-TDE and O-ROCKET, respectively). The incorporation of TDE and ROCKET methodologies is well-founded considering the previously discussed framework of Hydra, which combines the main strategies of dictionaries and convolutions (see Sect. 2). For the ROCKET and HYDRA methodologies, a cross-validation of the regularisation parameter λ (see Eq. (1)) is performed. The set of λ values to be tested is obtained according to $10^{-3+\frac{6i}{9}}$ where $i \in \{0, 1, \ldots, 9\}$. The optimal λ value is determined based on MAE for both nominal and ordinal approaches.

The results are evaluated in terms of the Correct Classification Rate (CCR) together with other four more appropriate metrics for ordinal problems: MAE, Averaged MAE (AMAE), Quadratic Weighted Kappa (QWK) and 1-OFF metrics. An in-depth description of these performance metrics can be found in [2].

Table 1. Information about the 21 univariate TSOC datasets considered in this work. #Train and #Test stand for the number of training and testing patterns, respectively, Q is the number of classes, and L is time series length.

Dataset	#Train	#Test	Q	L
DistalPhalanxOutlineAgeGroup	400	139	3	80
DistalPhalanxTW	400	139	6	80
EthanolLevel	504	500	4	1751
MiddlePhalanxOutlineAgeGroup	400	154	3	80
MiddlePhalanxTW	399	154	6	80
ProximalPhalanxOutlineAgeGroup	400	205	3	80
ProximalPhalanxTW	400	205	6	80
AAPL	1720	431	5	53
AMZN	1035	259	5	53
Covid3Month	140	61	5	84
GOOG	732	183	5	53
META	408	103	5	53
MSFT	1501	376	5	53
AcousticContaminationMadrid	166	72	5	365
DhakaHourlyAirQuality	1447	621	5	24
GasSensorArrayAcetone	324	140	3	7500
GasSensorArrayEthanol	324	140	3	7500
NaturalGasPricesSentiment	65	28	5	20
ParkingBirmingham	1391	597	5	14
WaveDataTension	1325	568	5	57
WindTurbinePower	596	256	5	144

4 Results

This section outlines the results of the proposed O-Hydra approach, utilising the experimental configurations detailed in Sect. 3. The results are presented as the Mean and Standard Deviation (STD) across 10 independent executions conducted across 21 univariate TSOC datasets (Mean_{STD}) in Table 2.

As observed, regarding the ordinal performance metrics, O-Hydra obtains the best results in terms of MAE, AMAE, and 1-OFF, securing the second-best performance in terms of QWK, closely following O-ROCKET, which achieves the top results. O-ROCKET also results as the second-best performer in terms of MAE, AMAE, and 1-OFF. Regarding CCR, O-Hydra once again achieves the best results, surpassing its nominal counterpart, Hydra, which might be expected to be the top performed in this nominal performance metric. This underscores the validity of using ordinal approaches when addressing TSOC problems.

Table 2. Results display the Mean and Standard Deviation (STD) of the 10 executions across the 21 univariate TSOC datasets of each method.

Method	MAE ($\downarrow$)	AMAE ($\downarrow$)	QWK ($\uparrow$)	1-OFF ($\uparrow$)	CCR ($\uparrow$)
Hydra	$0.592_{0.369}$	$0.793_{0.510}$	$0.527_{0.376}$	$0.871_{0.118}$	$0.584_{0.211}$
O-Hydra	$\mathbf{0.516_{0.322}}$	$\mathbf{0.708_{0.467}}$	$0.555_{0.371}$	$\mathbf{0.900_{0.102}}$	$\mathbf{0.596_{0.217}}$
O-ROCKET	$0.573_{0.296}$	$0.751_{0.389}$	$\mathbf{0.561_{0.292}}$	$0.895_{0.091}$	$0.548_{0.196}$
O-TDE	$0.661_{0.384}$	$0.890_{0.488}$	$0.454_{0.375}$	$0.851_{0.126}$	$0.537_{0.212}$
ROCKET	$0.694_{0.378}$	$0.883_{0.448}$	$0.465_{0.331}$	$0.841_{0.128}$	$0.524_{0.204}$
TDE	$0.677_{0.394}$	$0.901_{0.489}$	$0.448_{0.371}$	$0.844_{0.131}$	$0.536_{0.211}$

Furthermore, a summary of performance statistics in terms of MAE is illustrated in Fig. 1, generated using the multiple comparison matrix tool [12]. We observe significant differences between O-Hydra and the other methodologies, with the exception of O-ROCKET. This observation validates the objective of this work. Additionally, it is noteworthy that the original Hydra proposal notably outperforms both the dictionary-based TDE and the convolution-based ROCKET in their nominal versions. Another intriguing observation is that the ordinal counterparts of these approaches consistently outperform their nominal counterparts.

Mean-mae	O-Hydra -0.5158	O-Rocket -0.5732	Hydra -0.5919	O-TDE -0.6616	TDE -0.6767	Rocket -0.6945
O-Hydra -0.5158	Mean-Difference / r>c / r=c / r<c / Wilcoxon p-value	0.0574 / 15/1/5 / 0.0604	0.0761 / 16/1/4 / 0.0054	0.1458 / 17/0/4 / 0.0001	0.1609 / 17/0/4 / 0.0002	0.1787 / 19/0/2 / ≤ 1e-04
O-Rocket -0.5732	-0.0574 / 5/1/15 / 0.0604	-	0.0187 / 13/1/7 / 0.3133	0.0883 / 16/1/4 / 0.0091	0.1035 / 15/0/6 / 0.0142	0.1213 / 18/0/3 / 0.0001
Hydra -0.5919	-0.0761 / 4/1/16 / 0.0054	-0.0187 / 7/1/13 / 0.3133	-	0.0697 / 15/1/5 / 0.0049	0.0848 / 13/0/8 / 0.0043	0.1026 / 17/1/3 / 0.0003
O-TDE -0.6616	-0.1458 / 4/0/17 / 0.0001	-0.0883 / 4/1/16 / 0.0091	-0.0697 / 5/1/15 / 0.0049	-	0.0151 / 12/0/9 / 0.3205	0.0330 / 10/1/10 / 0.9723
TDE -0.6767	-0.1609 / 4/0/17 / 0.0002	-0.1035 / 6/0/15 / 0.0142	-0.0848 / 8/0/13 / 0.0043	-0.0151 / 9/0/12 / 0.3038	-	0.0178 / 10/0/11 / 0.7079
Rocket -0.6945	-0.1787 / 2/0/19 / ≤ 1e-04	-0.1213 / 3/0/18 / 0.0001	-0.1026 / 3/1/17 / 0.0003	-0.0330 / 10/1/10 / 0.9723	-0.0178 / 11/0/10 / 0.7079	If in bold, then p-value < 0.05

Mean-Difference scale: 0.2, 0.1, 0.0, -0.1, -0.2

Fig. 1. Summary performance statistics obtained by a multiple comparison tool [12].

5   Conclusions

This paper continues our efforts to advance research in the TSOC domain. TSOC involves the development of models that map time series data to discrete ordinal response variables. Thus far, only a few methodologies have been adapted from the nominal TSC area to TSOC. Notable among these are the dictionary-based Temporal Dictionary Ensemble (TDE) and the convolution-based RandOm Convolutional KErnel Transform (ROCKET) family. Their ordinal counterparts have shown significantly superior performance in terms of ordinal measures, which are appropriate as they take into account the ordering information inherent in the data. This work has introduced an ordinal hybrid approach to TSOC, which is a mixture of convolutional and dictionary-based techniques. The basis of this methodology, known as the Hybrid Dictionary-Rocket Architecture (Hydra) in the TSC community [6], has demonstrated competitive performance when coupled with the MultiROCKET method, ranking second-best and not significantly different from the top-performing technique, HIVE-COTE2 [15]. Hydra integrates two key aspects of dictionary methods: the formation of pattern groups approximating input time series and the use of pattern counts for classification. Similar to Rocket, Hydra transforms input time series using random convolutional kernels. The final classifier being either a ridge classifier or, for larger datasets, a logistic regression classifier. In this study, we present the ordinal variant of the Hydra approach, denoted as O-Hydra. The primary adaptation in O-Hydra lies in the use of the ordinal LogisticAT classifier as the final classifier. In terms of evaluation, O-Hydra has been compared against its nominal counterpart, exhibiting significantly superior performance. Additionally, O-Hydra has been compared against dictionary-based methods and their ordinal versions, TDE and O-TDE, as well as the convolution-based ROCKET approach. This evaluation has been conducted using a set of 21 univariate TSOC datasets, expanded from previous studies. The results underscored the superiority of the proposed O-Hydra not only over nominal Hydra but also over two prominent dictionary-based and convolution-based methods: TDE and ROCKET.

As future works, the existing methodologies in TSOC could be enhanced by focusing on the feature extraction phase or by using dilation. In the case of convolution-based approaches, considering features from the convolution that consider the ordinality of the output could be explored. In the case of dictionary-based methods, dilation has shown significant improvements, and may offer potential improvements when applied to ordinal dictionary-based approaches.

Acknowledgements. The present study has been supported by the "Agencia Estatal de Investigación (España)" (grant ref.: PID2020-115454GB-C22/AEI/10.13039/5011 00011033), the Spanish Ministry of Research and Innovation. David Guijo-Rubio has been supported by the MCIU/AEI/10.13039/501100011033 and European Union Next-GenerationEU/PRTR (grant ref.: JDC2022-048378-I).

References

1. Ayllón-Gavilán, R., Guijo-Rubio, D., Gutiérrez, P.A., Hervás-Martínez, C.: Assessing the efficient market hypothesis for cryptocurrencies with high-frequency data using time series classification. In: García Bringas, P., et al. (eds.) SOCO 2022. LNNS, vol. 531, pp. 146–155. Springer, Cham (2022). https://doi.org/10.1007/978-3-031-18050-7_14

2. Ayllón-Gavilán, R., Guijo-Rubio, D., Gutiérrez, P.A., Bagnall, A., Hervás-Martínez, C.: Convolutional and deep learning based techniques for time series ordinal classification. arXiv preprint arXiv:2306.10084 (2023)

3. Ayllón-Gavilán, R., Guijo-Rubio, D., Gutiérrez, P.A., Hervás-Martínez, C.: A dictionary-based approach to time series ordinal classification. In: Rojas, I., Joya, G., Catala, A. (eds.) IWANN 2023. LNCS, vol. 14135, pp. 541–552. Springer, Cham (2023). https://doi.org/10.1007/978-3-031-43078-7_44

4. Blázquez-García, A., Conde, A., Mori, U., Lozano, J.A.: A review on outlier/anomaly detection in time series data. ACM Comput. Surv. (CSUR) **54**(3), 1–33 (2021)

5. Dempster, A., Petitjean, F., Webb, G.I.: ROCKET: exceptionally fast and accurate time series classification using random convolutional kernels. Data Min. Knowl. Disc. **34**, 1454–1495 (2020)

6. Dempster, A., Schmidt, D.F., Webb, G.I.: Hydra: competing convolutional kernels for fast and accurate time series classification. Data Min. Knowl. Discov. **37**, 1–27 (2023)

7. Guijo-Rubio, D., et al.: Ordinal regression algorithms for the analysis of convective situations over Madrid-Barajas airport. Atmos. Res. **236**, 104798 (2020)

8. Guijo-Rubio, D., Durán-Rosal, A.M., Gutiérrez, P.A., Troncoso, A., Hervás-Martínez, C.: Time-series clustering based on the characterization of segment typologies. IEEE Trans. Cybern. **51**(11), 5409–5422 (2020)

9. Guijo-Rubio, D., Gutiérrez, P.A., Bagnall, A., Hervás-Martínez, C.: Time series ordinal classification via shapelets. In: 2020 International Joint Conference on Neural Networks (IJCNN), pp. 1–8. IEEE (2020)

10. Guijo-Rubio, D., Middlehurst, M., Arcencio, G., Silva, D.F., Bagnall, A.: Unsupervised feature based algorithms for time series extrinsic regression. Data Min. Knowl. Disc. 1–45 (2024). https://doi.org/10.1007/s10618-024-01027-w

11. Gutiérrez, P.A., Pérez-Ortiz, M., Sánchez-Monedero, J., Fernández-Navarro, F., Hervás-Martínez, C.: Ordinal regression methods: survey and experimental study. IEEE Trans. Knowl. Data Eng. **28**(1), 127–146 (2016)
12. Ismail-Fawaz, A., et al.: An approach to multiple comparison benchmark evaluations that is stable under manipulation of the comparate set (2023)
13. Large, J., Kemsley, E.K., Wellner, N., Goodall, I., Bagnall, A.: Detecting forged alcohol non-invasively through vibrational spectroscopy and machine learning. In: Phung, D., Tseng, V.S., Webb, G.I., Ho, B., Ganji, M., Rashidi, L. (eds.) PAKDD 2018, Part I. LNCS (LNAI), vol. 10937, pp. 298–309. Springer, Cham (2018). https://doi.org/10.1007/978-3-319-93034-3_24
14. Middlehurst, M., Large, J., Cawley, G., Bagnall, A.: The temporal dictionary ensemble (TDE) classifier for time series classification. In: Hutter, F., Kersting, K., Lijffijt, J., Valera, I. (eds.) ECML PKDD 2020. LNCS (LNAI), vol. 12457, pp. 660–676. Springer, Cham (2021). https://doi.org/10.1007/978-3-030-67658-2_38
15. Middlehurst, M., Schäfer, P., Bagnall, A.: Bake off redux: a review and experimental evaluation of recent time series classification algorithms. arXiv preprint arXiv:2304.13029 (2023)
16. Pedregosa, F., Bach, F., Gramfort, A.: On the consistency of ordinal regression methods. J. Mach. Learn. Res. **18**(1), 1769–1803 (2017)
17. Schäfer, P., Leser, U.: Fast and accurate time series classification with weasel. In: Proceedings of the 2017 ACM on Conference on Information and Knowledge Management, pp. 637–646 (2017)

Predicting Parkinson's Disease Progression: Analyzing Prodromal Stages Through Machine Learning

Maitane Martinez-Eguiluz[1](✉) [iD], Javier Muguerza[1] [iD], Olatz Arbelaitz[1] [iD], Ibai Gurrutxaga[1] [iD], Juan Carlos Gomez-Esteban[2,3,4] [iD], Ane Murueta-Goyena[2,3] [iD], and Iñigo Gabilondo[3,4,5] [iD]

[1] Department of Computer Architecture and Technology, University of the Basque Country, UPV/EHU, Donostia, Spain
{maitane.martineze,j.muguerza,olatz.arbelaitz,i.gurrutxaga}@ehu.eus
[2] Department of Neurosciences, University of the Basque Country, UPV/EHU, Leioa, Spain
ane.muruetagoyena@ehu.eus
[3] Neurodegenerative Diseases Group, Biobizkaia Health Research Institute, Barakaldo, Spain
[4] Department of Neurology, Cruces University Hospital, Barakaldo, Spain
{juancarlos.gomezesteban,inigo.gabilondocuellar}@osakidetza.eus
[5] Ikerbasque Basque Foundation of Science, Bilbao, Spain

Abstract. This study explores prodromal Parkinson's Disease (PD) by leveraging data from the Parkinson's Progression Markers Initiative (PPMI). The main goal was to discriminate between prodromals that phenoconverted to PD in 7 years to those that did not. Through feature selection, the system identified key first visit predictors of PD phenoconversion, encompassing demographic, clinical, and structural magnetic resonance imaging (MRI) data. Employing seven machine learning algorithms in standard and balanced forms, we find Support Vector Machine (balanced) as most effective for demographic and clinical data, and Logistic Regression (balanced) when adding thicknesses and volumes of MRI data. The metrics were improve in the second case (AUC ROC of 0.84). Significant predictors include olfactory dysfunction, motor symptoms, psychomotor speed, and third ventricle dilation.

Keywords: Prodromal Parkinson's disease · Machine Learning · MRI data

1 Introduction

Parkinson's Disease (PD) is the second most common neurodegenerative disorder [11], primarily affecting the elderly, with age being a significant risk factor. Diagnosis relies on clinical criteria such as bradykinesia and other motor symptoms, with a strong link to dopaminergic cell loss in the substantia nigra

A. Alonso-Betanzos et al. (Eds.): CAEPIA 2024, LNAI 14640, pp. 61–70, 2024.
https://doi.org/10.1007/978-3-031-62799-6_7

[5]. Recent insights challenge this traditional view, highlighting that significant neuropathological changes and nonmotor manifestations can occur well before classic motor symptoms [14], indicating a 'preclinical' (symptom-free) or 'prodromal' (exhibit various nonmotor symptoms and/or minor motor signs) phase of PD. This early phase is crucial for diagnosis and offers a potential window for intervention to slow disease progression [15]. It is important to highlight that prodromal PD encompasses a broad spectrum of phenotypes, including individuals with genetic risk factors or clinical characteristics predating PD onset, such as hyposmia (a reduced sense of smell) or REM sleep behavior disorder. It is worth noting that the penetrance of genetic risk factors is not complete, and the early clinical symptoms lack specificity for PD, making their individual contribution to PD risk estimation limited.

Neuroimaging, particularly magnetic resonance imaging (MRI), offers a pivotal tool for exploring the prodromal phase of PD, allowing for the detailed observation of structural brain changes. This capability facilitates early detection of neurodegenerative alterations, providing crucial insights into PD's progression before more evident symptoms emerge. Recent research in identifying prodromals that phenoconverted to PD has incorporated machine learning (ML) approaches. A specific study [13] used ML to examine diffusion MRI and clinical data for early PD detection, including assessments within a prodromal cohort. While various data types, such as electrocardiograms [6], have been explored, there appears to be a gap in studies using structural MRI data for this purpose. Consequently, accurately identifying PD phenoconversion during the prodromal stage continues to be a crucial yet challenging area for further exploration.

In this study, we integrated a set of clinical scales that assess both nonmotor and motor symptoms with structural MRI data at first visit. Our objective was to analyze the predictive performance of seven different machine learning algorithms in identifying prodromal individuals who phenoconverted to PD as opposed to those who did not, over a period of seven years.

The structure of the paper is as follows: Sect. 2 provides a detailed description of the database characteristics and the data pre-processing approaches. Section 3 discusses the machine learning methodologies and the evaluation criteria used in the experiments. The outcomes of these experiments are presented in Sect. 4. Underlying meaning of the research, along with an exploration of the limitations of this research, are presented in Sect. 5. The paper concludes with Sect. 6, which summarizes the key findings and implications.

2   Data

2.1   Database Description

The core database for this study is derived from the Parkinson's Progression Markers Initiative (PPMI) [9].[1] The PPMI, an extensive and ongoing study, is focused on identifying biomarkers that signal the progression of PD. The PPMI

---

[1] https://www.ppmi-info.org/.

database is characterized by its diversity in data types, encompassing demographic and clinical data, as well as MRI data. Leveraging these varied data sources, two distinct datasets were developed: the first one comprised exclusively demographic/clinical data at first visit, and the second one integrated both structural MRI and demographic/clinical data at first visit.

The study encompasses a cohort of prodromal subjects. This group includes those with genetic mutations in LRRK2, GBA, and SNCA genes, and clinical presentations like hyposmia or Rapid Eye Movement (REM) sleep behavior disorder. Among the prodromal subjects, a subgroup (n = 18) phenoconverted to PD over a 7-year observation period, while the remainder (n = 54) did not develop the disease within this timeframe. For detailed demographic and clinical characteristics of these groups, refer to Table 1.

Table 1. Demographic and clinical features of participants. Qualitative variables (genetic mutation, sex, race and handed) is expressed with proportion, whereas quantitative variables is expressed as mean (standard deviation). p-value is calculated using the t-test in quantitative and chi-square in the case of qualitative variables.

n°	NO-PHENOCNV	PHENOCNV	p-values
	54	18	
Genetic mutation	77.77%	11.11%	<0.01
UPSIT	31.17 ± 6.49	15.97 ± 5.39	<0.01
REM	4.33 ± 3.17	7.22 ± 4.22	<0.01
Age	62.15 ± 6.65	67.18 ± 6.19	<0.01
Sex (Male)	44.44%	77.78%	<0.01
Education years	17.28 ± 4.21	16.06 ± 3.67	0.275
Race (White, Black, Other)	96.30%, 1.85%, 1.85%	88.88%, 0%, 11.11%	0.013
Handed (Right, Left, Mixed)	81.48%, 12.96%, 5.56%	88.88%, 5.56%, 5.56%	0.194
MDS-UPDRS III	2.35 ± 2.95	6.44 ± 5.45	<0.01
MoCA	27.54 ± 1.95	26.44 ± 2.79	0.07

2.2   Demographic and Clinical Data

Demographic data includes age, years of education, sex, race, dominant hand, and familial history of PD. Regarding the clinical data, it encompasses a range of tests and questionnaires across different domains. **Olfactory Tests**: University of Pennsylvania Smell Identification Test (UPSIT); **Sleep-Related Questionnaires**: Rapid Eye Movement Sleep Behavior Disorder Screening Questionnaire (REM), Epworth Sleepiness Scale (ESS); **Cognitive Assessments**: Montreal Cognitive Assessment (MoCA), Hopkins Verbal Learning Test-Revised (HVLT-R), Benton Judgement of Line Orientation Test (BJLOT), Semantic Fluency Test (SFT), Letter Number Sequencing (LNS), Symbol Digit Modalities Test (SDMT); **Motor Tests**: Movement Disorder Society - Unified Parkinson's Disease Rating Scale (MDS-UPDRS), Hoehn & Yahr Scale (NHY), Modified Schwab

& England Activities of Daily Living (ADL); **Neuropsychiatric Evaluations**: Geriatric Depression Scale (GDS), State-Trait Anxiety Inventory (STAI), Questionnaire for Impulsive-Compulsive Disorders (QUIP); **Autonomic Function Tests**: Scale for Outcomes in Parkinson's Disease - Autonomic (SCOPA).

For nonmotor tests, aggregate scores were used, except for HVLT-R, where three distinct scores were calculated: Immediate/Total Recall (HVLT-R1), Discrimination Recognition (HVLT-R2), Retention (HVLT-R3). For motor tests, aggregate scores were used for ADL. Additionally, data from the first three parts of MDS-UPDRS were incorporated, separately and as the sum of all three parts. These parts encompass nonmotor experiences (MDS-UPDRS I), motor experiences of daily living (MDS-UPDRS II), and motor examination (MDS-UPDRS III). Notably, the MDS-UPDRS III data were specific to the unmedicated state. The Levodopa Equivalent Daily Dose (LEDD) data was also included to understand medication influences. Additionally, another variable (TD-PIGD) provided insight into whether patients belonged to the Tremor Dominant (TD) or Postural Instability and Gait Distress (PIGD) classifications.

2.3   Structural MRI Data

The methodology employed allowed the extraction of 98 brain volume and cortical thickness features from T1-weighted MRI scans. Initially, quality control measures led to the exclusion of three images due to duplication, incompleteness, and excessive noise, ensuring the use of high-quality images. The scans then underwent field bias correction with Advanced Normalization Tools [1]. Lastly, Freesurfer software [4] was used for feature extraction, including brain volumes and cortical thickness of anatomical regions defined by Desikan-Killiany MRI atlas, which were normalized against the estimated total intracranial volume to adjust for individual differences.

2.4   Pre-processing

In this study, data pre-processing was crucial to address common medical data challenges such as missing values and scale disparities. In total, 8 variables had 1 or 2 missing values, and those were handled using a median imputation strategy. Data standardization was achieved through z-score normalization, balancing the scales of different variables by adjusting each to have zero mean and unit variance. These steps aimed to enhance data quality and consistency, setting the stage for more effective and accurate analyses in later stages of the research.

3   Methodology

We first performed a feature selection, which helps reducing the dimensionality of the problem and identifying the most significant features. Then, we trained and validated various models.

3.1   Feature Selection

We tried several features selection options, such as Correlation Based Feature Selection, Boruta or PCA, but the best results were obtained with the following procedure. The first step in feature selection process involved calculating the Pearson correlation coefficient for each feature relative to the class (if a subject phenoconverted or not). The used implementation not only computes Pearson's correlation coefficient but also tests the hypothesis that the underlying distributions of the samples are uncorrelated and normally distributed. Typically, a lower p-value suggests that the observed correlation is not due to random chance, thus lending more credibility to the existence of an actual relationship between the feature and the class. The threshold used for discerning between selected and non-selected features was 0.05.

Given that multiple hypotheses are being tested (one for each feature), there's a risk of false discoveries - i.e., incorrectly identifying features as significant due to random chance. To mitigate this, we applied a False Discovery Rate (FDR) correction. FDR controls the expected proportion of incorrectly rejected null hypotheses (false discoveries) [3]. By doing so, the p-values are adjusted to reflect the likelihood of a feature being genuinely correlated with the class, not just appearing so due to multiple comparisons.

3.2   Classification Algorithms

Seven different models were trained to predict outcomes based on the selected features. These models include: Decision Tree (DT), K-Nearest Neighbors (KNN), Logistic Regression (LR), Multilayer Perceptron (MLP), Random Forest (RF), Support Vector Machine (SVM) and eXtreme Gradient Boosting (XGB).

Each of these models has unique characteristics and strengths, making this a comprehensive approach to finding the best predictive model for the data. To deal with class imbalance problem, *class weight* parameter was set to *balanced* in one iteration (for all models except MLP and KNN), thus giving more importance to the minority class in the training data, and left as default (*none*) in another iteration. The algorithms were implemented in Python, using the *sklearn* package [12]. In the case of XGB the xgb library was used. For all algorithms default parameters were used, except the case mentioned. Other oversampling techniques, such as SMOTE, were explored, but gave worse results.

3.3   Classification Performance Evaluation

We used a Leave-One-Out Cross-Validation (LOOCV) due to the limited data. We evaluate the models using the Area under the ROC Curve (AUC-ROC) metric [7]. The AUC-ROC is particularly useful for validating unbalanced classification problems because it evaluates the model's ability to distinguish between classes without being influenced by the distribution of class labels. For the best performance algorithms, we also validated with other metrics, such as Accuracy, Balanced Accuracy, F-score, Recall, Precision and Specificity.

3.4   Explanation

SHAP (SHapley Additive exPlanations) [8] algorithm was used to explain the best model's predictions. SHAP values are based on the concept of Shapley values from cooperative game theory. The algorithm calculates the contribution of each feature by comparing what a model predicts with and without the feature. This is done across all possible combinations of features, providing a detailed attribution of prediction. Each feature gets an importance value for a particular prediction, essentially explaining how much each feature contributes to the final decision.

4   Results

The demographic and clinical characteristics of prodromal PD patients who progressed to PD significantly differ in various aspects from those who did not convert over a span of 7 years, as shown in Table 1.

The initial stage of the experiments was dedicated to feature selection, as depicted in Fig. 1. In a primary stage, with only demographic and clinical data, 12 out of 29 variables were selected, encompassing factors like age, sex, UPSIT for olfactory tests, REM for sleep disorders, along with cognitive and motor assessments. Introduction of structural MRI data led to the selection of 9 out of 127 variables, notably excluding previously selected demographic and certain cognitive and motor variables in favor of highlighting the third ventricle's volume, a critical brain structure situated centrally.

We trained 7 algorithms using LOOCV and evaluated them with the ROC-AUC metric, adjusting the class weight parameter to *balanced* for some models. Overall performance was ROC-AUC $= 0.73 \pm 0.06$. As showing in Fig. 1, for DT, RF and XGB, adjusting the class weight did not increase performance. LR showed similar outcomes. However, SVM benefited from the *balanced* setting. Best performance was attained using SVM with a *balanced* setting for demographic and clinical data, and LR, also *balanced*, when incorporating structural MRI data. Table 2 displays the metrics for these top-performing algorithms. The inclusion of structural MRI data yielded a slight improvement in metrics.

Table 2. Metric of the best algorithms. SVM (class weight *balanced*) in the case of Demographic/Clinical data (Data $= 1$). LR (class weight *balanced*) in the case of Demographic/Clinical data + structural MRI (Data $= 2$).

Data	Algorithm	ROC AUC	Accuracy	Balanced Accuracy	F-score	Recall	Precision	Specificity
1	SVM	0.83	0.83	0.83	0.71	0.83	0.62	0.83
2	LR	0.84	0.85	0.84	0.73	0.83	0.65	0.85

The analysis of SHAP values revealed key variables impacting the likelihood of phenoconversion to PD as shown in Fig. 2. For demographic/clinical data via the SVM algorithm, UPSIT (olfactory dysfunction) emerged as the

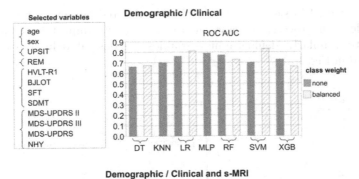

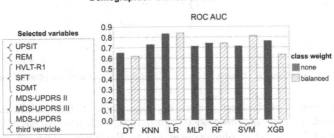

Fig. 1. Selected variables and ROC AUC of the train algorithm. *class weight* is the parameter that can be tuned to weight classes.

most critical predictor, where lower scores suggest a higher phenoconversion risk. MDS-UPDRS II, related to motor experiences, indicates that increased motor issues also favor phenoconversion likelihood. SDMT, assessing psychomotor speed, showed that lower scores are predictive of phenoconversion. Incorporating structural MRI data with LR algorithm, the volume of the third ventricle became a significant indicator, with increased volume (indicative of atrophy in the surrounding areas) being a strong phenoconversion predictor.

Regarding other motor variables, in Fig. 2(a) the NHY emerges as more significant, consequently diminishing the relative importance of MDS-UPDRS III, as both evaluate motor status. Without the NHY variable, MDS-UPDRS III gains prominence in Fig. 2(b). Although the MDS-UPDRS total score was selected during feature selection, it does not seem to offer additional insights to the algorithm, likely because it is a composite of Parts I, II, and III. Its selection is attributed to the influence of Parts II and III but does not provide extra information beyond these components.

In cognitive assessments, HVLT-R Immediate/Recall and SFT, both related to verbal memory, contribute valuable information across scenarios. However, BJLOT, focusing on visuospatial perception, has minimal impact on the model's decision-making, as evidenced in Fig. 2(a). Notably, BJLOT was not selected in scenarios combining demographic/clinical data with structural MRI, indicating its smaller relevance in this enriched dataset.

Finally, the REM sleep behavior variable exhibited minimal influence in the model's decision process, as shown in Fig. 2, with its impact being negligible in Fig. 2(b). Similarly, demographic variables demonstrated limited relevance, highlighted in Fig. 2(a).

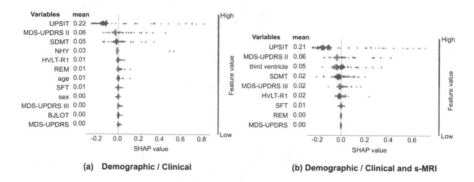

(a) **Demographic / Clinical**   (b) **Demographic / Clinical and s-MRI**

Fig. 2. SHAP values of the best performing algorithms. SHAP values highlight the influence of each variable on the model's prediction, with positive SHAP values suggesting a higher likelihood of phenoconversion to Parkinson's Disease, and negative values indicating a lower likelihood. Variables are ranked by their impact, with a wider range indicating greater importance. The mean absolute SHAP values, indicators of variables impact, corroborate the same order. The color scheme, from violet to blue, represents the variable's value, with violet denoting higher values and blue lower ones. (Color figure online)

5   Discussion

This study explored the progression of prodromal stages to PD over 7 years, employing a ML approach that included a preliminary feature selection phase. The LR algorithm with class weight balancing achieved the highest performance, incorporating variables such as olfactory dysfunction, REM sleep disorder, cognitive assessments, motor impairment tests, and the volume of the third ventricle, resulting in an AUC ROC of 0.84.

Regarding the difference between subjects who phenoconvert PD and those who did not, great heterogeneity was observed. The study analyzed various genetic mutations in subjects with prodromal PD. Among those who did not phenoconvert, 55.56% had LRRK2 mutations, 12.96% had GBA mutations, 1.85% had SNCA mutations, and 7.4% had both LRRK2 and GBA mutations. In contrast, among those who phenoconverted, only 11.11% exhibited LRRK2 mutations. This observations underlines the complexity inherent in the early stages of PD.

With regard to the performance, the effect of the balanced class weight depend on the algorithm. Some of them did not improve with this option. In the case of DT, its improvement can be less pronounced due to how they handle data distribution. DT's performance can vary significantly depending on the spatial distribution of the minority class in the feature space. On the other hand, in the case of RF and XGB, their resilience to class imbalance might stem from their inherent mechanisms for reshaping features and focusing on subsets of the data. These algorithms construct multiple DTs and employ techniques which can inherently adjust to and emphasize the minority class during the learning process, making them less reliant on external balancing methods. Finally, the balanced LR doesn't change the metrics due to the intrinsic robustness of the model against class imbalance, focusing on feature relevance and distribution rather than class proportions alone.

As for the most significant variables identified are linked to diminished olfactory function, motor symptoms, and psychomotor velocity. In the case of structural change, the third ventricle dilatation seems to be important. Interestingly, the REM sleep variable, despite being a criterion for identifying prodromal cases, shows minimal impact. Similarly, age, while a primary risk factor for the disease, does not emerge as a crucial variable. This highlights the complexity of factors influencing the progression to PD and suggests that the predictive importance of symptoms and risk factors can vary.

In a previous research [10] that explored nonmotor variables for early-stage PD prediction, olfactory dysfunction emerged as a significant indicator. However, unlike the SCOPA test's findings in that study, this aspect was not observed here. While the volume of the third ventricle has not been directly linked to early PD detection, existing literature [2] associates it with the disease's cognitive decline, underscoring its potential relevance in understanding PD's progression.

The primary limitation of this study is the dataset's size, despite utilizing the PPMI, one of the largest databases for prodromal PD subjects. Additionally, not tuning the algorithms' hyperparameters represents another constraint, as optimized hyperparameters could potentially enhance model performance. In future research, we plan to investigate additional databases and conduct a comparative analysis of feature selection algorithms, particularly the analysis of wrapper methods, to further refine our methodology.

6 Conclusion

This research enriches the comprehension of the prodromal phase in Parkinson's disease by combining clinical, demographic, and structural MRI data. Initially, a feature selection process was undertaken, followed by the application of machine learning algorithms and a subsequent interpretability analysis. This approach emphasized the critical roles of olfactory dysfunction, motor symptoms, psychomotor speed and third ventricle dilation as key predictive markers.

Acknowledgments. Maitane Martinez-Eguiluz is recepient of a predoctoral fellowship of the Basque Government (Grant PRE-2022-1-0204). This work was funded by Grant PID2021-123087OB-I00 funded by MICIU/AEI10.13039/501100011033 and, FEDER, UE; and Department of Economic Development and Competitiveness (ADIAN, IT1437-22) of the Basque Government; and the Gipuzkoas' network for Science, Technology and Innovation, ProPark project (DG23/04).

References

1. Avants, B.B., Tustison, N., Song, G.: Advanced normalization tools (ants). Insight j **2**(365), 1–35 (2009)
2. Behnke, S., et al.: Third ventricular width assessed by transcranial ultrasound correlates with cognitive performance in Parkinson's disease. Parkinsonism Relat. Disord. **66**, 68–73 (2019)
3. Benjamini, Y., Hochberg, Y.: Controlling the false discovery rate: a practical and powerful approach to multiple testing. J. Roy. Stat. Soc.: Ser. B (Methodol.) **57**(1), 289–300 (1995)
4. Fischl, B.: Freesurfer. Neuroimage **62**(2), 774–781 (2012)
5. Greffard, S., et al.: Motor score of the unified Parkinson disease rating scale as a good predictor of Lewy body-associated neuronal loss in the substantia Nigra. Arch. Neurol. **63**(4), 584–588 (2006)
6. Karabayir, I., et al.: Externally validated deep learning model to identify prodromal Parkinson's disease from electrocardiogram. Sci. Rep. **13**(1), 12290 (2023)
7. Lobo, J.M., Jiménez-Valverde, A., Real, R.: AUC: a misleading measure of the performance of predictive distribution models. Glob. Ecol. Biogeogr. **17**(2), 145–151 (2008)
8. Lundberg, S.M., Lee, S.I.: A unified approach to interpreting model predictions. In: Advances in Neural Information Processing Systems, vol. 30 (2017)
9. Marek, K., et al.: The Parkinson progression marker initiative (PPMI). Prog. Neurobiol. **95**(4), 629–635 (2011)
10. Martinez-Eguiluz, M., et al.: Diagnostic classification of Parkinson's disease based on non-motor manifestations and machine learning strategies. Neural Comput. Appl. **35**(8), 5603–5617 (2023)
11. Meara, J., Hobson, P.: Epidemiology of Parkinson's disease. Parkinson's Disease in the Older Patient, pp. 30–38 (2018)
12. Pedregosa, F., et al.: Scikit-learn: machine learning in Python. J. Mach. Learn. Res. **12**, 2825–2830 (2011)
13. Peña-Nogales, Ó., Ellmore, T.M., de Luis-García, R., Suescun, J., Giancardo, L.: Longitudinal connectomes as a candidate progression marker for prodromal Parkinson's disease. Front. Neurosci. **12**, 414158 (2019)
14. Pont-Sunyer, C., et al.: The onset of nonmotor symptoms in Parkinson's disease (the onset PD study). Mov. Disord. **30**(2), 229–237 (2015)
15. Rees, R.N., Noyce, A.J., Schrag, A.: The prodromes of Parkinson's disease. Eur. J. Neurosci. **49**(3), 320–327 (2019)

Ground-Level Ozone Forecasting Using Explainable Machine Learning

Angela Robledo Troncoso-García[1]([✉]) [iD], Manuel Jesús Jiménez-Navarro[2] [iD],
Francisco Martínez-Álvarez[1] [iD], and Alicia Troncoso[1] [iD]

[1] Data Science and Big Data Lab, Pablo de Olavide University, 41013 Sevilla, Spain
{artrogar,fmaralv,atrolor}@upo.es
[2] Department of Computer Science, University of Seville, 41012 Sevilla, Spain
mjimenez3@us.es

Abstract. The ozone concentration at ground level is a pivotal indicator of air quality, as elevated ozone levels can lead to adverse effects on the environment. In this study various machine learning models for ground-level ozone forecasting are optimised using a Bayesian technique. Predictions are obtained 24 h in advance using historical ozone data and related environmental variables, including meteorological measurements and other air quality indicators. The results indicated that the Extra Trees model emerges as the optimal solution, showcasing competitive performance alongside reasonable training times. Furthermore, an explainable artificial intelligence technique is applied to enhance the interpretability of model predictions, providing insights into the contribution of input features to the predictions computed by the model. The features identified as important, namely PM_{10}, air temperature and CO_2 concentration, are validated as key factors in the literature to forecast ground-level ozone concentration.

Keywords: Ozone concentration · Time series forecasting · Explainable artificial intelligence

1 Introduction

Air quality is a crucial aspect of environmental health, with atmospheric composition significantly impacting ecosystems and organisms. Ozone (O_3) plays a dual role as both a protective layer in the stratosphere and a potential hazard at ground level. While the ozone layer shields against harmful UV radiation, elevated concentrations of ground-level ozone can negatively affect human health, ecosystems, and agricultural output. This poses a significant challenge to air quality, particularly in urban areas with heavy traffic [1]. As concerns about atmospheric pollution and its adverse effects intensify, it has become imperative to develop precise and effective methods for accurate predictions of O_3 concentration in the air, as they enable proactive management strategies to mitigate pollution, such as coordinating traffic patterns. In this context, Machine Learning (ML) and Deep Learning (DL) techniques have emerged as a promising

A. Alonso-Betanzos et al. (Eds.): CAEPIA 2024, LNAI 14640, pp. 71–80, 2024.
https://doi.org/10.1007/978-3-031-62799-6_8

tool to improve prediction accuracy. However, environmental experts hesitate to fully embrace these techniques in real-world applications and policymaking due to their opaque nature.

This study aims to explore and assess the efficacy and efficiency of different ML models in predicting future ground-level O_3 concentration based on air quality and meteorological measurements over the past hours. Then, the model obtaining the best results is explained through an eXplainable Artificial Intelligence (XAI) technique based on quantitative explanation rules, denoted as RULEx, thus obtaining an accurate and interpretable framework for forecasting concentrations O_3.

The remainder of this paper is structured as follows. First, Sect. 2 summarises contributions related to O_3 forecasting found in the literature. Second, Sect. 3 introduces the proposed methodology, and third, Sect. 4 presents the results that have been obtained. Finally, Sect. 5 concludes the paper and leads to future work lines.

2   Related Work

Several approaches in the literature explored the integration of ML solutions for the forecasting of O_3 in the context of air pollution, with initiatives to improve prediction models, thus considering the complex interrelationships between air quality and meteorological elements. First, the authors in [2] conducted a comprehensive review focused on presenting the latest advances in the area, emphasising the nature of the models utilized and the input variables employed as input data. The model repertoire comprised Support Vector Machines (SVM), Artificial Neural Networks (ANN), decision trees, and hybrid models. The findings indicated that while SVM-based models outperformed others in accuracy, ANN are extensively employed in existing literature. Additionally, the analysis revealed that nitrogen oxides (NO_2, NO), particulate matter (PM_{10}, $PM_{2.5}$), and ozone (O_3) are the most frequently examined in the reviewed articles. Furthermore, in the paper presented in [3], the authors used meteorological data from Kennewick (USA) as input data to a hybrid approach combining different models, namely random forest and linear regression. The results showcased the system's reliability with significantly reduced computational resources. In this way, the benefits of introducing not only air pollution observances but also exogenous variables such as temperature or wind speed are highlighted in [4]. The application is carried out on a six-year data set of hourly O_3 concentrations and meteorological measurements from Béthune (France). The models were trained with only air observations and with these measurements combined with exogenous data, and the models trained with exogenous variables showed the best predictive power.

Additionally, Neural Networks (NN) are extensively utilized in various applications in the literature. For example, the authors of the article in [5] proposed an integrated model based on multilayer perceptron, combining available data from other environmental models and measurements on-site of meteorological and air pollution parameters in Slovenia. Validation results demonstrated that integrated models significantly improve O_3 forecasts and contribute to more effective alert systems. Moreover, a novel approach utilizing a spatiotemporal graph NN to predict O_3 concentration dynamics in urban areas, using meteorological and air quality data from Houston, Texas, was introduced in [7]. The research incorporated various configurations of time lags, and three forecast horizons (1, 3, 6 h ahead). The results demonstrated the efficacy of the proposed model in recognising intricate spatio-temporal patterns within the data. Another example is found in [6], where the authors introduced a comparative study between a hybrid nonlinear regression (NLR) model and a NN model, both tailored to predict next-day maximum 1-hour average ground-level O_3 concentrations in Louisville, USA, during 1998 and 1999. The NLR model demonstrated a slight superiority over the NN model using observed meteorological data. Furthermore, meteorological data and air pollutant observations were used as input to a DL model with long short-term memory (LSTM) layers in [8]. Predictions of O_3 concentrations are obtained for the next 48 h, thus improving both temporal and spatial air quality.

Finally, in terms of an XAI perspective, the tool denoted eXplaining Air Quality (AQX) was presented in [9] as a visual analytics system developed to assist experts in validating DL models with domain knowledge. Thus, multiple coordinated views were used to present input feature contributions across temporal and spatial dimensions. The methodology was tested using a case study in the field of O_3 forecasting, showing the effectiveness and utility of the tool. Furthermore, another DL approach has been developed in the domain of forecasting evapotranspiration [10], an ecological concern similar to the forecasting problem O_3. The authors optimized and trained a LSTM model, and explanations were obtained with SHapley Additive exPlanations (SHAP), aligning with existing literature on the primary significant exogenous features.

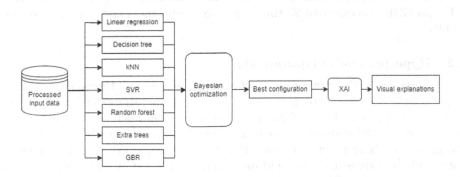

Fig. 1. Methodology workflow.

3   Materials and Methods

This paper introduces the application of a suite of ML models designed for O_3 forecasting, followed by an explanation of the best-performing model using an XAI technique. The overall methodology is depicted in Fig. 1, with each step elaborated in subsequent sections.

3.1   Machine Learning

ML models have consistently shown strong performance in the prediction of O_3 concentration. To identify the most effective option, various techniques, including Linear Regression (LR), Decision Trees (DT), k nearest neighbours (kNN), Support Vector Regression (SVR), Random Forest (RF), Extra Trees (ET), and Gradient Boosting Regression (GBR), are optimized and evaluated. The models are delineated as follows.

- **LR** models the relationship between the dependent variable and one or more independent variables by fitting a linear equation.
- **DT** divides the feature space into a set of regions and assigns a simple model to each region, making predictions based on the region the input falls into.
- **kNN** makes predictions by averaging the target values of the k-nearest data points in the feature space.
- **SVR** is a variant of the regression-adapted support vector machines.
- **RF** is an ensemble learning method that constructs a multitude of decision trees and outputs the mean prediction of each individual tree.
- **ET** is an extension of the Random Forest method, thus building decision trees from random training data samples, making it easier to train.
- **GBR** builds an ensemble of weak learners (typically decision trees) sequentially, each new model correcting the errors made by the previous ones, using a gradient descent method to minimize a loss function during training.

The stochastic approaches, including those based on trees, namely DT, RF, ET, and GBR, are executed 25 times to ensure robustness and reliability of the results.

3.2   Hyperparameter Optimization

The ML models underwent a process of optimization using a Bayesian technique to iteratively refine the hyperparameters governing the ML models' architecture and training process. This technique employs Bayesian inference to construct a probabilistic model of the objective function and utilizes this model to determine the most promising points. Optimization balances exploring uncertain regions with exploiting areas likely to yield improvement, ultimately converging toward the optimal solution. Then, the hyperparameters optimized and their range are detailed in Table 1. LR model has no parameters to optimize, and it serves as a baseline model in this study. Furthermore, optimization encompasses the input data window for all the models, including LR, thus refining the timeframe of the input window, and, as the data is hourly, this entails testing window sizes ranging from 24 to 72 h, covering every hourly increment in between.

Table 1. Hyperparameters ranges for each model optimization.

Model	Hyperparameters	Range
DT	max_depth	[2, 50]
kNN	k	[2, 7]
SVR	C	[0.0001, 5]
	epsilon	[0.0001, 1]
RF	max_depth	[2, 50]
	n_estimators	[10, 256]
ET	max_depth	[2, 50]
	n_estimators	[10, 256]
GBR	max_depth	[2, 50]
	n_estimators	[10, 256]

3.3 XAI

The XAI method used in this experiment is denoted as RULEx, presented in [11], and based on quantitative association rules (QARs), obtained with MOQAR method. MOQAR [12] is a multi-objective evolutionary algorithm applied for discovering QARs, to identify optimal configurations, with an approach specifically suitable for time series data because it can handle association rules in continuous intervals, thus allowing the capture of temporal relationships between events.

In this way, the RULEx technique aims to enhance the interpretability of time series forecasting through the visual representations of sets of rules, thus referring to patterns that capture relationships among variables. RULEx is a model-agnostic explainability technique, thus elucidating how the model works by illustrating the most important values for the time series forecasting task once the predictions have been obtained. The output is a chart-based representation colorized to reflect the significance of the input values in influencing the predictions for each distinct prediction horizon. RULEx has been recently applied to obtain time series explainability in [13].

4 Results

This section presents the results derived from this study. The experimental process involves fine-tuning the models delineated earlier. After that, the predictions generated by the optimal model are explained by employing the RULEx technique to offer interpretable explanations of the model's predictions.

4.1 Input Data

The input data set comprises a collection of hourly measurements that include air quality and meteorological data from 2006 to 2023. These measurements were recorded at a monitoring station located in the metropolitan area of Seville, Spain, at the coordinates 42.8748° N and 1.6256° W. The meteorological conditions included the average temperature, wind direction (DD), and wind speed (VV), and the air quality factors considered were carbon monoxide (CO), nitrogen dioxide (NO_2), and particles of $10\,\mu$m or less (PM_{10}). For more information about the data, [14] can be consulted. The O_3 measurements were also obtained using the reference monitoring method [15]. The model is trained with data from 2006 to 2021, hyperparameters are validated using data from 2022, and model performance is assessed on data from 2023. Furthermore, in this work, air quality measures and meteorological variables are used to forecast O_3 conditions for the next 24 h, equivalent to one day ahead. This approach incorporates historical data to predict future O_3 levels, enabling more accurate and timely forecasts.

4.2   Evaluation Metrics

The models' evaluation is conducted using metrics that are widely utilized in forecasting tasks, thus ensuring robustness and comparability across different methodologies, namely Mean Absolute Error (MAE), in Eq. (1), Root Mean Squared Error (RMSE), in Eq. (2), and R-squared (R2), in Eq. (3). MAE and RMSE metrics quantify the disparities between the predictions and the actual values, ranging from 0 to infinity depending on the data, and values closer to 0 indicate higher predictive precision. On the contrary, R2 ranges from 0 to 1, where 1 denotes the complete explanation of the dependent variable. The training time of each model is also measured on a machine with the following specifications: 8 GB RAM and 512 GB SSD disk. The mathematical expressions of the quality measures are described below, where y refers to actual data, $\hat{y}$ to predicted data, n is the total number of samples, and $\bar{y}$ is the mean value of the input samples.

$$MAE = \sum_{i=1}^{n} |y_i - \hat{y}_i| \tag{1}$$

$$RMSE = \sqrt{\frac{1}{n}\Sigma_{i=1}^{n}\left(y_i - \hat{y}_i\right)^2} \tag{2}$$

$$R^2 = 1 - \frac{\sum_{i=1}^{n}(y_i - \hat{y}_i)^2}{\sum_{i=1}^{n}(y_i - \bar{y})^2} \tag{3}$$

4.3   ML Optimization

In this section, the results of the Bayesian optimization process are introduced and compared using the evaluation metrics presented above.

The best parameters obtained for each model are presented in Table 2, and Table 3 outlines the error metrics and training times associated with each optimal configuration, ordered by RMSE. The variation in window size for each model

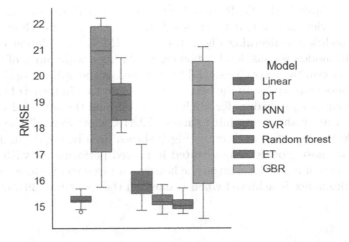

Fig. 2. RMSE boxplot for the Bayesian optimization process.

Table 2. Best hyperparameters configuration for each model.

Model	Window size	Hyperparameters
DT	44	{max_depth: 6}
kNN	38	{k: 6}
SVR	62	{C: 0.7020, epsilon: 0.1982}
RF	39	{max_depth: 27, n_estimators: 180}
ET	39	{max_depth: 27, n_estimators: 180}
GBR	66	{max_depth: 3, n_estimators: 180}

Table 3. Error metrics for the best configuration of each model.

Model	MAE	RMSE	R2	Time (s)
GBR	**11.38**	**14.55**	**0.60**	416.79
ET	11.57	14.73	**0.60**	52.41
LR	11.52	14.80	0.59	0.09
RF	11.75	14.88	0.59	186.14
DT	12.33	15.73	0.54	0.91
SVR	12.26	15.44	0.57	81.52
KNN	14.22	17.81	0.46	**0.01**

may stem from the distinct sensitivity of each algorithm to different lengths of window, as certain models need longer windows to capture patterns in the data. Then, Fig. 2 illustrates the variations of RMSE metric across all the different configurations of each model tested during the optimization phase.

Based on Table 3, the GBR model has the best performance in terms of evaluation metrics, however, it requires substantially more time than the other models. In addition, concerning Fig. 2, the mean RMSE for different configurations of GBR models is considerably higher, exhibiting a wide range of variation. With this concern, the Extra Trees (ET) is selected as the optimal option due to its performance comparable to the best GBR configuration in terms of error metrics, with slightly higher values for MAE and RMSE and the same R2 value, and with a significantly shorter training time of 52.41 s. Moreover, all the tried ET models collectively perform better, as Fig. 2 shows. Finally, regarding the input time window, most models demonstrated improved performance with approximately two days of input data, given the hourly data frequency. Notably, the ET optimal performance is achieved when trained on the preceding 39 h of data.

4.4 XAI

The selected model from the previous section, namely ET with a maximum depth of 27, 180 estimators, and 39 items as input time window, is elucidated through RULEx. A set of QARs is generated independently for each prediction horizon, utilizing both the real input data (each variable in each time window) and the predictions obtained by the ET model.

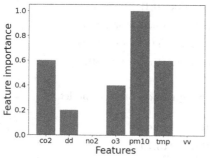

(a) Global influence of each feature.

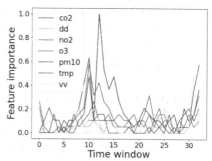

(b) Feature importance across time windows.

Fig. 3. XAI outputs.

Figure 3a summarizes the importance of each feature in determining the forecasts. The most significant feature discovered is PM_{10}, the variable that indicates the presence of particles smaller than 10 μm, and the past values of O_3 are the fourth feature in importance. These results align with the findings presented in the review paper in [2], whose analysis revealed that particulate matter (PM_{10}, $PM_{2.5}$), and O_3 are one the most frequently examined variable in estimating O_3 concentration. Moreover, in a city with a Mediterranean climate like Seville, characterized by warm or hot temperatures for most of the year (with a mean temperature of 20 °C), the temperature (tmp) also emerges as an important feature. Additionally, given that the data are from a metropolitan area with heavy traffic, the presence of CO_2 is also notable and significantly impacts O_3 concentration. Finally, the importance of wind direction (dd) may be attributed to the presence of both a large urban area and nearby countryside, thus assuming that if the wind is coming from the North-Est, air pollution will be higher, while when coming from the South and West, the air would be cleaner. On the other hand, Fig. 3b depicted the feature importance across the time windows, namely 39, given that measurements from the preceding 39 h have been utilized as input, thus capturing the temporal dimension of each variable. The peak importance values, particularly for CO_2, are concentrated between time windows 10 and 15, and these time intervals approximately correspond to the 24 h preceding the predicted O_3 concentration, indicating a high correlation between the current value and the same time interval from the previous day. Moreover, in the most recent time intervals (from 30 to 39 time window items), the most significant values are the wind velocity (vv) and PM_{10}, features that could represent the current contamination levels: the presence of high wind velocities indicates that strong winds could significantly alter ground-level O_3 concentration.

5   Conclusions and Future Works

Accurate O_3 forecasts are invaluable for effective pollution reduction efforts, and the acquisition of timely and precise information about O_3 levels can guide targeted interventions including emission reduction strategies, traffic management measures, and public health advisories, aimed at minimizing health risks and environmental impact associated with elevated O_3 levels. Besides, ML solutions have already demonstrated their effectiveness in ground-level O_3 concentration forecasting. Several models were tested in this study, and the best results were achieved with an Extra Trees model regarding evaluation metrics and training time. The explanations provided by the RULEx XAI technique illustrate that the model prioritizes features that align with the expertise of domain experts in the literature, namely the concentration of O_3 in past moments, the concentration of CO_2, PM_{10}, air temperature and wind direction. Finally, looking ahead, future research could explore the integration of predictive models with additional datasets, such as a wider range of meteorological variables or real-time satellite imagery, to enhance forecast accuracy and comprehensiveness.

Acknowledgements. The authors would like to thank the Spanish Ministry of Science and Innovation for the support within the projects PID2020-117954RB-C21 and TED2021-131311B-C22.

References

1. Hashim, B.M., Al-Naseri, S.K., Al-Maliki, A., Al-Ansari, N.: Impact of COVID-19 lockdown on NO2, O3, PM2.5 and PM10 concentrations and assessing air quality changes in Baghdad, Iraq. Sci. Total Environ. **754**, 141978 (2021)
2. Yafouz, A., Ahmed, A.N., Zaini, N.A., El-Shafie, A.: O_3 concentration forecasting based on artificial intelligence techniques: a systematic review. Water Air Soil Pollut. **232**, 1–29 (2021)
3. Fan, K., Dhammapala, R., Harrington, K., Lamastro, R., Lamb, B., Lee, Y.: Development of a machine learning approach for local-scale O_3 forecasting: application to Kennewick, WA. Front. Big Data **5**, 781309 (2022)
4. Damon, J., Guillas, S.: The inclusion of exogenous variables in functional autoregressive O_3 forecasting. Environmetrics **13**(7), 759–774 (2002)
5. Gradišar, D., Grašič, B., Božnar, M.Z., Mlakar, P., Kocijan, J.: Improving of local ozone forecasting by integrated models. Environ. Sci. Pollut. Res. **23**, 18439–18450 (2016)
6. Cobourn, W.G., Dolcine, L., French, M., Hubbard, M.C.: A comparison of nonlinear regression and neural network models for ground-level O_3 forecasting. J. Air Waste Manag. Assoc. **50**(11), 1999–2009 (2000)
7. Oliveira Santos, V., Costa Rocha, P.A., Scott, J., Van Griensven Thé, J., Gharabaghi, B.: Spatiotemporal air pollution forecasting in houston-TX: a case study for O_3 using deep graph neural networks. Atmosphere **14**(2), 308 (2023)
8. Sun, H., et al.: Improvement of $PM_{2.5}$ and O_3 forecasting by integration of 3D numerical simulation with deep learning techniques. Sustain. Cities Soc. **75**, 103372 (2021)
9. Palaniyappan Velumani, R., Xia, M., Han, J., Wang, C., Lau, A.K., Qu, H.: AQX: explaining air quality forecast for verifying domain knowledge using feature importance visualization. In: 27th International Conference on Intelligent User Interfaces, pp. 720–733 (2022)
10. Troncoso-García, A.R., Brito, I.S., Troncoso, A., Martínez-Álvarez, F.: Explainable hybrid deep learning and Coronavirus Optimization Algorithm for improving evapotranspiration forecasting. Comput. Electron. Agric. **215**, 108387 (2023)
11. Troncoso-García, A.R., Troncoso, A., Martínez-Ballesteros, M., Martínez-Álvarez, F.: Evolutionary computation to explain deep learning models for time series forecasting. In: Proceedings of the ACM/SIGAPP Symposium on Applied Computing, pp. 433–436 (2023)
12. Martínez-Ballesteros, M., Troncoso, A., Martínez-Álvarez, F., Riquelme, J.C.: Improving a multi-objective evolutionary algorithm to discover quantitative association rules. Knowl. Inf. Syst. **49**, 481–509 (2016)
13. Troncoso-García, A.R., Martínez-Ballesteros, M., Martínez-Álvarez, F., Troncoso, A.: A new approach based on association rules to add explainability to time series forecasting models. Inf. Fusion **94**, 169–180 (2023)
14. Gómez-Losada, A., Asencio-Cortés, G., Martínez-Álvarez, F., Riquelme, J.C.: A novel approach to forecast urban surface-level ozone considering heterogeneous locations and limited information. Environ. Model. Softw. **110**, 52–61 (2018)
15. Anav, A., et al.: Legislative and functional aspects of different metrics used for O_3 risk assessment to forests. Environ. Pollut. **295**, 118690 (2022)

Multi-Objective Lagged Feature Selection Based on Dependence Coefficient for Time-Series Forecasting

María Lourdes Linares-Barrera⬤, Manuel J. Jiménez Navarro⬤,
José C. Riquelme⬤, and María Martínez-Ballesteros(✉)⬤

Department of Computer Languages and Systems, University of Seville,
41012 Seville, Spain
{mlinares,mjimenez3,riquelme,mariamartinez}@us.es

Abstract. In the fast-evolving field of machine learning, the process of
feature selection is essential for reducing model complexity and enhancing interpretability. Within this context, filter methods have gained
recognition for their effectiveness in assessing features through statistical metrics. A recently introduced metric, the Conditional Dependence
Coefficient, aims to assess the dependence between subsets of features
and a target variable, enhancing our understanding of feature relevance.
This paper presents a novel feature selection approach that integrates
this statistical metric with a multi-objective evolutionary algorithm. This
strategy leverages the flexibility of evolutionary algorithms to efficiently
explore the feature space and employs an intuitive metric for identifying
pertinent features. Unlike many filter-based approaches, our method does
not require thresholds or percentiles related to the number of selected
features and evaluates the collective merit of feature subsets instead of
the significance of individual features. To address the forecasting challenge of identifying the appropriate time lags and features, we performed
experiments on eight distinct datasets containing multivariate time-series
data. Comparing our method against a baseline with no feature selection,
our results show solid performance in efficacy and a notable reduction in
model complexity.

Keywords: Feature Selection · Multi-objective Optimization ·
Genetic Algorithm · Neural Network · Time-Series Forecasting

1 Introduction

In today's data-driven landscape, where massive and real-time information
becomes the norm, datasets often contain a vast number of attributes. This situation demands advanced storage and processing capabilities to handle increased
data volumes and rapid and interpretable responses. In this context, feature
selection [3] allows the identification of the most relevant subset of features,
enabling a focus on a reduced set of variables while maintaining or enhancing
efficacy.

This process offers several benefits. Firstly, it enhances model interpretability [7], enabling experts to focus on meaningful insights. Secondly, it addresses the curse of dimensionality [17], reducing computational complexity and overfitting. Finally, eliminating irrelevant features prevents the need to sample data requiring extensive resources.

Feature selection remains a dynamic area of research. Despite the diverse range of approaches, it is possible to distinguish three distinct groups: filter, wrapper and embedded methods [4,10]. Within this domain, filter methods are gaining significant attention for their ability to quickly assess feature importance through statistical measures, but may overlook feature interactions.

This paper introduces MOLS (Multi-Objective Lag Selection), a novel filter feature selection algorithm that combines the Conditional Dependence Coefficient (CODEC) [1] with a multi-objective genetic algorithm. The CODEC metric evaluates the collective importance of a feature subset. This metric addresses the limitations of numerous filter techniques that primarily emphasize individual feature rankings.

The multi-objective genetic algorithm approach aims to balance model simplicity and interpretability by selecting a concise set of highly relevant features. Our proposal is based on the Pareto-optimal set and the NSGA-II algorithm [6], overcoming the limitations of traditional genetic algorithms that rely on weighted functions, leading to suboptimal trade-offs and sensitivity issues.

Given the complex relationships between variables and the significance of identifying key lags, time series forecasting provides an optimal scenario to evaluate our approach.

Therefore, the main contributions of this paper are:

- Introduction of a multi-objective filter method for feature selection that evaluates feature subsets collectively. Unlike several filter approaches, this method eliminates the need for hyperparameters that dictate the number of features to be selected, such as thresholds, percentiles, or a specific number of features.
- The proposal is applied over a neural network, leveraging the significant benefits that feature selection can provide. This model is further optimized via the Bayesian Optimization.
- Evaluation of the proposal effectiveness across eight diverse time-series datasets, covering various domains such as air pollution, electricity, and traffic forecasting. The results demonstrate competitive performance and a reduction in model complexity through feature selection.

The paper is organized into several sections. Section 2 reviews previous research on feature selection and Sect. 3 describes MOLS proposal. Section 4 outlines the experimental methodology applied and Sect. 5 presents the obtained results. Finally, Sect. 6 summarizes the main conclusions and suggests future research directions.

2   Related Works

As the demand for more interpretable and efficient models grows, there is a noticeable shift towards integrating feature selection methods into neural network architectures. A notable example of this trend is the work of Liu et al. [14], who combined a mutual information-based feature selection method with a hybrid deep neural network model to accurately forecast wind speed. Similarly, Kilincer et al. [12] have made a significant contribution by using recursive feature elimination with multilayer perceptron optimization to improve the detection of cybersecurity threats in healthcare systems.

Among feature selection strategies integrated on machine learning models, filter methods stand out for their versatility and computational efficiency. The CODEC metric, introduced in [1], marks a significant advancement in filter methods by efficiently detecting both linear and nonlinear dependencies.

Despite the potential of feature selection, optimizing search techniques within a vast feature space presents a considerable challenge. To overcome this, the adoption of bio-inspired algorithmic techniques has been suggested. Zhou et al. [19] proposed a genetic algorithm guided by a correlation matrix as a feature selection strategy. In a similar vein, Espinosa et al. [8] have incorporated a multi-objective evolutionary feature selection approach into an LSTM model, achieving notable improvements in air quality prediction in Italy. Our work similarly leverages a multi-objective evolutionary approach, combined with the CODEC metric, to enhance feature selection.

The importance of feature selection is underscored in various domains, particularly in the analysis of time-series data. The need to pinpoint relevant temporal points and tackle issues like temporal dependencies and seasonality is paramount. Addressing this need, in [15] is developed a two-stage feature selection process (correlation analysis and wrapper method utilizing a shallow neural network) for financial time series forecasting. Our research parallels these initiatives, concentrating on rigorously assessing our methodologies within the time-series domain.

3   Description of the Proposed MOLS Algorithm

We propose an evolutionary strategy-based method to identify the optimal feature subset. The main goal is to identify the subset of features maximizing CODEC value while keeping the number of features as small as possible.

The Conditional Dependence Coefficient (CODEC) [1] (see Eq. 1) assesses the relationship between a target variable Y and a feature set Z in a dataset of N instances. We focus on the unconditional version of CODEC, which evaluates the direct relationship without conditioning on additional variables. The formulation is as follows:

$$CODEC(Y, Z) := \frac{\sum_{i=1}^{N} \left(N \min \left\{ R_i, R_{M(i)} \right\} - L_i^2 \right)}{\sum_{i=1}^{N} L_i \left(N - L_i \right)} \tag{1}$$

In this formula, for each instance i we consider the following terms. R_i represents the rank of the Y value for the i-th instance. L_i represents the inverse rank of the Y value for the i-th instance. $M(i)$ represents the index of the nearest data point to the i-th instance, computed using only the dimensions defined by Z and Euclidean distance. The metric quantifies the strength of the relationship between Y and Z by assessing how Z influences ranks and positioning. In [1], the authors demonstrate that CODEC is a nonlinear generalization of partial R^2.

Our proposal is based on a multi-objective genetic algorithm based on Pareto front inspired by the NSGA-II algorithm.

1. **Initialization.** We start by generating an initial population of μ individuals at random, where each is codified by a binary vector ("1" for inclusion, "0" for exclusion of each feature).

2. **Evolutionary process.** The whole evolutionary process is repeated until the desired number of generations ($ngens$) is reached. At each iteration, we generate a new population through a series of steps:

   (a) **Offspring generation.** At each generation's outset, λ offspring are produced through the following evolutionary operations (only one at each time): crossover (chance $cxpb$), mutation (chance $mutpb$), or reproduction (chance $1 - mutpb - cxpb$).

   In crossover, two parents are randomly selected from the population, producing a single offspring using a two-point crossover mechanism. During mutation, each gene from a randomly selected individual have a probability ($gmutpb$) of flipping from 0 to 1 or vice versa, introducing variability. In reproduction, a random individual is cloned and the clone is added to the offspring, preserving genetic information.

   (b) **Evaluation and selection of subsequent population.** The offspring, combined with the current population, undergo evaluation. The top μ performers are selected for the next generation. Each individual is evaluated based on two criteria: its CODEC value (reflecting the dependence between the selected features and the target variable) and the number of features it represents.

   Individuals are sorted into layers called Pareto fronts. The first front contains individuals that are not dominated. Subsequent fronts are filled with individuals that are only dominated by those in the previous front(s).

   For the next generation, the top μ individuals are selected starting from the first front and moving on to the next ones as needed. If including an entire front would exceed the desired population size, the crowding distance within that front is used to choose individuals, ensuring the selection prioritizes diversity.

3. **Best solution selection.** Once the evolutionary process is completed, individuals within the population are classified into different Pareto fronts. The first front comprises non-dominated solutions, characterized by achieving an optimal balance between high CODEC values and a reduced number of features. The best individual on the first front is chosen based on the criterion of

Table 1. MOLS Parameter Settings.

Parameter	Default Value
Population size (μ)	50
Offspring size (λ)	50
Number of Generations ($ngens$)	20
Crossover Probability ($cxpb$)	0.5
Mutation Probability ($mutpb$)	0.5
Gene Mutation Probability ($gmutpb$)	0.2

having the minimum number of features. This selection provides an optimal balance between maintaining high dependency and ensuring model simplicity.

The parameters of the multiobjective genetic algorithm have been fixed (Table 1). Optionally, these parameters could be tuned, but our results (Sect. 5) suggest that the parameters are good enough to obtain competitive results.

4 Methodology and Experimentation

This section outlines the experimental methodology, details the learning model in Sect. 4.1 and the main phases of the approach in Sect. 4.2.

4.1 Model

As a base model, we selected a fully connected neural network architecture (MLP). It features one or two hidden layers, each containing 50 to 100 neurons. The Rectified Linear Unit (ReLU) activation function is used for its efficiency in speeding up convergence and reducing the vanishing gradient issue. The Adam optimizer is used for network optimization, with a learning rate set between 0.0001 and 0.01. This learning rate spectrum allows for a balanced approach to learning, adaptable to the unique demands of the problem at hand. Finally, to prevent overfitting, an early stopping mechanism is applied, stopping training if the validation loss fails to improve for 10 consecutive epochs.

4.2 Main Phases

1. **Preprocessing:** The initial dataset is segmented into three subsets: training (70%), validation (15%), and test sets (15%); ensuring unbiased model evaluation. As the algorithms require the lagged information, each time series is segmented into fixed-size, non-overlapping windows. Data from all channels are flattened into a one-dimensional vector. Standardization is also applied to address issues that arise from different scales and distributions.

2. **MLP hyperparameters tuning:** First, we perform MOLS feature selection on the training set and apply the selection over train and validation sets. To identify the optimal hyperparameters for the MLP, Bayesian optimization [16] is employed. This involves training models with a variety of configurations on the training set and assessing their performance on the validation set. The configuration that results in the lowest Mean Absolute Error (MAE) is considered optimal.
3. **Best model training and evaluation:** In this step, MOLS feature selection is applied. Then MLP is trained with the optimal hyperparameters and MAE is evaluated over the test set.

The experiment is carried out with and without feature selection and is repeated using 5 different random seeds.

5   Results and Discussion

This section presents the results, introducing the datasets in Sect. 5.1 and analyzing the effectiveness of the MOLS approach in Sect. 5.2.

5.1   Datasets

The proposal is evaluated in eight time series datasets. Preprocessing techniques are detailed in Sect. 4.2, focusing on windowing and channel flattening.

- **The Torneo dataset** [11] consists of four separate datasets, each focusing on a specific pollutant (CO, NO_2, O_3 or PM_{10}), gathered by hourly sensors in the Torneo region (Seville). The dataset consists of 7 variables (4 pollutants and 3 meteorological attributes) and a past history of 24 h (thereby resulting in a total of 168 features). The target variable is the level of pollutant for the next hour. Each dataset contains 2,798 instances and 168 features.
- **The Electricity dataset** [9] contains measurements of electricity consumption in Portugal for 321 different clients. A past history of 24 h is taken into account. The target is to predict the next hour for the first sampled client. It comprises 1,095 instances and 7,704 features.
- **The Traffic dataset** [5] details the road occupancy rates captured between 2015 and 2016 by sensors placed on highways in the San Francisco Bay Area at 10-minute intervals. It includes data from 862 sensors and 24 h of past history. The target consists of predicting the occupancy for the first sensor in the next hour. The dataset includes 730 instances and 20,688 features.
- **The ExchangeRate dataset** [13] covers daily exchange rate data for the period between 1990 and 2016 in eight countries: Australia, the United Kingdom, Canada, Switzerland, China, Japan, New Zealand, and Singapore. This dataset considers 8 countries, and a historical record of the 7 previous days is considered. The target of this dataset is to predict the value of the next hour for the first country. It is made up of 1080 instances and 56 features.

- **The ETTh2 dataset** [18] comprises data collected from an electrical transformer located in China, with hourly measurements spanning from July 2016 to July 2018. The dataset includes 7 variables (High Useful Load, High Useless Load, Middle Useful Load, Middle Useless Load, Low Useful Load, Low Useless Load, and Oil Temperature) and a historical record of 24 h is considered. The target is to predict the transformer oil temperature for the next hour. It contains 725 instances and 168 features.

5.2   Result and Analysis

Table 2 presents the effectiveness of our proposal compared to the results without using feature selection, based on the performance in terms of MAE and selected features. The entire experimentation process was repeated using 5 distinct random seeds to ensure the robustness and reliability of the results. The average MAE (Mean Absolute Error) and the average number of features from the 5 executions were recorded and are shown in Table 2.

Table 2. Average efficacy Results in Terms of MAE and Number of Features.

	MAE		# Features	
Dataset	MOLS	No Selection	MOLS	Total
ExchangeRate	0.007	0.006	9.8	56
TorneoCO	1.415	1.291	50.4	168
TorneoNO2	1.432	1.386	46.8	168
TorneoPM10	1.225	1.274	49.6	168
TorneoO3	1.362	1.375	48.6	168
ETTh2	1.875	1.897	50.2	168
Electricity	204.573	213.243	3611.6	7704
Traffic	0.007	0.009	9925.8	20688

In terms of MAE, our proposal exhibits superior performance compared to the approach without feature selection in five datasets, while obtaining a MAE close to the baseline method in the remaining three datasets. This underscores the strength of the CODEC metric in accurately capturing the dependence between subsets of features and the target variable. In particular, a significant enhancement was observed in the Electricity dataset. However, it should be mentioned that the results for TorneoCO were slightly worse. Furthermore, our proposal stands out by substantially simplifying the model, selecting fewer than half of the total features available in the datasets, and most cases selecting approximately 20–30% of the total features.

Figure 1 illustrates the progression of the MOLS algorithm throughout the feature selection process for one of the 5 random seeds executions considered, using the TorneoPM10 dataset. The first Pareto front fitness points is highlighted

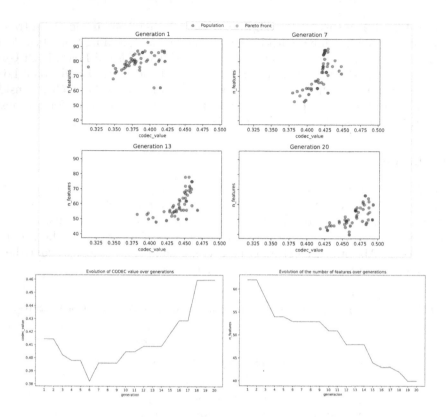

Fig. 1. MOLS selection on TorneoPM10 in one of the 5 random seeds executions.

in red, while the rest of individuals fitness is represented in black. It is evident that, across generations, individuals tend to converge towards the bottom-right corner of the graph. This indicates a tendency towards achieving a balance of higher CODEC values with a reduced number of features. At the end of the process, the MOLS algorithm successfully achieves a robust balance, thus ensuring effective and efficient feature selection.

The observed well-balanced relationship between the Mean Absolute Error (MAE) and the number of features underscores the potential of the multi-objective evolutionary approach to maintain or enhance effectiveness while reducing complexity.

To ensure the significance of the conclusions obtained, a statistical test [2] was applied to the results. Figure 2 presents the results of the Bayesian analysis comparing our methodology with the NoSelection (NS) method. With a 77% confidence level, we found that the NoSelection method results in a higher error. This results allow us to identify that there are significant differences between the methods compared.

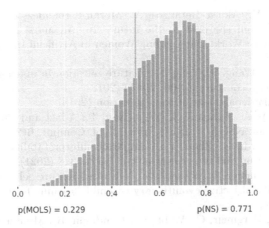

p(MOLS) = 0.229   p(NS) = 0.771

Fig. 2. Bayesian MAE comparison result.

6   Conclusions and Future Works

The paper presents MOLS, a novel approach that integrates the CODEC metric into a filter feature selection algorithm for time-series forecasting. MOLS aims to balance the feature dimension with the efficacy, addressing the challenges posed by datasets with numerous features. The key contributions include proposing a multi-objective filter selection method, applying a neural network model optimized via Bayesian Optimization, and evaluating the proposal across diverse time-series datasets. Results indicate that MOLS outperforms the approach without feature selection in terms of MAE in several datasets, achieving a significant reduction in the number of features while maintaining or improving model efficacy. Statistical analysis supports these findings. However, more research is needed to establish the significance conclusively.

Future work could focus on refining the MOLS algorithm, exploring additional datasets and models, and investigating other statistical metrics or optimization techniques. Additionally, extending the application of MOLS to different and more complex time-series forecasting problems could provide valuable insights into its effectiveness and versatility.

Acknowledgements. This research has been supported by the grant PID2020-117954RB-C22 funded by MICIU/AEI/10.13039/501100011033. This work has also been supported by TED2021-131311B-C21 funded by MICIU/AEI/10.13039/501100011033 and by the European Union NextGenerationEU/PRTR.

References

1. Azadkia, M., Chatterjee, S.: A simple measure of conditional dependence. Ann. Stat. **49**(6), 3070–3102 (2021)
2. Benavoli, A., Corani, G., Demsar, J., Zaffalon, M.: Time for a change: a tutorial for comparing multiple classifiers through Bayesian analysis. J. Mach. Learn. Res. **18**, 2653–2688 (2017)

3. Bolón-Canedo, V., Alonso-Betanzos, A., Morán-Fernández, L., Cancela, B.: Feature selection: from the past to the future. In: Advances in Selected Artificial Intelligence Areas: World Outstanding Women in Artificial Intelligence, pp. 11–34 (2022)
4. Cai, J., Luo, J., Wang, S., Yang, S.: Feature selection in machine learning: a new perspective. Neurocomputing **300**, 70–79 (2018)
5. CDT: California department of transportation (2015)
6. Deb, K., Pratap, A., Agarwal, S., Meyarivan, T.: A fast and elitist multiobjective genetic algorithm: NSGA-II. IEEE Trans. Evol. Comput. **6**(2), 182–197 (2002)
7. Dunn, J., Mingardi, L., Zhuo, Y.: Comparing interpretability and explainability for feature selection. arXiv preprint arXiv:2105.05328 (2021)
8. Espinosa, R., Jiménez, F., Palma, J.: Embedded feature selection in LSTM networks with multi-objective evolutionary ensemble learning for time series forecasting. arXiv (2023)
9. Godahewa, R., Bergmeir, C., Webb, G., Hyndman, R., Montero-Manso, P.: Electricity hourly dataset (2020)
10. Jiménez-Navarro, M.J., Martínez-Ballesteros, M., Brito, I., Martínez-Álvarez, F., Cortés, G.: Feature-aware drop layer (FADL): a nonparametric neural network layer for feature selection. In: GarcíaBringas, P., et al. (eds.) SOCO 2022. LNCS, vol. 531, pp. 557–566. Springer, Cham (2022). https://doi.org/10.1007/978-3-031-18050-7_54
11. Jiménez-Navarro, M., Martínez-Ballesteros, M., Martínez-Álvarez, F., Asencio-Cortés, G.: Explaining deep learning models for ozone pollution prediction via embedded feature selection. Appl. Soft Comput. 111504 (2024)
12. Kilincer, I., Ertam, F., Sengur, A., Tan, R., Acharya, U.: Automated detection of cybersecurity attacks in healthcare systems with recursive feature elimination and multilayer perceptron optimization. Biocybern. Biomed. Eng. **43**(1), 30–41 (2023)
13. Lai, G., Chang, W., Yang, Y., Liu, H.: Modeling long- and short-term temporal patterns with deep neural networks. In: Proceedings of the International ACM SIGIR Conference on Research and Development in Information Retrieval, pp. 95–104 (2018)
14. Liu, X., Zhang, H., Kong, X., Lee, K.: Wind speed forecasting using deep neural network with feature selection. Neurocomputing **397**, 393–403 (2020)
15. Niu, T., Wang, J., Lu, H., Yang, W., Du, P.: Developing a deep learning framework with two-stage feature selection for multivariate financial time series forecasting. Expert Syst. Appl. **148**, 113237 (2020)
16. Wu, J., Chen, X., Zhang, H., Xiong, L., Lei, H., Deng, S.: Hyperparameter optimization for machine learning models based on Bayesian optimization. J. Electron. Sci. Technol. **17**(1), 26–40 (2019)
17. Zebari, R., Abdulazeez, A., Zeebaree, D., Zebari, D., Saeed, J.: A comprehensive review of dimensionality reduction techniques for feature selection and feature extraction. J. Appl. Sci. Technol. Trends **1**(2), 56–70 (2020)
18. Zhou, H., et al.: Informer: beyond efficient transformer for long sequence time-series forecasting. In: Proceedings of AAAI Conference on Artificial Intelligence, vol. 35, pp. 11106–11115 (2021)
19. Zhou, J., Hua, Z.: A correlation guided genetic algorithm and its application to feature selection. Appl. Soft Comput. **123**, 108964 (2022)

FuSDG: A Proposal for a Fuzzy Assessment of Sustainable Development Goals Achievement

David A. Pelta(✉), Pavel Novoa-Hernández, and José Luis Verdegay

Department of Computer Science and A.I., Universidad de Granada,
18014 Granada, Spain
{dpelta,pavelnovoa,verdegay}@ugr.es

Abstract. The cornerstone of the 2030 Agenda for Sustainable Development are the 17 Sustainable development goals (SDGs). These goals are measured through 109 indicators and, in very basic terms, the degree of achievement of the 17 SDGs for a country, the so called SDG Index, is calculated with a weighted sum without taking into account any priorities among the goals.

Besides this, several facts are not considered: the different situations and priorities of every country, the different relevance that can be given to the SDGs and the potential imprecision in the data.

Here we propose a fuzzy alternative to the SDG Index, called FuSDG, having two main features: 1) it does not require an explicit set of weights to model priorities among SDGs, 2) it implicitly considers the imprecision in the input data, and explicitly in the output value.

A FuSDG value will be modelled with a triangular fuzzy number due to the reduced number of parameters required and the easy interpretation of its meaning. We illustrate the application of FuSDG over recent data, and we discuss potential issues.

Keywords: Sustainable development goals · fuzzy index · triangular fuzzy numbers

1 Introduction

The 2030 Sustainable Development Agenda, adopted by all UN Member States in 2015, provides a common framework for peace and prosperity for people and the planet, both now and for the future [2].

The 17 Sustainable Development Goals (SDGs) are the cornerstones of this Agenda, which offer the most practical and effective way to address the causes of violent conflicts, human rights abuses, climate change and environmental degradation, with a view to ensuring that there will be no one left behind at all. The Sustainable Development Goals (SDGs) are based on an understanding that sustainable development at all levels must integrate economic growth, social well-being and environmental protection.

A. Alonso-Betanzos et al. (Eds.): CAEPIA 2024, LNAI 14640, pp. 91–100, 2024.
https://doi.org/10.1007/978-3-031-62799-6_10

As it is well known, these SDGs are (as UN orders them): *"No poverty", "Zero hunger", "Good health and well-being", "Quality education", "Gender equality", "Clean water and sanitation", "Affordable and clean energy", "Decent work and economic growth", "Industry, innovation and infrastructure", "Reduced inequalities", "Sustainable cities and communities", "Responsible consumption and production", "Climate action", "Life below water", "Life on land", "Peace, justice, and strong institutions" "Partnerships for the goals".*

The "Europe Sustainable Development Report" [6] provides an annual overview of the European Union's progress towards the SDGs, as well as the progress of 38 individual European countries (including all EU countries, EU candidate countries, and regional partner countries) and highlights areas of success as well as opportunities for further improvement and uses the data to compare the progress of European sub-regions.

The degree of achievement of the SDGs by a country is measured by the SDG Index, where a score of 100 indicates that all SDGs have been achieved. The 2023/24 SDG Index for Europe comprises 109 indicators, derived from official and non-official statistics: for 95 of these, data is available from 2015.

Particularly, in the 2024 edition [6], one can read that

SDG progress in Europe has stalled since 2020. Even before the pandemic hit, progress in the EU was too slow to achieve all of the SDGs by 2030. Still, progress on the SDG Index was three times as fast over the period 2015–2019 (0.73 points per year) than over the period 2019-2022 (0.24 points per year).

The index is topped by Northern European countries. Finland ranks first for the fourth year in a row, followed by Sweden and Denmark - which all have scores close to or above 80 (out of 100).

The methodology for calculating the SDG Index is simple: firstly, the scores for each goal are calculated using the arithmetic mean of the scores of the indicators for that goal; secondly, these goal scores are then averaged across all 17 SDGs to obtain the SDG Index score. Equal weights were used for aggregating indicator scores into the goal scores, and for aggregating goal scores into the overall index score (See the Methodology section at [6]).

Due to the different characteristics of the countries in terms of size, population, location, political priorities, and so on, three elements can be problematic: the quality of the data, the simultaneous consideration of the 17 SDGs and the use of equal weights.

At a given time, not all the countries may agree on the most relevant SDG, nor in the possible preferences among them. Besides this, we recognize both the difficulty of agreeing in a specific set of weights and the need to be aware of the potential presence of imprecision in the data. This later aspect becomes clear if we check the description of some indicator. For example, one of the indicators for Goal 4 (Ensure inclusive and equitable quality education) is "Proportion of youth and adults with information and communications technology (ICT) skills, by type of skill"; or for Goal 1 (End poverty in all its forms everywhere), the indicator "Proportion of men, women and children of all ages living in poverty in all its dimensions according to national definitions" [5].

In this context, where many pieces of information have an obvious fuzzy nature, the aim of this contribution is to propose a Fuzzy SDG Index (FuSDG in what follows) to evaluate the level of achievement of a set of SDGs by a country. The calculation of FuSDG does not require an explicit set of weights but a prioritization of the goals. Besides, it considers implicitly the imprecision in the input data, while explicitly in the output representing the score as a triangular fuzzy number.

The paper is organized as follows. Section 2 presents the FuSDG and how to calculate it. Then, Sect. 3 illustrates the application of FuSDG in a case study with 20 countries and six SDG with a given prioritization. Different rankings are derived from FuSDG values and comparisons among them are performed. Also, in Sect. 4 an example using different prioritizations of the goals is provided to illustrate the changes implied in the FuSDG values. Finally, Sect. 5 is devoted to discussions and conclusions.

2   Definition of a Fuzzy SDG Index (FuSDG)

In this section, we propose to define the FuSDG index as a triangular fuzzy number (TFN, in what follows). So, we describe how every parameter is computed.

The calculation of the FuSDG for a given country requires the following information.

Firstly, a vector $V = \{v_1, v_2, \ldots, v_n\}$, where $v_i \in \Re$ represents the degree to which the country achieves the SDG i. All the SDGs or a subset of them can be considered. Secondly, it requires a preference order of the SDG defined as an ordinal relation among them denoted as $g_1 \succeq_p g_2 \succeq_p \ldots \succeq_p g_n$. The symbol $\succeq_p$ stands for "at least as preferred to".

In many situations, such order can be translated into a set of weights $w_1 \geq w_2 \geq \ldots \geq w_m$, $w_1 + \ldots + w_n = 1$ and $w_j \geq 0$ $(\forall j = 1, \ldots, n)$ and then a crisp SDG Index score of a country i can be calculated using a weighted sum model:

$$z_i(w) = \sum_{i=1}^{n} w_i v_i \tag{1}$$

where $z_i(w)$ is the scoring function for a country i and a given realization of the vector of weights $w = (w_1, \ldots, w_n)$. Using the so called ranked weights [1,9], specific values for w_i can be readily obtained.

But it is here where one of the motivations for proposing FuSDG arises. Let's suppose we consider three SDGs: g_1, g_2, g_3 and the following preference order: $g_2 \succeq_p g_1 \succeq_p g_3$. Then, the weights should satisfy $w_2 \geq w_1 \geq w_3$ and $w_1 + w_2 + w_3 = 1$. As the reader may notice, there are infinite sets of weights that satisfy those constraints. For example, $(1, 0, 0)$, $(1/2, 1/2, 0)$, $(1/3, 1/3, 1/3)$, $(0.7, 0.2, 0.1)$, $(0.65, 0.20, 0.15)$ and so on.

Due to potential measurements errors or lack of confidence in the data, we assume that the v_i values can be imprecise, and that they can be interpreted as "around v_i". In this case, it is clear that fuzzy numbers can be a good choice to model such kind of imprecision in the input data. However, we will not model this imprecision in explicit terms. As the input information available has single $v_i \in \Re$ values, we do not want to make an artificial "fuzzification" of the values.

In turn, we will consider such imprecision in the value given by the FuSDG.

The FuSDG of a country i is denoted as $\tilde{z}_i$. In order to avoid the introduction of (potentially unnecessary) layers of complexity we will represent $\tilde{z}_i$ as a triangular fuzzy number (TFN), which just require three values (a, b, c) for its definition. In what follows, the calculation of such values is shown.

Finally, let's consider the SDGs preference order is $g_1 \succeq_p g_2 \succeq_p \ldots \succeq_p g_n$.

Obtaining the support of the FuSDG

As we previously stated, there exist an infinite number of realizations of the w vector, thus leading to an infinite number of potential scores that a country can achieve. We are interested in two specific scores values: the minimum and the maximum. If we can calculate such values, then the support of the corresponding TFN can be readily obtained.

The minimum and maximum (crisp) scores that a country can achieve can be obtained by solving the two following linear programming problems where the decision variables are the weights:

$$
\min_w \; \mathbf{a} = \sum_{i=1}^{n} w_i v_i \qquad\qquad \max_w \; \mathbf{c} = \sum_{i=1}^{n} w_i v_i
$$

$$
s.t. \; w_1 \geq w_2 \geq \ldots \geq w_n \qquad\qquad s.t. \; w_1 \geq w_2 \geq \ldots \geq w_n
$$

$$
w_1 + w_2 + \ldots + w_n = 1 \qquad\qquad w_1 + w_2 + \ldots + w_n = 1
$$

The particular structure of both problems make them easy to solve, even without the need to run a conventional Linear Programming algorithm. More details about this are available in [7,10] and the references therein.

Now, two out of three values to define FuSDG are available: $\tilde{z}_i = (a, \_, c)$.

Obtaining the Core of the FuSDG

The last step for completing $\tilde{z}_i$ is the definition of value b.

In the context of multicriteria decision making, authors in [8] explored six different alternatives for such definition. The idea was to locate the core, at a particular score attained with a given set of weights. For example, using equal weights, or some definitions for ranked weights or just taking the center of the support. The results showed that, in terms of the ranking obtained for a set of alternatives, differences are very minor, thus recommending the use of simple approaches.

Although the use of the score obtained using equal weights is interesting (and easy to calculate), the resulting fuzzy numbers are hard to interpret. This is because the resulting numbers are not symmetric or, in some cases, the core lies at one of the extreme values of the support. That's why we propose to define $b = a + (c - a)/2$, i.e. at the center of the support. In this way, the classical interpretation of "around b" can be assigned to the FuSDG $\tilde{z}_i$.

Country	a	b	c	EW
SWE	0,65	0,73	0,81	0,81
DNK	0,64	0,73	0,82	0,82
IRL	0,65	0,72	0,78	0,78
FRA	0,63	0,70	0,78	0,75
DEU	0,60	0,69	0,79	0,75
PRT	0,62	0,68	0,73	0,72
HUN	0,60	0,67	0,74	0,71
POL	0,58	0,67	0,75	0,74
EUU	0,57	0,66	0,74	0,73
GRC	0,58	0,65	0,71	0,66
ITA	0,56	0,64	0,71	0,68
ESP	0,53	0,63	0,73	0,71
EST	0,52	0,61	0,70	0,70
ROU	0,56	0,61	0,65	0,57
FIN	0,43	0,60	0,77	0,77
BEL	0,42	0,58	0,74	0,72
NLD	0,34	0,55	0,76	0,76
BGR	0,48	0,54	0,60	0,57
GBR	0,33	0,53	0,72	0,72
TUR	0,42	0,52	0,62	0,55

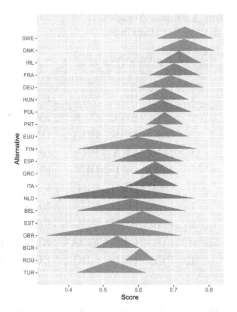

Fig. 1. In the left, FuSDG values for every country are shown. Column "EW" contains the score calculated using equal weights for all the SDGs considered. In the right, a graphical representation of the FuSDG values appears.

3   Case Study

As we stated before, the 2023/24 SDG Index for Europe comprises 109 indicators, derived from official and non-official statistics. For the sake of simplicity, we start here with the aggregated values for each of the 17 SDGs and we restricted to a set of 20 countries.

Considering the topics of SDGs, it is easy to understand that some priorities among them can be established. In fact, given the local context of every country, it is clear that the interest among them is not the same. For example, SDG 14 "Life below water" could be very relevant for a country in the sea shore, but less relevant for a country in the center of Europe. In this regard, a recent study by the World Economic Forum and Ipsos consultancy agency [3] asked 20,000 people in 28 countries which of the SDGs they thought were most important. The global priority ranking based on the average ranking of all 17 goals in the 28 countries surveyed was 2, 1, 3, 6, 8, 4, 13, 15, 14, 7, 16, 10, 11, 12, 5, 9, 17.

The six more relevant SDG were "Zero hunger" (2), "No poverty" (1), "Good health and well-being" (3), "Clean water and sanitation" (6), "Decent work and economic growth" (8) and "Quality education" (4). So, for illustrative purposes we will deal with these six SDGs.

In what follows, we will calculate the FuSDG value for 20 countries, using the preferences $g_2 \succeq_p g_1 \succeq_p g_3 \succeq_p g_6 \succeq_p g_8 \succeq_p g_4$.

Table 1. Equal Weights (EW), Conservative (based on a values), Neutral (b) and Optimistic (c) Rankings.

	Ranking (Positions 1 - 10)					Ranking (Positions 11 - 20)			
	EW	Cons.	Neutral	Optim.		EW	Cons.	Neutral	Optim.
1	DNK	IRL	SWE	DNK	11	GBR	ITA	ITA	BEL
2	SWE	SWE	DNK	SWE	12	PRT	ROU	ESP	ESP
3	IRL	DNK	IRL	DEU	13	HUN	ESP	EST	PRT
4	FIN	FRA	FRA	IRL	14	ESP	EST	ROU	GBR
5	NLD	PRT	DEU	FRA	15	EST	BGR	FIN	ITA
6	DEU	HUN	PRT	FIN	16	ITA	FIN	BEL	GRC
7	FRA	DEU	HUN	NLD	17	GRC	BEL	NLD	EST
8	POL	POL	POL	POL	18	ROU	TUR	BGR	ROU
9	EUU	GRC	EUU	HUN	19	BGR	NLD	GBR	TUR
10	BEL	EUU	GRC	EUU	20	TUR	GBR	TUR	BGR

Figure 1 shows the FuSDG value for every country. The fuzzy scores (their parameters) and their graphical representation are shown. The specific crisp score value attained for every country when using equal weights is displayed in the column "EW Score". The country labeled as "EUU" is a fictitious country constructed using the mean of the corresponding v_i values.

From these results, we derive three rankings, sorting the values according to each parameter of the FuSDG value. A conservative ranking (based on a), a neutral (on b) and an optimistic ranking (on c) are shown. For comparison purposes, we also derive a ranking from the attained scores using equal weights for the SDGs (no prioritization). The results are graphically shown in Fig. 3.

Looking at the plots, four countries seem to "break" the order in the Equal Weights and Optimistic rankings. These are FIN, NLD, BEL and GBR. All of them have quite wide support in their fuzzy scores in comparison with the other values. In these rankings, those countries seem to be in the wrong position. Intuitively, they should not be there. However, the conservative and neutral rankings look as one may expect.

Table 1 displays the ranking of the countries. Some basic facts are readily observed. DNK, SWE, and IRL are always at the TOP-4. EUU which is an "average" country, is always in the middle of the rankings. If we consider the EW ranking as the reference one, we observe that GRC goes from position 17 to the 9th in the Conservative ranking (or 10 for the Neutral one). In turn, FIN goes from 4 in EW to 16 in the Conservative ranking (or 15 in the Neutral one). The case in NLD is also notorious. It appears in the 5th position en EW, but in position 19 in the Conservative ranking (or 17 in the Neutral one). Something similar happens with BEL and GBR, which goes from positions 10 and 11 in EW to 17 and 20 in the conservative view, respectively.

Table 2. Kendall correlation coefficient of the rankings obtained from the different criteria.

Ranking	EW score	Cons.	Neutral
Cons	0.57	–	–
Neutral	0.57	0.66	–
Optim	0.51	0.58	0.66

Table 2 displays the Kendall's correlation coefficients among the rankings. In general, the values are quite low indicating that they are quite different. The most similar ones are the Neutral and Optimistic rankings, while the less similar ones are those obtained by the EW and Optimistic variants.

4   On the Impact of Prioritization of the SDG

The use of different prioritization of the SDGs implies changes in the support values of the TFN associated with the FuSDG. In turn, if the set of SDGs is fixed, the use of equal weights to make the aggregation always gives the same value. To illustrate the impact of the preferences/prioritization in the FuSDG values, we take a few countries and different preferences of the goals.

The countries considered are ESP, FIN, GBR and NLD and they will be analyzed according with the four different prioritization of six goals shown in Fig 2 (left). From one prioritization to another, just the relevance of two SDGs is exchanged.

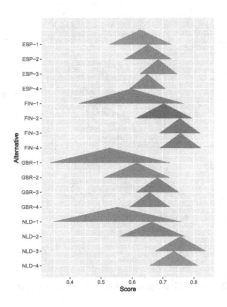

Prioritization Cases

1	2	3	4
ZH	NP	NP	NP
NP	ZH	GH	DW
GH	GH	ZH	ZH
CW	CW	CW	CW
DW	DW	DW	GH
QE	QE	QE	QE

Fig. 2. Prioritization cases and the corresponding Fuzzy-SDG Index for every country. Goals abbreviations are: ZH (Zero hunger), NP (No poverty), GH (Good healt), CW (Clean water). DW (Decent work), and QE (Quality Education).

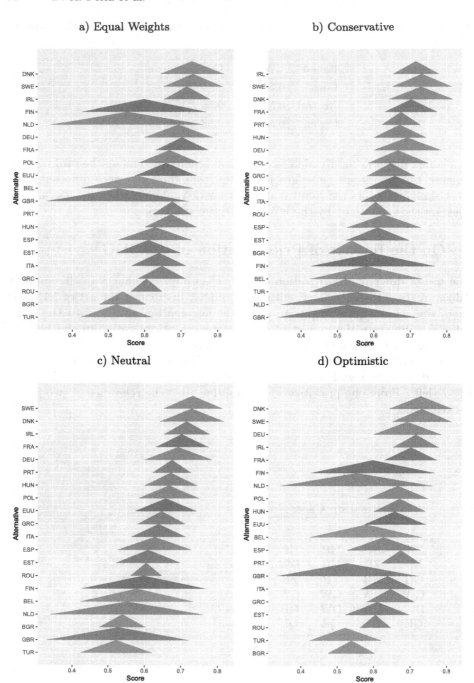

Fig. 3. FuSDG values sorted by different criteria. Colors are associated with countries.

Figure 2 (right) displays the corresponding results. The most notorious changes are observed from the first prioritization to the other ones. The reduction of the support of the FuSDG values from FIN-1, GBR-1 and NLD-1 to the other cases is almost about 50%. The main difference from case 1 to case 2 is the exchange of the first two SDGs.

The example shows that FuSDG values provide more information than a basic crisp score. For every case study we can observe both, the change in the support and the "displacement" of the fuzzy number. While the later has a clear meaning, the former deserves further discussion. Here, some of the ideas recently posed in [4] can be explored.

5   Discussion and Conclusions

In this contribution we proposed FuSDG, an index to assess the achievement of Sustainable Development Goals in terms of fuzzy numbers.

As the index is represented by means of symmetric triangular fuzzy numbers, the linguistic interpretation is straightforward: a value x is interpreted as "around x". We provided a simple mechanism to calculate the corresponding parameters and we showed its applications in various examples.

Although we are aware of the many ways available to compare fuzzy numbers and thus, construct different rankings, this is not the way we propose to explore. Comparing countries in terms of the achievements of the SDGs can be problematic, due to the many issues involved.

However, we envisage FuSDG as a useful tool to evaluate the behavior of a country along the time. In the last example, and when the priorities change, we observed both, the modifications in the support and the "displacement" of the fuzzy numbers. The later has a clear meaning: if the FuSDG is "moving" to the right, then the country is improving. The change in the support poses several questions with respect to its interpretation. For example, one may consider that the support of the FuSDG can be associated with the "certainty" of the value. But a wider support implies an increase or a decrease of such "certainty"?. Here one may be tempted to explore more sophisticated techniques to model the imprecision in the outputs, but a proper balance with the interpretation of results that non-experts can do from the values should be taken into account.

Acknowledgement. The authors acknowledge support from project PID2020-112754GB-I00, MCIN/AEI 347/10.13039/501100011033, Ministry of Science and Innovation, Spain.

Disclosure of Interests. The authors have no competing interests to declare that are relevant to the content of this article.

References

1. Barron, F.H., Barrett, B.E.: Decision quality using ranked attribute weights. Manag. Sci. **42**(11), 1515–1523 (1996). https://doi.org/10.1287/mnsc.42.11.1515
2. United Nations: Transforming our world: the 2030 Agenda for Sustainable Development. UN: New York, NY, USA (2015)
3. IPSOS Consultancy: Global public ranks ending hunger and poverty and ensuring healthy lives as top priorities among U.N. SDGs. https://www.weforum.org/agenda/2021/06/hunger-poverty-improve-health-survey/
4. de Hierro, A.F.R.L., et al.: On the notion of fuzzy dispersion measure and its application to triangular fuzzy numbers. Inf. Fusion **100**(101905), 101905 (2023)
5. Inter-Agency, on SDG Indicators (IAEG-SDGs).: The global indicator framework for Sustainable Development Goals (2017). https://unstats.un.org/sdgs/indicators/indicators-list/
6. Lafortune, G., Fuller, L., Kloke-Lesch, A., Koundouri, P., Riccaboni, A.: European elections, Europe's future and the Sustainable Development Goals. Europe sustainable development report 2023/24 (2024). https://doi.org/10.25546/104407, http://www.tara.tcd.ie/handle/2262/104407
7. Mármol, A.M., Puerto, J., Fernández, F.R.: The use of partial information on weights in multicriteria decision problems. J. Multi-Criteria Decis. Anal. **7**(6), 322–329 (1998). https://onlinelibrary.wiley.com/doi/pdf/10.1002/(SICI)1099-1360(199811)7:6<322::AID-MCDA203>3.0.CO;2-4
8. Novoa-Hernández, P., Pérez-Cañedo, B., Pelta, D.A., Verdegay, J.L.: Towards imprecise scores in multi-criteria decision making with ranked weights. In: Massanet, S., Montes, S., Ruiz-Aguilera, D., González-Hidalgo, M. (eds.) Fuzzy Logic and Technology, and Aggregation Operators. EUSFLAT AGOP 2023 2023. LNCS, vol. 14069, pp. 197–207. Springer, Cham (2023). https://doi.org/10.1007/978-3-031-39965-7_17
9. Stillwell, W.G., Seaver, D.A., Edwards, W.: A comparison of weight approximation techniques in multiattribute utility decision making. Org. Behav. Hum. Perform. **28**(1), 62–77 (1981). https://doi.org/10.1016/0030-5073(81)90015-5
10. Torres, M., Pelta, D.A., Lamata, M.T., Yager, R.R.: An approach to identify solutions of interest from multi and many-objective optimization problems. Neural Comput. Appl. **33**(7), 2471–2481 (2021). https://doi.org/10.1007/s00521-020-05140-x

A Surrogate Assisted Approach for Fitness Computation in Robust Optimization over Time

Pavel Novoa-Hernández[✉] [iD], Carlos Corona Cruz[iD], and David A. Pelta[iD]

Department of Computer Science and A.I., Universidad de Granada,
18014 Granada, Spain
{pavelnovoa,carloscruz,dpelta}@ugr.es

Abstract. One of the crucial aspects of solving robust optimization over time (ROOT) problems is to efficiently approximate the robustness of the solutions. However, current progress in this area has been scarce to date. To help bridge this gap, this paper proposes an alternative approach to one of the predominant frameworks in this field. Specifically, we decouple the fit and prediction of future environments that occur for each fitness evaluation by just evaluating previously fitted surrogate models. In this way, we globally approximate the robustness of the solutions by learning fitness functions, rather than point-wise predicting values during the execution of the algorithm. Preliminary results obtained from computational experiments indicate that this approach can achieve significantly superior performances to the existing framework, especially for specific surrogate model configurations. Furthermore, we show that in certain cases where our algorithms are less efficient than the existing approach, such inefficiency is compensated by improvements in error.

Keywords: robust optimization over time · radial basis function · surrogate optimization · autoregressive models

1 Introduction

In the context of dynamic optimization problems, where the fitness function changes with time, the goal is to find the optimal solution at the current time (i.e., before the change) [7]. As population-based techniques are usually applied to solve these problems, the field is known as Evolutionary Dynamic Optimization (EDO) [2, 8].

A recent topic in EDO is Robust Optimization Over Time (ROOT) [11, 14]. Unlike traditional dynamic problems, in ROOT problems the quality of a solution depends on its performance in the past, current, and future environments.

A discrete-time and continuous bounded search space ROOT problem can be formally defined as:

$$\max_{x \in \Omega} \mathcal{R}(x, t) \tag{1}$$

© The Author(s), under exclusive license to Springer Nature Switzerland AG 2024
A. Alonso-Betanzos et al. (Eds.): CAEPIA 2024, LNAI 14640, pp. 101–110, 2024.
https://doi.org/10.1007/978-3-031-62799-6_11

where $\Omega \subset \mathbb{R}^D$ is the search space and $x \in \Omega$ is a candidate solution. Value $t \in \mathbb{N}$ is the environment of the problem. The function $\mathcal{R}$ computes the *robustness* of a solution x in the environment t. The task is to find the set $X^* = \{x_t^* : t = 1, 2, \ldots, N\}$ such that x_t^* maximizes $\mathcal{R}$. Two definitions for $\mathcal{R}$ currently predominate: *average fitness* and *survival time*. In this paper, we focus on the former, which is defined as:

$$\mathcal{R}^a(x, t) = \frac{1}{W+1} \sum_{i=0}^{W} f_{t+i}(x) \tag{2}$$

where f_i is the objective function for the environment i, and W is the *time window*.

In general, the fitness functions f_{t+i} of the future environments are unknown, so the solving strategy must implement mechanisms to predict the values of these functions. A common approach is to rely on the performance of the solution in the past, to construct forecasting models (e.g., autoregressive models). Regardless of whether the past can be accurately evaluated, the task of predicting the future is very error-prone [9, 11].

Jin et al. [6] proposed an approach for solving ROOT problems. The main idea is that a solution's robustness is approximated by fitting a forecasting model using the history of past environments. Alternatively, Yazdani et al. [13] proposed to learn the characteristics of the search space during the run. This approach exploited information about the problem, such as the presence of peaks, that may be is not available in real-world problems. From this perspective, Jin's approach is more robust. However, it entails a significant computational overhead, since each function evaluation involves fitting a forecasting model.

In this context, the following question arises: *is it possible to find a less complex evaluation mechanism for robustness while maintaining performance levels comparable to Jin's approach?*

This aspect, which we consider crucial in ROOT, has been very little investigated so far. In addition to the previous contributions [6, 13], the efforts reported [3, 4] are also relevant, highlighting the complexity of this task in the absence of smooth transitions between environments. Specifically, [3] concluded that when this condition is not met, a sophisticated predictor such as Support Vector Regression is no better than a simple regression model. This motivated the proposal of artificial problems that allow these models to adequately capture the dynamics of the problem [4]. Similarly, in [9] how to approximate the fitness functions from the past environments was studied. The authors concluded that the contribution of surrogate models to the algorithm depended on problem characteristics, such as the number of local optima.

This contribution aims to present and evaluate a new approach assisted by surrogate models to model future environments. Instead of fitting a forecast model for every solution to predict its future fitness values, our approach constructs surrogate models of the future environment from a set of reference solutions. These surrogate models will allow the robustness of solutions to be approximated without fitting forecast models during the optimization, as suggested by

[6]. We have studied our proposal from computational experiments using ROOT problems with different time windows and using Jin's framework as a baseline for comparison.

The remainder of this paper was organized as follows. Section 2 delves into the proposed approach, which is analyzed in Sect. 3. Finally, Sect. 4 summarizes the main conclusions from our findings and future work.

2 Proposed Approach

In the so-called Jin's framework [6], the calculation of robustness implies fitting a forecast model at each evaluation of the objective function, thus incurring a significant computational cost. An alternative would be to decouple the fitting of these forecast models from the objective function evaluations.

In this sense, we propose to fit these forecast models before starting the optimization of each environment and based exclusively on a set of previously selected representative points of the search space. In this way, it is possible to build surrogate models of future environments that would interpolate any further evaluation during the optimization process.

Formally, let be a ROOT problem with a time window W. At the beginning of the execution, our approach creates (for one time only), a set $\mathbf{X}$ with N randomly generated D-dimensional points in the search space. We refer to $\mathbf{X}$ as the *reference points*. Since we are interested in covering as much of the search space as possible, these points should be evenly distributed. For example, using a technique such as Latin hypercube sampling or Sobol sampling [1].

Next, during the learning period of the algorithm (*cold start*) when there is not enough information to calculate robustness, we populate a matrix $\mathbf{Y}$ with the corresponding evaluations of the reference points in the first L environments. So, a value y_{ij} of $\mathbf{Y}$ stands for the fitness evaluation of the point $\mathbf{x}_i$ in the environment j. We will refer to $\mathbf{Y}$ as the *reference point history*.

Once the learning period is over, for each subsequent environment, we update $\mathbf{Y}$ by removing its first column and appending a new one $\mathbf{y}_t$ at the position L. Here, $\mathbf{y}_t$ is a column vector of dimension N of the evaluations of the reference points in the fitness function of the current environment.

The next step is fitting forecasting models $\Phi_{i,t}$ for each reference point i, that is, by using the row $\mathbf{y}_i$ from $\mathbf{Y}$ as input. This procedure is depicted as *step 1* in Fig. 1.

Then, we employ these models to forecast the fitness of each point i in the subsequent W environments (step 2, Fig. 1). This results in a $N \times W$ matrix $\tilde{\mathbf{Y}}_t$, which is used together with reference points for building W surrogate models. Specifically, each surrogate model $\tilde{f}_{t+i}$, $i = 1, \ldots, W$ is fitted using $\mathbf{X}$ and the j-th column of $\tilde{\mathbf{Y}}_t$ (step 3, Fig. 1). So after this process, we have an array of W surrogate models that will be used by an underlying EA to estimate the robustness of the solutions during the environment t.

Algorithm 1 shows our general framework for solving ROOT problems by incorporating surrogate models. Like Jin's framework [6], ours incorporates an

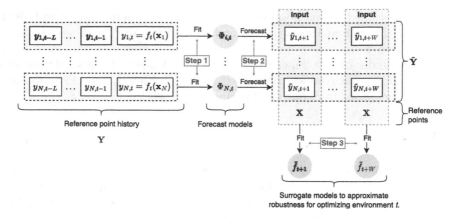

Fig. 1. Method for creating the surrogate models.

evolutionary algorithm (EA) for the optimization process within the current environment. We assume here that this EA implements mechanisms for detecting and reacting to changes.

In addition to decoupling the fitting of forecasting models during fitness assessment, our approach differs from Jin's in other respects worth noting. First, our approach *learns* future fitness functions, whereas Jin's approach only forecasts fitness values in the future. So, our robustness approximation can be viewed as a global approach, while that of Jin's is a local approach. Finally, since we rely on a set of reference points and their respective fitness values in the past, our approach does not require approximating the past with the hybrid approach proposed in Jin's. That is, by combining solution storage and surrogate model building [6]. In other words, our approach addresses the issue of modeling the past, which enables it to be applied to ROOT problems both assuming that the past is perfectly known and in problems where it is not [11].

3   Computational Experiments

To assess the benefits of our proposal, we make a set of computational experiments on three instances of the popular benchmark proposed by [5]- specifically, from the RMPB-I class. The configurations of these instances are summarized in Table 1. Note that the problem is a maximization problem with a 2-dimensional search space and a fitness landscape of 5 peaks per dimension. More details can be found in [5].

In this artificial problem, we can compute the optimal solution in terms of the robustness in each environment t as the fitness functions for the future environments are perfectly known. So, the true error of the algorithm can be

---

Algorithm 1: Proposed framework for solving ROOT problems.

---

1 $\mathbf{X} \leftarrow generateReferencePoints(N)$;
   // **Learning period**
2 **while** $t \leq L$ **do**
3   Evaluate $\mathbf{X}$ in f_t and store in $\mathbf{y}_t$;
4   Append $\mathbf{y}_t$ to $\mathbf{Y}$ as the column t;
5   **if** *a change is detected* **then**
6 | $t \leftarrow t+1$;
7   **end**
8   Run the EA using the fitness function of the current environment;
9 **end**
   // **Learning period is over**
10 **while** $t \leq T_{max}$ **do**
11   **if** *a change is detected* **then**
12   Evaluate $\mathbf{X}$ in f_t and store in $\mathbf{y}_t$;
13   Update $\mathbf{Y}$ with $\mathbf{y}_t$;
14   Fit N forecast models using $\mathbf{Y}$ (history of reference points);
15   Forecast the next W future fitnesses and record them in $\tilde{\mathbf{Y}}_t$;
16   Fit W surrogate models ($\tilde{f}_i$) from $\mathbf{X}$ and $\tilde{\mathbf{Y}}_t$;
17      $t \leftarrow t+1$;
18   **end**
19   Run the EA using the approximated robustness (Eq. 2 with $\tilde{f}_i$) as the fitness function.;
20 **end**

---

used as the performance measure. We opted for the error of the best solution before each change [11], which is averaged at the end of each run:

$$E_{best} = \frac{1}{T_{max}} \sum_{t=1}^{T_{max}} \left(|\mathcal{R}(\mathbf{c}^*, t) - \mathcal{R}(\mathbf{x}^*, t)| \right) \tag{3}$$

where $\mathcal{R}$ is the robustness calculated according to Eq. (2), $\mathbf{c}^*$ is the optimal solution of the problem and $\mathbf{x}^*$ the best solution found by the algorithm.

Table 1 shows that we explored three instances derived from varying the time window W. Note that this parameter defines how many alternative models have to be built.

To forecast future environments, we considered an autoregressive model with lag 5, which aligns with settings from previous research [5, 11].

We explored different variants for constructing the surrogate models of future environments. Specifically, we have considered different instances of Radial Basis Function (RBF) interpolation models by combining the parameters listed in Table 2. Each combination produces a different setting of a Differential Evolution (DE) algorithm (e.g. 8 settings) which is the EA technique used here. DE basic parameters are a population of 30 individuals, parameters $F = 1.0$, $CR = 0.5$, and mutation strategy $DE/rand/2$ [12].

Table 1. Parameter settings of the tested problems.

Parameter	Values
Number of peaks (m)	5
Dimension (D)	2
Search space	$[-25.0, 25.0] \times [-25.0, 25.0]$
Number of changes (T_{max})	50
Change frequency (Δe)	3000 function evaluations
Change type	Small step
Peaks' height range (h)	$[30.0, 70.0]$
Height severity $(h_{severity})$	5.0
Peaks' width range (w)	$[1.0, 13.0]$
Width severity $(w_{severity})$	0.5
Rotation angle range (θ)	$[-\pi, \pi]$
Angle severity $(\theta_{severity})$	1.0
Time window (W)	$\in \{2, 4, 6\}$
History size (period L)	12

Table 2. Parameter settings for the surrogate models.

Parameter	Values
Kernel	$\{Linear, Multiquadric\}$
Shape factor (ϵ)	0.1
Smoothing factor (ς)	0.5
Number of points (N)	$\in \{50, 100\}$
Neighbors proportion (ϑ)	$\in \{0.5, 1.0\}$

Within each environment (periods in which the problem does not change), the EA has a budget (Δe) of 3000 fitness evaluations of the current environment. To isolate the effects of our proposal, we will also assume that the algorithm can detect changes. Finally, we also measured the time in seconds consumed by the algorithm during its execution in each problem environment. At the end of each run, we averaged these values. Overall, 20 independent runs of the DE with each setting have been performed.

As a basis for comparison, we have implemented Jin's approach, which except for the mechanism to evaluate robustness, relies on the same configurations as the algorithms derived from our proposal. Furthermore, we assume that Jin's approach can accurately evaluate past environments, thus avoiding any effect of the past approximation mechanism implemented by that approach.

3.1   Computational Complexity

It is worthwhile to delve into the computational complexity of our proposal and that of Jin's approach. According to Jin [6], the complexity of fitting an autoregressive model is cubic in terms of the lag ψ, i.e. $O(\psi^3)$. Predicting from this already fitted model is linear in terms of the time window W, i.e., $O(W)$. So for Jin's approach, evaluating a solution has a cost of $O(\psi^3 + W + c_t)$, where c_t is the cost of evaluating the current environment. Being the dominant term ψ^3, it is reasonable to assume that its complexity is $O(\psi^3)$. Moreover, in an environment where the EA performs Δe evaluations, the complexity of Jin's is $O(\Delta e \cdot \psi^3)$.

In contrast, in our case, fitting a radial basis function model has a complexity of $O(N^3)$ [6] in terms of the number of radial functions (N). Once fitted, evaluating it has a linear cost in terms of N. More specifically, if a neighbor approach is used, then this complexity is reduced to $\vartheta \cdot N$, where the non-neighbor-based approach is equivalent to $\vartheta = 1.0$. Since W models are fitted, evaluating a solution using our approach will have a cost of $O(W \cdot \vartheta \cdot N + c_t)$, which leads to $O(W \cdot \vartheta \cdot N)$. Considering a whole environment, our approach has a complexity of $O(\Delta e \cdot W \cdot \vartheta \cdot N)$. This is because the entire construction of the surrogate models is left out of the optimization process carried out by the EA.

This implies our approach will be more computationally expensive when $W \cdot \vartheta \cdot N > \psi^3$. Based on the configurations used for W (Table 1) and the surrogate models (Table 2), we can at least expect our approach to be faster than Jin's on problems with $W = 2$ except for $\vartheta = 1.0$ and $N = 100$, and also on problems with $W = 4$, whenever $\vartheta = 0.5$ and $N = 50$.

3.2   Experiment Results

Figure 2 shows a summary, through a scatter plot, of the performance of the DE variants on the three problems considered. Each subplot corresponds to a problem with a specific time window, while every point reflects the position of a DE variant in terms of its execution time (x-axis) and its error (y-axis). Note that the DE variants are labeled following a nomenclature referring to the configuration of the surrogate models that they included. For example, *lin_50_0.5* corresponds to the DE that employed surrogate models with a *linear* kernel, 50 radial basis functions, and a neighborhood proportion of 0.5. Similarly, *mul_50_0.5* refers to a surrogate model with a multiquadric kernel and the same settings for parameters N and ϑ.

As Jin's approach is our baseline for comparison, we included two lines that intersect at the point corresponding to this algorithm, and which divide the graphs into four quadrants. See that the lower left quadrant corresponds to algorithms that outperform Jin's algorithm in both performance and runtime.

As we had anticipated in our complexity analysis, our algorithms are noticeably faster than Jin's on problems with $W \in \{2, 4\}$. In particular, for $W = 2$, all the variants exhibited lower average execution times than Jin's. As W increases, so did the execution times of our proposals, since more surrogate models are required to calculate the robustness of the solutions. However, our estimates overestimated these execution times, since surprisingly, for $W = 6$, the variants with $N = 50$ and $\vartheta = 0.5$, were faster than Jin's approach. A possible

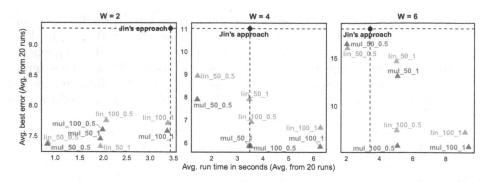

Fig. 2. Scatter plots of the average performance of the DE variants regarding the error and the run time, in problems with different time windows (W).

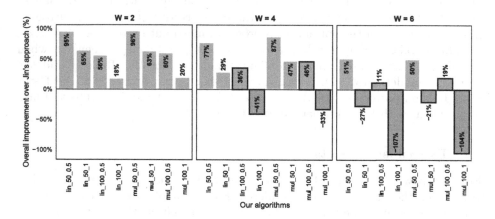

Fig. 3. Overall improvement of our proposal over Jin's approach in problems with different time windows (W).

explanation for this discrepancy lies in the implementation used to fit and evaluate the models[1].

However, what we did not expect was such a significant improvement in terms of the error. Regardless of the problem, all the DE variants fall below the dashed horizontal line, indicating the error of Jin's approach. Nevertheless, some variants are more sensitive to increasing W than others. This is the case of those that use $N = 50$, regardless of the kernel and the proportion of neighbors. On the contrary, those with 100 radial basis functions not only achieve better errors but are much more stable depending on the problem. Overall, the performances of our variants were significantly better than Jin's, as evidenced by a Friedman

---

[1] For surrogate modeling, we utilize Python's SciPy 1.12.0, built on NumPy 1.26.0. NumPy's optimizations, leveraging libraries like OpenBLAS and LAPACK, enhance linear algebra operations.

test p-value of less than 0.05 (omnibus test) and adjusted p-values of less than 0.05 from the Wilcoxon multiple comparisons test.

An important question here is to what extent improvements in error compensate for inefficiency. To answer this, we calculated the improvement rates of DE variants over Jin's for both error and runtime. To globally characterize the improvements, we consider both the error and the runtime rates. Thus, a positive value would indicate that our algorithms globally improve over Jin's approach. In particular, in cases where our algorithm was less efficient, a positive value indicates that the improvement in error rate compensates for the inefficiency. In contrast, a negative value means the opposite. Figure 3 summarizes this analysis through bar graphs corresponding to the overall improvement rates of our algorithms over Jin's algorithm. Note that, consistent with the first analysis, our variants improve Jin's on the problem with $W = 2$, but partially on problems with $W = 4$ and $W = 6$. Out of the 10 configurations that did not improve in runtime to Jin's approach, but did improve in performance, only 4 compensated for their inefficiency with improvements in error. These 10 configurations correspond to the black-bordered bars in Fig. 3.

4   Conclusion and Future Works

This proposal is an initial step towards the development of more sophisticated algorithms for solving ROOT problems. Nevertheless, we can draw some important conclusions from these preliminary results. The most important conclusion is that it is possible to separate the local fitting of prediction models from the robustness computation at run time. Our approach, based on surrogate models that are fitted before optimizing each environment, allows for achieving better performance, at least for the problems considered.

Additionally, the efficiency of the proposal deteriorates with the increase in the problem time window and the number of radial basis functions of the model. However, the sacrifice of this efficiency is compensated by the performance of the algorithm. There is no single surrogate model configuration that is optimal for all problems, considering both performance and execution time. Our findings suggest that an appropriate balance between these criteria can be achieved by carefully selecting the number of radial basis functions and the proportion of neighbors used to interpolate solutions.

Based on these results, we plan to extend our experimentation in the future. Firstly, it would be interesting to observe how the efficiency scales as a function of the number of dimensions of the search space, which increases the complexity of the reference points. Secondly, our proposal's sensitivity to the surrogate model parameters highlights the importance of designing strategies to learn these configurations at runtime. This is an issue that can be addressed from the perspective of self-adaptation [10].

Acknowledgments. Authors acknowledge support from project PID2020-112754GB-I00, MCIN/AEI 347/10.13039/501100011033, Ministry of Science and Innovation, Spain.

Disclosure of Interests. The authors have no competing interests to declare that are relevant to the content of this article.

References

1. Antoy, J.: Design of Experiments for Engineers and Scientists: Second Edition. Elsevier, Amsterdam (2014). https://doi.org/10.1016/C2012-0-03558-2
2. Cruz, C., González, J.R., Pelta, D.A.: Optimization in dynamic environments: a survey on problems, methods and measures. Soft Comput. **15**(7), 1427–1448 (2011). https://doi.org/10.1007/s00500-010-0681-0
3. Fox, M., Yang, S., Caraffini, F.: An experimental study of prediction methods in robust optimization over time. In: 2020 IEEE Congress on Evolutionary Computation (CEC), pp. 1–7, July 2020. https://doi.org/10.1109/CEC48606.2020.9185910
4. Fox, M., Yang, S., Caraffini, F.: A new moving peaks benchmark with attractors for dynamic evolutionary algorithms. Swarm Evolut. Comput. **74**, 101125 (2022). https://doi.org/10.1016/j.swevo.2022.101125
5. Fu, H., Sendhoff, B., Tang, K., Yao, X.: Robust optimization over time: problem difficulties and benchmark problems. IEEE Trans. Evol. Comput. **19**(5), 731–745 (2015). https://doi.org/10.1109/TEVC.2014.2377125
6. Jin, Y., Tang, K., Yu, X., Sendhoff, B., Yao, X.: A framework for finding robust optimal solutions over time. Memet. Comput. **5**(1), 3–18 (2013). https://doi.org/10.1007/s12293-012-0090-2
7. Kordestani, J.K., Ranginkaman, A.E., Meybodi, M.R., Novoa-Hernández, P.: A novel framework for improving multi-population algorithms for dynamic optimization problems: a scheduling approach. Swarm Evol. Comput. **44**, 788–805 (2019). https://doi.org/10.1016/j.swevo.2018.09.002
8. Nguyen, T.T., Yang, S., Branke, J.: Evolutionary dynamic optimization: a survey of the state of the art. Swarm Evol. Comput. **6**, 1–24 (2012)
9. Novoa-Hernández, P., Pelta, D.A., Corona, C.C.: Approximation models in robust optimization over time - an experimental study. In: 2018 IEEE Congress on Evolutionary Computation (CEC), pp. 1–6, July 2018. https://doi.org/10.1109/CEC.2018.8477670
10. Novoa-Hernández, P., Corona, C.C., Pelta, D.A.: Self-adaptation in dynamic environments - a survey and open issues. Int. J. Bio-Inspired Comput. **8**(1), 1–13 (2016). https://doi.org/10.1504/IJBIC.2016.074635
11. Novoa-Hernández, P., Puris, A., Pelta, D.A.: Robust optimization over time problems-characterization and literature review. Electronics **12**(22), 4609 (2023). https://doi.org/10.3390/electronics12224609
12. Opara, K.R., Arabas, J.: Differential evolution: a survey of theoretical analyses. Swarm Evolut. Comput. **44**, 546–558 (2019). https://doi.org/10.1016/j.swevo.2018.06.010
13. Yazdani, D., Nguyen, T., Branke, J.: Robust optimization over time by learning problem space characteristics. IEEE Trans. Evol. Comput. **23**(1), 143–155 (2019). https://doi.org/10.1109/TEVC.2018.2843566
14. Yazdani, D., et al.: Robust optimization over time: a critical review. IEEE Trans. Evolut. Comput. 1–21 (2023). https://doi.org/10.1109/tevc.2023.3306017

A Path Relinking-Based Approach for the Bi-Objective Double Floor Corridor Allocation Problem

Nicolás R. Uribe[iD], Alberto Herrán[iD], and J. Manuel Colmenar[(✉)][iD]

Department of Computer Science and Statistics, Universidad Rey Juan Carlos,
Móstoles, Spain
{nicolas.rodriguez,alberto.herran,josemanuel.colmenar}@urjc.es

Abstract. The Bi-Objective Double Floor Corridor Allocation Problem is one of the most recent incorporation to the family of Facility Layout Problems. This problem, which has been a challenge for exact and meta-heuristic approaches, involves optimizing the layout of the given facilities to minimize material handling cost and the length of the corridor considering more than one floor. This paper introduces a new approach based on the combination of two greedy methods and a path relinking implementation to tackle this problem. The experimental results show the superiority of our proposal in relation to the current state-of-the-art under different multi-objective metrics.

Keywords: Path Relinking · Bi-Objective optimization · Facility Layout Problem

1 Introduction

Facility Layout Problems (FLP) aim to optimize facility arrangements in order to minimize a certain objective function. This family of problems has a wide range of applications, such as manufacturing, delivery services, urban planning, and computer storage design [11]. Typically, three resolution approaches are found in the literature [2]: exact, heuristics, and machine learning approaches. Initial FLP research began with the Single Row Facility Layout Problem (SRFLP) [13], followed by the Double Row (DRFLP) [3] and Multiple Row (MRFLP) [7] versions, each with different row layouts and conditions. A significant variant is the Corridor Allocation Problem (CAP) [1], which is a DRFLP variant without spaces between facilities.

Previous papers dealt with one objective, the material handling cost (MHC). Recently, new variants of the problem have been studied where an additional objective is considered, such as the closeness rating (CR) [14] or the corridor length (CL) [8]. The Bi-Objective Corridor Allocation Problem (bCAP) [9] and Bi-Objective Double Floor Corridor Allocation Problem (bDFCAP) [6] involve optimizing facility layout for MHC and CL. The latter is a two-floor variant

© The Author(s), under exclusive license to Springer Nature Switzerland AG 2024
A. Alonso-Betanzos et al. (Eds.): CAEPIA 2024, LNAI 14640, pp. 111–120, 2024.
https://doi.org/10.1007/978-3-031-62799-6_12

of bCAP, which was tackled by means of a Mixed Integer Linear Programming and a Memetic Algorithm (combining a Genetic Algorithm and Variable Neighborhood Search) in the previous work, providing results for instances up to size 30. In this paper, we study the bDFCAP proposing a metaheuristic algorithm based on the combination of a greedy constructive method and Path Relinking. This approach has obtained competitive results in relation to the state-of-the-art method in the studied instances.

The remaining sections of this paper are organized as follows. In Sect. 2, we present the description of the problem. In Sect. 3, our optimization proposal is described. In Sect. 4, we provide an analysis of our results and compare them with the state of the art. Finally, in Sect. 5, we present our conclusions and future work.

2 Problem Description

The bDFCAP considers a layout with two floors: the lower and the upper ones. In each floor, facilities can be located at both sides of a corridor without allowing any gap between two adjacent facilities in a row. In addition, there is an elevator on the side where the origin of the four rows is set, allowing the flow of material between facilities located on different floors (see Fig. 1, where the origin is set on the left-hand side). The objective is to arrange all the facilities in the layout minimizing both, the overall MHC, defined as the weighted sum of the center-to-center distances between each pair of facilities in the layout, and the CL, defined as the length of the longest row. Notice that the distance between facilities in different floors must consider the route through the elevator.

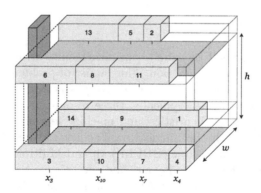

Fig. 1. Layout with two floors and one corridor per floor. Facility 3 is located in the first row of the first floor ($f_3 = 1$, $r_3 = 1$). Similarly, facility 14 has ($f_{14} = 1$, $r_{14} = 2$), facility 6 has ($f_6 = 2$, $r_6 = 1$), facility 13 has ($f_{13} = 2$, $r_{13} = 2$), and so on.

More formally, given a set F of n facilities, $n = |F|$, where each $i \in F$ has an associated length l_i; the flow cost per unit distance c_{ij} between each pair of facilities $i, j \in F$; and a layout with two floors (floors 1 and 2, separated by a height h), and two rows in each floor (rows 1 and 2, separated by a corridor of width w); the bDFCAP consist in finding an assignment of facilities to floors $f : F \rightarrow \{1, 2\}$ and rows $r : F \rightarrow \{1, 2\}$, and a vector $x \in \mathbb{R}^n$ with the center positions of all the facilities in the layout (measured from the common fixed left origin where the elevator is located) that minimizes both the total MHC and CL. Mathematically:

$$\min \ \mathcal{F}(f, r, x) = \{\mathcal{F}_{MHC}, \mathcal{F}_{CL}\} \tag{1a}$$

$$\text{s.t.} \ \mathcal{F}_{MHC} = \sum_{\substack{i,j \in F \\ i < j}} c_{ij} d_{ij} \tag{1b}$$

$$\mathcal{F}_{CL} = max(L_{11}, L_{12}, L_{21}, L_{22}) \tag{1c}$$

$$|x_i - x_j| \geq (l_i + l_j)/2 \qquad i, j \in F, \ i < j, \ r_i = r_j \tag{1d}$$

$$d_{ij} = |x_i - x_j| \qquad i, j \in F, \ i < j, \ r_i = r_j \tag{1e}$$

$$d_{ij} = |x_i - x_j| + w \qquad i, j \in F, \ i < j, \ f_i = f_j, \ r_i \neq r_j \tag{1f}$$

$$d_{ij} = x_i + x_j + w + h \qquad i, j \in F, \ i < j, \ f_i \neq f_j \tag{1g}$$

$$L_{ab} = \sum_{\substack{i \in F \\ f_i = a \land r_i = b}} l_i \qquad a, b \in \{1, 2\} \tag{1h}$$

Equations (1b) and (1c) represent the MHC and CL objectives, respectively. Equation (1d) avoids the overlapping between two adjacent facilities in the same row. Equations (1e) to (1g) compute the distance between two facilities in three different situations: (1e) located in the same row; (1f) located in different rows of the same floor; and (1g) located in different floors. Finally, Eq. (1h) computes the length of each row.

3 Optimization Proposal

This paper introduces a Path Relinking (PR) approach to tackle the bDFCAP problem. Originally conceptualized as a method to combine intensification and diversification strategies within Tabu Search [12], PR is based on the notion of establishing a trajectory between two solutions. The aim is to discover potential solutions while traversing this trajectory. The process involves incremental integration of the features of a second high-quality solution, known as the guide solution, into a first solution, known as the initial solution. Given that both solutions are of considerable quality, the expected outcome is that exploration along the generated path will venture into new and valuable areas of the search space.

3.1 Bi-Objective PR

In single-objective problems, determining the superiority of one solution over another is straightforward. For minimization problems, the solution with the lowest value is preferable, while in maximization problems, the highest value prevails. However, in multi-objective problems, the comparison involves multiple objective functions. Specifically, in this context, we are dealing with two functions that need to be minimized. A solution can either dominate, be dominated by, or be non-dominated with respect to another. To be more precise, a solution φ_1 is said to dominate another solution φ_2 (denoted as $\varphi_1 \prec \varphi_2$) if for every objective function $\mathcal{F}_i$, φ_1 is either better or equal, and there is at least one objective function where φ_1 is better. This concept is formally defined in Eq. (2).

$$\varphi_1 \prec \varphi_2 \; if$$
$$\forall i \in \{1..k\} : \mathcal{F}_i(\varphi_1) \leq \mathcal{F}_i(\varphi_2) \qquad (2)$$
$$\wedge \; \exists i \in \{1..k\} : \mathcal{F}_i(\varphi_1) < \mathcal{F}_i(\varphi_2)$$

Since our algorithm deals with multiple solutions at the same time, they must be organized within a suitable data structure. For this purpose, we will utilize a set named as *ND*, designated for storing only non-dominated solutions. To incorporate a new solution φ into this collection, we will employ an Update function. This function will first determine whether φ is dominated by any existing member of the set. Should φ not be dominated, the function will proceed to evaluate all present solutions within the set, excluding any dominated by φ.

3.2   Path Relinking

Our PR proposal creates a path between two solutions φ and χ by iteratively including in φ elements from χ. The method starts using *insert* moves to balance the rows from the initial solution to the guide solution. Then, it applies *interchange* moves to match the guide solution. Moreover, the method tries to update the *ND* set with all the solutions generated in the path.

Figure 2 shows an example of the whole procedure using the instance S9H, where an initial solution φ (in the top part of the figure) will be modified until reaching the guide solution χ (at bottom). Our idea behind the *insert* move is to ensure that each row in the initial solution matches the size of its corresponding row in the guide solution. For this purpose, let us define a vector N_φ with the number of facilities in each row of φ, hence, in this example, $N_\varphi = \{4, 3, 1, 1\}$ and $N_\chi = \{2, 2, 3, 2\}$. Then, in order to balance the number of facilities in each row of φ, all the candidate *insert* moves at each iteration are those insertions of facilities from a row $row1$ with $N_\varphi(row1) > N_\chi(row1)$ to a row $row2$ with $N_\varphi(row2) < N_\chi(row2)$. In this example, facilities 6, 2 and 4 in $row1$ of φ (not present in $row1$ of χ) are candidate facilities to be inserted in rows 3 and/or 4. Similarly, the three facilities in $row2$ of φ (not present in $row2$ of χ) can be removed but, in this case, only facilities 1 and 8 can be inserted in $row3$. Figure 2 shows below the initial solution two *insert* moves among the six possible moves. Moreover, we intend to benefit from placing a facility in the identical location as it appears in the guide solution (facility 6 inserted at the beginning of $row3$, and facilities 2 and 4 at the end or beginning of $row4$, respectively). Once we have all the solutions resulting after the possible insertions at each iteration

(6 in this case), the method selects one of the solutions at random to belong to the path and continue the procedure. The selected solutions, which belong to the path, are highlighted in red in the figure. This phase of the process continues until each row in the initial solution matches the size of its corresponding row in the guide solution, ending in what we call the intermediate solution.

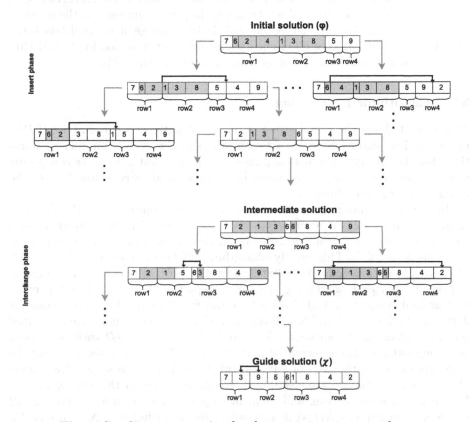

Fig. 2. Graphic representation for the PathRelinking procedure.

The second phase of the PR procedure compares the intermediate solution with the guide solution to match the position of all the facilities in both solutions. Therefore, it analyzes all the facilities in φ to check if they are located at the same position in χ, otherwise an interchange is needed to match this facility in both solutions. Following the example in Fig. 2, only five facilities from the intermediate solution (2, 1, 3, 5 and 9) can exchange its position in φ at the first iteration of the second phase. Then, the procedure selects one of these moves using a given function, following a Greedy Randomized Adaptive Search Procedure (GRASP) methodology [5]. In this case, the greedy function of a candidate move $g(move)$ is the objective function of the resulting solution after the interchange move, and the selected move is randomly chosen from a restricted candidate list built including all the candidate moves with $g(move) \leq g_{min} + \alpha \cdot$ $(g_{max} - g_{min})$. Hence, the randomness/greediness of the procedure is controlled by the α parameter ($\alpha = 0$ purely random, $\alpha = 1$ purely greedy). Once the move is applied, the resulting solution is added to the path, and the procedure continues after it.

We have encapsulated the whole PR procedure in a method `PathRelinking`(φ, χ, α, *func*), where φ is the initial solution, χ is the guide solution, α is the parameter required by the GRASP methodology of the interchange phase, and *func* is the objective function (MHC or CL) to be used as the greedy function by the GRASP. The method will return the set of solutions selected for the path.

3.3   Algorithmic Description

Algorithm 1 shows the pseudo-code of our Bi-objective Path Relinking (BPR) proposal. The algorithm receives two input parameters: the number of iterations for the greedy construction phase, *maxCons*; and a value α controlling random/greedy selection of the move to be performed at each iteration of the `PathRelinking` procedure.

In step 1, we initialize our set of non-dominated solutions, called *ND*, to an empty set. In step 2, we generate *maxCons* solutions with the `Greedy` method considering MHC and store them in S_1. In step 3, we repeat the same process but considering CL. This greedy algorithm will be later explained. Next, in steps 4 to 7, we proceed with a `PathRelinking` process between each solution φ from S_1 and each solution χ from S_2 (steps 6 and 7) and then the other way around (steps 8 and 9). Notice that the first and third methods consider MHC, while the second and fourth consider CL. These steps generate the initial set of non-dominated solutions *ND*. In step 10, we update *ND* with the sets of non-dominated solutions generated in steps 6 to 9. Notice that the value for the third parameter in the uses of `PathRelinking` is 1 in these steps. The reason of this value is that we want the most greedy behavior in this phase. In step 11, we set *improve* to true, and then, in step 12, we enter a loop. The aim of this loop is to improve *ND* while new solutions are included in *ND*. In step 13, we set *improve* to false. In step 14 to step 19 we repeat a similar procedure for the `PathRelinking`, but instead of using S_1 and S_2, using the solutions in *ND*. Notice that in step 20 we Update *ND'* instead of the original *ND*. In step 21 if *ND'* and *ND* are different, we set *ND* to *ND'* in step 23. Finally, in step 24, we return the final set of non-dominated solutions *ND*.

Regarding the `Greedy` algorithm, it generates *maxCons* solutions based on a greedy strategy. Firstly, it selects four random facilities and places them in each row. Then, the remaining facilities are placed in the solution considering the indicated objective function as greedy criteria, either MHC or CL.

Algorithm 1: BPR($maxCons, \alpha$)

---

1 $ND \leftarrow \emptyset$
2 $S_1 \leftarrow$ Greedy($maxCons, MHC$)
3 $S_2 \leftarrow$ Greedy($maxCons, CL$)
4 **for** $\varphi \in S_1$ **do**
5 $\quad$ **for** $\chi \in S_2$ **do**
6 $\quad\quad$ $P_1 \leftarrow$ PathRelinking($\varphi, \chi, 1, MHC$)
7 $\quad\quad$ $P_2 \leftarrow$ PathRelinking($\varphi, \chi, 1, CL$)
8 $\quad\quad$ $P_3 \leftarrow$ PathRelinking($\chi, \varphi, 1, MHC$)
9 $\quad\quad$ $P_4 \leftarrow$ PathRelinking($\chi, \varphi, 1, CL$)
10 $\quad\quad$ $ND \leftarrow$ Update($ND \cup P_1 \cup P_2 \cup P_3 \cup P_4$)

11 $improve \leftarrow$ **true**
12 **while** $improve$ **do**
13 $\quad$ $improve \leftarrow$ **false**
14 $\quad$ **for** $i = 1$ **to** $|ND| - 1$ **do**
15 $\quad\quad$ **for** $j = i + 1$ **to** $|ND|$ **do**
16 $\quad\quad\quad$ $P_1 \leftarrow$ PathRelinking($ND[i], ND[j], \alpha, MHC$)
17 $\quad\quad\quad$ $P_2 \leftarrow$ PathRelinking($ND[i], ND[j], \alpha, CL$)
18 $\quad\quad\quad$ $P_3 \leftarrow$ PathRelinking($ND[j], ND[i], \alpha, MHC$)
19 $\quad\quad\quad$ $P_4 \leftarrow$ PathRelinking($ND[j], ND[i], \alpha, CL$)
20 $\quad\quad\quad$ $ND' \leftarrow$ Update($ND \cup P_1 \cup P_2 \cup P_3 \cup P_4$)

21 $\quad$ **if** ($ND \neq ND'$) **then**
22 $\quad\quad$ $improve \leftarrow$ **true**
23 $\quad\quad$ $ND \leftarrow ND'$

24 **return** ND

---

4 Results

In this section, we present our experimental findings and subsequently benchmark them against the state of the art. We provide our results through various metrics to facilitate a clearer comparison. The parameter values used in the execution of our algorithm are the following: $maxCons = 5 \cdot n$, where n is the size of the instance, and $\alpha = RND$, where RND means that there is a random value $[0, 1]$ for each iteration.

This research evaluates the results using literature multi-objective metrics [10] [15], where each metric calculates different values, such as the dominance, the distance between solutions, etc. Except for the Hypervolume, these metrics require a comparison between two sets of non-dominated solutions. For each problem instance, we compiled a *reference set* of non-dominated solutions by aggregating the results from the state-of-the-art and our algorithm.

The coverage metric $C(X, Y)$ assesses the proportion of solutions from algorithm X that weakly dominate those from algorithm Y, with $C(X, Y) = 1$ suggesting that all solutions from Y are weakly dominated by those from X. We define coverage as $C(Ref, Alg)$, where Ref is the reference set. Hypervolume

(HV) measures the objective space volume occupied by a set of non-dominated solutions. The epsilon metric (ϵ) quantifies the minimum distance needed to reach solutions from a set of non-dominated solutions to the reference set. Generational (GD), inverse generational (IGD), and additive inverse generational ($IGD+$) distances quantify the divergence of solutions from the reference set, each with its distinct, but similar, calculation methodology. We also considered the number of solutions in each set, labeled as $Size$, and the spread (Δ), which are the size of the set, and the average distance between adjacent solutions, respectively. Also, we compare the computational time in seconds (T(s)).

These metrics were calculated using the *jMetal* [4] framework. For all metrics but HV and $Size$, lower values indicate better results.

We compare our algorithm proposal, named *BPR*, with the algorithm in [6]. The authors propose a memetic algorithm, composed by a Genetic Algorithm with Variable Neighborhood Search (GAVNS). Table 1 displays the performance of both algorithms. There are 22 instances in the state of the art, and we have split them in 4 sets, depending on the size of the instance, for a better comparison. In addition, the total average is calculated for each metric. In the first set, our proposal obtains better results for the $HV, GD, Size$ and time. In the second set, we obtain better results for the $GD, Size$ and Δ. It is the only set in which we obtain HV worse than GAVNS and better results in Δ. For the third and fourth sets, our approach reaches better results in $HV, \epsilon, GD, Size$, and $T(s)$. It is important to note that we have spent only 12%, 6%, 16% and 20% of the execution time of the state of the art, respectively. In conclusion, we obtain better results in HV, ϵ, GD and $Size$, spending only 20% of the execution time of the GAVNS on average.

In addition, we also include Fig. 3 as a graphic representation of the results for both algorithms in instance N30_05. In blue, we have the results for the GAVNS algorithm, and in red, for our proposal. In the ordinates, the values for CL are represented, while in the abscissas, the values for MHC. It is worth mentioning that GAVNS obtains better values in both ends, mainly in the end for MHC, where our proposal is still far from those solutions. However, our

Table 1. Overview for both algorithms for each set and each metric.

Set	Algorithm	C(Ref, Alg)	HV	ϵ	GD	IGD	IGD+	Size	Δ	T(s)
[9, 12]	BPR	0.24	**0.49**	0.10	**1227.35**	1088.17	3000.07	**7**	1.00	**4.67**
	GAVNS	**0.02**	0.47	**0.09**	1304.81	**1069.81**	**2955.10**	6	**0.98**	38.45
[13, 20]	BPR	0.52	0.49	0.12	**1781.97**	1548.09	5699.38	**12**	**0.98**	**48.33**
	GAVNS	**0.04**	**0.52**	**0.11**	1943.87	**1525.20**	**5616.89**	10	0.99	773.89
[25]	BPR	0.43	**0.41**	**0.04**	**3178.81**	2958.89	14203.25	**23**	0.95	**443.40**
	GAVNS	**0.10**	0.39	0.09	5067.48	**2939.09**	**14118.05**	9	**0.93**	2803.09
[30]	BPR	0.52	**0.37**	**0.10**	**6525.34**	5975.67	26476.98	**18**	0.96	**1227.80**
	GAVNS	**0.13**	0.34	0.12	9019.89	**5912.30**	**26193.00**	9	**0.95**	4967.20
Total	BPR	0.42	**0.45**	**0.09**	**3026.21**	2749.56	11618.08	**14**	0.98	**394.27**
	GAVNS	**0.07**	0.43	0.10	4087.68	**2719.41**	**11499.42**	8	**0.96**	1987.52

algorithm obtains non-dominated solutions in the middle of the front. Although we have represented one of the largest solutions, the performance is similar in the other instances.

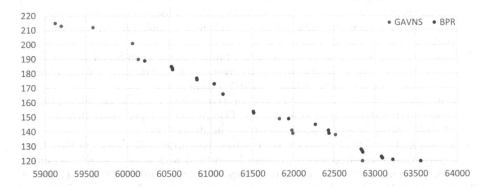

Fig. 3. Representation of the results for both algorithms in instance N30_05.

5 Conclusions and Future Work

The Bi-Objective Double Floor Corridor Allocation Problem has been introduced in the recent literature. This paper details the implementation of a meta-heuristic algorithm that utilizes the Path Relinking technique as alternative to the state of the art. Our proposal obtained competitive results in eight different multi-objective metrics spending a 20% of the time of the previous work.

Looking ahead, our research will focus on incorporating an External Path Relinking technique in order to improve the search on the ends of the front, where the previous approach obtains a good behavior. Moreover, our aim is to enhance our findings by improving aspects like coverage or execution time.

Acknowledgements. This work has been partially supported by the Spanish Ministerio de Ciencia e Innovación (MCIN/AEI/10.13039/501100011033) under grant refs. RED2022-134480-T, PID2021-126605NB-I00 and by ERDF A way of making Europe; and Generalitat Valenciana with grant ref. CIAICO/2021/224.

References

1. Amaral, A.R.: The corridor allocation problem. Computers & Operations Research **39**(12), 3325–3330 (2012)
2. Burggräf, P., Wagner, J., Heinbach, B.: Bibliometric study on the use of machine learning as resolution technique for facility layout problems. IEEE Access **9**, 22569–22586 (2021). https://doi.org/10.1109/ACCESS.2021.3054563
3. Chung, J., Tanchoco, J.: The double row layout problem. Int. J. Prod. Res. **48**(3), 709–727 (2010). https://doi.org/10.1080/00207540802192126

4. Durillo, J.J., Nebro, A.J.: jmetal: A java framework for multi-objective optimization. Adv. Eng. Softw. **42**(10), 760–771 (2011)
5. Feo, T., Resende, M.: A probabilistic heuristic for a computationally difficult set covering problem. Oper. Res. Lett. **8**, 67–71 (1989)
6. Guan, C., Zhang, Z., Gong, J., Liu, S.: Mixed integer linear programming model and an effective algorithm for the bi-objective double-floor corridor allocation problem. Comput. Oper. Res. **132**, 105283 (2021). https://doi.org/10.1016/j.cor.2021.105283
7. Hungerländer, P., Anjos, M.F.: A semidefinite optimization-based approach for global optimization of multi-row facility layout. Eur. J. Oper. Res. **245**(1), 46–61 (2015). https://doi.org/10.1016/j.ejor.2015.02.049
8. Kalita, Z., Datta, D.: Solving the bi-objective corridor allocation problem using a permutation-based genetic algorithm. Computers & Operations Research **52**, 123–134 (2014). https://doi.org/10.1016/j.cor.2014.07.008
9. Kalita, Z., Datta, D., Palubeckis, G.: Bi-objective corridor allocation problem using a permutation-based genetic algorithm hybridized with a local search technique. Soft. Comput. **23**(3), 961–986 (2019). https://doi.org/10.1007/s00500-017-2807-0
10. Knowles, J.D., Thiele, L., Zitzler, E.: A tutorial on the performance assessment of stochastic multiobjective optimizers, vol. 214. ETH Zurich (2006)
11. Pablo Pérez-Gosende, J.M., Díaz-Madroñero, M.: Facility layout planning. An extended literature review. Int. J. Prod. Res. **59**(12), 3777–3816 (2021). https://doi.org/10.1080/00207543.2021.1897176
12. Resende, M.G., Ribeiro, C.C.: Scatter Search and Path Relinking: Advances and Applications, pp. 1–37. Springer US, Boston, MA (2010)
13. Simmons, D.M.: One-dimensional space allocation: An ordering algorithm. Oper. Res. **17**(5), 812–826 (1969)
14. Singh, D., Ingole, S.: Multi-objective facility layout problems using BBO, NSBBO and NSGA-II metaheuristic algorithms. International Journal of Industrial Engineering Computations pp. 239–262 (2019)
15. Zitzler, E., Thiele, L., Laumanns, M., Fonseca, C., da Fonseca, V.: Performance assessment of multiobjective optimizers: an analysis and review. IEEE Trans. Evol. Comput. **7**(2), 117–132 (2003)

An Experimental Comparison of Qiskit and Pennylane for Hybrid Quantum-Classical Support Vector Machines

Francesc Rodríguez-Díaz[1]([✉])[iD], José Francisco Torres[1][iD],
David Gutiérrez-Avilés[2][iD], Alicia Troncoso[1][iD],
and Francisco Martínez-Álvarez[1][iD]

[1] Data Science and Big Data Lab, Pablo de Olavide University, Seville, Spain
`{froddia,jftormal,atrolor,fmaralv}@upo.es`
[2] Department of Computer Science, University of Seville, Seville, Spain
`dgutierrez3@us.es`

Abstract. Quantum computing holds great promise for enhancing machine learning algorithms, particularly by integrating classical and quantum techniques. This study compares two prominent quantum development frameworks, Qiskit and Pennylane, focusing on their suitability for hybrid quantum-classical support vector machines with quantum kernels. Our analysis reveals that Qiskit requires less theoretical information to be used, while Pennylane demonstrates superior performance in terms of execution time. Although both frameworks exhibit variances, our experiments reveal that Qiskit consistently yields superior classification accuracy compared to Pennylane when training classifiers with quantum kernels. Additionally, our results suggest that the performance of both frameworks remains stable for up to 20 qubits, indicating their suitability for practical applications. Overall, our findings provide valuable insights into the strengths and limitations of Qiskit and Pennylane for hybrid quantum-classical machine learning.

Keywords: Quantum Computing · Quantum Support Vector Machine · Quantum Kernel · Hybrid Quantum-Classical Algorithms

1 Introduction

Quantum computing, with its inherent parallel processing capabilities, offers a quantum advantage over classical computing. Its potential to drive breakthroughs across various science and engineering domains is widely acknowledged. Machine learning emerges as a pivotal domain poised to leverage the power of quantum computing. Despite the successful development of numerous machine learning algorithms, such as support vector machines or neural networks, over recent decades, their training processes are often protracted. Moreover, tackling today's vast datasets exacerbates the computational intensity of these algorithms.

© The Author(s), under exclusive license to Springer Nature Switzerland AG 2024
A. Alonso-Betanzos et al. (Eds.): CAEPIA 2024, LNAI 14640, pp. 121–130, 2024.
https://doi.org/10.1007/978-3-031-62799-6_13

This paper compares Qiskit and Pennylane, two prominent quantum development frameworks, focusing on their features and performance in the context of hybrid quantum-classical support vector machines (SVMs) with quantum kernels. Support vector machines are widely used in classical machine learning for classification tasks, and their extension to utilize quantum kernels offers a pathway to exploit the computational advantages of quantum systems.

The motivation behind this comparative study stems from the rapid growth and diversification of quantum computing frameworks, each offering unique features and capabilities. As the field of quantum computing continues to evolve rapidly, new frameworks and libraries are constantly being developed, each offering unique capabilities and approaches. Understanding the strengths and weaknesses of these frameworks allows researchers and practitioners to make informed decisions when selecting the most suitable tool for their specific quantum computing tasks. Furthermore, by examining the features and performance of existing frameworks, we gain valuable insights into emerging trends and best practices in quantum algorithm development. This comparative analysis serves not only to guide current research and development efforts but also to shape the future direction of quantum computing frameworks, ultimately advancing the field as a whole.

Qiskit [5], developed by IBM, and Pennylane [2], developed by Xanadu, represent two prominent open-source platforms for quantum programming, each with its tools, libraries, and community support. Understanding the strengths and limitations of these frameworks is crucial for researchers and practitioners aiming to harness quantum computing for practical applications, particularly in machine learning. Thus, the primary objective of this paper is to provide a comprehensive comparison between Qiskit and Pennylane in the context of hybrid quantum-classical support vector machines with quantum kernels. Specifically, we aim to:

1. Evaluate the ease of use and accessibility of both frameworks for developing hybrid quantum-classical algorithms.
2. Compare the performance of Qiskit and Pennylane in terms of execution time and resource utilization for training and testing SVMs with quantum kernels.
3. Assess the scalability and flexibility of each framework for handling increasingly complex quantum-classical workflows.
4. Highlight any unique features or advantages Qiskit and Pennylane offer that may be relevant to hybrid quantum-classical machine learning applications.

The remainder of this paper is organized as follows. Section 2 briefly overviews existing quantum computing and hybrid quantum-classical frameworks. Section 4 describes the fundamentals of Qiskit and Pennylane, covering their respective architectures, features, and programming interfaces. Section 5 presents the results achieved, followed by a comprehensive discussion. Finally, Sect. 6 concludes the paper with a summary of findings and avenues for future research.

2   Related Works

Diverse frameworks and libraries mark the landscape of quantum computing, each offering unique features and capabilities for developing and executing quantum algorithms. In this section, we provide an overview of several prominent quantum computing frameworks and libraries, including Qiskit, Pennylane, Q#, Cirq, Wolfram Quantum, Amazon Braket, Strawberry Fields, TensorFlow Quantum, and OpenFermion. We discuss each framework's architecture, features, and suitability for various quantum computing tasks. Additionally, we highlight the pros and cons of each framework to aid researchers and practitioners in selecting the most suitable tool for their specific needs.

Qiskit [5], developed by IBM, is a comprehensive open-source quantum computing framework that provides tools for quantum circuit construction, simulation, and execution. It offers a user-friendly programming interface and extensive documentation, making it accessible to both beginners and experienced users. Qiskit also supports hybrid quantum-classical computing and integrates with classical machine learning libraries for hybrid quantum-classical algorithms. However, its performance on certain tasks may vary and have scalability and resource utilization limitations.

Pennylane [2], developed by Xanadu, is a quantum machine learning library focusing on differentiable programming and hybrid quantum-classical computing. It offers seamless integration with popular machine learning libraries like TensorFlow and PyTorch, enabling the development of hybrid quantum-classical algorithms. Pennylane's strength lies in its efficient optimization techniques and support for various quantum hardware platforms. However, it may have a steeper learning curve compared to some other frameworks, and its ecosystem is relatively smaller.

Q# [7] is a quantum-focused programming language developed by Microsoft that provides a high-level programming model for quantum algorithms. It offers seamless integration with classical languages like C# and Python. One of its strengths lies in strong support for quantum simulation and debugging tools. However, its ecosystem is relatively smaller compared to other frameworks.

Cirq [4], an open-source quantum computing framework developed by Google, allows researchers to design, simulate, and execute quantum circuits. Despite a steeper learning curve compared to higher-level quantum programming languages, Cirq offers flexibility and modular architecture for building custom quantum algorithms. However, it may lack some tooling and visualization capabilities present in other frameworks.

Wolfram Quantum [9], part of the Wolfram Language ecosystem with full integration into Mathematica, provides tools for symbolic quantum computation, quantum circuit simulation, and algorithm development. Its integration with Wolfram Language's extensive mathematical and computational capabilities offers high-level symbolic manipulation of quantum expressions. However, Wolfram Quantum may have limited support for quantum hardware interfaces compared to other frameworks.

Amazon Braket [1], an AWS quantum computing service, offers access to quantum hardware from multiple vendors and provides a development environment for quantum algorithms. While it integrates seamlessly with AWS infrastructure for scalable and cloud-based computing, it may be perceived as a relatively new platform with evolving features. Additionally, the pricing model could be prohibitive for some users.

Strawberry Fields [6], an open-source quantum programming library developed by Xanadu, focuses on continuous-variable quantum computing and integrates with Pennylane for hybrid quantum-classical computing. Its specialization in continuous-variable quantum computing and integration with Pennylane make it suitable for quantum photonic systems. However, its applicability to discrete-variable quantum computing tasks may be limited.

TensorFlow Quantum [3], an open-source library developed by Google and others, enables researchers to construct hybrid quantum-classical models using TensorFlow. While TFQ integrates with TensorFlow for scalable and efficient machine learning workflows, its complex integration with quantum simulators and hardware may require familiarity with TensorFlow and quantum computing concepts.

3   Fundamentals

3.1   Quantum Fundamentals

This subsection will briefly explain some quantum concepts, such as a qubit, a quantum circuit, or a feature map.

First, a quantum bit or qubit is the fundamental unit of quantum information in quantum computing. Unlike classical bits, which can exist in one of two states (0 or 1), qubits can exist simultaneously in a superposition of both states, thanks to the principles of quantum mechanics. This unique property allows quantum computers to perform calculations in parallel and potentially solve certain problems much more efficiently than classical computers. Equation (1) shows the representation of a qubit.

$$|\psi\rangle = \alpha|0\rangle + \beta|1\rangle \tag{1}$$

where α and β are complex probability amplitudes. Furthermore, α and β are constrained by Eq. (2):

$$|\alpha|^2 + |\beta|^2 = 1 \tag{2}$$

The previous equation means that the sum of the probabilities squared must be equal to 1.

A quantum circuit is a graphical representation of a sequence of quantum operations performed on qubits. These operations can include simple operations like applying a gate (analogous to a classical logic state) to a single qubit or more complex operations involving multiple qubits. Quantum circuits are analogous to classical in digital electronics but operate according to the principles of quantum mechanics.

Finally, we move on to explain the feature map. Initially, our datasets consist of traditional binary bits, not quantum bits or qubits, needing the translation of classical information into quantum information for quantum computing utilization. This transformation is fundamental for developing a robust quantum or hybrid quantum model. Typically, this conversion is known as data encoding, data embedding, or feature mapping, a pivotal step in the quantum machine learning pipeline. Feature mapping is a familiar concept in conventional machine learning; however, translating data into quantum states is unique to quantum computing, as classical machine learning exclusively deals with data in a classical context.

3.2 Support Vector Machines

The Support Vector Machines (SVM) algorithm is a supervised learning model for classification and regression tasks. The primary concept behind SVM is identifying the hyperplane that best separates the data classes within the feature space. In binary classification scenarios, the goal is to find the hyperplane that maintains the maximum distance (margin) from the nearest data points of each class, known as support vectors. This margin is critical because the greater it is, the more reliable the classification will be for new data.

SVM employs mathematical techniques to maximize this margin and determine the hyperplane's position. When data are not linearly separable in their original space, SVM uses a kernel function to transform them into a higher-dimensional space where linear separation is possible. This ability allows SVM to handle complex and nonlinear problems effectively. In Eq. (3), one observes the equation of a kernel.

$$k(\vec{x_i}, \vec{x_j}) = \langle f(\vec{x_i}), f(\vec{x_j}) \rangle \tag{3}$$

4 Methodology

In this section, we present the methodology followed during the experimentation. Firstly, it is important to mention that we adhered to the basic workflow of machine learning. This entails a series of steps outlined as follows.

Initially, data preprocessing was conducted to prepare them for subsequent analysis and modeling. Subsequently, we proceeded with the model training and testing phase. During this stage, a portion of the preprocessed data was used for training, while another portion was reserved for performance evaluation. We employed the hold-out technique with a 70% split for training and a 30% split for testing.

Upon completion of the previous phase, model validation was carried out. In this stage, the model's ability to generalize to unseen data was evaluated using the subset set aside for testing. Finally, an analysis of the results obtained by the model was performed. This included the evaluation of performance metrics available in the results section.

The novel aspect being presented is using a classical SVM alongside the computational power provided by quantum computing [8]. This is depicted in Fig. 1, where it can be observed how the classical SVM algorithm is injected with a quantum kernel generated from a quantum machine, thus creating a hybrid algorithm. The one provided by the Sklearn library was employed for the classical algorithm due to its ease of integration with the quantum kernel. Subsequently, each part of the diagram will be described in detail.

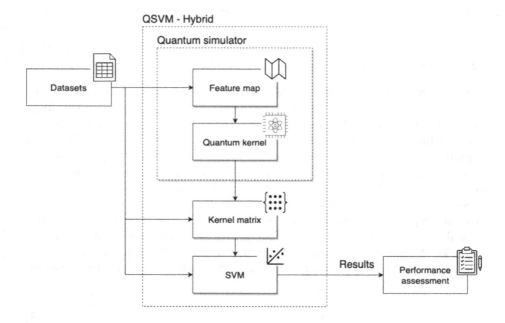

Fig. 1. Methodology employed.

The first step is to define the feature map of the problem. The quantum circuit representing this map can be observed in Fig. 2.

Upon examining the circuit, we observe a series of wires corresponding to the dataset's features. A qubit represents each wire, and the circuit should be interpreted from the bottom to the top to determine the qubit order, followed by reading from left to right to establish the sequence of gate operations.

Once we have constructed the feature map of the problem, the next step is to prepare the quantum kernel, which uses the former. This quantum kernel is equivalent to the classical kernel, as it is merely a function used to transform the input data space into a new space where it may be easier to separate the data into categories. The sole difference is that the new space is quantum.

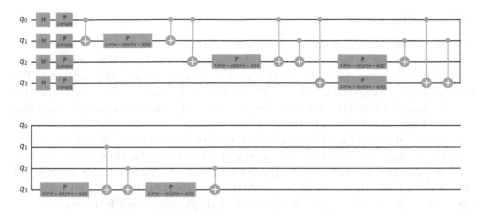

Fig. 2. Quantum circuit for feature mapping.

The final step to complete the quantum kernel is to prepare the quantum simulators where both the kernel and the aforementioned circuit will be executed. The execution is conducted on a simulated quantum machine facilitated by the capabilities provided by both frameworks. Simulation is employed due to the limitations of accessing real quantum machines, including the high costs and limited accessibility.

In our case, we have chosen to employ the most basic simulators. The use of these simulators mitigates the need for datasets with high dimensionality. If a more powerful simulator is desired, one can utilize the simulator provided by the Qiskit_aer library.

When we have created the quantum kernel, the next step is to generate the kernel matrix. Much like its classical counterpart, this matrix is a square matrix in which each element represents the result of applying the kernel function to a pair of points in the training set. The only difference with its quantum version is that it involves using quantum states.

Finally, we need to pass the kernel matrix and the training data to the classical SVC algorithm, which will then generate predictions using the test set. Subsequently, a series of metrics are applied to the results produced by the hybrid model to evaluate the predictions' quality and performance.

5   Results

This section introduces the datasets employed during the experimental phase, including multi-class and binary classification datasets, each accompanied by a brief description. Additionally, we detail the results obtained for these datasets, as well as the metrics used to evaluate the performance of the hybrid models. Furthermore, a brief explanation of each metric utilized is provided.

5.1   Quality Parameters

In binary classification tasks, where the goal is to classify instances into one of two classes, it is essential to evaluate the performance of a predictive model using various metrics. Commonly used performance metrics include true positives (TP), false positives (FP), true negatives (TN), and false negatives (FN). These metrics provide insights into the model's ability to correctly classify instances belonging to each class and help quantify different types of classification errors. Additionally, sensitivity (Sens) and specificity (Spec) measure the model's ability to correctly identify positive and negative instances, respectively. Furthermore, positive predictive value (PPV) and negative predictive value (NPV) assess the accuracy of the model's positive and negative predictions, respectively, among all instances classified as positive or negative. Equations (4)–(8) show their formulas.

$$Sens = \frac{TP}{TP + FN} \tag{4}$$

$$Spec = \frac{TN}{TN + FP} \tag{5}$$

$$PPV = \frac{TP}{TP + FP} \tag{6}$$

$$NPV = \frac{TN}{TN + FN} \tag{7}$$

$$Accuracy = \frac{TP + TN}{TP + TN + FP + FN} \tag{8}$$

5.2   Dataset Description

The datasets used for experimentation comprised the Iris dataset and ad_hoc_data. The Iris dataset consists of 150 instances of 5 features, with three distinct values for the class column. The second dataset is derived from a function provided by Qiskit to create a synthetic dataset. This dataset was generated with 200 instances across 4 features, featuring two possible values for the target column. These datasets were chosen due to constraints posed by the simulators employed. For instance, Qiskit's default simulator has a maximum capacity of 20 qubits, limiting the use of larger datasets.

5.3   Discussion

Table 1 provides a detailed comparative analysis of the performance of a hybrid algorithm, specifically the SVM with a quantum kernel, applied to the most basic simulators of the two frameworks in use. The algorithm has been evaluated using the datasets described in the previous section.

For Qiskit, the performance on the Iris dataset shows an accuracy of 86.66%. Specificity, positive predictive value (PPV), and negative predictive value (NPV) are also high for the three classes of the Iris dataset, demonstrating a strong discriminate ability and reliability in predicting both positive and negative outcomes. However, for the ad_hoc_data dataset, accuracy drops to 68.33%, with a decrease in sensitivity and specificity compared to the Iris dataset, indicating potential challenges in generalizing the model to this more complex or less structured dataset.

On the other hand, Pennylane shows a lower accuracy on the Iris dataset with 75.55%. Sensitivity ans specificity vary across the classes, with some classes exhibiting higher sensitivity but lower specificity compared to Qiskit. For the ad_hoc_data dataset, accuracy falls to 55%, with a decrease in sensitivity and specificity compared to the Iris dataset, indicating lower predictive capacity for this dataset.

In terms of execution time, Qiskit consistently shows longer times than Pennylane. For instance, Qiskit takes 41 s for the Iris dataset, while Pennylane takes only 21 s. This pattern is maintained across the tests, suggesting that Pennylane could offer an advantage in computational efficiency.

In summary, Qiskit delivers better performance in classification metrics, particularly with the Iris dataset, but at the expense of longer execution times. Pennylane may be preferable when execution time is critical, although this may involve a trade-off with accuracy and other performance metrics. These differences can be crucial when choosing the appropriate library for practical applications of quantum algorithms, depending on whether the priority is precision or speed.

Table 1. Performance comparison of Qiskit and Pennylane frameworks.

Framework	Dataset	Class	Acc. (%)	Sens.	Spec.	PPV	NPV	Ex. time (s)
Qiskit	Iris	Setosa	86.66	0.87	1.00	1.00	0.93	41
		Versicolor		0.76	0.96	0.92	0.87	
		Virginica		1.00	0.84	0.70	1.00	
	Ad_hoc_data	Binary	68.33	0.66	0.70	0.68	0.67	53
Pennylane	Iris	Setosa	75.55	1.00	0.96	0.94	1.00	21
		Versicolor		0.72	0.79	0.53	0.90	
		Virginica		0.55	0.88	0.76	0.75	
	Ad_hoc_data	Binary	55.00	0.56	0.53	0.54	0.55	36

6   Conclusions

This study compared Qiskit and Pennylane in the context of hybrid quantum-classical (SVMs with quantum kernels). Our investigation evaluated both frameworks' ease of use, scalability and performance for developing and executing quantum-classical machine learning algorithms. Our analysis revealed several key findings. First, Qiskit emerged as the more user-friendly framework, offering an intuitive and well-documented programming interface. Its extensive library of quantum algorithms and built-in tools for quantum circuit visualization and simulation make it an accessible choice for both beginners and experienced users. Second, Pennylane demonstrated superior performance in terms of execution time, consistently outperforming Qiskit across various experimental setups. This advantage can be attributed to Pennylane's efficient quantum circuit optimization techniques and lightweight computational overhead. Third, while both frameworks exhibit variances, our experiments reveal that Qiskit consistently yields superior classification accuracy compared to Pennylane when training classifiers with quantum kernels. Fourth, Our experiments indicated that Qiskit and Pennylane exhibit stable performance for up to 20 qubits, highlighting their scalability for practical applications. Future research directions include exploring optimization techniques to enhance the performance of Qiskit and investigating the scalability of both frameworks for larger quantum-classical workflows.

Acknowledgments. The authors thank the Spanish Ministry of Science and Innovation for the support within the projects PID2020-117954RB-C21 and TED2021-131311B-C22.

References

1. Amazon Web Services: Amazon Braket: Research quantum algorithms and test quantum computers (2022). https://aws.amazon.com/braket/. Accessed February 2024
2. Bergholm, V., et al.: Pennylane: automatic differentiation of hybrid quantum-classical computations (2018). https://pennylane.ai/. Accessed February 2024
3. Broughton, M., et al.: TensorFlow quantum: a software framework for quantum machine learning (2020). https://doi.org/10.48550/arXiv.2003.02989. Accessed February 2024
4. Google: Cirq: Quantum AI open-source framework (2022). https://quantumai.google/cirq. Accessed February 2024
5. IBM Quantum: Qiskit: an open-source framework for quantum computing (2022). https://qiskit.org/. Accessed February 2024
6. Killoran, N., et al.: Strawberry fields: a software platform for photonic quantum computing. Quantum **3**, 129 (2019)
7. Microsoft: Q#: Microsoft's quantum-focused programming language (2022). https://docs.microsoft.com/en-us/quantum/?view=qsharp-preview.   Accessed February 2024
8. Rebentrost, P., Mohseni, M., Lloyd, S.: Quantum support vector machine for big data classification. Phys. Rev. Lett. **113**, 130503 (2014)
9. Wolfram Research: Wolfram Quantum Computation Framework (2022). https://wolfr.am/wolfram-quantum. Accessed February 2024

Preserving the Essential Features in CNNs: Pruning and Analysis

Clara I. López-González[1]([✉])(iD), María J. Gómez-Silva[2](iD),
Eva Besada-Portas[2](iD), and Gonzalo Pajares[3](iD)

[1] Department of Software Engineering and Artificial Intelligence,
Complutense University of Madrid, 28040 Madrid, Spain
`claraisl@ucm.es`
[2] Department of Computer Architecture and Automation,
Complutense University of Madrid, 28040 Madrid, Spain
`{mgomez77,ebesada}@ucm.es`
[3] Institute for Knowledge Technology, Complutense University of Madrid,
28040 Madrid, Spain
`pajares@ucm.es`

Abstract. The exceptional performance of Convolutional Neural Networks (CNNs) entails increasing requirements in computing power and storage. While several efficient compression methods have been developed, there is no consideration on which features are removed or preserved, which can affect pruning. In this paper, we propose a novel filter pruning strategy, named Layer Factor Analysis one to one (LFA1-1), that, relying on explainability, selects the filters that best retain the essential features underlying convolutional layers. We provide insights about the relevance of preserving these features and verify its relationship with compressed network's performance. The explanatory analysis carried out allows us to justify pruning efficiency and detect problematic parts. Experiments with VGG-16 on CIFAR-10 are conducted in order to validate our approach. Quantitative and qualitative comparisons with methods in the literature uncover pruning properties and prove the effectiveness of our proposal, which reaches a 89.1% parameters and 83.8% FLOPs reduction with the lowest accuracy drop.

Keywords: Convolutional Neural Networks · Explainable Artificial Intelligence · Compression Methods · Factor Analysis

1 Introduction

In recent years, Convolutional Neural Networks (CNNs) have proven incredible performance in a wide variety of computer vision tasks, from classification, to object detection, and image segmentation. They have surpassed traditional methods, which do not achieve such generalization capabilities. Nevertheless, the enormous computational cost and storage required for deep networks constitutes a challenge when dealing with resource-constrained devices, such as mobile

© The Author(s), under exclusive license to Springer Nature Switzerland AG 2024
A. Alonso-Betanzos et al. (Eds.): CAEPIA 2024, LNAI 14640, pp. 131–141, 2024.
https://doi.org/10.1007/978-3-031-62799-6_14

devices or on-board systems for autonomous vehicles. As a result, compression methods have been under development for some time now. Starting from a pre-trained CNN, these techniques achieve a large reduction of parameters and float-ing point operations (FLOPs[1]), with negligible accuracy loss.

Firsts works [2,6] prune individual weights, giving rise to sparse models that require concrete software and hardware. Consequently, recent research focuses on filter pruning approaches, which remove the whole convolutional kernel. In general, these methods are based on defining metrics of importance for filters (or, equivalently, channels) and removing the less relevant ones. The values of the metrics can be obtained from the filter weights, for example with the l_1 norm [8] or cosine similarity [1]. Activation maps are considered too. The work in [3] computes the average percentage of zeros on these maps, while [15] defines relevance in terms of feature maps information. Other techniques combine both strategies, such as [7] which introduces diversity and similarity-aware selection. Different approaches involve reconstruction-based methods [10] or scaling factors in objective functions [9], among others.

In spite of their success, pruning methods neither take into account nor ana-lyze which characteristics are being removed or preserved. This knowledge is determinant, since, depending on the dataset, some features will be more impor-tant than others in the prediction. While a selection criterion works well with certain datasets, it may not be suitable for others by not prioritizing the appro-priate features, as analyzed in [11]. This drives our work, where we define a pruning strategy that retains as many learned features as possible, and compare well-known methods in terms of how many of these features they preserve.

Thanks to explainable Artificial Intelligence (xAI, [13]), it is possible to study and understand what CNNs have learned. These techniques can be used not only to interpret network predictions, but also to improve its performance or related processes, such as pruning. This motivates our proposal, where we employ Explainable Layer Factor Analysis method (ELFA-CNNs, [12]) to obtain a few essential features underlying the convolutional layers that guide pruning. It is worth noting that, unlike ELFA, our goal is pruning, and we do not make use of its explanatory strategy, but only of the parameters provided by its model to elaborate a new compression technique and our own explanatory analysis.

In particular, we propose a novel filter pruning method, named Layer Factor Analysis one to one (LFA1-1), which, based on the parameters provided by ELFA, selects those filters that best cover the essential features. We hypothesize that retaining as many latent features as possible leads to better performance on the compressed models. Thanks to the explanatory analysis conducted, we are able to validate this statement, justify the efficiency of well-known pruning approaches, and detect where problems arise in adverse cases. Although works such as [16] quantify filters relevance based on xAI, we look for learned features, whereas [16] only deals with pruning, without reaching state-of-the-art rates.

Experiments with VGG-16 on CIFAR-10, one of the most analyzed both in pruning and explainability frameworks, were carried out to prove the effectiveness

---

[1] We only consider FLOPs of convolutional operations, including multiplication and addition, as it is commonly used for comparison.

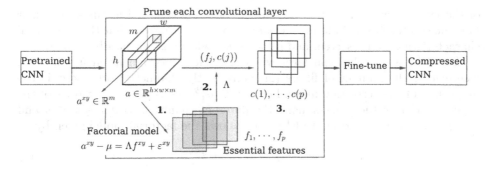

Fig. 1. Flowchart of the proposed pruning method.

of our approach. Comparisons with methods in the literature validate our proposal, which achieves almost 89.1% parameters and 83.8% FLOPs reduction with the lowest accuracy drop. The explanatory study conducted uncovers properties of pruning methods, contributing to a better understanding.

The major contributions and novelties of this article are the following:

1. The design of a novel CNN filter pruning strategy based on explainability, which maintains the underlying essential features.
2. The analysis and evidence of the importance of preserving these essential characteristics for the performance of compressed networks.
3. The explanation of the success of well-known filter pruning criteria in terms of the retained features, as well as the detection of problematic parts.

The paper is organized as follows. Section 2 focuses on the first contribution and presents our filter pruning strategy. Section 3 addresses the experiments conducted and analyzes the effectiveness of our approach. Section 4 delves into the importance of retaining essential features, taking care of the remaining contributions. Finally, Sect. 5 draws the conclusions and some future work.

2   Filter Pruning Strategy

This section introduces our filter pruning approach, which retains the essential characteristics underlying layers. As shown in Fig. 1, given a pretrained CNN, each convolutional layer is pruned. Then, we fine-tune the compressed model to recover performance.

2.1   Layer Essential Features

In order to define a strategy that preserves the learned features, we must first find them. The xAI field often assumes that each filter matches a single feature. In addition to being incorrect [14], the large amount of filters makes it difficult to identify the most relevant characteristics for network learning. This is why ELFA-CNNs [12] is considered. Based on Factor Analysis (FA), it obtains a summary of the layer knowledge by finding a few underlying essential features and their influence on the original filters. Our aim is to prune CNNs so that these essential characteristics are preserved, and network knowledge is not hardly damage.

Let $\mathcal{C}$ be a convolutional layer whose output a has dimension $h \times w \times m$, where m is the number of filters (or equivalently channels) and $h \times w$ is the dimension of the activation maps. Let $a^{xy} = (a_1^{xy}, \cdots, a_m^{xy})$ be the values of the (x, y) location of these maps along the different channels, with $1 \leq x \leq h$ and $1 \leq y \leq w$. Then, according to ELFA, $\mathcal{C}$ follows the factorial model given by

$$a^{xy} - \mu = \Lambda f^{xy} + \varepsilon^{xy}, \tag{1}$$

where $\mu = (\mu_1, \cdots, \mu_m)$, with μ_j being the mean of the jth activation map. The variables $f^{xy} = (f_1^{xy}, \cdots, f_p^{xy}) \in \mathbb{R}^p$, with $p < m$, represent the p latent features. Meanwhile, $\varepsilon^{xy} \in \mathbb{R}^m$ is a vector of unobserved perturbations or errors.

The matrix $\Lambda \in \mathcal{M}_{m,p}$, called loading matrix, describes how much these essential features influence the original channels. Indeed, Λ equals the correlation matrix between both. It is this parameter, and not the whole ELFA strategy, that inspires our compression method, which also aims at a totally different objective. After pruning, Λ can be used to quantify the influence of the essential features in the remaining filters. This will allow us to analyze the different performances in compression approaches, as shown in Sect. 4.

2.2 Pruning Method

In light of the advantages of filter pruning, we remove whole convolutional filters and their corresponding connections to adjacent layers. Given a convolution with m filters, the proposed strategy consists of the following steps (shown in Fig. 1):

1. Obtain the essential features underlying that layer $f_1, \ldots, f_p$ (see eq. (1)).
2. For each latent feature f_j, select the filter/channel $c(j)$ that represents it better (see Eq. (2)). Thus, we obtain one to one pairs of the form $(f_j, c(j))$.
3. Remove the $m - p$ non selected channels. In this way, we preserve as many filters as essential features have been obtained, $p < m$.

We do not prioritize some features over others because we believe that, whenever possible, it is better to store all the prior knowledge. When selecting the most representative filters, we hope that a small fine-tuning will be enough for the layer to readjust without losing the already learned features, leading to better performance. The analysis of Sect. 4 will prove the above statements.

Note that our proposal, denoted hereafter by LFA1-1 (Layer Factor Analysis one to one), as opposed to many pruning methods, is not based on computing filter's importance scores and removing those with low values. As mentioned above, these strategies do not ensure that the remaining filters cover all latent characteristics. Section 4 exposes that, depending on which essential features are preserved, they may lead to poor performance recovery.

Pairing Essential Features and Channels. Given a latent feature, to find the filter/channel that represents it better, we rely on the matrix $\Lambda \in \mathcal{M}_{m,p}$ of equation (1). Each column, $\lambda_{\bullet j} = (\lambda_{1j}, \cdots, \lambda_{mj})^\top$ with $1 \leq j \leq p$, determines the impact of the jth essential feature f_j on the channels $c_1, \ldots, c_m$. Thus, the one with the maximum impact (positive or negative) is chosen, denoted by $c(j)$

$$c(j) := \{c_k \mid 1 \leq k \leq m \quad \text{and} \quad \lambda_{kj} = \max_{1 \leq i \leq m}\{|\lambda_{ij}|\}\}. \tag{2}$$

If already selected, choose the next with highest $|\lambda_{ij}|$.[2] This leads to the pairs $\{(f_j, c(j))\}_{j=1}^p$, taking over the method's second step.

Fine-Tuning. Because of the damage that filter pruning causes to generalization ability, fine-tuning is a fundamental step in any compression method. It can be conducted iteratively, i.e., retraining each time a layer is pruned; or as a final step, after all the layers have been pruned. We choose the later, since iterative fine-tuning can be time consuming due to the complexity of datasets or CNNs. Moreover, pruning all layers at once provides a clearer idea of the resilience of the compressed network. In general, fewer epochs than the quantity employed to train the original model are used.

3   Experiments and Results

In this section we validate our proposal and compare it with other state-of-the-art methods, proving its effectiveness. The experimental settings are presented first, followed by the pruning configuration. Then, several compression methods are considered for comparison. An in-depth analysis is performed in Sect. 4.

Finally, it is worth noting that all the experiments are conducted within Matlab and executed on a i9.10900X CPU 3.70 GHz with 46 GB of RAM and NVIDIA GeForce RTX 3080 GPU.

3.1   Experimental Setting

Experiments are carried out with VGG-16 [8], which consists of 13 convolutional layers followed by batch normalization and ReLU. Due to its widespread use in pruning framework, the results are easily comparable between strategies. It is trained from scratch with the following training options: sgdm optimizer with momentum of 0.9, 10^{-3} learning rate dropping every 25 epochs by a factor of 3×10^{-3}, weight decay of 10^{-3}, with 80 epochs and 128 mini-batchsize. Regarding the final fine-tuning after the pruning, 40 epochs (half of the original) are used.

As dataset, CIFAR-10 [5] is employed. It contains 60000 images of 32×32, divided into 40000 for training (67%), 10000 for testing (16.5%) and 10000 for validation (16.5%), randomly and proportionally picked with 10 different classes. Random horizontal and vertical reflections are used for data augmentation. In addition to being widely used, its simplicity allows for explanatory analyses that uncover properties of pruning methods, as shown in Sect. 4.

---

[2] It should be noted that it was not necessary in practice.

3.2 Pruning Setting

This section presents the setting used to obtain the essential latent features via ELFA-CCNs (first step of our proposal). For each convolutional layer, the factorial model given by Eq. (1) is estimated with the parameters of the original paper for VGG-16 on CIFAR-10 [12]. As detailed there, this is the model that satisfies the quality requirements and has the lowest number p of essential features, achieved with Kaiser's method [4], the Standard Error Scree criterion [17], or the 25%-50% of the given channels, depending on the layer (Table 1). We choose to be a bit more lax with the quality bounds. In particular, $D_1 \geq 0.6$, $D_> \geq 0.85$, and $\gamma_j^2 \geq 0.75$. As explained in [12], this can be done as far as the model is useful and minimum fit requirements are accomplished. We make use of the results in [12, Appendix A.3] to justify this small adjustment. Thus, fewer latent features are obtained without harming the quality of the factorial model.

3.3 Comparing Different Filter Selection Criteria

We compare our proposal with other strategies in order to demonstrate its validity. Several methods in the literature are based on the elimination of the filters with the lowest importance score, defined by certain criteria. To properly analyze how pruning affects the essential features, the pruning setting is kept as similar to ours as possible. In each layer we prune the same number of filters as in our approach. That is, $m - p$, where m is the number of filters and p the number of latent features estimated. Then, we select which filters are removed according to the method's importance criteria. This is a balanced solution that let us compare pruning and learning performance. Since this implies that all the methods evaluated will prune the same percentage of parameters, we could focus on testing the effectiveness of the proposal in terms of the final accuracy.

The following selection criteria are considered: standard deviation of activation maps (Std), l_1 norm of filter's weights (L1, [8]), sparsity of activation maps (APoZ, [3]), redundancy of feature maps (FeatStats, [7]), feature maps entropy information (FmInfo, [15]), and mean of activation maps (MeanAct).

3.4 Results

Following Sect. 3.2, we estimate the essential features for each convolutional layer. Table 1 shows the number of features obtained, compared to that of original filters. The summary involved in considering the latent characteristics is obvious. Once we have the number of channels to retain, we proceed with the pruning as explained in Sect. 2.2 and 3.3.

The performance of the compressed network, according to the different strategies considered, is summarized in Table 2. It shows the percentage by which the accuracy, parameters, and FLOPs have decreased w.r.t the baseline model. The latter metrics are also included on top of the table for better comprehension. The last column is the average time it takes to segment an image, which has been obtained with the entire test set.

Table 1. Number of underlying essential features for each convolutional layer of VGG-16 on CIFAR-10, and the method employed to compute it: (K) Kaiser, (S) Standard error scree method or (x%) just the x% of the given channels.

Layers	cv1_1	cv1_2	cv2_1	cv2_2	cv3_1	cv3_2	cv3_3	cv41	cv4_2	cv4_3	cv5_1	cv5_2	cv5_3
Channels	64	64	128	128	256	256	256	512	512	512	512	512	512
Features	12 (S)	25 (S)	44 (K)	64 (S)	128 (50%)	128 (50%)	128 (50%)	150 (K)	270 (S)	128 (25%)	128 (25%)	126 (S)	46 (S)

Table 2. Results of pruned VGG-16 on CIFAR-10. Acc. is short of accuracy and Param. of parameters. ↓ indicates the drop percent between pruned and original models.

Original: Acc = 85.05%, Param = 14.9M, FLOPs = 6.26×10^8, time = 6.8×10^{-3} s				
Method	Acc. ↓(%)	Param. ↓(%)	FLOPs ↓(%)	time ($\times 10^{-3}$ s)
LFA1-1	**0.97**			**3.7**
Std	2.76			4.4
L1 [8]	0.99			4.4
APoZ [3]	1.94	89.1	83.8	4.4
FeatStats [7]	1.31			4.2
FmInfo. [15]	3.19			4.1
MeanAct	1.79			4.3

Despite the huge drop in parameters and FLOPs (the same in all methods as explained in Sect. 3.3), LFA1-1 and L1 show no significant decrease in accuracy, less than 1% and with the former being the best. This lies below the mean (1.85%). On the contrary, the rest of the strategies (excluding FeatStats) present almost a 2% accuracy reduction (above the mean), being even more than a 3% for FmInfo. It should be noted that this second group coincides with those criteria that only include activation maps in their computations. A thoughtful analysis of these relationships is presented in Sect. 4. Finally, the drop in parameters and FLOPs is evidenced by the decrease in segmentation time by almost half, with LFA1-1 below the mean (4.2) and the variance being low (0.12).

4 Discussion on the Importance of Retaining the Essential Features

Taking advantage of the information gathered on the loading matrix, it is used to study how different pruning criteria affect the essential features. As will be shown, this validates the assumption that preserving as many latent features as possible leads to better performance on the compressed networks.

Given a convolutional layer, we remove from the loading matrix Λ the rows corresponding to the deleted channels, and compare this pruned matrix with the original. Figure 2 displays a visual representation for each of the pruning strategies in the first convolution. Note that rows correspond to channels, and columns to latent features. These pruned matrices represent the correlation between the essential features and the remaining channels. The more dispersed they are, the more distributed the influence of latent characteristics in those channels will be.

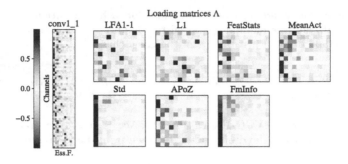

Fig. 2. Original (left) and pruned (right) Λ matrices for the first convolutional layer of VGG-16 on CIFAR-10. Λ is the correlation matrix between channels (rows) and essential features (columns). Large absolute values reveal the influence of these features.

Clearly, LFA1-1 and L1 exhibit the greatest dispersion, encompassing all the columns. That is, after pruning, these approaches preserve virtually all of the essential features. This uniformity is reduced for FeatStats, APoZ, and MeanAct, where the strong values are accumulated in the first columns. As a result, the last essential features (columns) are not represented in the pruned layer, losing this knowledge. An extreme case is that of Std and FmInfo, where the retained channels relate almost only to the first latent feature, forgetting the others.

A quantitative analysis completes the previous one by testing whether the pruned matrices are uniformly distributed. First, we compute the mean $M(f_j)$ of each column (feature), given by $M(f_j) = (1/m) \sum_{i=1}^{m} |\lambda_{ij}|$. If the matrix values are spread out, we expect these means $M(f_1), \ldots, M(f_p)$ to be similar. Therefore, the smaller the standard deviation S of the vector of means, the more distributed the influences of the essential features are, where

$$S^2 = \frac{1}{p-1} \sum_{j=1}^{p} \left(M(f_j) - \overline{M(f_j)} \right)^2, \quad \text{with } \overline{M(f_j)} = \frac{1}{p} \sum_{j=1}^{p} M(f_j). \quad (3)$$

This uniformity test, whose results are shown in Fig. 3, allows us to analyze deeper convolutions, as the large number of channels prevents us from doing so visually. The first and last layers manifest the same pattern. The low S values of LFA1-1 and L1 exhibit their ability to retain a wide variety of the essential features, unlike the other methods. We observe that this tendency of preserving the influence of the essential characteristics after pruning agrees with the results of Table 2. The strategies with better pruning performance coincide with those where the remaining filters cover more essential features. Meanwhile, middle layers present similar S values for all methods. Perhaps, other test will yield more information. We conclude that the cause of the poorer performance of methods such as APoZ, Std, or FmInfo, comes from the first layer. There, these strategies fail to preserve the influence of enough essential characteristics, focusing on only one in the most extreme cases (see Fig. 2). This is in line with the work of [11], which shows that the standard deviation highlights color detectors over others.

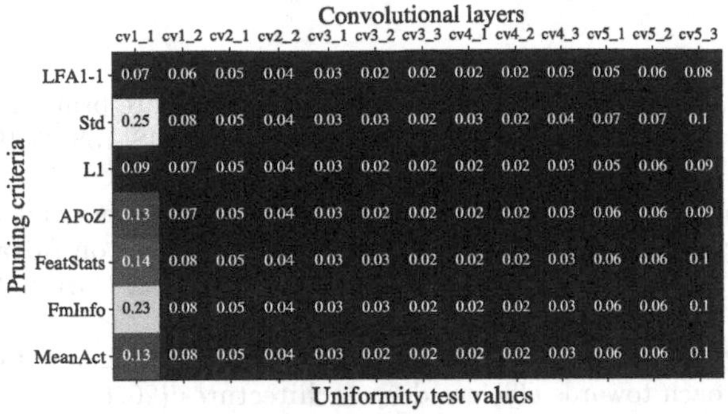

Convolutional layers

Pruning criteria	cv1_1	cv1_2	cv2_1	cv2_2	cv3_1	cv3_2	cv3_3	cv4_1	cv4_2	cv4_3	cv5_1	cv5_2	cv5_3
LFA1-1	0.07	0.06	0.05	0.04	0.03	0.02	0.02	0.02	0.02	0.03	0.05	0.06	0.08
Std	0.25	0.08	0.05	0.04	0.03	0.03	0.02	0.03	0.02	0.04	0.07	0.07	0.1
L1	0.09	0.07	0.05	0.04	0.03	0.02	0.02	0.02	0.02	0.03	0.05	0.06	0.09
APoZ	0.13	0.07	0.05	0.04	0.03	0.02	0.02	0.02	0.02	0.03	0.06	0.06	0.09
FeatStats	0.14	0.08	0.05	0.04	0.03	0.03	0.02	0.02	0.02	0.03	0.06	0.06	0.1
FmInfo	0.23	0.08	0.05	0.04	0.03	0.03	0.02	0.02	0.02	0.03	0.06	0.06	0.1
MeanAct	0.13	0.08	0.05	0.04	0.03	0.02	0.02	0.02	0.02	0.03	0.06	0.06	0.1

Uniformity test values

Fig. 3. Uniformity test (3) results for the pruned Λ matrices of VGG-16 on CIFAR-10. Low values imply more dispersion in correlations between channels and latent features.

All in all, the above analyses expose the importance of retaining essential and adequate features when pruning. Besides, in the case of CIFAR-10, criteria based on activation maps do not adequately prioritize the important channels.

5 Conclusion

In this paper, we propose a novel filter pruning strategy, named LFA1-1, that effectively prunes CNNs, through an explanatory approach, and retains essential features. We provide insights about the importance of preserving these features and prove that it is related to the compressed network performance. Qualitative and quantitative comparisons with other pruning methods are conducted.

In the future, we would like to perform a deeper study, considering other complex CNN models (residual, inception), datasets (more images and classes), usual pruning method modes, and extending the analysis on the preserved features using more explainable parameters and metrics. In addition, the use of our approach for a more selective pruning, prioritizing for example the removal of counterproductive characteristics, is also worthy to be investigated.

Acknowledgments. The authors acknowledge support from the following Research Projects: IA-GES-BLOOM-CM (Y2020/TCS-6420) funded by Comunidad Autónoma de Madrid, INSERTION (PID20211-27648OB-C33) funded by the Spanish Ministry of Science, and SMART-BLOOMS (TED2021-130123B-I00) funded by the Spanish Ministry of Science and the European Union NextGeneration. The first author, Clara I. López-González, is supported by a FPU Ph.D. scholarship from the Spanish Ministry of Universities. The authors thank the anonymous referees for their very valuable comments and suggestions.

Disclosure of Interests. The authors have no competing interests to declare that are relevant to the content of this article.

References

1. Ayinde, B.O., Inanc, T., Zurada, J.M.: Redundant feature pruning for accelerated inference in deep neural networks. Neural Netw. **118**, 148–158 (2019). https://doi.org/10.1016/j.neunet.2019.04.021
2. Han, S., Pool, J., Tran, J., Dally, W.: Learning both weights and connections for efficient neural network. In: Proceedings of the Conference on Advances in Neural Information Processing Systems, vol. 28, pp. 1135—1143. Curran Associates, Inc. (2015)
3. Hu, H., Peng, R., Tai, Y.W., Tang, C.K.: Network trimming: a data-driven neuron pruning approach towards efficient deep architectures (2016)
4. Kaiser, H.F.: The application of electronic computers to factor analysis. Educ. Psychol. Meas. **20**(1), 141–151 (1960). https://doi.org/10.1177/001316446002000116
5. Krizhevsky, A.: Learning multiple layers of features from tiny images (2009)
6. LeCun, Y., Denker, J., Solla, S.: Optimal brain damage. In: Proceedings of the Conference on Advances in Neural Information Processing Systems, vol. 2, pp. 598—605. Morgan-Kaufmann (1989)
7. Li, H., Ma, C., Xu, W., Liu, X.: Feature statistics guided efficient filter pruning. In: Proceedings of the Twenty-Ninth International Joint Conference on Artificial Intelligence, pp. 2619–2625. IJCAI (2020). https://doi.org/10.24963/ijcai.2020/363
8. Li, H., Kadav, A., Durdanovic, I., Samet, H., Graf, H.P.: Pruning filters for efficient ConvNets (2017). https://doi.org/10.48550/arXiv.1608.08710
9. Liu, Z., Li, J., Shen, Z., Huang, G., Yan, S., Zhang, C.: Learning efficient convolutional networks through network slimming. In: 2017 IEEE International Conference on Computer Vision (ICCV), pp. 2755–2763 (2017). https://doi.org/10.1109/ICCV.2017.298
10. Luo, J.H., Wu, J., Lin, W.: ThiNet: a filter level pruning method for deep neural network compression. In: 2017 IEEE International Conference on Computer Vision (ICCV), pp. 5068–5076. IEEE Computer Society (2017). https://doi.org/10.1109/iccv.2017.541
11. López-González, C.I., Gascó, E., Barrientos-Espillco, F., Besada-Portas, E., Pajares, G.: Filter pruning for convolutional neural networks in semantic image segmentation. Neural Netw. **169**, 713–732 (2024). https://doi.org/10.1016/j.neunet.2023.11.010
12. López-González, C.I., Gómez-Silva, M.J., Besada-Portas, E., Pajares, G.: Layer factor analysis in convolutional neural networks for explainability. Appl. Soft Comput. **150**, 111094 (2024). https://doi.org/10.1016/j.asoc.2023.111094
13. Minh, D., Wang, H.X., Li, Y.F., Nguyen, T.N.: Explainable artificial intelligence: a comprehensive review. Artif. Intell. Rev. **55**(5), 3503–3568 (2021). https://doi.org/10.1007/s10462-021-10088-y
14. Nguyen, A., Yosinski, J., Clune, J.: Multifaceted feature visualization: uncovering the different types of features learned by each neuron in deep neural networks. In: Visualization for Deep Learning Workshop at International Conference on Machine Learning (2016)
15. Shao, L., et al.: Filter pruning via measuring feature map information. Sensors **21**(19), 6601 (2021). https://doi.org/10.3390/s21196601

16. Yeom, S.K., et al.: Pruning by explaining: a novel criterion for deep neural network pruning. Pattern Recogn. **115**, 107899 (2021). https://doi.org/10.1016/j.patcog.2021.107899
17. Zoski, K.W., Jurs, S.: An objective counterpart to the visual scree test for factor analysis: the standard error scree. Educ. Psychol. Meas. **56**(3), 443–451 (1996). https://doi.org/10.1177/0013164496056003006

Iterated Local Search for the Facility Location Problem with Limited Choice Rule

Enrique García-Galán⬛, Alberto Herrán⬛, and J. Manuel Colmenar$^{(\boxtimes)}$⬛

Universidad Rey Juan Carlos, Calle Tulipán s/n, Móstoles, Madrid, Spain
{enrique.garciag,alberto.herran,josemanuel.colmenar}@urjc.es

Abstract. Facility location problems cover a great variety of different real-life scenarios. Among them, it is usual to consider distances between facilities and/or distances with clients in order to determine the best location for them. However, a different problem arises when the distribution of clients among the open facilities is considered and the cost of opening the facilities is also taken into account. In this paper, we study a problem with these features, the Facility Location problem with Limited Choice rule. We propose a first metaheuristic approach to this problem by means of an Iterated Local Search, which is able to obtain similar results than the state of the art spending shorter execution times.

Keywords: Iterated local search · Facility location problem · Limited choice rule

1 Introduction

Facility location problems form a family that comprises the model and resolution of many different real-world problems where the shared feature is the need to determine the location of a given number of facilities under a particular set of constraints. Depending on the defined scenario, different objective functions are considered. Healthcare facility location, trying to reduce different features related to the relationship between health providers and patients [1], facility location considering pollution [9] and obnoxious facility location, trying to distribute the annoying effect of the facilities [2] are some of the most recent topics that nowadays coexist with the classical facility location problems [10]. In fact, the family is divided into different categories of problems like the continuous Covering Location Problems, Discrete Network Location Models, or Competitive Facility Location problems, among others [3].

The problem we tackle in this work, namely the Facility Location problem with Limited Choice rule (FLLC), belongs to the category of the Competitive Facility Location problems (CFL). In CFL choice models are applied to estimate the expected revenue and/or the expected market share when a company plans to introduce a service to a market by opening a set of facilities from some predetermined sites. Once some facilities are open, customer zones split the buying

power among their *consideration set* (the subset of open facilities that the customers are willing to patronize according to their utility) plus an outside option
(not using the service or seeking the service from other providers). The objective of FLLC is to maximize the expected profit of the company, that takes into
account the revenue and the fixed cost of facilities, by determining the optimal
location for the facilities.

The version of the problem that we have studied was proposed in [5]. Here,
the problem was defined and a mathematical model was presented, proposing a
generalized Benders decomposition scheme which is compared with two state-
of-the-art methods: a branch-and-cut approach based on outer approximation,
and a mixed-integer conic quadratic program.

In this work we propose an Iterated Local Search (ILS) algorithm that is
able to obtain competitive results for the FLLC problem in relation to the
state of the art spending shorter computation times. The ILS proposal begins
with a constructive algorithm based on the Greedy Randomized Adaptive Local
Search Procedure (GRASP) strategy, followed by a custom best-improvement
local search, and helped with a fast perturbation method, all of the tailored
to this problem. The experimental results show that our proposal is able to
obtain the same number of best results as the state of the art spending shorter
computation times.

The paper is organized as follows: the problem is formally described in Sect. 2,
our algorithmic proposal is detailed in Sect. 3, the experimental experience is
explained and analyzed in Sect. 4, and the conclusions are drawn in Sect. 5, also
pointing out future work.

2   Formal Description of the Problem

The FLLC can be formally described as follows. Let J be a set of m candidate
facilities, $m = |J|$, that a company can open to offer some service to a set I of
n customer zones, $n = |I|$. Each facility $j \in J$ has a fixed opening cost, f_j, and
an attractiveness A_j. Each customer zone $i \in I$ has a buying power, b_i, and a
maximum number of facilities in its consideration set γ_i. Moreover, given the
distance between a customer zone and a facility, d_{ij}, the utility of a facility j to
the customer zone i is $u_{ij} = A_j/d_{ij}^2$ and, besides the facilities, there is an outside
utility, u_{i0}.

Defining a binary variable $x_j \in \{0, 1\}$ for each facility (equal to 1 if facility
j is open, 0 otherwise), and additional binary variables $y_{ij} \in \{0, 1\}$ (equal to
1 if facility j is in the consideration set of customer i, 0 otherwise), the FLLC
can be mathematically formulated by Eq. (1), where $\pi_{ij} = u_{ij}/u_{i0}$. The first
term in Eq. (1a) is the expected revenue collected by the new facilities, while
the second one is the fixed cost of opening the facilities. Equation (1b) avoids
unopen facilities j in the consideration set of a customer zone i. Equation (1c)
restricts the size of the consideration set of a customer zone i to γ_i.

$$\max \ \mathcal{F}(x,y) = \sum_{i \in I} b_i \frac{\sum_{j \in J} \pi_{ij} y_{ij}}{\sum_{j \in J} \pi_{ij} y_{ij} + 1} - \sum_{j \in J} f_j x_j \tag{1a}$$

$$\text{s.t.} \ y_{ij} \leq x_j \qquad\qquad\qquad \forall i \in I, \ j \in J \tag{1b}$$

$$\sum_{j \in J} y_{ij} \leq \gamma_i \qquad\qquad\qquad \forall i \in I \tag{1c}$$

As described in [5], this model states that customers first rank the open facilities according to the utility of facilities to customers from the largest to the smallest and then pick the first γ_i facilities from the sorted list into this set. Then, defining φ as the set of open facilities and χ_i as the consideration set a customer zone $i \in I$, the mathematical model described above can be rewritten as shown in Eq. (2):

$$\max \ \mathcal{F}(\varphi) = \sum_{i \in I} b_i \frac{\sum_{j \in \chi_i} \pi_{ij}}{\sum_{j \in \chi_i} \pi_{ij} + 1} - \sum_{j \in \varphi} f_j \tag{2a}$$

$$\text{s.t.} \ |\chi_i| = \gamma_i \qquad\qquad\qquad \forall i \in I \tag{2b}$$

which is useful to explain the procedures of our metaheuristic proposal. Notice how the only decision variable is the set of open facilities φ, since once this set is fixed, each customer zone $i \in I$ populates its consideration set χ_i including the γ_i facilities $j \in \varphi$ with the best utility relative to customer i, u_{ij}.

3   Iterated Local Search

Iterated Local Search (ILS) is a stochastic metaheuristic with several applications to different combinatorial optimization problems [6,7]. It iteratively applies a local search procedure to a perturbed solution of the incumbent one to escape from local optima. This metaheuristic has four different components: (1) a constructive method to generate the initial solution, (2) a local search procedure to improve the current solution, (3) a perturbation strategy to generate a new starting solution for the local search, and (4) an acceptance criteria to select the solution the ILS continues the search from. It effectively combines the intensification provided by a local search procedure with the diversification introduced by the perturbation strategy.

Algorithm 1 shows the pseudo-code of our ILS proposal inside a multi-start schema (MsILS), which runs the standard ILS t_{max} times returning the best solution found among all runs. The loop starts in step 2 by constructing an initial solution with the constructive method later described in Algorithm 2 and improving its quality in step 3 by means of the local search procedure later described in Algorithm 3. Then, it enters a loop that restarts the local search from a new solution with a perturbation procedure in step 6 that removes one facility at random. The acceptance criteria is checked until there is no improvement after k_{max} iterations. Finally, steps 13 to 14 update the best solution found in the overall procedure.

Algorithm 1: MsILS(α,k_{max},t_{max})

---

1 **for** $t = 1$ **to** t_{max} **do**
2 | $\varphi \leftarrow$ Constructive(α)
3 | $\varphi \leftarrow$ LocalSearch(φ)
4 | $k \leftarrow 0$
5 | **while** $k < k_{max}$ **do**
6 | | $\varphi' \leftarrow$ Perturbation(φ)
7 | | $\varphi' \leftarrow$ LocalSearch(φ')
8 | | **if** $\mathcal{F}(\varphi') > \mathcal{F}(\varphi)$ **then**
9 | | | $\varphi \leftarrow \varphi'$
10 | | | $k \leftarrow 0$
11 | | **else**
12 | | | $k \leftarrow k + 1$
13 | **if** $\mathcal{F}(\varphi) > \mathcal{F}(\varphi^\star)$ **then**
14 | | $\varphi^\star \leftarrow \varphi$
15 **return** $\varphi^\star$

Algorithm 2 shows the method used to construct an initial solution, which follows a Greedy Randomized Adaptive Search Procedure (GRASP) methodology [4]. It starts with a partial solution φ_p with no facilities, which represents that all the facilities are closed. Then, it enters a loop that opens a new facility while there is an improvement on the solution quality. At each iteration, the candidate facility to be incorporated on the partial solution is selected following a random-greedy strategy. Hence, the best solution in terms of a greedy function is selected from a restricted candidate list (RCL), which is created randomly selecting facilities from the candidate list (CL) according to the parameter α. Notice that the greedy function $\mathcal{G}_{add}$ in step 7 is the objective function after adding the candidate facility j' to the partial solution φ_p.

Algorithm 3 shows the pseudo-code of the local search procedure to improve the current solution. It tries to add the best facility to the current solution at each iteration until there is no improvement on the solution quality (steps 5 to 12). Then, it follows the same procedure but removing facilities (steps 14 to 21). Notice the analogous greedy function $\mathcal{G}_{rem}$ on removing facility j'. The procedure continues until there is no change on the current solution after sequentially applying the above *add* and *remove* procedures.

Algorithm 2: CONSTRUCTIVE(α)

1 $\varphi_p \leftarrow \emptyset$
2 $CL \leftarrow J$
3 **repeat**
4 $\quad$ *improve* $\leftarrow$ **false**
5 $\quad$ *size* $\leftarrow$ **max**($\lfloor \alpha \cdot |CL| \rfloor, 1$)
6 $\quad$ $RCL \leftarrow$ SelectRandomSet($CL, size$)
7 $\quad$ $j \leftarrow \underset{j' \in RCL}{\arg\max}\ \mathcal{G}_{add}(\varphi_p, j')$
8 $\quad$ $\varphi_p \leftarrow \varphi_p \cup \{j\}$
9 $\quad$ $CL \leftarrow CL \setminus \{j\}$
10 $\quad$ **if** $\mathcal{F}(\varphi_p) > \mathcal{F}(\varphi)$ **then**
11 $\quad\quad$ $\varphi \leftarrow \varphi_p$
12 $\quad\quad$ *improve* $\leftarrow$ **true**
13 **until** *improve* = **false**
14 **return** φ

Algorithm 3: LOCALSEARCH(φ)

1 *improve* $\leftarrow$ **true**
2 **while** *improve* **do**
3 $\quad$ *improve* $\leftarrow$ **false**
4 $\quad$ *continue* $\leftarrow$ **true**
5 $\quad$ **while** *continue* **do**
6 $\quad\quad$ *continue* $\leftarrow$ **false**
7 $\quad\quad$ $j \leftarrow \underset{j' \in J \setminus \varphi}{\arg\max}\ \mathcal{G}_{add}(\varphi, j')$
8 $\quad\quad$ $\varphi' \leftarrow \varphi \cup \{j\}$
9 $\quad\quad$ **if** $\mathcal{F}(\varphi') > \mathcal{F}(\varphi)$ **then**
10 $\quad\quad\quad$ *continue* $\leftarrow$ **true**
11 $\quad\quad\quad$ *improve* $\leftarrow$ **true**
12 $\quad\quad\quad$ $\varphi \leftarrow \varphi'$
13 $\quad$ *continue* $\leftarrow$ **true**
14 $\quad$ **while** *continue* **do**
15 $\quad\quad$ *continue* $\leftarrow$ **false**
16 $\quad\quad$ $j \leftarrow \underset{j' \in \varphi}{\arg\max}\ \mathcal{G}_{rem}(\varphi, j')$
17 $\quad\quad$ $\varphi' \leftarrow \varphi \setminus \{j\}$
18 $\quad\quad$ **if** $\mathcal{F}(\varphi') > \mathcal{F}(\varphi)$ **then**
19 $\quad\quad\quad$ *continue* $\leftarrow$ **true**
20 $\quad\quad\quad$ *improve* $\leftarrow$ **true**
21 $\quad\quad\quad$ $\varphi \leftarrow \varphi'$
22 **return** φ

4   Computational Experiments

To assess the computational efficiency of our MsILS approach against the previous algorithm, denoted as BC-Benders, we conducted experiments using three different datasets studied in [5]. Set $R1$ has a total of 135 ($5 \times 9 \times 3$) instances corresponding to 5 different distributions of $I = 100$ customer zones and $J = 100$ facilities on a square area $[0, 1000]^2$, 9 values of $\gamma \in \{1, 2, 3, 4, 5, 7, 10, 20, nh\}$ and 3 different values of the opening cost $f \in \{500, 1000, 2000\}$ each. The value $\gamma = nh$ means that γ_i is generated from an integer uniform distribution $[1, 39]$ for all $i \in I$. Set $R2$ has 90 ($5 \times 9 \times 2$) instances generated with the same procedure as $R1$ but using $I = 200$ and $f \in \{500, 2000\}$. Finally, set $R3$ contains 24 bigger instances with $I \in \{800, 1000\}$, $J \in \{100, 150, 200\}$ and $f = 2000$. Moreover, all the customer zones have a buying power $b_i \in [10, 1000]$, $A_j = 1, \forall j \in J$ ($u_{ij} = A_j / d_{ij}^2$), and $u_{i0} = 1/100^2$ for $R1$ and $R2$, and $u_{i0} = 1/50^2$ for $R3$.

All the experiments were executed on the same machine, an AMD EPYC 7282 processor with 32GB of RAM running Kubuntu 22.04. We used Gurobi 10.0.1 as an exact solver for BC-Benders using the Python code kindly provided by the authors of [5], and Java Temurin 17.0.6 using the MORK framework [8] for our MsILS proposal. BC-Benders was executed with a time limit of 7200 s for each instance. Regarding MsILS, we experimentally checked that $t_{max} = 50$ executions and $k_{max} = 50$ iterations without improvement at each execution were enough to achieve good results in a reasonable CPU time.

Table 1 shows the aggregated results for each different instance category in both algorithms. We can see the average cost, denoted as *Cost*, the average time in seconds, *CPU(s)*, and the number of times the best cost value was reached, *#Best*. Best results are highlighted in bold font. Before breaking down into each instance category, we can see that the new proposal is faster than the previous one, spending less than 45% of the time of the previous method. We can also see that in $R3$ we have improved the number of best results, 23 out of 24, but the average cost is not better. This result happens because BC-Benders gets the best solution in one of the instances by bigger difference than the instances where MsILS gets the best solution. In addition, we have found a best value in $R3$ not reported previously.

Table 1. Comparison between BC-Benders and MsILS. Each row show the averaged cost, CPU time and number of best over all the instances in each set. Best values for the metrics are highlighted with **bold font**.

Instance set	BC-Benders			MsILS		
	Cost	CPU(s)	#Best	Cost	CPU(s)	#Best
$R1$	20542.09	68.9	129	**20542.14**	**57.8**	**135**
$R2$	53349.70	527.7	85	**53350.28**	**160.8**	**90**
$R3$	**160440.80**	2251.7	21	160432.70	**1054.7**	**23**
Average	**78110.86**	949.4	78	78108.37	**424.4**	**83**

Table 2 shows the detailed results for *R1*. Here we can see that the cost of both algorithms is similar in every instance. For small γ values BC-Benders is faster and returns the best value. However, when γ increases, both algorithms report a higher computational time, showing a direct relationship between γ and computational time. This relationship arises that given the gap between the slowest and fastest time of BC-Benders is wider than for MsILS, BC-Benders has a steeper slope ending up timing out on big instances with big γ.

Table 2. Comparison between BC-Benders and MsILS for *R1*. Each row show the averaged values of the 5 different instances for every value of f and γ. In this set $I = 100$ and $J = 100$ for all the instances. Best values for the metrics are highlighted with **bold**.

Instance		BC-Benders		MsILS	
f	γ	Cost	CPU(s)	Cost	CPU(s)
500	1	24739.88	**5.9**	**24740.30**	24.2
	2	**27035.17**	**11.2**	**27035.17**	30.2
	3	**28015.83**	**12.9**	**28015.83**	37.4
	4	**28594.87**	**17.3**	**28594.87**	43.3
	5	28985.39	**22.2**	28985.46	51.7
	7	**29496.50**	**36.3**	**29496.50**	73.1
	10	**29951.44**	**65.6**	**29951.44**	95.4
	20	30532.72	545.6	**30532.90**	**183.9**
	nh	**29605.16**	104.2	**29605.16**	117.4
1000	1	**17253.63**	**8.5**	**17253.63**	17.8
	2	**19552.12**	**10.2**	**19552.12**	23.7
	3	**20568.52**	**14.6**	**20568.52**	31.8
	4	**21176.23**	**22.0**	**21176.23**	39.3
	5	21604.04	**32.5**	**21604.20**	45.7
	7	**22162.49**	**36.7**	**22162.49**	62.0
	10	**22635.39**	**83.8**	**22635.39**	86.3
	20	**22857.04**	260.4	**22857.04**	**116.0**
	nh	22119.63	**73.6**	22119.73	83.5
2000	1	**8764.35**	11.6	**8764.35**	12.8
	2	**10723.84**	13.5	**10723.84**	20.2
	3	**11682.42**	19.6	**11682.42**	28.8
	4	**12220.86**	28.8	**12220.86**	35.7
	5	12591.93	**37.7**	12592.29	44.2
	7	**13041.59**	87.5	**13041.59**	**61.2**
	10	**13101.51**	113.8	**13101.51**	**69.8**
	20	**13101.51**	123.3	**13101.51**	**71.0**
	nh	**12522.35**	60.5	**12522.35**	**54.7**
Average		20542.09	68.9	**20542.14**	**57.8**

Table 3 shows the results for *R2*, where we can see a similar behavior than in the case of *R1*. Due to the larger size of the instances, BC-Benders spends more execution time on the largest ones, ramping up on the highest two γ values. When γ is equal to 20 we can observe the biggest difference, getting the same value in a forth of the time for f equals to 500. For f equals to 2000 the time improves a thirteenth of the previous algorithm.

Table 3. Comparison between BC-Benders and MsILS for *R2*. Each row show the averaged values of the 5 different instances for every value of f and γ. In this set $I = 200$ and $J = 100$ for all the instances. Best values for the metrics are highlighted with **bold**.

Instance		BC-Benders		MsILS	
f	γ	Cost	CPU(s)	Cost	CPU(s)
500	1	57936.22	**11.1**	**57937.06**	62.7
	2	63367.91	**26.6**	**63368.02**	79.7
	3	**65599.75**	**35.0**	**65599.75**	94.5
	4	**66872.21**	**47.1**	**66872.21**	116.8
	5	**67709.33**	**72.5**	**67709.33**	132.4
	7	**68788.68**	**138.9**	**68788.68**	176.8
	10	**69712.48**	351.1	**69712.48**	**238.2**
	20	**71063.56**	2100.0	**71063.56**	**456.3**
	nh	**69666.79**	499.8	**69666.79**	**395.0**
2000	1	**31358.33**	**15.3**	**31358.33**	31.2
	2	**36427.57**	**28.6**	**36427.57**	50.2
	3	**38749.97**	**58.7**	**38749.97**	66.0
	4	**40099.63**	117.0	**40099.63**	**85.6**
	5	**41041.99**	178.3	**41041.99**	**101.6**
	7	42253.87	395.0	42254.43	**141.8**
	10	**43304.00**	828.5	**43304.00**	**190.5**
	20	43851.18	3729.9	43860.09	**280.6**
	nh	**42491.12**	864.5	**42491.12**	**193.7**
Average		53349.70	527.7	53350.28	**160.8**

Finally, Table 4 shows the results for *R3*. Again, the performance is similar than in the case of *R1* and *R2*. As seen in the Table, the cases where γ is 1 or the number of facilities is small, BC-Benders returns the best value in a shorter time than MsILS. In all the other cases it seems to be a limitation for the algorithm. When this situation happens our proposal shines, and MsILS is able to reach a better results in a shorter time. The instance where we improve the state of the art can be seen with the following configuration $I = 1000, J = 200, \gamma = 3$.

Table 4. Comparison between BC-Benders and MsILS for *R3*. In this set $f = 2000$ for all the instances. Best values for the metrics are highlighted with **bold**.

Instance			BC-Benders		MsILS	
I	*J*	γ	Cost	CPU(s)	Cost	CPU(s)
800	100	1	**105658.10**	**35.8**	**105658.10**	280.1
		2	**130863.87**	**65.9**	**130863.87**	394.8
		3	**142928.31**	**119.7**	**142928.31**	561.5
		nh	137478.80	**92.6**	**137488.92**	579.3
800	150	1	115828.71	**63.7**	115831.47	592.4
		2	**140123.73**	**403.4**	**140123.73**	811.2
		3	**151499.70**	2464.5	**151499.70**	**953.1**
		nh	**145946.18**	3233.3	**145946.18**	**1199.2**
800	200	1	**116529.11**	**169.2**	**116529.11**	917.4
		2	**141522.83**	2764.1	**141522.83**	**1397.0**
		3	**152755.87**	7200.0	**152755.87**	**1822.8**
		nh	**147439.31**	5386.8	**147439.31**	**1874.0**
1000	100	1	**150424.50**	**40.2**	**150424.50**	270.7
		2	**182178.91**	**58.1**	**182178.91**	405.8
		3	**196973.75**	**95.1**	**196973.75**	494.2
		nh	**188693.30**	**91.1**	**188693.30**	539.5
1000	150	1	**155644.48**	**69.3**	**155644.48**	718.4
		2	**187760.49**	**616.8**	**187760.49**	1150.8
		3	**202301.40**	7200.0	**202301.40**	**1590.4**
		nh	**195306.86**	1399.5	**195306.86**	**1349.8**
1000	200	1	**161635.27**	**870.9**	161355.47	1100.3
		2	**193401.57**	7200.0	**193401.57**	**1764.1**
		3	207445.43	7200.0	207518.14	**2313.3**
		nh	**200238.63**	7200.0	**200238.63**	**2232.5**
Average			**160440.80**	2251.7	160432.70	**1054.7**

5   Conclusions and Future Work

The Facility Location problem with Limited Choice rule has been previously studied by means of the combination of an exact method with some heuristic help. In this paper, we propose the first metaheuristic approach to this complex problem by means of an Iterated Local Search method. To this aim, we have defined a constructive procedure, a best-improvement local search and a perturbation method able to efficiently traverse the space of solutions.

Considering this approach as a preliminary work on this problem, we obtained similar results than the state of the art in terms of objective function values, reaching the same number of best solutions as the previous work on the studied instances and obtaining a new best result. Moreover, our proposal is able to obtain these results spending, on average, 44% of the time spent by the state-of-the-art method using the same experimental machine.

Currently, our efforts are focused on improving the results by applying more complex algorithms and different neighborhood explorations.

Acknowledgements. This work has been partially supported by the Spanish Ministerio de Ciencia e Innovación (MCIN/AEI/10.13039/501100011033) under grant refs. RED2022-134480-T, PID2021-126605NB-I00 and by ERDF A way of making Europe; and Generalitat Valenciana with grant ref. CIAICO/2021/224.

References

1. Ahmadi-Javid, A., Seyedi, P., Syam, S.S.: A survey of healthcare facility location. Comput. Oper. Res. **79**, 223–263 (2017)
2. Church, R.L., Drezner, Z.: Review of obnoxious facilities location problems. Comput. Oper. Res. **138**, 105468 (2022)
3. Drezner, Z., Hamacher, H.W.: Facility Location: Applications and Theory. Springer, Heidelberg (2004)
4. Feo, T., Resende, M.: A probabilistic heuristic for a computationally difficult set covering problem. Oper. Res. Lett. **8**, 67–71 (1989)
5. Lin, Y.H., Tian, Q.: Branch-and-cut approach based on generalized benders decomposition for facility location with limited choice rule. Eur. J. Oper. Res. **293**(1), 109–119 (2021)
6. Lourenço, H.R., Martin, O.C., Stützle, T.: Iterated Local Search, pp. 320–353. Springer, Boston (2003). https://doi.org/10.1007/0-306-48056-5_11
7. Lourenço, H.R., Martin, O.C., Stützle, T.: Iterated local search: framework and applications. In: Gendreau, M., Potvin, J.Y. (eds.) Handbook of Metaheuristics, vol. 146, pp. 129–168. Springer, Cham (2019). https://doi.org/10.1007/978-1-4419-1665-5_12
8. Martín-Santamaría, R., Cavero, S., Herrán, A., Duarte, A., Colmenar, J.M.: A practical methodology for reproducible experimentation: an application to the Double-row Facility Layout Problem. In: Evolutionary Computation, pp. 1–35 (2022)
9. Mechouar, Y., Hovelaque, V., Gaigne, C.: Effect of raw material substitution on the facility location decision under a carbon tax policy. EURO J. Transport. Logist. **11**, 100061 (2022)
10. Melo, M.T., Nickel, S., Saldanha-Da-Gama, F.: Facility location and supply chain management-a review. Eur. J. Oper. Res. **196**(2), 401–412 (2009)

Driven PCTBagging: Seeking Greater Discriminating Capacity for the Same Level of Interpretability

Jesús María Pérez[✉][iD], Olatz Arbelaitz[iD], and Javier Muguerza[iD]

Department of Computer Architecture and Technology, University of the Basque
Country UPV/EHU, Manuel Lardizabal 1, 20018 Donostia, Spain
{txus.perez,olatz.arbelaitz,j.muguerza}@ehu.eus
http://www.aldapa.eus/

Abstract. The partial consolidated tree bagging (PCTBagging) was
presented as a multiple classifier that, based on a parameter, the consolidation percentage, can exploit more the possibilities of the inner ensembles, and obtain higher levels of interpretability, or can exploit more the
possibilities of the ensembles, and obtain higher discriminant capacity.
Thus, at the extreme values, with a consolidation percentage of 100% it
obtains a consolidated tree (CTC algorithm) and with 0% consolidation
it obtains a Bagging. For intermediate values, the consolidated tree is
collapsed to the number of internal nodes corresponding to the percentage value, selecting the biggest possible nodes. In this paper we propose
a strategy to directly develop the partial consolidated tree, i.e. without
the need to build the complete consolidated tree and, in addition, we
explore up to 4 other different criteria, besides the size of the nodes, to
decide which will be the next node to be developed in the partial consolidated tree: Pre-order, Gain ratio, Gain ratio × Size, and, Level by level.
The results show that the use of different criteria affects the discriminant
capacity of the classifier for the same level of interpretability, and that
this effect is greater the higher the percentage of consolidation is.

Keywords: Comprehensible classifiers · Consolidation · Ensembles

1 Introduction

Nowadays artificial intelligence is present in multiple contexts of our lives. To
a large extent this has been possible thanks to the great advances made in the
area of machine learning, specifically in the field of deep neural networks or
Deep Learning. These algorithms build classifiers with high reliability in their
predictions but do not provide an explanation as to why they have generated that
particular output for the input provided making them not suitable for certain
domains. Because of this, great efforts are being made to obtain classifiers with
explanatory capabilities [1,10,11].

Rule induction algorithms, such as decision trees or rule sets, are an alternative to produce models that are interpretable by humans [5]. Multiple proposals

A. Alonso-Betanzos et al. (Eds.): CAEPIA 2024, LNAI 14640, pp. 152–161, 2024.
https://doi.org/10.1007/978-3-031-62799-6_16

have been carried out to improve the predictive capacity of this type of classifiers, most of them based on the combination of multiple classifiers ('ensembles') obtained as a result of a resampling process of the original sample. One of the best known and most widely used ensembles is Bagging, and, as Leo Breiman said in [4], when we combine 50 decision trees via voting to make a prediction: "What one gains is increased accuracy. What one loses, with the trees, is a simple and interpretable structure". In this regard, in [13] an algorithm was proposed, the consolidated tree construction (CTC) algorithm, which introduces the techniques used by Bagging to generate the ensemble in the construction of the decision tree itself (which gave rise to the term 'inner ensembles'). In this case, based on a set of samples, the algorithm is able to build a single tree, and therefore, it does not lose the explanatory capacity. Although CTC algorithm performs better than simple decision trees [14], it does not reach the prediction level of Bagging [12].

Recently, a hybrid approach between CTC and Bagging was proposed, the PCTBagging [9]. This algorithm has a parameter, the consolidation percentage, which allows the user to indicate the number of internal nodes (the ones that will give the explanation) to be consolidated. This will be the partially consolidated tree (PCT), which will have a structure common to all the trees associated with Bagging. From this point onwards, all these trees are developed independently as in Bagging. In this way, when the consolidation percentage is 0%, a Bagging ensemble is obtained and when it is 100%, a CTC tree. The paper shows that this parameter gives the user the option to search for the desired trade-off between interpretability and discriminant capacity. An implementation of this algorithm can be found as an official package of the popular WEKA framework [6], J48PartiallyConsolidated[1,2].

In this algorithm, a complete consolidated tree is first built to calculate, according to the value of the consolidation percentage parameter specified by the user, the number of internal nodes in the tree that should be maintained for all the trees in the inner ensemble. Following with the example of the paper (Fig. 1), if the complete consolidated tree has 10 internal nodes and the value of the consolidation percentage is 60%, 6 internal nodes will be kept and the rest will be removed. But, one question arises in this process, which 6 nodes will be kept and which ones will be removed? In [9] the criterion used was the size of the nodes, i.e., the number of cases they contain. In this way, starting from the root node (which contains all the cases of the sample), all the internal nodes are ordered from largest to smallest and the 6 largest nodes will be the ones to keep as part of the explanation of the final classifier and, the rest will be collapsed in the consolidated tree. From this point on, Bagging will be applied, maintaining the 60% of all trees identical to that of the consolidated tree.

This work improves and extends the PCTBagging algorithm making more efficient the construction of the partially consolidated trees, and, including more criteria in the process of selecting the inner nodes to be consolidated. On the

---

[1] https://weka.sourceforge.io/packageMetaData/J48PartiallyConsolidated/

[2] We are trying to update this package with the proposal of this paper.

one hand, from a practical point of view, the strategy for the construction of the partially consolidated tree is very laborious in terms of computational cost and time, since it is always necessary to first, construct the complete consolidated tree to know the number of internal nodes it contains and then, apply the consolidation percentage. However, a much more practical use of this algorithm would be to indicate a concrete value of the number of internal nodes that we want to obtain as an explanation of our classifier, independently of the number of nodes that the complete consolidated tree would have, and to build the consolidated tree only up to the specified number of nodes. In many cases, a partial tree of as few as 5 internal nodes may provide sufficient explanation for the user's interests. Even one might be sufficient in some contexts.

The first contribution of this work is, precisely, to change the way to express the number of nodes to be consolidated in the CTC algorithm. The new version will allow to express this value as an absolute value, instead of as a percentage. This change implies switching from a recursive implementation to an iterative implementation of the function that builds the consolidated tree.

On the other hand, since the consolidated tree developed in this algorithm is partial, as is the case in the PART algorithm [7], the decision of which is the next node to be developed is of vital importance. The new proposal includes several criteria, in addition to the node size, that could be more adequate to the specific data used to induce the consolidated tree. The inclusion of this new degree of freedom in the construction of the partial consolidated tree may mean that the classifiers generated could have a clearer and more stable explanation, and a higher predictive capacity than that achieved by the node size criterion.

In this work 4 new criteria, in addition to Size, are proposed to decide which will be the next node to be developed in the consolidated tree: Pre-order, Gain ratio, Gain ratio × Size, and, Level by level. To evaluate the performance of this new proposal, a set of experiments were performed on 33 two-class-imbalanced dataset extracted from the KEEL repository. The results were compared from 3 points of view using a 5-fold cross-validation methodology executed 20 times (20 × 5CV): discriminating capacity, the complexity of the explanation provided, and the computational cost of building the classifiers.

The rest of the paper is organized as follows. Section 2 details the related work. Section 3 explains the Driven PCTBagging version proposed in this paper. Section 4 defines the experimental methodology. Section 5 lays out the obtained results. Finally, conclusions are drawn in Sect. 6.

2   Related Work on PCTBagging

This section, briefly describes the learning algorithms that serve as the basis for partially consolidated tree bagging algorithm.

In order to build a (partially or not) consolidated tree, we first need an algorithm for building a decision tree. The first algorithm to be consolidated was the well-known C4.5 decision tree induction algorithm [15] which has been widely used as a base algorithm in countless proposals for building multiple classifier systems [2–4].

'Bootstrap aggregating' (Bagging) [4] was proposed as an ensemble aggregating multiple C4.5 decision trees (although any other base algorithm can be used), independently created from bootstrap samples. It is in the process of classifying a new case that all classifiers are involved in order to finally assign it the most voted class.

The CTC algorithm [13,14] was designed to obtain the predictive capacity of an ensemble built based on a set of samples such as Bagging, but without losing the explanation of the classification, i.e. creating a tree that agglutinates the information of all the samples. In this case, the voting process, instead of being carried out in the classification phase, occurs every time it is necessary to decide which will be the predictor variable that will divide the current node during the construction of the tree.

The variable that splits a node in a consolidated tree is the variable that has been chosen the most times to split the same node in each of the trees associated to the sample set. In the CTC this same variable will split the consolidated tree and all the trees associated to the sample set. In this way, when the construction process is finished, all the trees will have the same structure. In PCTBagging [9], the idea is to start building the consolidated tree as in the CTC, but only up to a certain node. At this point, the construction of the consolidated tree is stopped, leaving it as a partial tree, and the rest of the trees associated to the samples continue to be constructed independently, applying C4.5 to each one, as is done in Bagging. Hence the partially consolidated tree bagging. Thus we obtain an explanation of the classification with the partially consolidated tree and the classification process of new cases is performed with the rest of the trees as in Bagging.

3   Driven PCTBagging

The original strategy for the construction of PCTBagging consists of first constructing a complete consolidated tree, then collapsing the tree until a specific number of internal nodes, and from that point onwards applying Bagging. The number of nodes is determined by a percentage value with respect to the total number of nodes of the complete consolidated tree (the consolidation percentage). However, we can use different criteria to 'drive' the construction of such a partial tree, giving priority to the development of one child node over another. In the original PCTBagging the node size was used. In this paper we propose 4 new criteria, in addition to size, to drive the development of the partial consolidated tree:

- *Size*: Node size or number of cases belonging to the node. This is the original criterion in PCTBagging, but in this case the implementation of the function that develops the tree is iterative instead of recursive.
- *Gain ratio*: In this case it is proposed to use the value of the same criterion (split function) used by C4.5 to choose the candidate variable that will split a node, the gain ratio. In the PART and BFPART rule induction algorithms [7], this criterion is also used to decide which is the next node to develop in the partial tree that will compose each rule.

- *Gain ratio* × *Size*: Sometimes, very small nodes obtain very high gain ratio values and, however, very large nodes obtain very low values. Being two interesting aspects in the construction of a tree, a combination of both via multiplication could be a good heuristic to explore.
- *Pre-order*: Most decision tree construction algorithms such as C4.5 develop the tree by traversing it in pre-order, i.e., descending as far as possible through the first child node until it is no longer possible, then moving on to the sibling node and so on until the whole tree has been completed. Normally, the order of the child nodes depends only on how the description of the values taken by the variable that divides the node has been done.
- *Level by level*: Instead of indicating how many nodes we want to develop and deciding which is the next node to develop at each step, another possibility is to indicate the number of levels we want to develop. Instead of developing in depth, we develop all the child nodes of each level up to the indicated level.

4   Experimental Methodology

The experiments were performed with the databases of one of the KEEL repository contexts used in the works [5] and [9], specifically 33 two-class datasets representing the problem of class imbalance (with a proportion of minority class examples between 0.77% (min) and 35.51% (max), 17.61% on average, detailed description in additional material[3]). Due to the size of the minority class, a 5-fold cross-validation methodology was used 20 times (20 × 5CV) to estimate the generalization capacity of the classifiers, as well as other metrics.

The main objective of this paper is to analyse how the criteria used to choose the next node to be developed in the partial consolidated tree affects the performance of the final classifier. We want to analyse how the discriminant capacity changes if we have chosen for example 5 internal nodes driven by size or if they have been chosen by gain ratio.

We want to try with different values of the number of nodes used to consolidate the partial tree, but we do not know a priori how many nodes the consolidated tree obtained for each dataset will have. For this reason, we have added an option in the Driven PCTBagging implementation where the number of internal nodes of the partial consolidated tree can also be indicated as a percentage of the total number of nodes of the complete consolidated tree, just as in the original PCTBagging [9].

This will allow us to do the same scanning of values for all datasets (regardless of the size of their trees) in percent, from 0 to 100%, so that the results of the 33 datasets are comparable.

The analysis of the results, therefore, will be similar to that done in [9], i.e., based on the percentage of consolidation. However, in this work the range of values sampled for a given dataset is much larger than in [9]. In both works the final trees associated with the PCTBagging are pruned (default option in

---

[3] http://www.aldapa.eus/res/2024/DrivenPCTBag

C4.5) but, however, there is a notable difference in the construction of the previous consolidated tree: in [9] it is also pruned whereas in the present work it is unpruned. This implies that the scanning from 0% to 100% reaches up to 36.4 internal nodes (on average for the 33 datasets), when in [9] it reached only 8 nodes (also on average). In other words, this work explores a range of values 4 times wider.

We compare the results of the 5 versions of Driven PCTBagging as the consolidation percentage varies in addition to its direct competitors (pruned and unpruned versions): C4.5, CTC and Bagging. Regarding the resampling strategy for these algorithms, we have chosen the best one for each of them based on what we know. We used 50 bootstrap samples for Bagging (widely accepted value [3]). However, for CTC and PCTBagging, we use balanced subsamples where the number of subsamples is determined by the distribution of classes in the dataset (based on the coverage concept defined in [8]). The number of subsamples for the 33 data sets ranges from 6 to 585, with a mean of 56 and a median of 23.

Being the datasets used unbalanced we evaluated the performance of the classifiers based on the area under the ROC curve (AUC). However, we are also interested in metrics that focus on the accuracy obtained for single classes, mainly in the minority class, such as balanced accuracy and sensitivity (or True Positive Rate).

The complexity of the explanation provided is measured with the number of internal nodes within the decision trees what is straightforward for C4.5 and CTC. For the case of PCTBagging we will also measure the number of nodes of the partial consolidated tree (like in [9]). However, in this work we have tried to estimate the complexity of the set of trees that constitute the multiple classifier in Bagging and in PCTBagging. In particular, we counted the number of nodes of all the decision trees of the multiple classifier and calculated the average value.

Finally, the computational cost is defined as the time taken to build the classifiers (elapsed time training), measured in seconds.

5   Experimental Results

In order to better understand the experiment performed, we will first show the results related to the structural complexity of the classifiers built. Figure 1 shows the average value of the number of internal nodes for the 33 datasets obtained for each of the compared algorithms. The results associated with each dataset for each algorithm can be found in the tables of the additional material website (See footnote 3).

As can be seen in the figure, there are 6 horizontal lines that correspond to the C4.5, CTC and Bagging algorithms (pruned(continuous lines) and unpruned (dash doted lines) versions), for which the consolidation percentage parameter does not affect. The rest of the curves (lines) correspond to results of the PCT-Bagging variants: on the one hand, the continuous lines on the diagonal of the figure ranging from 0 nodes (0%) to 36.4 (100%) that correspond to the partial

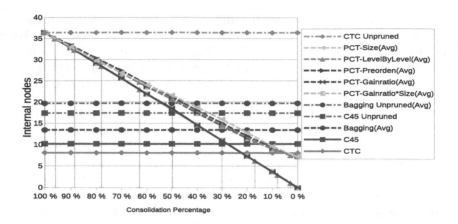

Fig. 1. Average values of the number of internal nodes for the 33 datasets

consolidated tree values (as expected, all of them coincide in their values and, therefore, all appear one on top of the other in the figure. Their names have been removed from the legend due to space problems) and, on the other hand, the dashed lines starting from 7.22 (0%) and varying up to 36.4 (100%), which correspond to the average value of the number of internal nodes of all the trees of the PCTBagging ensemble (marked with (Avg) in the legend).

The 'Level by level' variant of PCTBagging requires further explanation. The number of levels to be developed is indicated based on a percentage value with respect to the total number of levels in the consolidated tree. In order to show the results of this variant together with the other variants where the results vary according to the percentage of consolidated nodes (not levels), for each value of the percentage of levels we have counted the number of nodes that the partial tree has and calculated the percentage that this value represents with respect to the total number of nodes in the tree. For example, for the 33 datasets, the consolidated trees with 10% of the levels partially developed have on average 1.03 internal nodes, what corresponds to 2.83% of the nodes of the tree. When developed up to 20% of the levels, they have 2.91 nodes, i.e. 7.99% of the total nodes and for 30 % of the levels, 16.91 % of the nodes, and so on. These values have been highlighted in Fig. 1 with a dotted line from the x-axis to the triangle symbol that identifies the PCT-LevelByLevel in the figure.

As can be seen in Fig. 1, CTC is the algorithm that obtains the simplest trees (8.07 on average), followed by C4.5 (10.17) and then Bagging (13.41). The partially consolidated trees of all PCTBagging variants range from 0 to 36.4, just the size of the CTC Unpruned trees. Finally, the average size of the PCTBagging ensemble trees, for each consolidation percentage value, does not vary much for the 5 PCTBagging criteria used. When the consolidation percentage is 0%, the mean value of the ensemble trees is 7.22, very close to that of the CTC pruned. Recall here that all the trees in the PCTBagging ensemble are pruned in this work. As the consolidation percentage increases, the average number

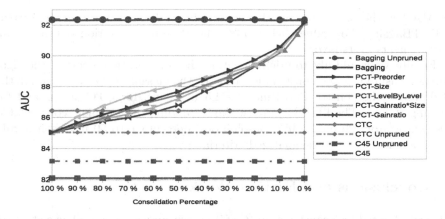

Fig. 2. Average AUC values for the 33 datasets

of nodes of the ensemble trees of all the PCTBagging gets closer to the size of the partial consolidated tree of the same PCTBagging. Finally, when the consolidation percentage is 100%, the pruned trees associated with the ensemble do not grow larger than the CTC Unpruned itself, as can be seen in the upper left corner of Fig. 1.

Regarding the discriminant capacity of the compared classifiers, Fig. 2 shows the mean AUC values obtained for the 33 datasets. The best values are obtained by Bagging (more so for Unpruned) whereas the worst values are obtained by C4.5 (pruned and unpruned). The pruned CTC has a good result as a simple decision tree and the 5 variants of PCTBagging vary from the result of the Unpruned CTC (100%) to almost the result of Bagging (0%). All PCTBagging variants with a consolidation percentage below 50% perform better than CTC. We have to remember here that Bagging is constructed with 50 bootstrap samples and, however, all PCTBagging variants (as well as CTC itself) are constructed with balanced subsamples, where the number of samples used depends on the proportion of cases of the minority class of each dataset. We believe that this resampling is key for obtaining good results with CTC and PCTBagging in contexts of unbalanced datasets, and it makes the results in terms of accuracy of the minority class (True Positive Rate) increase notably. The average TPR values of C4.5 and Bagging (pruned and unpruned) range between 64.46 and 66.64, while those of CTC and PCTBagging vary from 78.49 to 87.21 (see the additional material website (See footnote 3) for details).

Regarding the difference in results for PCTBagging variants, for the same value of consolidation percentage, i.e., for the same level of interpretability, Fig. 2 shows that when the consolidation percentage is low no major differences appear but from 40% onwards they become bigger to finally converge at 100%. The larger the partially consolidated tree, the more it affects the criteria used to determine the next node to develop. Curiously, for values greater than 50% of consolidation, the variant that obtains the highest discriminant capacity (based on AUC) is the one that uses the size of the nodes, i.e. the original variant of PCTBagging. For values below 40%, the Pre-order criterion obtains small improvements in its favor.

Finally, we would like to briefly mention the computational cost of the algorithms measured as the construction time of the classifiers. On average for the 33 datasets, the construction time of C4.5 is 10 ms, for CTC 40 ms and for Bagging 190 ms. The PCTBagging (without building the complete consolidated tree) varies from 20 ms for 0% consolidation percentage to 50 ms, with hardly any difference between the analyzed criteria.

6   Conclusions and Further Work

The consolidated tree construction (CTC) algorithm was proposed as a strategy for obtaining a decision tree using techniques from ensembles as Bagging but without losing interpretability. In order to increase the discriminant capacity of this classifier, at the sacrifice of interpretability, the partial consolidated tree Bagging (PCTBagging), allows the user to indicate a percentage of the number of internal nodes of the consolidated tree to be built (this will provide the explanation of the classification), from which the trees of the ensemble will be developed independently as in Bagging (obtaining a greater discriminant capacity). To do this, however, the complete consolidated tree had to be constructed first and then the tree had to be pruned or collapsed to the number of nodes indicated by the consolidation percentage parameter. In this work we propose to build the partial consolidated tree directly, based on the number of nodes to consolidate as an absolute value, without the need to build the complete consolidated tree, and then apply Bagging. In addition, we have analyzed the effect of using up to 5 different criteria for choosing the next node to develop in the partially consolidated tree. The results show that for the same level of interpretability, the discriminant capacity changes depending on the criterion used. The differences are more noticeable from values higher than 30% of consolidated nodes, being the Size criterion the one that obtains the best AUC values. The gain ratio criterion is the one that obtains the worst values for the same level of interpretability. As future work, we would like to analyze the behavior of PCTBagging with bootstrap samples as used by Bagging (instead of balanced subsamples) and compare its efficiency on both unbalanced and standard datasets. Another line of work we want to explore is to use other ensembles, such as boosting or random forest, instead of bagging, to be applied after the construction of the partial consolidated tree and give rise to PCTEnsembles.

Acknowledgments. This work was partially funded by grant PID2021-123087OB-I00 funded by MCIN/AEI/ 10.13039/501100011033 and, ERDF A way of making Europe, and by the Department of Education, Universities and Research of the Basque Government (ADIAN, IT-1437-22). We would like to thank our former undergraduate student Josué Cabezas, who participated in the implementation of the Driven PCTBagging algorithm for the WEKA platform.

References

1. Alatrany, A.S., Khan, W., Hussain, A., Kolivand, H., Al-Jumeily, D.: An explainable machine learning approach for Alzheimer's disease classification. Sci. Rep. **14**(1), 2637 (2024). https://doi.org/10.1038/s41598-024-51985-w
2. Banfield, R.E., Hall, L.O., Bowyer, K.W., Kegelmeyer, W.: A comparison of decision tree ensemble creation techniques. IEEE Trans. Pattern Anal. Mach. Intell. **29**(1), 173–180 (2007). https://doi.org/10.1109/TPAMI.2007.2
3. Bauer, E., Kohavi, R.: An empirical comparison of voting classification algorithms: bagging, boosting, and variants. Mach. Learn. **36**(1–2), 105–139 (1999). https://doi.org/10.1023/A:1007515423169
4. Breiman, L.: Bagging predictors. Mach. Learn. **24**(2), 123–140 (1996). https://doi.org/10.1023/A:1018054314350
5. Fernández, A., García, S., Luengo, J., Bernadó-Mansilla, E., Herrera, F.: Genetics-based machine learning for rule induction: state of the art, taxonomy, and comparative study. IEEE Trans. Evol. Comput. **14**(6), 913–941 (2010). https://doi.org/10.1109/TEVC.2009.2039140
6. Frank, E., Hall, M.A., Witten, I.H.: The WEKA Workbench, chap. Online Appendix, 4th edn. Morgan Kaufmann (2016). https://www.cs.waikato.ac.nz/ml/weka/Witten_et_al_2016_appendix.pdf
7. Ibarguren, I., Lasarguren, A., Pérez, J.M., Muguerza, J., Gurrutxaga, I., Arbelaitz, O.: BFPART: best-first PART. Inf. Sci. **367–368**, 927–952 (2016). https://doi.org/10.1016/j.ins.2016.07.023
8. Ibarguren, I., Pérez, J.M., Muguerza, J., Gurrutxaga, I., Arbelaitz, O.: Coverage-based resampling: building robust consolidated decision trees. Knowl.-Based Syst. **79**, 51–67 (2015). https://doi.org/10.1016/j.knosys.2014.12.023
9. Ibarguren, I., Pérez, J.M., Muguerza, J., Arbelaitz, O., Yera, A.: PCTBagging: from inner ensembles to ensembles. A trade-off between discriminating capacity and interpretability. Inf. Sci. **583**, 219–238 (2022). https://doi.org/10.1016/j.ins.2021.11.010
10. Khosravi, H., et al.: Explainable artificial intelligence in education. Comput. Educ. Artif. Intell. **3**, 100074 (2022). https://doi.org/10.1016/j.caeai.2022.100074
11. Love, P.E., Fang, W., Matthews, J., Porter, S., Luo, H., Ding, L.: Explainable artificial intelligence (XAI): precepts, models, and opportunities for research in construction. Adv. Eng. Inform. **57**, 102024 (2023). https://doi.org/10.1016/j.aei.2023.102024
12. Pérez, J.M., et al.: Consolidated trees versus bagging when explanation is required. Computing **89**, 113–145 (2010). https://doi.org/10.1007/s00607-010-0094-z
13. Pérez, J.M., Muguerza, J., Arbelaitz, O., Gurrutxaga, I.: A new algorithm to build consolidated trees: study of the error rate and steadiness. In: Kłopotek, M.A., Wierzchoń, S.T., Trojanowski, K. (eds.) Intelligent Information Processing and Web Mining. AINSC, vol. 25, pp. 79–88. Springer, Heidelberg (2004). https://doi.org/10.1007/978-3-540-39985-8_9
14. Pérez, J.M., Muguerza, J., Arbelaitz, O., Gurrutxaga, I., Martín, J.I.: Combining multiple class distribution modified subsamples in a single tree. Pattern Recogn. Lett. **28**(4), 414–422 (2007). https://doi.org/10.1016/j.patrec.2006.08.013
15. Quinlan, J.R.: C4.5: Programs for Machine Learning. Morgan Kaufmann (1993)

Semi-supervised Learning Methods for Semantic Segmentation of Polyps

Adrián Inés$^{(\boxtimes)}$ [iD], César Domínguez [iD], Jónathan Heras [iD], Eloy Mata [iD], and Vico Pascual [iD]

Department of Mathematics and Computer Science, Universidad de La Rioja, Logroño, Spain
{adines,cesar.dominguez,jonathan.heras,eloy.mata,mvico}@unirioja.es

Abstract. Nowadays, colorectal cancer is one of the most common cancers, and early detection would greatly help improve patient survival. The current methods used by physicians to detect it are based on the visual detection of polyps in colonoscopy, a task that can be tackled by means of semantic segmentation methods. However, the amount of data necessary to train deep learning models for these problems is a barrier for their adoption. In this work, we study the application of different semi-supervised learning techniques to this problem when we have a small amount of annotated data. In this study, we have used the Kvasir-SEG data set, taking only 60 and 120 annotated images and studying the behaviour of the Data Distillation, Model Distillation, and Data & Model distillation methods in both cases, using 10 different architectures. The results show that as we increase the number of initially annotated data, most models obtained better results, but two of them performed worse in the baseline case. Furthermore, we can conclude that the Data Distillation method increases the performance of the models a 48.6% and 30.6% on average using 60 and 120 annotated images respectively. Finally, using only 12% of the annotated data and applying Data Distillation, the results obtained are not very far from those obtained by training the models with the fully annotated dataset. For all these reasons, we conclude that the Data Distillation method is a good tool in semantic segmentation problems when the number of initially annotated images is small.

Keywords: Semantic Segmentation · Semi-Supervised Learning · Distillation methods · Gastrointestinal disease

1 Introduction

Cancer is the main cause of death in the world, with almost 10 million deaths in 2020 [22]. It is estimated that one in five inhabitants of the planet suffers from it at some point in their life and it is expected that more than 30 new million people will be affected by this disease by 2040 [22]. Among all the types of cancer that exist, colorectal cancer is one of the most important, being the second most common in women and the third most common among men [21]. One of the most important indicators of colorectal cancer is the existence of polyps, which are an abnormal growth of mucous membrane tissue that lines the inside of the gastrointestinal tract and, sometimes, can be cancerous. Early detection of these polyps has a huge impact on the survival of people suffering this type of cancer, so it is essential to detect and remove these polyps at an early stage [8].

The gold standard for detecting these polyps is colonoscopy [17]. In fact, polyps are detected for almost 50% of 50-year-olds who undergo this procedure. However, a colonoscopy is a visual test that is tedious, time-consuming, requires expert knowledge, and is subject to clinician bias and inter-observer variation. In addition, several studies manifest that between 14% and 30% of polyps are not detected using this procedure [24]. Therefore, the use of different techniques that allow the automatic detection of polyps at an early stage can play a crucial role in the prevention of colorectal cancer and patients' survival. This polyp detection can be seen as a semantic segmentation problem, which consists of assigning each pixel in the image a predefined label [7], in this case polyp or background.

Currently, deep learning methods are the state of the art approach to address semantic segmentation problems in medicine; for instance, deep cascade neural networks have been used to segment gliomas in the brain from MRI images [4], Soulami et al. used a U-Net model to segment mammograms [20], and, finally, Mei et al. and Wu et al. do a survey of polyps segmentation in [14] and [25] respectively. However, one of the main barriers to successfully apply these deep learning methods is the need of a large amount of annotated data. This annotation process means a considerable effort for experts. A solution proposed in the literature to deal with this challenge is the use of semi-supervised methods that allow us to extract knowledge from annotated and unannotated data, reducing the amount of annotated data necessary to train these models [27]. Among semi-supervised methods, distillation methods are a well known technique widely applied in classification problems [12]; however, its application in the context of semantic segmentation is not straightforward. In some works, distillation techniques have been used for semantic segmentation problems, for instance, in [1] Amirkhani et al. applied a teacher-student approach via multi teacher knowledge distillation; You et al. [26] developed a framework that employs unsupervised training using Contrastive Voxel-Wise Representation Distillation to increase the performance of models in semantic segmentation problems; a knowledge distillation method using a novel loss term for solving unpaired multi-modal segmentation was developed in [5]; and a pixel-wise similarity distillation module that utilises residual attention maps to capture more detailed spatial dependencies across multiple layers was proposed in [6]. In most of these papers, a teacher-student-based approach is used, in which a large model, teacher, is trained on a large dataset and its knowledge is distilled to a smaller model, student, on the target problem. However, there are not many examples where two semi-supervised techniques (data distillation and model distillation) widely used for image classification are applied to deal with semantic segmentation problems.

In this paper, we conduct a study of different distillation methods applied to the context of polyp segmentation. In particular, the contribution of this work is threefold. First, we study the performance of several state-of-the-art segmentation models when applied to polyp segmentation working with a small amount of images. Second, we study three semi-supervised learning techniques based on the distillation method to analyse the improvement that can be achieved for polyp segmentation. Finally, all the code associated with this project has been publicly released in GitHub[1] so the proposed methods can be applied to other contexts.

The rest of the paper is organised as follows: in Sect. 2, we describe the biological and computational materials and methods employed in our work. Subsequently, in Sect. 3, the results of the experiments are presented and discussed. The paper ends with a section with the final conclusions and the further work.

2   Materials and Methods

2.1   Dataset

As we have explained in the introduction, the objective of this work is to test the performance of distillation techniques when applied to the semantic segmentation of polyps. To this aim, we have selected the widely used Kvasir-SEG dataset [13].

The Kvasir-SEG dataset has 1,000 colonoscopy images with polyps, from the Kvasir-V2 dataset [16], see Fig. 1. These images range in size from 332×487 to 1920×1072 pixels, and images are encoded using JPG compression. For their annotation, a team was formed with an engineer and a doctor who manually outlined the margins of all the polyps in the 1,000 images. The annotations were subsequently reviewed by an experienced gastroenterologist. These annotations were exported to a 1-bit colour depth image, with the polyp in white and the background in black, see Fig. 1. This data is organised into two folders: one for the images and another for the corresponding masks, each data sharing the name and encoding (JPG).

In order to evaluate the different methods we have randomly selected 20 images that form our test set. With the remaining 980 images, we have conducted two experiments. In the first experiment, we have randomly picked 60 images that form our training set, having a typical split of 75–25 train-validation, leaving the remaining 920 images unlabelled and used for applying semi-supervised learning methods. In the second experiment, we have proceed in the same way but randomly picking 120 images for training, having a split of 85–15 train-validation.

2.2   Base Training Procedure

We have studied the behaviour of 10 different semantic segmentation networks, see Table 1. All the networks used in our experiments are implemented in Pytorch [15], and have been trained thanks to the functionality of the FastAI library [10] using a GPU Nvidia RTX 2080 Ti with 11 GB RAM.

---

[1] https://github.com/adines/polyp-semi-seg.

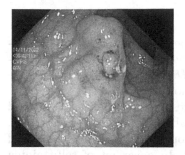 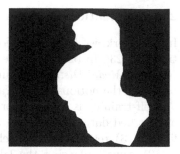

Fig. 1. Example of an image of the Kvasir-SEG dataset on the left and its respective mask on the right. The black colour on the mask represents the background and the white colour represents the segmented polyp.

Table 1. Segmentation architectures and backbones used int his work along with their FLOPS and parameters.

Architecture	Backbone	FLOPS (G)	Parameters (M)
CGNet	CGNet	1.4	0.5
DeepLabV3+	ResNet50	14.8	28.7
DenseASPP	ResNet50	14.1	29.1
FPENet	FPENet	0.3	0.1
HRNet	hrnet_w48	36.6	65.8
LEDNet	ResNet50	2.5	2.3
MANet	ResNet50	29.1	147.4
OCNet	ResNet50	16.9	35.9
PAN	ResNet50	13.6	24.3
U-Net	ResNet50	48.5	13.4

In order to train the models, we have used the transfer-learning method presented in [10]. This is a two-stage procedure that starts from a model pretrained, and can be summarised as follows. In the first stage, we replace the head of the model (that is, the layers that give us the classification of each pixel of the image), with a new head adapted to the number of classes of each particular dataset. Then, we train these new layers (the rest of the layers stay frozen) with the data of each particular dataset for two epochs. In the second stage, we unfreeze the whole model and retrain all the layers of the model with the new data for twenty epochs. In order to find a suitable learning rate for both the first and second stages, we select the learning rate that decreases the loss to the minimum possible value using the algorithm presented in [19]. Moreover, we employ early stopping based on monitoring the Dice coefficient, and data augmentation [18] (using flips, rotations, zooms and lighting transformations) to prevent overfitting.

2.3   Distillation Methods

In this work, we have analysed different semi-supervised methods based in distillation [23]. In particular, we will compare three different methods: *Data Distillation*, *Model Distillation*, and *Data & Model Distillation*; these methods are based on the notions of self-training and distillation.

Self-training is a basic approach that (1) defines a base model that is trained on labelled data, (2) uses the model to predict labels for unlabelled data, and, finally, (3) retrains the model with the most confident predictions produced in (2); thus, enlarging the labelled training set. In a variant of self-training called distillation [9], a big model is used for (1) and (2), whereas a faster and smaller model than the model trained in (1) is employed in (3). Data and model distillation are also two forms of self-training. In the case of Data Distillation [11] (1) a base model is trained, (2) this model is used to label new images using multiple transformations of each image, and (3) a new model is trained in both, the initial labelled images and the automatically annotated images in (2), see Fig. 2. In the case of Model Distillation [2] (1) several models are trained in the initial annotated images, (2) these model are ensembled to label new images, and (3) a new model is trained in both, the initial labelled images and the automatically annotated images in (2), see Fig. 3. Both techniques can also be combined in a technique called Data & Model Distillation [11], see Fig. 4. In order to train both the base models used in the semi-supervised methods and the target models obtained from Step (3), we have used the two-phase training procedure explained in the previous section.

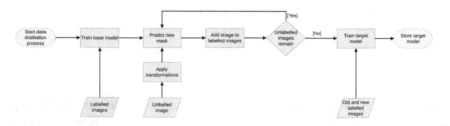

Fig. 2. Data Distillation method workflow.

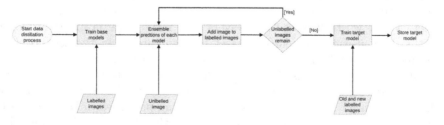

Fig. 3. Model Distillation method workflow.

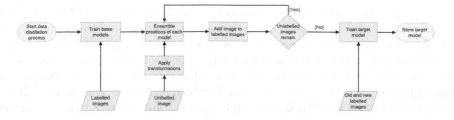

Fig. 4. Data & Model Distillation method workflow.

From the proposed distillation methods, we have conducted the following semi-supervised learning experiments. First of all, we have tested the performance of the aforementioned semantic segmentation networks when the number of annotated data is scarce. In the second experiment, we have applied Data Distillation by taking as base model the best model obtained in the previous approach and using 5 different transformations (horizontal flips, vertical flips, horizontal and vertical flips, blurring and gamma correction). In the third experiment, we have used a combination of the three models with the best performance in the first approach; that is, we applied Model Distillation. The fourth experiment uses Data & Model distillation; that is a mixture of the previous two approaches, based on the three best models of the first approach and the 5 transformations used in the Data Distillation. Finally, we have tested the performance of the networks using the full annotated data set, to see what is the maximum performance that could be obtained with each network. These experiments have been compared using the Dice coefficient [3] that is defined as follows:

$$Dice\ score\ (A, B) = \frac{2\mid A \cap B \mid}{\mid A \mid + \mid B \mid}$$

where A and B are the ground truth and the predicted area respectively.

3   Results

In this section, we show the results obtained in the different experiments. We have carried out the first block of experiments using only 60 annotated images as a training set and, leaving the rest of the images unlabelled to evaluate the distillation methods. In view of these experiments, see Table 2, we can confirm that the models are not accurate when applying plain training with a small dataset of images, being HRNet the only model that achieved a Dice score over 65%. We focus now on the results obtained by the different distillation methods. We can conclude that the Data Distillation method increases the performance of most models greatly (48.6% on average). In particular, the U–Net architecture increased its performance a 183.5% reaching a dice score of 73.95%; this fact is due to the large size of the network and the need for a greater number of data for its training. On the contrary, the Model Distillation and Data & Model Distillation approaches did not improve the results of the models, worsening the performance of the models in almost all cases. This may be because, by combining the predictions of 3 base models, which have a low Dice score (HRNet 65.87, CGNet 57.63 and MANet 56.35); the annotations obtained are not correct and worsen the performance of the new trained models.

In the second set of experiments, we have worked with 120 annotated images as a training set, twice as many as in the previous case, to check whether increasing the number of initially annotated images also improves the performance of the models and distillation methods. As we can see in Table 3, if we increase the number of initially annotated images, the base performance of the models improves in almost all cases, with the exception of DenseASPP and FPENet. Furthermore, the same pattern is repeated as in the previous case, obtaining good results in the case of the Data Distillation method, but not for the Model Distillation and Model & Data Distillation methods. Namely, with the Data Distillation method, an improvement of 30.6% on average with respect to the base training is again obtained. The best results are again obtained using the U-Net architecture and the Data Distillation method.

Table 2. Dice coefficient for each architecture and each distillation method, using 60 annotated images. Best result is highlighted in bold face.

Model	Baseline	Data Dist.	Model Dist.	Data-Model Dist.
CGNet	57.63	73.34	14.9	37.42
DeepLab	44.58	68.5	37.37	34.01
DenseASPP	46.94	70.45	0	0
FPENet	46.98	61.88	39.52	**44.27**
HRNet	**65.87**	66.62	14.5	3.22
LEDNet	38.47	69.05	29.8	17.75
MANet	56.35	70.71	0	0
OCNet	42.67	67.47	29.98	3.13
PAN	44.72	33.83	7.49	9.12
U-Net	26.08	**73.95**	**43.27**	0.8

Table 3. Dice coefficient for each architecture and each distillation method, using 120 annotated images. Best result is highlighted in bold face.

Model	Baseline	Data Dist.	Model Dist.	Data-Model Dist.
CGNet	58.51	74.89	44.11	**51.88**
DeepLab	50.61	79.3	41.8	42.95
DenseASPP	41.23	74.83	41.79	36.06
FPENet	38.63	66.97	31.55	42.38
HRNet	70.11	72.14	**46.13**	21.12
LEDNet	39.88	50.77	4.45	17.99
MANet	60.18	70.74	43.07	3.6
OCNet	44.94	68.95	6.72	5.4
PAN	59.45	37.01	0.01	9.2
U-Net	**76.98**	**79.45**	36.2	34.56

Finally, we have compared the performance of the methods studied in the first two experiments with respect to training the models with the fully annotated dataset. Specifically, in Table 4, we show the best result obtained by each model in each of the experiment blocks compared to the value obtained when training such a network with the fully annotated dataset. In view of these results, we can conclude that in most cases as we increase the number of images initially annotated, we obtain better results, with increases of up to 15.8% in the best case. Furthermore, in many cases the result obtained with 12.24% of the annotated dataset, 120 images, is close to the result obtained when training the same model with the fully annotated dataset.

Table 4. Comparison of the best results obtained with 60 annotated images, 120 annotated images and the fully annotated dataset (980 images). Best result highlighted in bold face.

Model	60 Images	120 Images	Full
CGNet	73.34	74.89	89.32
DeepLab	68.5	79.3	86.84
DenseASPP	70.45	74.83	72.32
FPENet	61.88	66.97	78.81
HRNet	66.62	72.14	72.43
LEDNet	69.05	50.77	47.36
MANet	70.71	70.74	65.22
OCNet	67.47	68.95	86.25
PAN	44.72	59.45	36.06
U-Net	**73.95**	**79.45**	**89.33**

4   Conclusions and Further Work

In this work, we have studied the application of different distillation techniques; namely, Data Distillation and Model Distillation techniques, to the semantic segmentation of polyps. Firstly, we have verified that as we increase the number of initially annotated data, the performance of the models is improved. Secondly, we have shown that the Data Distillation method serves to improve the initial models by increasing the performance of the models by an average of 48.6% with respect to the baseline training when using 60 annotated images, and by 30.6% when using 120. Finally, we can conclude that using only a 12% of the annotated data and applying Data Distillation, the results obtained are close from those obtained by training the models with the fully annotated dataset, and even in some cases improving them. For all these reasons, we can conclude that the Data Distillation method is a good tool in semantic segmentation problems when the number of initially annotated images is scarce, as occurs in many problems in the biomedical field. On the contrary, the results obtained with the Model Distillation and Data & Model Distillation methods show that these methods are not useful in this context.

In the future, we want to study how semi-supervised methods can help in other semantic segmentation problems where annotated data is scarce. In addition, we want to create a tool that allows users to use these semi-supervised methods in a simple way.

Acknowledgements. Partially supported by Ministerio de Ciencia e Innovación [PID2020-115225RB-I00/AEI/10.13039/501100011033], and by Agencia de Desarrollo Econonómico de La Rioja [ADER 2022-I-IDI-00015].

References

1. Amirkhani, A., Khosravian, A., Masih-Tehrani, M., Kashiani, H.: Robust semantic segmentation with multi-teacher knowledge distillation. IEEE Access **9**, 119049–119066 (2021). https://doi.org/10.1109/ACCESS.2021.3107841
2. Bucila, C., Caruana, R., Niculescu-Mizil, A.: Model compression: making big, slow models practical. In: 12th International Conference on Knowledge Discovery and Data Mining, KDD 2006, pp. 535–541 (2006)
3. Carass, A., et al.: Evaluating white matter lesion segmentations with refined Sørensen-Dice analysis. Sci. Rep. **10**(1), 8242 (2020)
4. Cui, S., Mao, L., Jiang, J., Liu, C., Xiong, S., et al.: Automatic semantic segmentation of brain gliomas from MRI images using a deep cascaded neural network. J. Healthc. Eng. **2018**, 4940593 (2018)
5. Dou, Q., Liu, Q., Heng, P.A., Glocker, B.: Unpaired multi-modal segmentation via knowledge distillation. IEEE Trans. Med. Imaging **39**(7), 2415–2425 (2020). https://doi.org/10.1109/TMI.2019.2963882
6. Feng, Y., Sun, X., Diao, W., Li, J., Gao, X.: Double similarity distillation for semantic image segmentation. IEEE Trans. Image Process. **30**, 5363–5376 (2021). https://doi.org/10.1109/TIP.2021.3083113

7. Gonzalez, R., Woods, R.: Digital Image Processing. Prentice Hall, Upper Saddle River (2002)
8. Haggar, F.A., Boushey, R.P.: Colorectal cancer epidemiology: incidence, mortality, survival, and risk factors. Clin. Colon. Rectal. Surg. **22**(04), 191–197 (2009)
9. Hinton, G., et al.: Distilling the knowledge in a neural network (2015)
10. Howard, J., Gugger, S.: Fastai: a layered API for deep learning. Information **11**, 108 (2020). https://doi.org/10.3390/info11020108
11. Huang, R., Noble, J.A., Namburete, A.I.L.: Omni-supervised learning: scaling up to large unlabelled medical datasets. In: Frangi, A.F., Schnabel, J.A., Davatzikos, C., Alberola-López, C., Fichtinger, G. (eds.) MICCAI 2018. LNCS, vol. 11070, pp. 572–580. Springer, Cham (2018). https://doi.org/10.1007/978-3-030-00928-1_65
12. Inés, A., Domínguez, C., Heras, J., Mata, E., Pascual, V.: Biomedical image classification made easier thanks to transfer and semi-supervised learning. Comput. Methods Programs Biomed. **198**, 105782 (2021)
13. Jha, D., et al.: Kvasir-SEG: a segmented polyp dataset. In: Ro, Y.M., et al. (eds.) MMM 2020. LNCS, vol. 11962, pp. 451–462. Springer, Cham (2020). https://doi.org/10.1007/978-3-030-37734-2_37
14. Mei, J., et al.: A survey on deep learning for polyp segmentation: techniques, challenges and future trends (2024)
15. Paszke, A., et al.: PyTorch: an imperative style, high-performance deep learning library. In: Wallach, H., Larochelle, H., Beygelzimer, A., d'Alché-Buc, F., Fox, E., Garnett, R. (eds.) Advances in Neural Information Processing Systems, vol. 32, pp. 8024–8035. Curran Associates, Inc. (2019)
16. Pogorelov, K., et al.: KVASIR: a multi-class image dataset for computer aided gastrointestinal disease detection. In: Proceedings of the 8th ACM on Multimedia Systems Conference, MMSys 2017, pp. 164–169. ACM, New York (2017). https://doi.org/10.1145/3083187.3083212
17. Secretariat, M.A.: Screening methods for early detection of colorectal cancers and polyps: summary of evidence-based analyses. Ontario Health Technol. Assess. Ser. **9**(6), 1 (2009)
18. Simard, P., Steinkraus, D., Platt, J.C.: Best practices for convolutional neural networks applied to visual document analysis. In: Proceedings of the 12th International Conference on Document Analysis and Recognition (ICDAR 2003), vol. 2, pp. 958–964 (2003)
19. Smith, L.: Cyclical learning rates for training neural networks. In: IEEE Winter Conference on Applications of Computer Vision, WACV 2017, pp. 464–472 (2017). https://doi.org/10.1109/WACV.2017.58
20. Soulami, K.B., Kaabouch, N., Saidi, M.N., Tamtaoui, A.: Breast cancer: one-stage automated detection, segmentation, and classification of digital mammograms using UNet model based-semantic segmentation. Biomed. Sig. Process. Control **66**, 102481 (2021)
21. Sung, H., et al.: Global cancer statistics 2020: GLOBOCAN estimates of incidence and mortality worldwide for 36 cancers in 185 countries. CA: A Cancer J. Clin. **71**(3), 209–249 (2021)
22. The Cancer Atlas: The burden of cancer (2024). https://canceratlas.cancer.org/the-burden/the-burden-of-cancer/
23. Triguero, I., et al.: Self-labeled techniques for semi-supervised learning: taxonomy, software and empirical study. Knowl. Inf. Syst. **42**, 245–284 (2015). https://doi.org/10.1007/s10115-013-0706-y
24. Van Rijn, J.C., et al.: Polyp miss rate determined by tandem colonoscopy: a systematic review. Official J. Am. Coll. Gastroenterol.—ACG **101**(2), 343–350 (2006)

25. Wu, Z., Lv, F., Chen, C., Hao, A., Li, S.: Colorectal polyp segmentation in the deep learning era: a comprehensive survey (2024)
26. You, C., Zhou, Y., Zhao, R., Staib, L., Duncan, J.S.: SimCVD: simple contrastive voxel-wise representation distillation for semi-supervised medical image segmentation. IEEE Trans. Med. Imaging **41**(9), 2228–2237 (2022). https://doi.org/10.1109/TMI.2022.3161829
27. Zhu, X., Goldberg, A.B.: Introduction to Semi-Supervised Learning. Synthesis Lectures on Artificial Intelligence and Machine Learning. Morgan & Claypool Publishers (2009)

Community-Based Topic Modeling
with Contextual Outlier Handling

Cesar Andrade[1]([✉]) [iD], Rita P. Ribeiro[1,3] [iD], and João Gama[2,3] [iD]

[1] Computer Science Department, Faculty of Sciences, University of Porto,
4169-007 Porto, Portugal
up202101459@edu.fc.up.pt
[2] Faculty of Economics, University of Porto, 4200-464 Porto, Portugal
[3] INESC TEC, Porto, Portugal

Abstract. E-commerce has become an essential aspect of modern life, providing consumers globally with convenience and accessibility. However, the high volume of short and noisy product descriptions in text streams of massive e-commerce platforms translates into an increased number of clusters, presenting challenges for standard model-based stream clustering algorithms. Standard LDA-based methods often lead to clusters dominated by single elements, effectively failing to manage datasets with varied cluster sizes. Our proposed Community-Based Topic Modeling with Contextual Outlier Handling (CB-TMCOH) algorithm introduces an approach to outlier detection in text data using transformer models for similarity calculations and graph-based clustering. This method efficiently separates outliers and improves clustering in large text datasets, demonstrating its utility not only in e-commerce applications but also proving effective for news and tweets datasets.

Keywords: Short Text Stream Clustering · Contextual Outliers · Bert

1 Introduction

The surge in online shopping has spotlighted the critical role of product descriptions in e-commerce platforms, where clear and informative descriptions significantly influence consumer decisions and enhance user experience. However, the vast and diverse nature of these descriptions, often generated by numerous users across various marketplaces, introduces a significant challenge. These user-generated descriptions are not standardized and frequently include abbreviations, leading to a complex array of data that requires sophisticated handling.

Clustering is a pivotal technique in managing product descriptions, serving multiple purposes such as product recommendation, efficient product grouping for search engines, and fraud detection systems. Among the clustering methods, Latent Dirichlet Allocation (LDA) [1–4] has gained traction for unsupervised clustering tasks.

Guided by the Brazilian NF-e Project, which manages unstructured, noisy, short-text data in e-commerce environments, Andrade et al. [5] proposed the

A. Alonso-Betanzos et al. (Eds.): CAEPIA 2024, LNAI 14640, pp. 173–183, 2024.
https://doi.org/10.1007/978-3-031-62799-6_18

Topic Model with Contextual Outlier Handling (TMCOH), which enhanced the application of LDA for clustering, with a focus on contextual outlier detection. It utilizes pre-trained DistilBert embeddings to enhance its clustering capability. However, their evaluations indicate that leveraging this pre-trained model does not yield significant comparative improvements compared to TFIDF.

We introduce CB-TMCOH, a novel approach based on TMCOH, which employs community cluster formation to address contextual outliers. By grouping such outliers based on contextual similarities, we enhance outlier detection and management using fine-tuned DistilBert embeddings for similarity analysis.

This paper is organized as follows. We review related work in Sect. 2, present our method in Sect. 3, and detail our experimental study and dataset in Sect. 4. We report the results of our experimental study in Sect. 5 and conclude the paper with suggestions for future research directions in Sect. 6.

2   Related Work

In the realm of clustering short text streams, two prominent areas of study emerge similarity-based and model-based approaches. Similarity-based clustering hinges on pairwise similarities, while model-based clustering relies on statistical models that define data distribution.

Recent advances, incorporating pre-trained language models like BERT [6] coupled with clustering algorithms such as HDBSCAN [7], have showcased promise in text clustering tasks. BERT generates contextual embeddings, allowing deeper context understanding and language structure modeling [8]. These embeddings serve as inputs for clustering algorithms. Studie [9] has demonstrated the superiority of combining BERT embeddings and HDBSCAN for short text clustering over traditional methods.

Latent Dirichlet Allocation (LDA) [10] is a model-based stream clustering technique that has inspired numerous extensions to address challenges related to topic evolution, semantic representation, and the dynamic nature of text streams. Initially, models like DCT [11] aimed to simplify topic assignments by assigning a single topic to each document but lacked adaptability to changing topic counts. In response, MSTREAM [4] emerged, managing topic counts by discarding outdated batch documents and adapting to evolving topics. However, MSTREAM's reliance on single-term document representation limited its ability to navigate semantic spaces effectively, impacting cluster purity. DCSS [3] and FASTSTREAM [2] marked significant milestones by demonstrating superior stability and adaptability and introducing efficiency improvements, respectively.

Recent models like OSDM [1] and OSGM [12] introduced evolving term co-occurrence matrices to capture dynamic semantic representation, presenting innovative approaches to understanding term relationships. Despite these advancements, challenges in managing cluster quality and performance persist due to data scale. Kumar et al. [13] continue with EINDM, incorporating a context-enhanced Dirichlet approach for improved clustering accuracy, leveraging window-based semantic term representations and episodic inference.

Andrade et al. [5] introduced the TMCOH method to handle contextual outliers and large datasets. It integrates the Dirichlet process with contextual outlier detection, building upon the MSTREAM model. While it excels at processing smaller clusters and contextual outliers, incorporating BERT embeddings yielded limited benefits.

3   Our Proposal

In response to the limitation of TMCOH [5], we propose a new approach that leverages the capabilities of pre-trained BERT models beyond mere embeddings. We introduce the CB-TMCOH, a new method of detecting outliers in text data using pairwise similarity measurements. As illustrated in Fig. 1, it operates by taking a random sample from a collection of documents and applying the one-pass DPMM [14] clustering method to assign initial clusters to the documents in the sample. It then employs a combination of transformer-based similarity evaluation and graph-based clustering techniques to identify clusters in a corpus of documents.

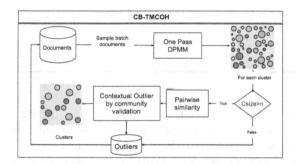

Fig. 1. CB-TMCOH Method.

Algorithm 1 presents the CB-TMCOH. Initially, it compares all documents pairwise to calculate similarity scores using a pre-trained transformer model. These scores are then used to construct a graph, where each document represents a node, and edges signify document similarity. The Louvain algorithm is applied to this graph to detect clusters or communities, with a threshold determining which pairs of documents are connected by edges. Resulting clusters are assigned new labels, augmented by pre-existing ones to ensure uniqueness. Our method can filter out outliers by labelling clusters that appear only once, effectively tagging them as outliers. The algorithm concludes by providing updated cluster labels for each document, facilitating grouping similar texts while concurrently identifying outliers.

For sentence similarity evaluation, the CB-TMCOH method repurposes the DistilBERT model, originally developed for general NLP tasks, to specialize

---

Algorithm 1: CB-TMCOH - based on MSTREAM [4]

Input : $\vec{d}$ - documents, c_{size} - threshold for cluster size, b_{size} - initial batch size, thr -
similarity threshold

Output : $\vec{Z}$ - cluster assignments for documents

1 **begin**
2   **while** $|\vec{d}| > 0$ **do**
3      $\vec{d_t}$ = Sample b_{size} from $\vec{d}$
4   Remove $\vec{d_t}$ from $\vec{d}$
5      $\vec{z_t}$ = MSTREAM($\vec{d_t}$) // cluster assignments for documents in bach t
6   **for** *each cluster* $z \in \vec{z_t}$ **do**
7   **if** $|z| < c_{size}$ **then**
8   **for** *each document* $d \in z$ **do**
9   Append d to $\vec{d}$
10   **end**
11   Remove z from $\vec{z_t}$
12   **else**
13          $simScores$ = PAIRWISESIMILARITY(z)
14          $\vec{z_r}, \vec{o}$ = COMMUNITYVALIDATION($z, simScores, thr$)
15   **for** *each document* $d \in \vec{o}$ **do**
16   Append d to $\vec{d}$
17   Remove d from $\vec{z_t}$
18   **end**
19   Remove z from $\vec{z_t}$
20   Append $\vec{z_r}$ to $\vec{z_t}$
21   **end**
22   **end**
23   b_{size} = ADAPTATIVEBATCHSIZE()
24   Append $\vec{z_t}$ to $\vec{Z}$
25   **end**
26   **return** $\vec{Z}$
27 **end**

---

in sentence similarity classification. We adapted DistilBERT, which was not initially designed for direct sentence similarity assessment, by training it on triplets of sentences labelled with their similarity. Through fine-tuning, Distil-BERT learned to discern semantic similarities and differences between sentences. This effectively transformed it into a sentence similarity classifier, showcasing the adaptability of transformer-based models for specialized tasks like sentence similarity analysis in NLP.

4 Experimental Study

In this experimental study, we investigate the impact of integrating a BERT-based similarity classifier on the efficacy of cluster formation using Latent Dirichlet Allocation (LDA) methods and community analysis through the Louvain algorithm. Our focus is on evaluating the performance of the CB-TMCOH method and understanding how a finely tuned similarity classifier influences community formation.

4.1 The Datasets

We used diverse real-world short text datasets listed in Table 1.

Algorithm 2: COMMUNITYVALIDATION

Input   : z - clusters, simScores - similarity scores, thr - the threshold for similarity
Output : $\vec{z_r}$ - refined clusters, $\vec{o}$ - indices of outlier sentences
1 **begin**
2 $\quad$ G = EmptyGraph()
3 $\quad$ Add documents in z as nodes to G
4 $\quad$ **for** *every pair (s1, s2) of z* **do**
5 $\quad\quad$ **if** *simScores(s1, s2)* $\geq$ *thr* **then**
6 $\quad\quad\quad|\quad$ Add edge between s1 and s2 to G
7 $\quad\quad$ **end**
8 $\quad$ **end**
9 $\quad$ $\vec{z_r}$ = LouvainCommunityDetection(G)
10 $\quad$ $\vec{o}$ = []
11 $\quad$ **for** *each cluster z in* $\vec{z_r}$ **do**
12 $\quad\quad$ **if** $|z|$ == 1 **then**
13 $\quad\quad\quad$ Append z to $\vec{o}$
14 $\quad\quad\quad$ Remove z from $\vec{z_r}$
15 $\quad\quad$ **end**
16 $\quad$ **end**
17 $\quad$ **return** $\vec{z_r}$, $\vec{o}$
18 **end**

Namely, the two datasets referred to in Andrade et al. [5] concerning the Brazilian NF-e Project They contain product descriptions that concisely summarise invoice items, while NCM (Nomenclatura Comum do Mercosul) categorize products for customs purposes. NCM codes are represented in two formats:

- NCM4: the first 4 digits of the NCM code, giving a broad product category.
- NCM8: the full 8-digit code, offering detailed classification information.

From public datasets, we utilized four real-world short text datasets, comprising two primary datasets and their temporal variants, as follows:

- Tweets: tweets from 269 queries from the TREC 2011–2015[1] microblog track.
- News: news headlines organized into 152 clusters and collect by [15].
- Tweets-T and News-T: temporal variants for the time-sensitive nature of topics created by ordering the original datasets by topic, divided into 16 segments, and shuffled independently.

4.2   Experimental Setup

We explored various techniques and methods to assess their effectiveness in clustering, focusing on LDA methods. In our case study, we evaluated clustering performance using hyper-parameters outlined in Table 2.

We assessed results using standard metrics: Homogeneity (H), Completeness (C), Normalized Mutual Information (NMI), and Purity (P). H measures cluster purity, while C assesses class representation within clusters. NMI provides a score reflecting the similarity between true and assigned labels. P evaluates clustering quality based on dominant class proportion. Additionally, we used AIC to evaluate tradeoff between the Homogeneity (H) and the number of clusters (K),

---

[1] http://trec.nist.gov/data/microblog.html.

Table 1. Characteristics of the datasets, where D represents the number of documents, K the number of clusters, V the size of the vocabulary, and "Avg Len" the average length of the documents.

Dataset	D	K	V	Avg Len
NCM4	475,565	706	3,076,252	6.47
NCM8	475,565	2,404	3,076,252	6.47
News	11,109	152	8,110	6.23
News-T	11,109	147	8,110	6.23
Tweets	30,322	269	12,301	7.97
Tweets-T	30,322	265	12,301	7.97

Table 2. Clustering Methods and Hyper-parameters

Method	Hyper-parameters
MSTREAM	$\alpha = 0.07$, $\beta = 0.002$, iterations $= 1$
DCSS	$\alpha = 0.07$, $\beta = 0.002$
OSDM	$\alpha = 0.04$, $\beta = 5e^{-4}$
EINDM	$\alpha = 0.04$, $\beta = 5e^{-4}$, $\lambda = 6e^{-6}$, $\Gamma = -1$, $\rho = 60$, $\psi = 500$
TMCOH	$c_{size} = 2$, $\alpha = 0.07$, $\beta = 0.002$, $b_{size} = 1000$
CB-TMCOH	$c_{size} = 2$, $\alpha = 0.07$, $\beta = 0.002$, $b_{size} = 1000$

as [16], balancing model fit and complexity for better analysis. We also report the number of clusters (k) and the number of true labels (kTrue).

Our experimental protocol for the CB-TMCOH method employed different strategies tailored to each dataset to ensure optimal performance. Specifically, for the NCM4 and NCM8 datasets, a similarity classifier was trained on 20 million instances. A classifier similarity threshold of 0.9. For other datasets such as News, News-T, Tweets, and Tweets-T, the similarity classifier was trained with 1 million instances. A higher classifier DistilBERT similarity threshold of 0.99 was employed to delineate communities. For the models MSTREAM, DCSS, OSDM, and EINDM, the selection of parameters such as α (document-topic density), β (topic-word density), λ (decay value), Γ (feature threshold), ρ (episodic memory), and ψ (episodic memory batch) is based on the recommendations provided by their respective authors.

5   Results

5.1   NCM4 and NCM8 Datasets

In our evaluation of clustering methods across datasets, we observed varied performance among different LDA approaches (Table 3).

Cluster Formation: According to Fig. 2, MSTREAM consistently generates a notable number of single-element clusters, particularly evident in the NCM4

Table 3. Performance measures obtained per dataset and by the LDA method.

Dataset	Method	H	C	NMI	P	AIC	k	kTrue
NCM4	TMCOH	0.831	0.773	0.801	0.602	**−0.678**	119	121
	DCSS	0.337	0.552	0.413	0.224	−0.660	110	214
	CB-TMCOH	**0.910**	**0.777**	**0.838**	0.796	−0.637	151	117
	FASTSTREAM	0.703	0.626	0.662	0.499	−0.335	379	214
	MSTREAM	0.969	0.690	0.807	**0.917**	0.174	779	214
	OSDM	0.545	0.513	0.528	0.502	2.131	2671	706
NCM8	TMCOH	0.839	**0.860**	0.849	0.565	**−0.678**	120	181
	DCSS	0.372	0.705	0.481	0.201	−0.658	110	387
	CB-TMCOH	0.914	0.849	**0.880**	0.783	−0.636	152	166
	FASTSTREAM	0.731	0.750	0.740	0.481	−0.337	378	387
	MSTREAM	**0.968**	0.796	0.873	**0.899**	0.175	779	387
	OSDM	0.566	0.597	0.581	0.423	2.135	2663	2404

and NCM8 datasets. This suggests a tendency towards fragmented clustering. In contrast, CB-TMCOH achieves a more balanced performance, effectively mitigating overly fragmented clusters while maintaining reasonable cluster purity. However, it tends to form smaller clusters.

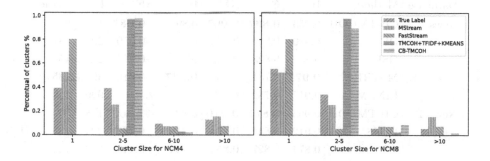

Fig. 2. Comparison of cluster sizes by True Label and clustering methods for NCM4 and NCM8 datasets at all batches.

Model Evaluation and Performance Comparison: AIC analysis highlights CB-TMCOH and TMCOH's superior efficiency compared to MSTREAM, indicating better optimization of cluster numbers without sacrificing model complexity. This underscores their ability to capture data structure effectively while avoiding overfitting. Additionally, CB-TMCOH outperforms existing LDA methods like TMCOH and FASTSTREAM, particularly regarding Completeness and Purity. This demonstrates its effectiveness in grouping similar elements while ensuring class exclusivity within clusters.

Overall Analysis: Our proposal exhibits enhanced performance over TMCOH, showcasing a better balance of NMI and purity. However, it forms smaller clusters than TMCOH, indicating a nuanced clustering behaviour favouring more cohesive groupings. CB-TMCOH maintains balanced performance across different datasets, even in more complex clustering scenarios like the NCM8 dataset. This underscores its versatility and effectiveness across varied data structures. In summary, our discussion highlights the strengths of CB-TMCOH in achieving balanced and effective clustering outcomes across diverse datasets while acknowledging its preference for smaller, more cohesive clusters. Integrating model evaluation with performance comparisons provides a comprehensive understanding of CB-TMCOH's capabilities and limitations.

5.2   News and Tweets Datasets

In this section, we analyze the clustering performance on News and Tweets datasets, focusing on the CB-TMCOH method and its comparison with other established LDA methods. The evaluation is consolidated into a table that offers a view of performance metrics across these datasets.

Table 4 serves as the basis for comparing the our method against others like DCSS, OSDM, MSTREAM, and EINDM across the News, News-T, Tweets, and Tweets-T datasets.

Table 4. Performance comparison of various methods on different datasets

Database	Method	H	C	NMI	Purity	AIC	k	kTrue
News	CB-TMCOH	0.953	**0.867**	**0.907**	0.895	**−0.987**	145	93
	DCSS	0.910	0.840	0.873	0.812	−0.680	226	137
	OSDM	0.884	0.823	0.852	0.808	−0.414	292	152
	MSTREAM	**0.971**	0.781	0.866	**0.937**	−0.015	393	135
	EINDM	0.917	0.782	0.844	0.854	2.303	999	152
News-T	CB-TMCOH	0.953	**0.871**	**0.910**	0.897	**−1.063**	148	95
	DCSS	0.912	0.841	0.875	0.819	−0.723	224	135
	OSDM	0.874	0.827	0.850	0.794	−0.419	286	151
	MSTREAM	**0.971**	0.779	0.865	**0.935**	0.076	394	136
	EINDM	0.951	0.793	0.865	0.922	2.245	870	152
Tweets	CB-TMCOH	0.920	**0.922**	**0.918**	0.832	**−0.762**	106	92
	DCSS	0.890	0.869	0.879	0.762	−0.606	231	205
	OSDM	0.891	0.856	0.873	0.830	−0.378	418	264
	MSTREAM	**0.975**	0.789	0.872	**0.936**	−0.229	536	204
	EINDM	0.953	0.759	0.845	0.917	2.388	2680	269
Tweets-T	CB-TMCOH	0.920	**0.918**	**0.916**	0.827	**−0.798**	110	95
	DCSS	0.892	0.870	0.880	0.766	−0.627	231	203
	OSDM	0.893	0.859	0.876	0.838	−0.368	418	259
	MSTREAM	**0.975**	0.790	0.872	**0.935**	−0.203	534	204
	EINDM	0.973	0.769	0.859	0.953	2.376	2398	269

AIC: The AIC values highlight the CB-TMCOH efficiency across News and Tweets datasets. Notably, it exhibits the lowest AIC scores, indicating an optimal balance between data fit and model simplicity.

Batch versus Online: The analysis of AIC values and the number of clusters reveals that while batch methods like CB-TMCOH, DCSS, and MSTREAM show greater efficiency for batch data, as seen through lower AIC values, online methods such as EINDM form a larger number of clusters with higher AICs when considering the entire dataset. This distinction does not merely suggest inefficiency on the part of online methods but highlights their capability to adapt and respond to the full scope of continuously evolving data. Thus, when selecting between batch and online methods, it's crucial to weigh model efficiency within batch data against the broader adaptability and responsiveness to the whole dataset offered by online methods.

Overall Analysis: In the News dataset, CB-TMCOH achieves notable scores, with an NMI of 0.907 and a Purity of 0.895, indicating its effective clustering performance. This method excels in these metrics and demonstrates robustness across different datasets, as evidenced by its performance in the Tweets dataset, where it achieves an NMI of 0.918 and a Purity of 0.832.

Moreover, the table extends the analysis to include a comparison with additional LDA methods, revealing that our approach consistently performs well. It demonstrates competitive or superior performance in NMI and Purity metrics, particularly standing out in the News-T dataset with an NMI of 0.910 and a Purity of 0.897. This suggests CB-TMCOH's capability in clustering, matching or surpassing other methods in all metrics.

6   Conclusions

The CB-TMCOH algorithm, an evolution of the previously proposed TMCOH algorithm, effectively employs pre-trained BERT models for enhanced text data clustering. The Louvain algorithm innovatively detects outliers through pairwise similarity measurements and graph-based community detection. This method efficiently handles dynamic and short content datasets, outperforming existing LDA methods.

Our method excels in clustering complex datasets, especially in product descriptions, compared to more straightforward news and tweet data. Its advanced outlier detection and community identification capabilities are particularly effective in navigating the nuanced language of product descriptions, showcasing its potential in detailed data analysis applications like e-commerce and targeted marketing.

Acknowledgments. The authors wish to clarify that the first author received support from Amazonas State Government/Brazil for this research project.

References

1. Kumar, J., Shao, J., Uddin, S., Ali, W.: An online semantic-enhanced Dirichlet model for short text stream clustering. In: Proceedings of the 58th Annual Meeting of the Association for Computational Linguistics, pp. 766–776. Association for Computational Linguistics (2020)
2. Rakib, M.R.H., Asaduzzaman, M.: Fast clustering of short text streams using efficient cluster indexing and dynamic similarity thresholds. CoRR abs/2101.08595 (2021)
3. Xu, Y., Wang, S., Zhang, S., Wang, F.: Dynamic clustering for short text stream based on Dirichlet process. IEEE Access 10, 22852–22865 (2022)
4. Yin, J., Wang, J., Xu, W., Gao, M.: Model-based clustering of short text streams. In: 27th ACM International Conference on Information and Knowledge Management, pp. 697–706. ACM (2018)
5. Andrade, C., Ribeiro, R.P., Gama, J.: Topic model with contextual outlier handling: a study on electronic invoice product descriptions. In: Moniz, N., Vale, Z., Cascalho, J., Silva, C., Sebastião, R. (eds.) EPIA 2023. LNCS, vol. 14115, pp. 365–377. Springer, Cham (2023). https://doi.org/10.1007/978-3-031-49008-8_29
6. Devlin, J., Chang, M.-W., Lee, K., Toutanova, K.: BERT: pre-training of deep bidirectional transformers for language understanding. arXiv preprint arXiv:1810.04805 (2018)
7. Campello, R.J.G.B., Moulavi, D., Sander, J.: Density-based clustering based on hierarchical density estimates. In: Pei, J., Tseng, V.S., Cao, L., Motoda, H., Xu, G. (eds.) PAKDD 2013. LNCS (LNAI), vol. 7819, pp. 160–172. Springer, Heidelberg (2013). https://doi.org/10.1007/978-3-642-37456-2_14
8. Dai, Z., Callan, J.: Deeper text understanding for IR with contextual neural language modeling. In: Proceedings of the 42nd International ACM SIGIR Conference on Research and Development in Information Retrieval (2019)
9. Eklund, A., Forsman, M.: Topic modelling by clustering language model embeddings: human validation on an industry dataset. In: Proceedings of the 2022 Conference on Empirical Methods in Natural Language Processing: Industry Track, pp. 635–643 (2022)
10. Blei, D.M., Ng, A.Y., Jordan, M.I.: Latent Dirichlet allocation. J. Mach. Learn. Res. 3, 993–1022 (2003)
11. Liang, S., Yilmaz, E., Kanoulas, E.: Dynamic clustering of streaming short documents. In: Proceedings of the 22nd ACM SIGKDD International Conference on Knowledge Discovery and Data Mining, pp. 995–1004 (2016)
12. Kumar, J., Din, S.U., Yang, Q., Kumar, R., Shao, J.: An online semantic-enhanced graphical model for evolving short text stream clustering. IEEE Trans. Cybern. 52(12), 13809–13820 (2021)
13. Kumar, J., Shao, J., Kumar, R., Din, S.U., Mawuli, C.B., Yang, Q.: A context-enhanced Dirichlet model for online clustering in short text streams. Expert Syst. Appl. 228, 120262 (2023)
14. Yin, J., Wang, J.: A model-based approach for text clustering with outlier detection. In: 2016 IEEE 32nd International Conference on Data Engineering (ICDE), pp. 625–636. IEEE (2016)

15. Yin, J., Wang, J.: A Dirichlet multinomial mixture model-based approach for short text clustering. In: Proceedings of the 20th ACM SIGKDD International Conference on Knowledge Discovery and Data Mining, pp. 233–242 (2014)
16. Andrade, T., Cancela, B., Gama, J.: Discovering locations and habits from human mobility data. Ann. Telecommun. **75**, 505–521 (2020). https://doi.org/10.1007/s12243-020-00807-x

Toward Explaining Competitive Success in League of Legends: A Machine Learning Analysis

Francisco Javier Galán-Sales[(✉)] [iD], María Lourdes Linares-Barrera[iD],
Pablo Reina-Jiménez[iD], Ana Rodríguez-López[iD],
and Manuel Jesús Jiménez-Navarro[iD]

Department of Computer Languages and Systems, University of Seville,
41012 Seville, Spain
fgsales@us.es

Abstract. Machine learning techniques have recently transformed the way we analyze competitive games. However, accurately detecting the impact of different insights on match outcomes remains a challenge. This study focuses on League of Legends, a popular multiplayer online battle arena game known for its strategic depth and teamwork requirements. We aim to understand how various actions and strategies influence match results, using a dataset from professional tournaments. Factors like "building damage", "total gold", and "assists" are analyzed as predictors. We employ tree-based and linear models to predict outcomes, supplemented by SHapley Additive exPlanations for explaining both local and global model outcomes. Our article offers a generalizable match analysis approach, compares explainable methods, and delves into key determinants of victory. The results, showcasing a remarkable 98.8% accuracy with the top-performing model, provide strong support for our conclusions, underlining their reliability.

Keywords: Performance analysis · esports · feature importance · explainable machine learning

1 Introduction

League of Legends (LoL), a multiplayer online battle arena (MOBA) game developed by Riot Games[1], has become the cornerstone of competitive gaming. The game involves two teams of five players, each aiming to destroy the opposing Nexus, located in their base. Players choose from various Champions, categorized into roles like tanks, damage dealers, and supports, reflecting the diverse positions found in traditional sports. The gameplay takes place on the "Summoner's Rift" map, where strategic teamwork is crucial. As the game progresses, Champions grow stronger and unlock new abilities, emphasizing the importance of evolving strategies and team plays.

---

[1] https://www.riotgames.com.

The impact of LoL on esports is profound, with a large global audience and professional leagues worldwide, likening it to traditional sports in terms of structure, sponsorship, and player development. The strategic depth and team dynamics of the game resemble those in traditional sports, where success relies on well-coordinated team strategies and continuous skill development. The professional ecosystem in LoL, featuring players, coaches, analysts, and fans, mirrors that of traditional sports, requiring similar physical and mental skills. The major tournaments attract large audiences and significant financial stakes, highlighting its broad appeal and economic influence in the sports world.

Victory in LoL relies on a blend of strategic execution, individual skill, and team coordination, where success is achieved by leveraging team strengths and exploiting the weaknesses of opponents from champion selection through in-game strategies. Crucial elements include resource management, control of key map objectives, and balancing aggressive tactics with strategic caution. Analyzing player performance to identify strengths and weaknesses is vital in refining team strategies and maintaining a competitive edge. This continual adaptation and understanding of various factors play a fundamental role in determining match outcomes in the dynamic environment of professional LoL [5].

In our study to identify key factors affecting outcomes in LoL, advanced machine learning techniques such as SHAP [9] (SHapley Additive exPlanations), tree-based models, and linear models are being utilized. SHAP is instrumental in providing local interpretability by valuing the impact of each feature on specific predictions, offering detailed insights into player behaviors and in-game dynamics. Concurrently, tree-based models like Random Forests and Gradient Boosting Machines analyze the global importance of features across matches to identify consistent trends. Linear models complement these by establishing direct relationships between features and outcomes, providing clear, interpretable insights. This integrated approach, combining local and global perspectives with linear analysis, is designed to thoroughly uncover decisive factors in the game.

In summary, the main contributions of this paper are the following:

- A generalizable methodology for match analysis in the context of LoL.
- An extensive comparative of well-known explainable methods including a hyperparameter optimization process.
- Consistent analysis of the key aspects that determine the victory or defeat from global to local explanations using SHAP.

The paper is structured as follows. Section 1 introduces LoL and its impact on esports, setting the stage for the machine learning analysis of game outcomes. Section 2 discusses comparative studies between esports and traditional sports, along with methodologies in esports analytics. Section 3 details the methodology, including dataset, models, experimental setup, evaluation metrics, and analysis workflow. Section 4 delves into results, analyzing global factors' influence, role importance, and specific game scenarios, showcasing model effectiveness and strategic insights. Conclusions are drawn in Sect. 5.

2   Related Work

When exploring the relationship between esports and traditional sports, comparative studies have become increasingly important. These analyses explore how traditional sports strategies, team dynamics, and performance metrics are mirrored or differ in the esports arena, particularly in games like LoL. This research area offers valuable information on the evolving nature of competitive gaming and its place within the broader context of sports. In [8], a Bayesian state-space model is introduced to differentiate team talent from randomness across sports, providing new metrics for assessing team strength and competitiveness. A framework for the evaluation of soccer players is introduced in [1], which includes a language to describe individual actions and a method to value these actions based on the impact and context of the game, thus enhancing the assessment of the total offensive and defensive contributions of a player. Performance indicators that differentiate winning and losing teams are identified in [4] in both regular season and playoff basketball games, while [7] builds and compares methods to predict the outcomes of basketball games too.

In the rapidly evolving field of esports analytics, a growing body of research is dedicated to understanding and improving various aspects of competitive gaming. In MOBA esports analytics, diverse methodologies have emerged. One study highlights the significant impact of the "Carry" role in LoL on team performance using logistic regression [3]. Another explores the prediction of wins in real time in professional Dota2 matches, achieving significant accuracy with machine learning models [6]. A third study in LoL focuses on predicting match outcomes based on the experience of the players with selected champions, using a deep neural network to reveal the importance of individual champion skill [2].

In esports analytics for other genres, one study introduces a comprehensive framework for player evaluation in Counter-Strike: Global Offensive, a tactical shooter, utilizing advanced data models and graph measures [12]. Another explores the use of multi-agent reinforcement learning in StarCraft II, with the AlphaStar agent achieving the highest level, showcasing the potential of AI in complex gaming environments [11].

3   Methodology

In this section, we detail the methodology adopted for our analysis of LoL matches, structured into five key subsections: Dataset, Models, Experimental Settings, Evaluation Metrics, and Workflow. Initially, in Sect. 3.1, we delve into the specifics of the dataset we have gathered. This is followed by Sect. 3.2, where we detail the analytical models employed. Subsequently, Sect. 3.3 covers our experimental setup, including the data preparation strategies and the division process to train and test the models. Section 3.4 outlines the metrics we have chosen for assessing the performance of our models. Lastly, Sect. 3.5 provides a comprehensive overview of our data processing workflow, illustrating the step-by-step approach taken in our analysis.

3.1 Dataset

The dataset for this study was sourced through the public Riot API, encompassing both regional and international LoL tournaments from 2019 to the present. Each match in the dataset provides comprehensive details, including the participating teams, key statistics such as match start time, duration, winning team, total kills, and captured structures. Additionally, the dataset offers in-depth player-specific data, such as the position played by each player along with their main performance metrics.

Teams start on either the Blue side (bottom left corner) or the Red side (top right corner), with slight map differences affecting strategies and objective control. The game features five main roles: Top Laners, often durable fighters or tanks, hold the isolated top lane; Mid Laners, typically high-damage or control mages, occupy the central lane with access to the whole map; Junglers roam the space between lanes, securing neutral objectives and assisting lanes; Bot Laners, which usually focus on dealing physical damage from the bot lane; and Supports, paired with Bot Laners, provide utility through healing, vision, and crowd control.

The dataset is balanced, showing an even split of match outcomes between the Blue and Red sides, ensuring unbiased analysis and model training. It includes the five main roles (Top, Mid, Jungle, Bot, and Support), providing a thorough coverage of the game dynamics and player strategies for in-depth analysis.

3.2 Models

Some of the most common and high-quality models used during experimentation have been selected from simpler to complex ones.

Decision trees (DT) are a fundamental algorithm in machine learning that is intuitive to understand and interpret. The hyperparameters selected to optimize are: maximum depth [1, 100], splitter [best or random], and criterion [entropy, log loss, or gini].

Random Forest (RF) is an ensemble learning method that constructs multiple decision trees trained on a random subset of features and aggregates their predictions. The hyperparameters selected to optimize are: Number of estimators [10, 500], maximum depth [1, 100], and criterion [entropy, log loss, or gini].

SGD is an iterative optimization algorithm commonly used to train machine learning models which, in our case, is a linear model. The hyperparameters selected to optimize are: loss function [hinge, log loss, huber, or squared hinge], penalty [l1 or l2], and regularization factor [0.001, 1].

A perceptron is a single-layer neural network with binary output (0 or 1) that is used for binary classification tasks. The hyperparameters selected to optimize are: penalty [l1 or l2], regularization factor [0.001, 1], and maximum iterations [5, 50].

XGBoost is an optimized gradient boosting library that builds an ensemble of weak learners sequentially. The hyperparameters selected to optimize are: Number of estimators [10, 500] and maximum depth [1, 100].

3.3   Experimental Settings

The dataset was divided, with 80% randomly selected for training and the remaining 20% allocated for testing. To prepare the data for analysis, the statistics of each player were transformed into differential values compared to their corresponding opponent in the same position. The data were then normalized using the MinMax scaling method. Furthermore, a stratified k-fold validation approach was used in the training set, with k set as 5, to ensure that each fold is a good representative of the entire dataset, providing a more reliable and unbiased evaluation of the performance. This method is particularly useful for maintaining the proportion of samples for each class, which is crucial in datasets with unbalanced class distributions.

3.4   Evaluation Metrics

To assess the quality of the models, we have chosen efficacy and efficiency metrics.

We chose accuracy as our efficacy metric for its simplicity and direct reflection of model performance, given our balanced dataset. Training time, measured in minutes, was selected to evaluate efficiency, considering the practical need for frequent model updates in esports analytics. These metrics offer a succinct evaluation of model effectiveness and computational demands.

3.5   Hyperparameter Optimization

To finalize the methodology, we summarize the optimization process aimed at obtaining the best models.

We have chosen Bayesian optimization [10], a widely used method to optimize hyperparameters. This choice is motivated by its recent remarkable results in the literature and its proven performance. Bayesian optimization constructs a probabilistic surrogate model of the objective function and iteratively selects the next point for evaluation by balancing exploration and exploitation. In our case, we have selected the upper confidence bound acquisition function, with a value of λ of 2.576, known for its generally good performance.

For each dataset and model, the optimization process begins by sampling combinations of hyperparameters from distributions specified in Sect. 3.2. Subsequently, a model is created, fitted, and evaluated for each fold using the sampled hyperparameters. Subsequently, the efficacy metrics are calculated and averaged across folds, and the top configuration is selected for each model. Finally, the best models are evaluated on the test set, and the Shapley values are obtained.

4   Results

In this section, the results of the analysis are divided into four sections. Firstly, Sect. 4.1 summarizes the efficacy and efficiency obtained from the best models. Section 4.2 evaluates the most important factors that influence games. Second, Sect. 4.3 evaluates the importance of every role. Finally, Sect. 4.4 shows two specific examples in which the games were unbalanced and balanced, respectively.

4.1   Best Models

Table 1 presents the optimal metrics achieved by each model in terms of accuracy and time to fitting. Our methodology utilizes a stratified k-fold approach for evaluation, hence the inclusion of standard deviations across the folds for each metric.

Table 1. Efficacy and efficiency metrics for the best models. Note that the standard deviation of the k-fold evaluation is reported between parenthesis.

Model	Accuracy (%)	Fit time (m)
XGBoost	98.8 (± 0.2)	1.35 (± 0.03)
Random Forest	98.5 (± 0.2)	9.47 (± 0.14)
SGD	98.1 (± 0.2)	0.05 (± 0.01)
Decision tree	96.5 (± 0.5)	2.30 (± 0.12)
Perceptron	80.8 (± 12.7)	0.08 (± 0.03)

The XGBoost model performs best, boasting an impressive approximate accuracy of 99%, with a standard deviation of 0.2%. This suggests consistent results in different folds. Although the random forest model demonstrates similar efficacy, its fit time is significantly longer, approximately seven times that of the XGBoost model.

Both the SGD and DT models achieve commendable results, showcasing competitive efficiency. Interestingly, despite both being tree-based methods, the DT model takes longer to train compared to XGBoost. On the contrary, the Perceptron yields the least favorable results with the highest variance. This suggests sensitivity to hyperparameters, which makes it unsuitable for this particular problem.

4.2   Global Analysis

Figure 1 illustrates the significance of the top 15 features after applying the methodology, organized by their average Shapley values. Each feature is labeled with the game position it references, shown in parentheses. The color and intensity of the points represent their values, while their position on the x-axis reflects the Shapley value. Negative Shapley values indicate a contribution to the blue team, whereas positive values denote a contribution to the red team.

Globally, we can categorize features into two types: those that contribute positively to their team and those that have a negative impact. For example, a team member who inflicts more damage to buildings or accumulates higher total gold is likely to perform well, while a high number of deaths suggests poorer performance.

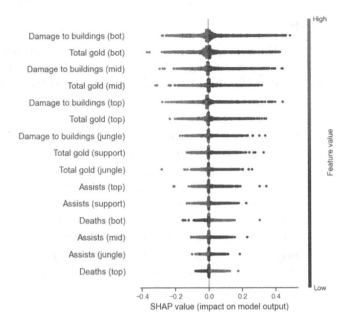

Fig. 1. Top global feature importances for the best models on the test set.

Specifically, damage to buildings and total gold appear to be the most influential features, reflecting a summary of player performance. It is noteworthy that player assists seem to carry more weight than kills, suggesting a game emphasis on strategic plays benefiting the team rather than individual advantages.

It is important to recognize that the impact of features is not consistent across the board. For example, in Damage to buildings (bot), there are instances of high values with positive impacts and vice versa. This suggests that the impact is contingent on the performance of other team members, indicating that good individual performance may not necessarily lead to victory.

As the best method used was a tree-based model, Fig. 2 shows the importance of the features based on the information gained. In this context, the most influential features are Assists and the total gold of the support. Generally, the most critical features align closely with those in Fig. 1, albeit with a different ranking. It is crucial to note that while this importance is related, it is not identical to Shapely values.

4.3   Role Analysis

In this section the influence of every position is studied. For that purpose, the influence calculated by the Shapley values for every sample of every position in the test set has been averaged.

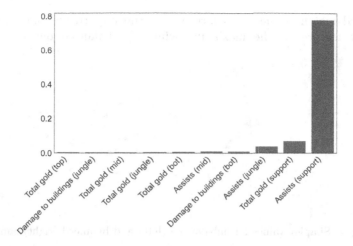

Fig. 2. Top global feature importances based on the importance gain of the XGBoost model.

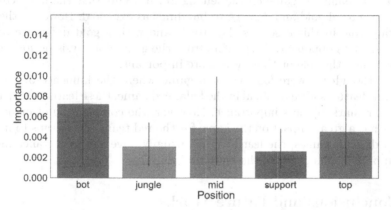

Fig. 3. Top global feature importances based on the averaged Shapley importance by role.

Figure 3 shows a bar plot with the average value and its 95% confidence interval is represented as an error bar. We can observe that the most important position in this case is the "bot" lane. This is the expected result, as this role usually is in charge of causing most of the damage in the fights and determining the results. The mid and top positions have a similar importance as they also have an important role in the fights causing damage or being the tank. Lastly, the jungle and support positions seem to be less relevant to determine the victory.

4.4   Local Analysis

In this case, the analysis is performed in two specific matches from the test set. Specifically, an unbalanced and a balanced match are shown in Fig. 4. The unbalanced match studies a scenario where the importance sum of the most important features is the maximum, while the balanced one considers the minimum.

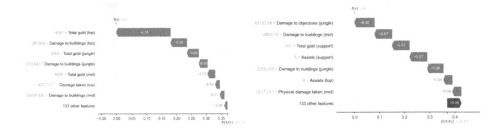

Fig. 4. Shapley values for unbalanced (left) and balanced (right) games.

In the unbalanced game on the left figure, it seems that the most common features are total gold and damage to buildings as expected. However, the most important role in this case was the "top" lane with a gold difference of 4041 compared to its opponent. This differs from the general analysis performed previously, where the role of "bot" was more important.

Even though we were looking for a game where the influence of the most important features were minimal in the balanced game, these features still appear but with remarkably less importance. However, the combination of many other features has a great impact on the game for the red team. This seems to indicate that, in difficult games, the features that usually have less importance increase their impact on the result of the match.

5 Conclusions and Future Works

In this work, the key factors that influence the outcomes in League of Legends (LoL) matches are analyzed using advanced machine learning techniques. Using a dataset from LoL tournaments and several well-known models, the study analyzes the results of matches, identifies influential factors, and assesses the importance of the role.

The results show that the XGBoost model performs best, achieving an approximate accuracy 99%, with features such as damage to buildings and total gold emerging as crucial determinants of match outcomes. Role analysis reveals that positions such as "bot" (Bottom lane) have a significant impact, underscoring the importance of strategic positioning and performance.

Future work will explore how success factors evolve over the years and impact outcomes at various game stages. We also plan to create a dynamic, fair ELO system, refining team and player performance assessment by incorporating new metrics and adjusting for key factors.

Acknowledgements. The authors would like to thank the Spanish Ministry of Science and Innovation for the support under the projects PID2020-117954RB-C22, TED2021-131311B-C21 funded by MCIU/AEI/10.13039/501100011033 and by the European Union - NextGenerationEU/PRTR and also thanks to Riot Games for the provided data.

References

1. Decroos, T., Bransen, L., Van Haaren, J., Davis, J.: Actions speak louder than goals: valuing player actions in soccer. In: Proceedings of the 25th ACM SIGKDD International Conference on Knowledge Discovery & Data Mining, pp. 1851–1861 (2019)
2. Do, T.D., Wang, S.I., Yu, D.S., McMillian, M.G., McMahan, R.P.: Using machine learning to predict game outcomes based on player-champion experience in league of legends. In: Proceedings of the 16th International Conference on the Foundations of Digital Games, pp. 1–5 (2021)
3. Eaton, J.A., Sangster, M.D.D., Renaud, M., Mendonca, D.J., Gray, W.D.: Carrying the team: the importance of one player's survival for team success in league of legends. In: Proceedings of the Human Factors and Ergonomics Society Annual Meeting, vol. 61, pp. 272–276 (2017)
4. García, J., Ibáñez, S.J., De Santos, R.M., Leite, N., Sampaio, J.: Identifying basketball performance indicators in regular season and playoff games. J. Hum. Kinet. **36**, 161 (2013)
5. Hitar-Garcia, J.A., Moran-Fernandez, L., Bolon-Canedo, V.: Machine learning methods for predicting league of legends game outcome. IEEE Trans. Games **15**(2), 171–181 (2022)
6. Hodge, V.J., Devlin, S., Sephton, N., Block, F., Cowling, P.I., Drachen, A.: Win prediction in multiplayer Esports: live professional match prediction. IEEE Trans. Games **13**(4), 368–379 (2019)
7. Lampis, T., Ioannis, N., Vasilios, V., Stavrianna, D.: Predictions of European basketball match results with machine learning algorithms. J. Sports Anal. **9**, 1–20 (2023)
8. Lopez, M.J., Matthews, G.J., Baumer, B.S.: How often does the best team win? a unified approach to understanding randomness in north American sport. Ann. Appl. Stat. **12**(4), 2483–2516 (2018)
9. Lundberg, S.M., Lee, S.: A Unified Approach to Interpreting Model Predictions. In: Advances in Neural Information Processing Systems, vol. 30, pp. 4765–4774. Curran Associates, Inc. (2017)
10. Snoek, J., Larochelle, H., Adams, R.P.: Practical Bayesian Optimization of Machine Learning Algorithms. In: Proceedings of the Advances in Neural Information Processing Systems, pp. 1723–1731 (2012)
11. Vinyals, O., et al.: Grandmaster level in starcraft ii using multi-agent reinforcement learning. Nature **575**(7782), 350–354 (2019)
12. Xenopoulos, P., Doraiswamy, H., Silva, C.: Valuing player actions in counter-strike: global offensive. In: 2020 IEEE international conference on big data (big data), pp. 1283–1292. IEEE (2020)

Reconstruction-Based Anomaly Detection in Wind Turbine Operation Time Series Using Generative Models

Amaia Abanda[1(✉)] [iD], Ainhoa Pujana[1] [iD], and Javier Del Ser[1,2] [iD]

[1] TECNALIA, Basque Research and Technology Alliance (BRTA),
48160 Derio, Spain
{amaia.abanda,ainhoa.pujana,javier.delser}@tecnalia.com
[2] Department of Communications Engineering, University of the Basque Country
(UPV/EHU), 48013 Bilbao, Spain

Abstract. Unsupervised time series anomaly detection is a common tasks in many real world problems, in which the normal/anomaly labels are extremely unbalanced. In this work, we propose to use three generative models (namely, a basic autoencoder, a transformer autoencoder and a diffusion model) for a reconstruction-based anomaly detection pipeline applied to failure detection in wind turbine operation time series. Our experiments show that the transformer autoencoder yields the most accurate reconstructions of the original time series, whereas the diffusion model is not able to obtain good reconstructions. The reconstruction error, which is used as an anomaly score, seems to follow different distributions for the anomalies and for the normal data in 2 of the 3 models, which is confirmed by our quantitative evaluation. The transformer autoencoder is the best performing generative model, achieving a AUC score of 0.98 in the detection of the anomalies. However, the same result is obtained by standard (i.e. non-generative) outlier detection algorithms, exposing that although the anomalies in this problem are sequence anomalies – with a temporal nature –, they can be effectively modeled and detected as point outliers.

Keywords: Time series · Anomaly detection · Generative models · Reconstruction · Wind Turbine

1 Introduction

Time series data mining [1] is a increasing research topic due to the vast amount of temporal data collected everyday in a diversity of application domains. Some examples of real-world time series include the evolution of a market in finance, the monitoring of vital sings of a patient in the medical domain, or measurements taken by sensors from a industrial process or asset [2].

Time series data mining involves various tasks aimed at extracting meaningful patterns, trends, and insights from sequential data points over time. The most

A. Alonso-Betanzos et al. (Eds.): CAEPIA 2024, LNAI 14640, pp. 194–203, 2024.
https://doi.org/10.1007/978-3-031-62799-6_20

popular tasks include time series forecasting [3], classification [4], clustering [5] and anomaly detection [6]. This work focuses on time series anomaly detection (hereafter referred to as TSAD), defined as the task of identifying patterns in time series data that significantly deviate from their expected normal behavior.

TSAD is a challenging task that nowadays generates great interest among researchers and practitioners due to the complexity of the task itself and the variety of strategies proposed to tackle it effectively. First it is important to note that the concept of *anomaly* can be broadly defined in time series data. As such, anomalies can be categorized into multiple groups depending on several characteristics: regarding the nature of the anomaly, they can be semantic anomalies or non-contextual anomalies. For instance, in the renowned NYC taxi demand dataset studied in [7], semantic anomalies are defined as the increase of taxi demand in particular days such as thanksgiving or Christmas. Non-contextual anomalies refer to those that do not take into account information from external sources and only consider a data-driven perspective. Depending of the length of the anomaly we may encounter point anomalies, sequence anomalies or time series anomalies. Point anomalies refer to single outlier points that do not follow the normal distribution of the data. Sequence anomalies are specific for time series and refer to patterns or subseries that do not conform to the statistical pattern of the time series. In the case of time series anomalies, the time series as a whole is identified as an anomaly, that hence can only be detected when the input data consist of multivariate time series.

One of the most popular applications of TSAD is failure detection in remote systems that are subject to minimal or even null human supervision. In this setting, it becomes paramount to devise data-based pipelines to automatically identify failures from data, so that on-site inspections of the faulty asset can be performed. This is the case of wind turbines, which are often installed in remote areas due to their wind regime and its potential to produce wind energy. However, the distant location of wind turbine deployments often comes along with the necessity to endow these installations with the capability to diagnose their operation autonomously, so that maintenance and repair visits are only scheduled when needed.

In the above context, this work addresses a sequence anomaly detection problem formulated over wind turbine real-world time series for the detection of overheating failures. The main contribution of the study is the exploration of modern deep generative models for the detection of these anomalies in an unsupervised learning fashion. To this end, we thoroughly describe these models, and show experimentally that the reconstruction error is a reliable indicator of the anomaly score needed to make a decision on their anomalous nature. We further compare these models and other non-generative outlier detection techniques in terms of detection performance, concluding that even if we deal with sequence-based anomalies, they can be effectively modeled as point outliers by non-generative approaches, achieving higher detection scores than their generative counterparts. Our results suggest that further study is needed towards mapping the statistical characteristics of the anomaly to be detected and the effectiveness of TSAD choices. The rest of this work is organized as follows: in Sect. 2 we provide a short background on wind turbine failure detection and time series anomaly detection. Then, Sect. 3 presents the methodology followed in our experiments. Section 4 presents and discusses the results of our experiments. Finally, Sect. 5 draws conclusions and some research lines departing from our findings.

2   Background

In this section, we provide a brief introduction to TSAD (Sect. 2.1), followed by a comment on some relevant works related to the detection of failures in wind turbines (Sect. 2.2). Finally, we cast the contribution of this paper within the reviewed literature.

2.1   Anomaly Detection in Time Series

TSAD is a long-standing research topic in the literature, in which a plethora of different approaches have been contributed to solve this problem. In general, TSAD methods can be grouped into statistics-based, classification-based, forecasting-based and reconstruction-based methods [16].

On one hand, statistics-based methods are classical unsupervised learning approaches that define an anomaly as a value that significantly deviates from the normal distribution of the data. Methods that follow this first strategy include techniques hinging on time series decomposition or extreme value theory [17]. Since anomaly data is usually very scarce, supervised methods would require specific methods for extremely unbalance data. As such, classification-based methods often rely on a semi-supervised approach, in which the normal distribution of the data is learnt with a one-class classifier, so that anything that deviates from this learned distribution is considered an anomaly. An example that follows this methodology is the One-Class SVM (OCSVM). Forecasting-based methods, instead, rely on the assumption that the error of the prediction made by a forecasting method in an anomalous point is higher that the error of the prediction in a normal point. A example is the proposal by Pena *et. al* in [18], where ARIMA forecasters are used for anomaly detection. Lastly, reconstruction-based method, mostly employ deep neural networks that learn to reconstruct inputs for anomaly detection. In those approaches, the network is learnt over the normal time series, assuming that the reconstruction error would be higher for the anomalies than for the normal points. The most popular reconstruction-based TSAD methods include autoencoders (AE) [19], while generative networks such as generative adversarial networks (GAN) [20] have also been satisfactorily applied, mostly over well-known synthetic benchmarks.

2.2   Failure Detection in Wind Turbines

Predictive maintenance is one of the most relevant tasks in the wind energy sector due to the high cost of unplanned downtimes and the reparation of some assets. The increased monitoring of all components in a wind turbine and the proliferation of sensors in these assets have resulted in a great amount of collected data. As a result, AI methods for predictive maintenance and failure diagnosis have progressively become prevalent in real-world setups [8].

From the algorithmic perspective, the author of [9] states that almost 60% of methods proposed in the literature use classification, while the rest rely on regression. In the specific task of failure detection, most of the proposed methods employ statistical o classical approaches [10] such as PCA or wavelet transform [11], or standard classification models [12]. More recently, deep learning based methods have been proposed for failure detection problems [14]. Most of these methods employ a forecasting based approach for the detection of failures [15]. To the best of our knowledge, only a single work has proposed a reconstruction-based approach for gearbox failure detection [13]. Failure detection in wind turbines has not been approached yet with modern generative AI methods.

Contribution: This work explores, for the first time in the literature, the use of modern generative models for reconstruction-based time series anomaly detection for wind turbines overheating failure diagnosis. A second differential aspect of our work w.r.t. related literature is the comparison of such generative models against other non-reconstruction based anomaly detectors. As shown by our results, the relatively better performance of non-generative anomaly detectors serves as a catalyst for future research towards establishing a connection between the nature of the anomaly to be detected and the adequacy of one TSAD approach or another.

3   Methodology

The methodology used in this work to detect the failures in wind turbine time series is based on the reconstruction error. This is an unsupervised approach, in which the distribution of normal time series is learned by using deep generative neural networks. Specifically, we first split the time series in sub-sequences by sliding window. Then, the distribution of normal time series is characterized by training a generative model using only windows that contain non-anomalous data. Lastly, the reconstruction error is computed for some time series in the test set that contains anomalies and normal data. Our hypothesis is that anomalies should yield larger reconstruction errors than normal sub-sequences.

In particular, three deep generative models are considered is this work: a basic autoencoder (BAE), a transformer autoencoder (TAE), and a diffusion model (DM):

- **BAE**: The basic autoencoder aims at compressing the input data into a low-dimensional latent space, and at decoding this representation back to the original space. The BAE is composed of an encoder with two one-dimensional convolutional layers with ReLU activation and dropout, and a decoder with the same structure but with transposed convolutional layers. It is trained to minimize the Mean Squared Error (MSE) distance between the original time series and their reconstructions.

- **TAE**: The transformer autoencoder is a variant of BAE that uses the Transformer architecture instead of conventional neural networks. In this case, the architecture begins with a linear layer, followed by a positional encoding layer. The encoder consists of a transformer encoder layer, and the resulting encoded memory is then summarized by taking the mean along the time dimension. The decoder utilizes a similar structure with a transformer decoder layer.
- **DM**: Diffusion models are the most novel generative networks, having gained great momentum in the current landscape of text-to-image modeling. These networks successively add Gaussian perturbations to the input data, until the input becomes pure Gaussian noise. Then, a denoising neural network recovers the original data by inverting the noise process back to the original input. The denoising network is a U-Net with classic ResNet blocks and a weight standardized convolutional layer.

4 Experimental Setup and Results

This section provides a detailed description of the dataset employed (Sect. 4.1), the experimentation setup (Sect. 4.2), and the presentation and discussion of the obtained results (Sect. 4.3). All the source code and experimentation details are available at Gitlab[1].

4.1 Dataset

Our dataset is extracted from the SCADA data of a real-world 2MW wind turbine. It comprises a longitudinal 3-dimensional time series, where the three dimensions refer to average value of three parameters measured in a wind turbine: wind speed, mechanical torque in the generator shaft and nacelle temperature. They are 10-minutely measurements of 5 years between 2016 and 2021, containing some missing data. The distribution of normality and failure points is extremely unbalanced, with only 15 anomaly sequences. These anomaly sequences are of different lengths, from 50 min to 6 h.

4.2 Experimental Evaluation

For the experimentation, the data is first partitioned to yield train and test partitions taking into account the temporal nature of the data (i.e. by sequence, not by point). Moreover, the split should be in such a way that in the train partition there are only non-anomalous points, while in the test set there are normality and anomaly points. Lastly, the train set should be significantly larger than the test set. Taking into account all these restrictions, we define the partition manually, taking for the test the 15 anomaly sequences and one month forward and one month backward of each anomaly. Thus, we obtained a partition such that the train partition contains 115,462 measurements, while the test contains 59,875 measurements (including the 15 anomalous sequences).

---

[1] https://git.code.tecnalia.com/amaia.abanda/berezia_anomaly_diffusion.

The evaluation metric employed to measure the performance of the different methods is the Area Under the Receiver Operating Characteristic curve (AUC). This is the area under the ROC curve, a representation of the trade-off between true positive rate (sensitivity) and false positive rate (1-specificity) at various threshold settings. A higher AUC value, closer to 1, indicates better discrimination, while an AUC of 0.5 suggests performance comparable to random chance. The AUC metric is particularly useful when dealing with imbalanced datasets or when the specific choice of the classification threshold is not critical. Hence, given a reconstruction error for each point, the ROC is computed for different thresholds in the reconstruction error to compute the AUC.

To avoid any bias in the comparison, the hyper-parameter of the models have been tuned. The hyper-parameters to be optimized in the case of the BAE and TAE are: the batch size in the set $(32, 64, 128)$, the window size in the set $(60, 120, 240)$ and the learning rate within $(1e-7, 1e-5, 1e-3)$. In the case of the DM, we have also optimized the noise steps and denosing steps within the values $(20, 50, 100)$. We have set the maximum number of epochs to 1000, but with a early stopping if the loss does not improve in the last 50 epochs. We have performed a random hyper-parameter search, selecting for each model the best configuration, namely: for the BAE a learning rate of 1e-5, a window size of 120 and a batch size of 32; for the TAE, a learning rate of 1e-5, a window size of 120 and a batch size of 128; and in the case of DM, a learning rate of 1e-3, window size of 240, batch size of 64, 50 noise steps, and 100 denoising steps.

4.3   Results and Discussion

Each model has a different reconstruction strategy, which may lead to difference anomaly detection performance scores. To delve into this, we first discuss on Fig. 1, which shows some examples of the reconstruction errors reported by the considered models in a particular instance of the test set (in the three dimensions). It can be observed that the model that most accurately reconstructs the time series is TAE, followed by BAE. DM fails to achieve accurately reconstructed versions of the depicted time series which, as is next presented, gives rise to poor detection statistics.

The following step in our discussion on our experiments consists of visualizing the distribution of the reconstruction error of the normal points and the anomaly points in the test set (Fig. 2). In these plots we notice that, in the case of BAE and TAE, the distribution of the reconstruction error in the anomalies is centered in the right tail of the distribution of the normal points. This suggests that the anomalous points follow a different distribution, and hence should be easily identified. In the case of DM, instead, the distribution of the error in the anomaly points seems to follow the same distribution as the normal points, so in line with our previous intuition, we can expect DM to perform worse when isolating the anomalies from the data corresponding to the regular operation of the asset.

Lastly, we have performed 10 repetitions of each method with its best hyper-parameter configuration in order to account for the randomness of their training procedure. In order to have a comparative with other types of anomaly detection

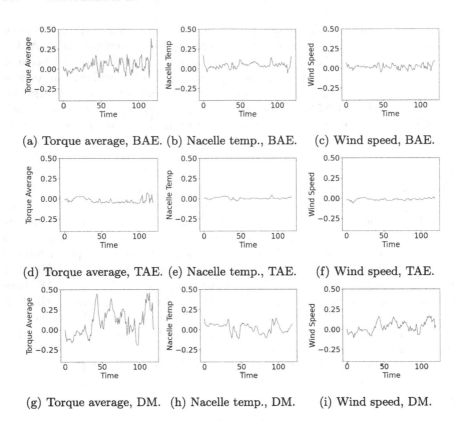

(a) Torque average, BAE. (b) Nacelle temp., BAE.   (c) Wind speed, BAE.

(d) Torque average, TAE. (e) Nacelle temp., TAE.   (f) Wind speed, TAE.

(g) Torque average, DM. (h) Nacelle temp., DM.   (i) Wind speed, DM.

Fig. 1. Reconstruction error reported by the BAE (top row), TAE (middle row) and DM (bottom row) for the three dimensions of a time series in the test set.

methods, we have performed the same experimentation with some benchmark outlier detection algorithms [21]: Histogram-base Outlier Detection (HBOS), Cluster-based Local Outlier Factor (CLOF), Isolation Forest (IFORST) and One-Class SVM (OCSVM). Table 1 shows the mean AUC and the standard deviation (between parenthesis) of each model with the best configuration. As expected, among the generative models TAE is the best performing model, followed by BAE. As expected, DM obtains the worst performance within all the considered methods. Interestingly, the benchmark methods attain very competitive results, since all outperform DM, while 3 out of 4 outperform two of the generative models.

With the aim of visualizing in detail the behavior of each model, Fig. 3 displays the mean and standard deviation of the ROC curves among 10 repetitions. The dark line indicates the mean ROC value over 10 repetitions, while the shaded region denotes the standard deviation. The curves of HBOS and OCSVM are not shadowed because they are deterministic and, thus, their results do not variate among iterations.

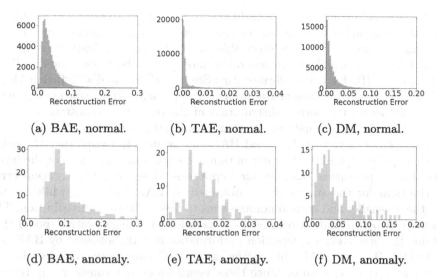

(a) BAE, normal.   (b) TAE, normal.   (c) DM, normal.

(d) BAE, anomaly.   (e) TAE, anomaly.   (f) DM, anomaly.

Fig. 2. Reconstruction error distribution for normal data.

Table 1. AUC results for each model.

	AUC
BAE	0.93 (0.01)
TAE	**0.98 (0.01)**
DM	0.76 (0.05)
HBOS	0.95 (0.01)
CLOF	**0.98 (0.01)**
IFORST	**0.98 (0.01)**
OCSVM	0.87 (0.01)

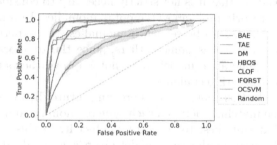

Fig. 3. ROC curves for the proposed models.

It can be seen that although some methods obtain similar AUC scores, the curves are different. TAE is the model that reaches the best false positive and true positive ratio (in the upper left corner). In the same manner, the curves show that HBOS works better for the false positive rate region than BAE, while BAE achieves better true positive rates than OCSVM. Benchmark models do not consider the temporal information since they consider each tuple of points (Torque average, nacelle temperature, wind speed) independently. In this way, the good performance of these models indicate that, in this problem, it is necessary to consider the anomalies neither as temporal nor as sequence-based, but rather as point anomalies.

5 Conclusions and Future Work

In this work, we have explored modern generative models for a reconstruction-based anomaly detection in wind turbine operation. The anomalies refer to overheating failure in the wind turbine, and as often in real-world problems, the dataset is highly unbalanced. In this context, an unsupervised reconstruction based approach is specially suitable, since the model is learned using only normal data. Specifically, three generative models have been considered: a Basic AutoEncoder (BAE), a Transformer AutoEncoder (TAE) and a Diffusion Model (DM). The underlying idea of the proposed approach is that, since the generative model learns the normal distribution of the data, the reconstruction error should be higher in anomaly points than in normal points.

The results show that TAE and BAE can accurately reconstruct the original time series, while DM does not obtain accurate reconstructions of the input data. Our experiments validate our hypothesis: different reconstruction error distributions for the anomalies are obtained by BAE and TAE, while for the DM the anomalies and normal points seems to follow the same distribution. The discussed experimentation results also conclude that the generative model that obtains the best anomaly detection performance is TAE, followed by BAE and lastly DM. However, TAE obtains the same AUC score than some benchmark outlier detection algorithms. Since these baselines do not consider any temporal information when detecting anomalies, the main conclusion drawn from our study is that it is not strictly necessary to consider the anomalies of this specific real-world problem as temporal anomalies. In other words, even if the anomalies are known to be sequence anomalies, the experimentation show that they can be modeled as point outliers, since the temporal information provided within the generative models does not improve the performance obtained by simpler benchmark techniques.

In this context, an interesting future direction of research could be to study the matching between each type of anomaly and the anomaly detection strategy that suits best to accurately detect it. In this sense, having a proxy that helps the user to choose a model given a anomaly detection dataset could be very useful for real-world applications.

Acknowledgments. This work has been supported by the Basque Government through the ELKARTEK funding program (ref. KK-2023/00012, BEREZ-IA). J. Del Ser also acknowledges the financial help from the same institution through the consolidated research group MATHMODE (IT1456-22). A. Abanda and A. Pujana are also supported by the IA4TES (Artificial Intelligence for Sustainable Energy Transition), funded by the Ministry of Economic Affairs and Digial Transformation within the project IA4TES MIA.2021.M04.0008.

References

1. Esling, P., et al.: Time-series data mining. ACM Comput. Surv. **45**(1), 1–34 (2012)
2. Diez-Olivan, A., et al.: Data fusion and machine learning for industrial prognosis: trends and perspectives towards industry 4.0. Inf. Fusion **50**, 92–111 (2019)
3. De Gooijer, J.G., et al.: 25 years of time series forecasting. Int. J. Forecast. **22**(3), 443–473 (2006)

4. Abanda, A., Mori, U., Lozano, J.A.: A review on distance based time series classification. Data Min. Knowl. Disc. **33**(2), 378–412 (2018). https://doi.org/10.1007/s10618-018-0596-4
5. Liao, T.W.: Clustering of time series data-a survey. Pattern Recogn. **38**(11), 1857–1874 (2005)
6. Blázquez-García, A. et al.: A review on outlier/anomaly detection in time series data. ACM Comput. Surv. (CSUR) **54**(3), 1–33 (2021)
7. Hagan, R.D., et al.: Classification and anomaly detection in traffic patterns of New York city taxis: a case study in compound analytics. In: IEEE IPDPSW (2018)
8. Maron, J., et al.: Artificial intelligence-based condition monitoring and predictive maintenance framework for wind turbines. In: Journal of Physics: Conference Series, vol. 2151, no. 1 (2022)
9. Stetco, A., et al.: Machine learning methods for wind turbine condition monitoring: a review. Renew. Energy **133**, 620–635 (2019)
10. Kim, K., et al.: Use of SCADA data for failure detection in wind turbines. In: Energy sustainability, vol. 54686 (2011)
11. Teng, W., et al.: Multi-fault detection and failure analysis of wind turbine gearbox using complex wavelet transform. Renew. Energy **93**, 591–598 (2016)
12. Santos, P., et al.: An SVM-based solution for fault detection in wind turbines. Sensors **15**(3), 5627–5648 (2015)
13. Yang, L., et al.: Wind turbine gearbox failure detection based on SCADA data: a deep learning-based approach. IEEE Trans. Instrum. Measur. **70**, 1–11 (2020)
14. Helbing, G., et al.: Deep learning for fault detection in wind turbines. Renew. Sustain. Energy Rev. **98**, 189–198 (2018)
15. Brandao, R.M., et al.: Application of neural networks for failure detection on wind turbines. In: IEEE Trondheim PowerTech (2011)
16. Liu, S., et al.: Time series anomaly detection with adversarial reconstruction networks. IEEE Trans. Knowl. Data Eng. **35**(4), 4293–4306 (2022)
17. Siffer, A., Fouque, P. A., Termier, A., Largouet, C.: Anomaly detection in streams with extreme value theory. In: ACM SIGKDD (2017)
18. Pena, E.H., et al.: Anomaly detection using forecasting methods arima and hwds. In: 32nd SCCC IEEE (2013)
19. Yin, C., et al.: Anomaly detection based on convolutional recurrent autoencoder for IoT time series. IEEE Trans. Syst. Man Cybern. Syst. **52**(1), 112–122 (2020)
20. Geiger, A., et al.: Tadgan: time series anomaly detection using generative adversarial networks. In: 2020 IEEE International Conference on Big Data (Big Data), IEEE (2020)
21. Zhao, Y., et al.: PyOD: a python toolbox for scalable outlier detection. J. Mach. Learn. Res. (JMLR) **20**(96), 1–7 (2019)

Multi-class and Multi-label Classification of an Assembly Task in Manufacturing

Manuel García-Domínguez[1(✉)] [ID], Jónathan Heras Vicente[1] [ID],
Roberto Marani[2] [ID], and Tiziana D'Orazio[2] [ID]

[1] Department of Mathematics and Computer Science, Universidad de La Rioja,
La Rioja, Spain
{manuel.garciad,jonathan.heras}@unirioja.es
[2] Institute of Intelligent Industrial Technologies and Systems for Advanced
Manufacturing, National Research Council of Italy, Bari, Italy
{roberto.marani,tiziana.dorazio}@stiima.cnr.it

Abstract. Human action monitoring is a tool that could help improve performance and efficiency in industrial assembly. Monitoring actions is a very complicated task to solve due to the complexity of the tasks to be classified added to the lack of data within the sector. Human action monitoring in the industrial environment is a complex problem to perform due to the difficulty of differentiating very complex tasks. Current methods are able to solve the problem of simple tasks while having difficulties during task transitions. Our approach aims to solve the problem of action classification in the industrial domain using deep learning models. By creating a multi-label classification model, we obtain a multi-label accuracy of 94.48% on a set of 12 tasks in the assembly of an industrial tool. The lessons learned in this work can serve as a basis for the construction of deep learning models for classifying complex actions in real time of industrial assembling tasks.

Keywords: Human monitoring · Deep Learning · Image classification · Multi-label classification

1 Introduction

Human action recognition is an active field that has considerably growth in the last few years thanks to the advancements in deep learning methods [12, 16], and the wide-spread usage of low-cost video cameras [10]. Human action recognition has applications in many areas including video-surveillance, safety and smart home security, ambient assisted living and health-care. The field of assembly task recognition in industrial environments could also benefit from human action recognition tasks to improve efficiency, effectiveness, and safety, as well as enhance cooperation between humans and cobots [1,5,14]; however, research in this field is limited due to the lack of public datasets, the similarity of the tasks that are studied and the complexity of these tasks that often require the manipulation of parts and tools.

A. Alonso-Betanzos et al. (Eds.): CAEPIA 2024, LNAI 14640, pp. 204–212, 2024.
https://doi.org/10.1007/978-3-031-62799-6_21

In the literature, we can find several projects that aim to address the complexities of recognizing actions in the dynamic environments of task recognition in industrial environments. One notable project by Wang et al. used a CNN to directly predict actions from individual frames; however, a drawback of this approach is that it does not take into account temporal information and the absence of consideration for transitions between actions, as it relies on a single label per frame during training [15]. Another approach, proposed by Zhang et al., focused on mitigating the issue of action transitions by employing a bi-stream CNN; but, their method omits a preliminary step to extract the person's skeleton, which could introduce noise in action recognition [18]. Finally, Lee et al. presented a compelling idea by collecting skeletons over multiple frames to generate an RGB image for action recognition; despite its innovativeness, the approach's reliance on a single label during network training poses challenges in predicting action transitions [6]. The limitations of these works underscore the need for more robust methods that consider both temporal dynamics and accurate feature extraction for enhanced action recognition in industrial settings.

To address the limitations identified in existing approaches for task recognition in manufacturing, a multi-label approach from videos emerges as a crucial solution. While prior projects have made noteworthy attempts using CNNs to predict actions directly from individual frames, in this paper we propose an approach based on a multi-label classification of a sequence of frames from an assembly task. In particular, the contributions of this paper are:

- We propose a methodology to convert a sequence of frames to a single image based on the positions of the skeleton of a worker in an assembly task.
- From the aforementioned images, we conduct a study of several multi-class and multi-label models to classify the action (or actions) conducted on the sequence of frames associated with the image.
- Finally, we publicly release all the code and models in https://github.com/ManuGar/Multi-label_classification.

The rest of this paper is organized as follows. In the next section, we present the dataset of videos from an assembly task used for our experiments, the method used to convert a sequence of frames from those videos into images, and the training process used to train the multi-class and multi-label models from those images. Subsequently, we analyse the results obtain by those models. The paper ends with the conclusions and further work.

2   Materials and Methods

In our work, we have used the Human Action Multi-Modal Monitoring in Manufacturing (HA4M) dataset [2], a collection of multi-modal data relative to actions performed by different subjects building an Epicyclic Gear Train (EGT). The assembly of an EGT involves three phases (Fig. 1): first, Blocks 1 and 2 are assembled separately and then they are combined. The EGT is made up of a total of 13 components: eight components to build Block 1, four components to build Block 2, and a cover to assemble Block 1 and Block 2. Finally, two screws fix the two blocks with an Allen key, thus obtaining the EGT. In Fig. 1, the two supports used to facilitate the assembly of each block are also shown. The total number of actions to build the EGT is 12; namely, there are four actions for building Block 1: pick up/place carrier (action 1), pick up/place gear bearings (action 2), pick up/place planet gears (action 3) and pick up/place carrier shaft (action 4); four actions for building block 2: pick up/place sun shaft (action 5), pick up/place sun gear (action 6), pick up/place sun gear bearing (action 7) and pick up/place ring bear (action 8); and four actions for assembling the two blocks and completing the EGT: pick up block 2 and place it on block 1 (action 9), pick up/place cover (action 10), pick up/place screw and pick up allen key (action 11), turn both screws, return allen key and the EGT (action 12). Some actions are performed several times as there are more components of the same type to be assembled: actions 2 and 3 are executed three times, whereas action 11 is repeated twice. Finally, a "don't care" action has been added to include transitions or unexpected events such as the loss of a component during the assembly process.

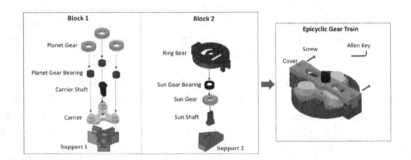

Fig. 1. Components of the EGT that is built on the HA4M dataset.

The dataset consists of 217 videos where one person appears assembling the EGT (note that only a person appears per video) and each frame of the dataset is annotated with one of the 12 actions previously explained. The dataset divided into 80% for training and 20% for testing in such a way that the same person cannot be in both sets simultaneously. The acquisition of the videos was carried out with a depth camera, specifically a Microsoft Azure Kinect, which allows simultaneous acquisition of RGB and depth images, and also automatically generates the skeleton associated with the person who appears in the recording. Using the skeletons provided in the dataset, we propose a method to construct an RGB image from a sequence of frames based on the approach proposed on the Skepxels project [7]; the main difference with that approach is that our method focuses on the top part of the body since the bottom part of the worker is covered by a table (see Fig. 2) and therefore such information can be ignored.

Fig. 2. Frames of two different scenarios in the HA4M dataset.

In order to convert a sequence of frames from the H4AM dataset to an image, we proceed as follows. Given a sequence of frames $F_0, \ldots, F_n$ (where $n > 1$), and $S_0, \ldots, S_n$ the skeletons associated respectively with each frame, we build an RGB image of size $n \times 45$ where the i-th row of the image corresponds with the skeleton S_i, and each column represent a joint of the skeleton. Joints are a set of key points from the skeleton (see Fig. 3) that serve to represent a specific body part storing its three-dimensional coordinates (X, Y, Z). In our case, after normalizing the spatial coordinates to the range between 0 and 255, they are used to represent a pixel value in the RGB colour space. As we have previously mentioned, only the joints from the upper body provide relevant information for our problem, and to build the row associated with a skeleton; namely, they will be traversed in a specific order to keep information about which joints are more related to each other. Given the skeleton S_i, the route of the joints will begin at the naval spine; it will reach the neck, go through the left arm, return to the neck, head and finally the right arm. With this route there are some joints that appear several times but that are necessary to give us information about what other joints they are related to. Once the tour has been completed, we obtain a list of 45 3D points that form the i-th row of the image.

It is worth noting that the proposed method can be applied to sequences of frames of any length; therefore, a study was conducted to determine the number of frames to use in order to build the images. The study consisted of calculating the mean and mode of the frames it takes for the tasks to be performed. The results obtained were 77 frames for the mean and 38 frames for the mode. Another parameter to consider when translating videos into images is the stride; that is, the number of frames that will be skipped to generate the next image. In other words, if the first image represents from frame 0 to 76, using a stride of 20 frames, the second image will represent from frame 19 to 96; and so on. Based on this study, we have built two different datasets. The former consist of images containing 77 frames and the latter contains 38 frames per image; in both of them, we have used a stride of 20 frames. In order to annotate the images, we consider two versions per each dataset: a multi-class dataset and a multi-label dataset. In the multi-class dataset, each image is annotated with the class associated with the majority of frames that form it; whereas, in the multi-label dataset, each image is annotated with the set of classes associated with all the frames that were used to build it. Finally, the division of the dataset is given

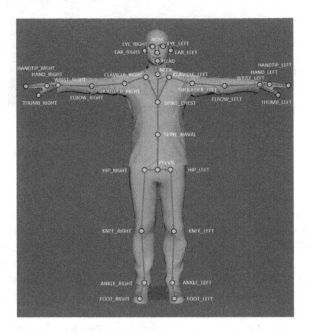

Fig. 3. Figure of the skeleton and joints captured by the Microsoft Azure Kinect camera.

by the original division from the source dataset having 80% of the images (7543 images in 77 frames dataset and 25112 images in 38 frames dataset) for training and 20% for testing (2783 images on 77 frames dataset and 7726 images on 38 frames dataset).

From the generated dataset, we have trained several multi-class and multi-label models. In both cases, we have used 5 convolutional architectures: Hrnetw [13], ResnetRS [4], Convnext [8], Resnest [17], and EfficientNet [9]. All models are implemented in Pytorch and have been trained using the functionality of the Fastai and Timm libraries on an Nvidia RTX 2080 Ti GPU. The heads of these architectures have been adapted respectively to the multi-class and multi-label task (the difference between these approaches is that in multi-class classification, the prediction is about a problem with several different classes; whereas the multi-label classification refers to the fact that images can belong to more than one class). In order to train the models, we have used the transfer-learning method presented in [3]. This is a two-stage procedure that starts from a model pretrained in the ImageNet challenge, and can be summarised as follows. In the first stage, we replaced the head of the model (that is, the layers that give us the classification of the images), with a new head adapted to the number of classes of the dataset. Then, we trained these new layers (the rest of the layers stayed frozen) with the data of each particular dataset for two epochs. In the second stage, we unfreezed the whole model and retrained all the layers of the model with the new data for 300 epochs. In order to find a suitable learning rate for both the first and second stage, we used cyclical learning rates for optimisation [11]. Moreover, we employed early stopping based on monitoring the accuracy. Finally, in order to evaluate the models, we used the accuracy and F1-score for evaluating both the multi-class and multi-label models. All the code used for training these models is available at the project webpage.

3   Results

In this section, we explain the results obtained with the two versions of the dataset and for the multi-class and multi-label tasks. We start by analysing the results obtained for the multi-class classification problem for both the 77 frames dataset and the 38 frames dataset, see Table 1. For the 77 frames dataset, the models exhibit varying levels of performance being ResnetRS the model that consistently outperforms the rest in both frame settings in terms of accuracy (77.97%) and F1 score (73.37%); the Hrnet model also performs quite well, showing competitive results. A more fine-grained analysis of the errors produced by the ResnetRS model can be seen in the associated confusion matrix, see Fig. 4. From such a confusion matrix, we can notice that the model is able to distinguish among the majority of the classes; however, the model gets confused with tasks pick up/place Screw and pick up Allen key (action 11), and turn both screws (action 12); two really similar actions.

If we focus now on the reduction from 77 frames to 38 frames, this generally means a slight increase in the accuracy for most models; the exception is the ResnetRS model that experiences a significant drop in accuracy from 77.97% to 63.23%. The increment in the results might happen due to the fact that an image coming from 38 frames usually contain 1 action; whereas images coming from 77 frames are generated from frames representing multiple actions. Hence, in this context when working with a multi-class setting is usually better to work with images generated from less frames even if this means a longer training process since more images are generated.

Table 1. Results for the multi-class classification task.

	77 Frames		38 Frames	
	Accuracy	F1 score	Accuracy	F1 score
ResnetRS	**77.97**	**73.37**	63.23	65.03
Convnext	67.37	61.87	68.42	63.04
EfficientNet	66.37	58.77	68.96	64.57
Resnest	67.19	62.63	69.07	64.87
Hrnet	68.95	63.79	**69.47**	**65.11**

Focusing now on the multi-label problem, we analyze the results obtained, see Table 2. For the 77 frames dataset, the models obtain similar results in terms

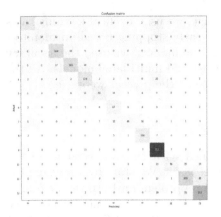 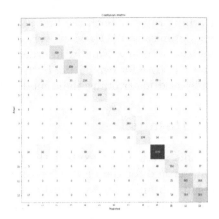

Fig. 4. Confusion matrix for multi-class classification problem. **Left.** Results with ResnetRS model on the dataset of 77 frames per image. **Right.** Results with Hrnet model on the dataset of 38 frames per image.

of multi-label accuracy, with Hrnet being the model with the best accuracy (94.48%). However, we see a variation in performance in the F1 score metric. The model with the highest F1 score is Resnest (67.11%). The rest of the models, except for Convnext (56.32%), also obtain good performance in this metric. A more fine-grained analysis of the errors produced by the Hrnet model can be seen in the associated task prediction process, see Fig. 5. We can see that the model is able to clearly distinguish the shorter tasks. However, it starts to have more difficulty in predicting the longer tasks (pick up block 2 and place it on block 1 (action 9), pick up/place cover (action 10), pick up/place screw and pick up allen key (action 11), turn both screws, return allen key and the EGT (action 12)).

Table 2. Results for multi-label classification

	77 Frames		38 Frames	
	Accuracy	F1 score	Accuracy	F1 score
ResnetRS	94.31	65.81	52.36	61.32
Convnext	93.52	56.32	47.75	57.13
EfficientNet	94.06	63.45	51.25	60.94
Resnest	94.42	67.11	55.92	66.29
Hrnet	94.48	66.46	53.02	65.23

Regarding the 38 frames dataset, we see that the results decrease both in multi-label accuracy and F1 score. In the case of accuracy, the reduction is notable, going from 94.48% in Hrnet to 55.92% in Resnest. In terms of F1 score,

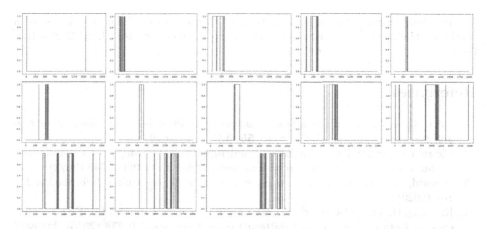

Fig. 5. Task prediction process performed throughout the video of a part assembly.

we also appreciate a slight decrease in the results, except for Convnext which improves from 56.32% to 57.13%. In this case, it can be seen that the models trained on the 38 frames dataset have not been able to correctly learn to differentiate between tasks or the transitions between them.

4 Conclusions and Further Work

In this paper, we have addressed the problem of assembly task classification in the industrial domain using two different approaches, one based on multi-class classification and the other in multi-label classification; as far as we are aware, this is the first time that the multi-label approach has been used for human monitoring of assembly tasks. In order to use state-of-the-art classification models in our context, we have proposed an approach to convert a sequence of skeleton frames into an image based on the position of the joints of the skeletons. The results achieved with our methods show that it is interesting to use the multi-label approach because the models are able to obtain more temporal information, which helps them in predicting the transition between tasks. Hence, this work is a step towards the development of models that can predict the action that are conducting the workers so a cobot might help them.

As future work, we have to study the possibility of providing more information to the models so that they are able to differentiate those tasks that are similar. Additionally, it would also be interesting to develop explainability models to provide users with more information about what is being done. Finally, we are interested in implementing our models in a real scenario, for this we want to provide more information about the execution time. In this way we can check the performance of the models to make modifications to the models so that they work in real time.

Acknowledgements. Partially supported by Ministerio de Ciencia e Innovación [PID2020-115225RB-I00 / AEI / 10.13039/501100011033], and by ADER 2022-I-IDI-00015.

References

1. Chen, C., et al.: Repetitive assembly action recognition based on object detection and pose estimation. J. Manuf. Syst. **55**, 325–333 (2020)
2. Cicirelli, G., et al.: The ha4m dataset: multi-modal monitoring of an assembly task for human action recognition in manufacturing. Sci. Data **9**(1), 745 (2022)
3. Howard, J., Gugger, S.: Fastai: a layered API for deep learning. Information **11**, 108 (2020)
4. Kaiming, H., et al.: Deep residual learning for image recognition. In: IEEE Conference on Computer Vision and Pattern Recognition, pp. 770–778 (2016). https://doi.org/10.1109/CVPR.2016.90
5. Kobayashi, T., et al.: Fine-grained action recognition in assembly work scenes by drawing attention to the hands. In: 2019 15th International Conference on Signal-Image Technology & Internet-Based Systems (SITIS), pp. 440–446. IEEE (2019)
6. Lee, J., Ahn, B.: Real-time human action recognition with a low-cost RGB camera and mobile robot platform. Sensors **20**(10), 2886 (2020)
7. Liu, J., Akhtar, N., Mian, A.: Skepxels: spatio-temporal image representation of human skeleton joints for action recognition. In: CVPR Workshops, pp. 10–19 (2019)
8. Liu, Z., et al.: A convnet for the 2020s. In: CVF Conference on Computer Vision and Pattern Recognition (CVPR), vol. 2, p. 7, IEEE (2022)
9. Mingxing, T., Le, Q.V.: Efficientnet: Rethinking model scaling for convolutional neural networks. In: International Conference on Machine Learning, vol. 97, pp. 6105–6114 (2019). https://doi.org/10.48550/arXiv.1905.11946
10. Sarkar, A., et al.: 3d human action recognition: through the eyes of researchers. Expert Syst. Appl. **193**, 116424 (2022)
11. Smith, L.: Cyclical learning rates for training neural networks. In: IEEE Winter Conference on Applications of Computer Vision, pp. 464–472 (2017)
12. Wang, J., et al.: Deep learning for sensor-based activity recognition: a survey. Pattern Recogn. Lett. **119**, 3–11 (2019)
13. Wang, J., et al.: Deep high-resolution representation learning for visual recognition. IEEE Trans. Pattern Anal. Mach. Intell. (2020). https://doi.org/10.1109/tpami. 2020.2983686
14. Wang, L., et al.: Symbiotic human-robot collaborative assembly. CIRP Ann. **68**(2), 701–726 (2019)
15. Wang, P., et al.: Deep learning-based human motion recognition for predictive context-aware human-robot collaboration. CIRP Ann. **67**(1), 17–20 (2018)
16. Zhang, H., et al.: A comprehensive survey of vision-based human action recognition methods. Sensors **19**(5), 1005 (2019)
17. Zhang, H., et al.: Resnest: split-attention networks (2020). https://doi.org/10. 48550/arXiv.2004.08955
18. Zhang, J., Wang, P, Gao, R.: Hybrid machine learning for human action recognition and prediction in assembly. Robot. Comput.-Integr. Manuf. **72**, 102184 (2021)

Image Processing and Deep Learning Methods for the Semantic Segmentation of Blastocyst Structures

María Villota[1,2]([✉]) [iD], Jacobo Ayensa-Jiménez[1,2] [iD], Manuel Doblaré[1,2] [iD],
and Jónathan Heras[3] [iD]

[1] Institute for Health Research Aragón (IIS Aragón), Aragón, Spain
mvillota@iisaragon.es
[2] Aragón Institute of Engineering Research (I3A), University of Zaragoza,
Aragón, Spain
{jacoboaj,mdoblare}@unizar.es
[3] Department of Mathematics and Computer Science, University of La Rioja,
La Rioja, Spain
jonathan.heras@unirioja.es

Abstract. Embryo selection is an indispensable step to ensure the success of in vitro fertilization. There are two techniques to perform embryo selection: preimplantation genetic screening and embryo morphological grading. However, even with these techniques, the embryo implantation probability is barely 65% making extremely difficult to evaluate their implantation potential. This is mainly due to the lack of markers, and the subjectivity associated with experience, judgment, and training of the embryologists. Computer vision and deep learning methods can help to automatically identify those markers with methods such as the segmentation of the embryo structures to offer detailed, quantitative, and objective assessments; and with that, information to predict the pregnancy outcome of embryos. In this paper, we present different methods capable of segmenting the components of an embryo (namely, the Trophectoderm, the Inner Cell Mass and the Zona Pellucida) with Dice scores ranging from 0.85 to 0.89, and openly release the code so that anyone can use it and replicate the results. These models are a first step towards a more objective evaluation of the embryos' implantation potential.

Keywords: In vitro fertilization · Blastocyst segmentation · Semantic Segmentation

1 Introduction

Infertility is a problem worldwide that affects between 10 and 15% of all couples, and both men and women [10]. In vitro fertilization (IVF) is an effective solution which keeps on growing despite the negative trend in the birth rate [10]. Given the importance of this technique, a great research effort has resulted in

A. Alonso-Betanzos et al. (Eds.): CAEPIA 2024, LNAI 14640, pp. 213–222, 2024.
https://doi.org/10.1007/978-3-031-62799-6_22

enormous advances in both IVF techniques and procedures. However, there are still many unknowns in this field, such as, the embryo selection [5,25]. In such a process, several eggs are fertilized to compensate for the fact that not all embryos develop with implantation potential [5], and they are cultured until they reach the blastocyst stage (5th or 6th day after fertilization). The blastocyst is the first morphologically differentiated state of the embryo, wherein cellular structures are arranged in four regions: the Zona Pellucida (ZP), the Trophectoderm (TE), which surrounds the Blastocoel (BC) and the Inner Cell Mass (ICM) [20] (see Fig. 1).

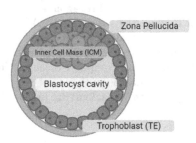

Fig. 1. Blastocyst Structure

Once the fertilized eggs reach the blastocyst stage, there are two techniques for selecting which embryos will be implanted. The former is known as *Preimplantation Genetic Screening (PGS)*, an excellent method for predicting non-implanting embryos [17]. However, the use of this technology remains low due to its cost [17] and its invasive nature — cells are taken from the embryo at a very early stage and it is possible that cells with important genetic material are collected, making the embryo unimplantable. Therefore, when using this technique, it is extremely important to avoid cells from the ICM because they will be the cells of the embryo's body [19]. Due to these reasons, the current standard for embryo selection is *embryo morphological grading*, a technique based on visual inspection of morphological characteristics and development rate of blastocyst structures [5]. Unfortunately, the criteria employed in embryo morphological grading are not clearly established, and they are based on experience, judgment, and training of the embryologists; making this process completely subjective.

This lack of knowledge has a strong impact on the success of the process, since the probability of pregnancy of an embryo with the best characteristics barely exceeds 65%. These data are less encouraging when considering the success of the pregnancy (only 50% of the embryos considered as excellent end with a birth). These probabilities are even lower when considering embryos of poorer quality [25]. Hence, it is necessary to search for a quantitative and objective evaluation procedure for embryo selection in order to increase the probability of success. Computer vision methods can help towards that aim. A first step to reach such goal is the automatic identification of different structures of a blastocyst stage embryo in order to obtain detailed information of the embryo and thus be able to perform a quantitative analysis; and this is the goal of this paper. In particular, the contribution of this work is threefold.

- To analyze several image processing algorithms and deep learning methods to segment different structures of a blastocyst stage embryo.
- To replicate state-of-the-art works for the segmentation of different structures of a blastocyst stage embryo whose code was not publicly released.
- To open-source all our code at https://github.com/mavillot/Blastocyst-Seg; so, it can help in embryo selection research.

2   Related Work

Despite the importance and growing influence of IVF, the research works that try to make more objective this process are not very numerous and can be divided into two distinct lines of research: one through image processing techniques, and the more recent one using Deep Learning models.

The works on image processing techniques use classical algorithms such as active contour models [11], textures [16], watershed segmentation [21], the level-set method [4] or ellipse fitting methods [24]. In those algorithms, different thresholds and parameters are manually fixed, making generalization to images with different properties possible but very costly since it is a matter of finding parameters that work with these new properties. Another disadvantage of those algorithms is that there is not a single method able to perform simultaneous detection of multiple structures; and, therefore, for each structure there is a different procedure.

A recent approach to deal with the drawbacks of the classical image processing methods, is the usage of convolutional neural network. In [3], five binary images were generated per blastocyst image and they propose a neural network that classifies each pixel into these 5 classes (ZP, TE, ICM, BC and background) according to a feature vector. In [1], a multiscale aggregation semantic segmentation network was trained for segmenting all the components of a blastocyst. In [12], a deep Hierarchical Neural Network for segmenting the ZP was proposed. Hua Wang [22] used the I2C module for segmenting the ZP, TE and ICM. A two layer feedforward backpropagation neural network was trained using the derived features of discrete cosine transform coefficients in [8]. Harun implemented a deep neural network based on the Residual Dilated U-Net for segmenting the TE and ICM [6] and Kheradmand et. al proposed a Fully Convolutional Network to segment the ICM [7]. Finally, [18] proposed a segmentation of the TE using a Retinex algorithm. As a summary of the results achieved in these works, most of use the dataset from [24] for training, reaching performances that range from 0.64 to 0.74 in the Jaccard index for the ZP structure, from 0.59 to 0.85 for the TE, and from 0.48 to 0.89 for the ICM structure. Among their limitations, we can mention the absence of code and models to replicate the results (except for [1]), also most of the studies do not segment all the blastocysts' components but just focus on only one or two structures, and, finally, they have been trained with the only public database (except for [3]) so they suffer from the domain-shift problem. In this work, we address the former two limitations, whereas the latter remains as further work.

3   Materials and Methods

In this section, we present both the dataset and computational methods used in our work.

3.1   Data Source

As in most studies available in the literature on the segmentation of blastocyst structures, we have employed the dataset presented in [24]. This database consists of 249 images of blastocyst stage embryos manually annotated by experts from the Pacific Centre for Reproductive Medicine (PCRM) in Canada. The annotations consist of the segmentation of three different regions (ZP, TE, ICM) of the blastocyst, a classification of the degree of TE and ICM, and also the outcome of implantation. This dataset does not present any split, therefore, each paper performs a different training-test division; but usually, a division of 85% for training and 15% for test is conducted [6,13], and the same percentages are used in our work.

From such a dataset, and following the two existing lines of research, we have performed blastocyst segmentation using both image processing methods and deep learning methods.

3.2   Proposal Description

First of all, we have replicated the image processing pipeline proposed in [16,24] using Python as programming language, and publicly released the code. Here, we briefly provide an overview of the method. Specific details can be found in the original paper, and our implementation in our GitHub repository. The proposed method is unsupervised since it does not require a training process, and consists of three different procedures (one per structure). For the ZP, the points of the inner and outer contour of the ZP are obtained by performing different operations on the image, including phase congruency in 6 orientations, convex hull, Canny edges and Watershed segmentation; subsequently, those points are fit by least squares to an ellipse for the inner contour of the ZP and another for the outer contour. Once both ellipses have been calculated, the ZP is perfectly delimited as the region between the inner ellipse and the outer ellipse. For the TE and ICM structures, the first steps of the segmentation procedure are common. Namely, the image is divided into small regions using the Watershed segmentation algorithm, and then the segmented regions are classified based on their texture into two classes: textured or smooth. Biologically, TE always appears at the edge of the blastocyst and ICM in a more central position; therefore, textured regions adjacent to the inner edge of ZP are associated with TE and textured regions in the center are associated with ICM. These regions will form the seeds to segment TE and ICM. In the case of the TE, all regions that have low intensity and are connected to the TE seed are aggregated, and the edges of the formed area are extracted using the edge linking algorithm developed by Kovesi [9]. For the ICM structure, regions are iteratively added to the ICM seed if they verify a texture-based similarity condition and a 8-connectivity condition.

In addition, we have analyzed several deep learning architectures for segmenting the blastocyst structures. The state-of-the-art results based on this kind of methods were obtained by an autoencoder architecture proposed by Harun [6] that is able to segment both the TE and ICM at the same time. However, neither the code or the models associated with such a work are available. Therefore, we started by replicating and open-sourcing such an architecture using the Keras framework — the hyperparameters used to train this models were a 0.05 in dropout, a learning rate of 10^{-4}, and loss function and callbacks that were proposed in [6].

Moreover, we also trained different models using three standard segmentation architectures (U-Net [15], Hrnet [23], and DeepLab [2]) implemented in Pytorch. The three models were trained for 45 epochs using an NVIDIA GeForce RTX 3060 GPU. These three models are trained to segment the three blastocysts' structures at the same time.

3.3 Experimentation Setup

First, since there is not a pre-defined split of the dataset, we conducted a k-fold cross-validation [14] (with $k = 10$) on the full dataset and using our implementation of the Harun's architecture [6] to study whether different train/test set splits make the results to vary significantly. The second part of our analysis consisted in studying the mean and standard deviation when evaluating the 10-fold cross validation on the testing set of all the different architectures — our implementation of the Harun's architecture is only evaluated on the TE and ICM structures since in the original paper did not segment the ZP structure. The next stage of our study was focused on comparing the best trained model from each family studied in the previous step with the results presented in the literature; in addition, we included our implemented image processing pipeline. Finally, both the image processing pipeline and the deep learning models were evaluated using as metrics the per pixel accuracy, precision, recall, and specificity, as well as, the Dice coefficient and Jaccard index.

4 Results and Discussion

In this section, we show the results obtained with the methods explained above. In Table 1 the 10-fold cross-validation in the full dataset is shown. As we can see, there are small values for the standard deviation; so, we can conclude that the division of the dataset does not have an impact on the performance of the models; and therefore, for the rest of the study we use a random split of 85% for training and 15% for testing.

The mean and standard deviation of the 10-fold is displayed in Table 2. The Hrnet and DeepLab models achieved the best results for the three blastocysts structures, reaching Dice coefficient values over 0.8 in the three structures.

Table 1. 10-fold cross validation in dataset

	Accuracy	Precision	Recall	Specificity	Dice Coeff	Jaccard idx
TE	0.96 ± 0.01	0.79 ± 0.03	0.90 ± 0.05	0.970 ± 0.006	0.72 ± 0.04	0.83 ± 0.03
ICM	0.97 ± 0.01	0.87 ± 0.04	0.74 ± 0.08	0.994 ± 0.002	0.77 ± 0.07	0.68 ± 0.07

However, it is worth noticing that the comparison of our methods with those presented in the literature is not completely fair, since some of those works use their own datasets to conduct the validation [7,8,11,18], test on 67% of the data [12] or train on a private dataset and test on the public dataset [3]; and none of them provide their code or models; so, here we just report the results provided in those papers.

We start by comparing the results obtained for the ZP structure and those presented in the literature [3,8,12] — the results presented in [24] were not included in our comparison since they use different metrics. As can be seen in Table 3, our segmentation models are the most accurate with a higher accuracy and precision; besides, our Hrnet and DeepLab models obtained a higher Jaccard index, which shows a bigger similarity between the predicted and the ground truth masks. Nevertheless, none of our models can overcome the recall achieved in [8]. It is also worth noting that all deep learning models achieved better results than those obtained by the image processing pipeline. Finally, even if the results obtained by Farias et al. [3] are worse than other approaches, they trained their models with a different dataset, and validated their model in the dataset from [24]; so that approach seems to generalize to unseen data.

Regarding the TE structure, there are several works that propose methods for segmenting this structure, see Table 4. The best results reported in the literature are those obtained by Harun [6]; however, our replicated version of such a model was not able to achieve the same results, although it is very competitive with the others segmentation models. The results obtained by our deep learning segmentation models are close to those obtained by Harun's work, and are better than the rest of the state of the art works. In addition, even if the image processing pipeline achieved worse results than our deep learning models, it is competitive with the deep learning models available in the literature.

We finish this part of the study with the ICM. This structure is the most important of the three structures, since the body of the future fetus will come out of it; hence, its correct detection is crucial, not only to make a good grading but also to ensure the integrity of the embryo using PGS. In the PGS procedure, cells are taken from the embryo to make a biopsy; taking cells belonging to the

Table 2. 10-fold cross validation in Blastocyst's structures.

Structure	Model	Accuracy	Precision	Recall	Specificity	Dice Coeff	Jaccard idx
ZP	Unet	0.958 ± 0.002	0.90 ± 0.01	0.77 ± 0.02	0.989 ± 0.002	0.83 ± 0.01	0.72 ± 0.01
	Hrnet	0.967 ± 0.001	0.93 ± 0.01	0.835 ± 0.003	0.989 ± 0.001	0.874 ± 0.003	0.784 ± 0.004
	DeepLab	0.967 ± 0.001	0.93 ± 0.01	0.83 ± 0.01	0.990 ± 0.001	0.873 ± 0.004	0.78 ± 0.01
TE	Unet	0.958 ± 0.003	0.84 ± 0.02	0.77 ± 0.02	0.98 ± 0.003	0.79 ± 0.01	0.67 ± 0.02
	Hrnet	0.968 ± 0.001	0.89 ± 0.01	0.81 ± 0.01	0.987 ± 0.001	0.843 ± 0.003	0.733 ± 0.004
	DeepLab	0.967 ± 0.001	0.89 ± 0.01	0.81 ± 0.01	0.987 ± 0.001	0.84 ± 0.01	0.73 ± 0.01
	Harun [6]	0.957 ± 0.002	0.79 ± 0.01	0.84 ± 0.04	0.972 ± 0.003	0.80 ± 0.02	0.68 ± 0.02
ICM	Unet	0.975 ± 0.003	0.89 ± 0.02	0.75 ± 0.05	0.993 ± 0.002	0.79 ± 0.03	0.69 ± 0.04
	Hrnet	0.982 ± 0.001	0.90 ± 0.01	0.85 ± 0.02	0.993 ± 0.001	0.87 ± 0.02	0.78 ± 0.02
	DeepLab	0.982 ± 0.002	0.91 ± 0.01	0.86 ± 0.02	0.992 ± 0.001	0.87 ± 0.01	0.79 ± 0.02
	Harun [6]	0.968 ± 0.004	0.85 ± 0.03	0.67 ± 0.08	0.994 ± 0.002	0.71 ± 0.06	0.61 ± 0.06

Table 3. Comparison of our best ZP models with the literature. Best in bold.

	Accuracy	Precision	Recall	Specificity	Dice Coeff	Jaccard idx
Kheradmand et al. [8]	0.92	0.80	0.81	–	–	0.64
Red et al. [12]	0.95	0.79	0.91	–	–	0.74
Farias et al. [3]	0.94	0.85	0.69	0.98	0.75	–
Image Processing	0.91	0.79	0.62	0.97	0.67	0.53
Unet	0.96	0.90	0.79	0.99	0.84	0.74
Hrnet	**0.97**	**0.93**	**0.84**	**0.99**	**0.89**	**0.79**
DeepLab	0.97	0.93	0.84	0.99	0.88	0.79

ICM could give rise to future viability problems; so, it is necessary that those cells do not belong to the ICM. This condition makes recall to be the most important metric to look at when analyzing segmentation models. Among our models, the best results were obtained with the DeepLab architecture, which is among the top 3 models in the state of the art.

A visual comparison of the implemented methods is shown in Table 6. As a summary, the results achieved by our models are similar or even better than those presented in the literature. Moreover, the deep learning approach obtains slightly better results than our image processing pipeline. However, the image processing pipeline should not be discarded, since in such approach, when generalizing to new images, only a parameter adjustment would be necessary; whereas for the deep learning model it would be necessary to retrain the network with similar images.

Table 4. Comparison of our best TE models with the literature. Best in bold.

	Accuracy	Precision	Recall	Specificity	Dice Coeff	Jaccard idx
Saeedi et al. [16]	0.86	0.69	0.89	0.86	0.77	–
Singh et al. [18]	0.87	0.71	0.83	–	0.77	0.62
Kheradmand et al. [8]	0.9	0.69	0.80	–	0.74	0.59
Harun et al. [6]	**0.98**	**0.92**	**0.93**	–	**0.92**	**0.85**
Farias et al. [3]	0.93	0.80	0.59	0.98	0.67	–
Image Processing	0.91	0.78	0.91	0.91	0.69	0.55
Unet	0.96	0.86	0.79	0.98	0.81	0.69
Hrnet	0.97	0.89	0.82	**0.99**	0.85	0.74
DeepLab	0.97	0.89	0.82	0.99	0.85	0.74
Harun (replicated)	0.96	0.78	0.88	0.97	0.82	0.71

Table 5. Comparison of our best ICM models with the literature. Best in bold.

	Accuracy	Precision	Recall	Specificity	Dice Coeff	Jaccard idx
Saeedi et al. [16]	0.91	0.77	0.84	0.92	0.79	–
Saeedi et al. [16] with DRLS	0.93	0.84	0.78	0.96	0.83	–
Kheradmand et al. [8]	0.93	0.76	0.56	–	0.64	0.48
Kheradmand et al. [7]	0.96	–	–	–	0.87	0.77
Rad et al. [11]	–	0.79	0.87	–	0.83	0.70
Rad et al. [13]	0.98	0.89	0.92	–	0.90	0.82
Harun et al. [6]	**0.99**	**0.95**	**0.94**	–	**0.94**	**0.89**
Farias et al. [3]	0.96	0.87	0.62	0.99	0.67	–
Image Processing	0.93	0.79	0.86	0.95	0.64	0.49
Unet	0.98	0.91	0.81	0.99	0.83	0.74
Hrnet	0.98	0.90	0.87	**0.99**	0.88	0.80
DeepLab	0.98	0.91	0.88	0.99	0.88	0.80
Harun (replicated)	0.98	0.87	0.88	0.99	0.86	0.77

Table 6. Predictions of the different methods in a test image

5   Conclusions and Further Work

The automatic identification of the embryo structures is necessary to study their implantation potential; and it is key to improve embryo selection techniques such as PGS and embryo morphological grading. The methods available in the literature to carry out this task do not provide a segmentation of all the structures, do not indicate how they have divided the dataset, nor do they provide the code of their models.

In this work, we have studied the importance of the dataset division in training and test set; and also the consistency of the different model families trained in our work. Our best model, based on the DeepLab architecture, achieves Dice scores over 0.8 for the segmentation of the Trophectoderm, the Inner Cell Mass, and the Zona Pellucida. Moreover, we have publicly released the code and the developed models, so anyone can easily replicate our results and use them for their own research.

As further work, we want to test our tools with embryo images captured in different conditions. Moreover, we are interested in obtaining information not only from the embryo at the blastocyst stage but also from fertilization until that moment. Thanks to such quantitative information, we will have tools that help in the prediction of the implantation potential, and serve embryologists to increase the success rate of in vitro fertilization.

Acknowledgments. This work was partially supported by Grant PID2020-115225RB-I00 funded by MCIN/AEI/10.13039/501100011033, and Agencia de Desarrollo Económico de La Rioja ADER 2022-I-IDI-00015.

References

1. Arsalan, M., et al.: Human blastocyst components detection using multiscale aggregation semantic segmentation network for embryonic analysis. Biomedicines **10**(7) (2022)
2. Chen, L.C., et al.: DeepLab: Semantic image segmentation with deep convolutional nets, Atrous convolution, and fully connected CRFs (2017)
3. Farias, A.F.S., et al.: Automated identification of blastocyst regions at different development stages. Sci. Rep. **13**(1) (2023)
4. Filho, E.S., et al.: A method for semi-automatic grading of human blastocyst microscope images. Hum.Reprod. **27**(9), 2641–2648 (2012)
5. Hardarson, T., et al.: The blastocyst. Human Reproduction **27**(suppl_1), i72–i91 (08 2012)
6. Harun, M.Y., et al.: Inner cell mass and trophectoderm segmentation in human blastocyst images using deep neural network. In: 2019 IEEE 13th International Conference on Nano/Molecular Medicine & Engineering (NANOMED), pp. 214–219 (2019)
7. Kheradmand, S., et al.: Inner cell mass segmentation in human HMC embryo images using fully convolutional network. In: 2017 IEEE International Conference on Image Processing (ICIP), pp. 1752–1756 (2017)

8. Kheradmand, S., et al.: Human blastocyst segmentation using neural network. In: 2016 IEEE Canadian Conference on Electrical and Computer Engineering (CCECE), pp. 1–4 (2016)
9. Kovesi, P.: MatLab and octave functions for computer vision and image processing. https://www.peterkovesi.com/matlabfns/
10. Marte Myhre, R., Ritsa, S.: Development of in vitro fertilization, a very important part of human reproductive medicine, in the last 40 years. Int. J. Women's Health Wellness **5**(1) (2019)
11. Rad, R.M., et al.: Coarse-to-fine texture analysis for inner cell mass identification in human blastocyst microscopic images. In: 2017 Seventh International Conference on Image Processing Theory, Tools and Applications (IPTA), pp. 1–5 (2017)
12. Rad, R.M., et al.: Human blastocyst's zona pellucida segmentation via boosting ensemble of complementary learning. Inform. Med. Unlocked **13**, 112–121 (2018)
13. Rad, R.M., et al.: Multi-resolutional ensemble of stacked dilated U-Net for inner cell mass segmentation in human embryonic images. In: 2018 25th IEEE International Conference on Image Processing (ICIP), pp. 3518–3522 (2018)
14. Refaeilzadeh, P., et al.: Cross-Validation, pp. 532–538. Springer, US, Boston, MA (2009)
15. Ronneberger, O., et al.: U-Net: convolutional networks for biomedical image segmentation (2015)
16. Saeedi, P., et al.: Automatic identification of human blastocyst components via texture. IEEE Trans. Biomed. Eng. **64**(12), 2968–2978 (2017). https://doi.org/10.1109/TBME.2017.2759665
17. Scott, R.T., et al.: Comprehensive chromosome screening is highly predictive of the reproductive potential of human embryos: a prospective, blinded, nonselection study. Fertil. Steril. **97**(4), 870–875 (2012)
18. Singh, A., et al.: Automatic segmentation of trophectoderm in microscopic images of human blastocysts. IEEE Trans. Biomed. Eng. **62**(1), 382–393 (2015)
19. Tarín, J.J., Handyside, A.H.: Embryo biopsy strategies for preimplantation diagnosis. Fertil. Steril. **59**(5), 943–952 (1993)
20. Trounson, A., Conti, A.: Research in human in-vitro fertilisation and embryo transfer. BMJ **285**(6337), 244–248 (1982)
21. VerMilyea, M., et al.: Development of an artificial intelligence-based assessment model for prediction of embryo viability using static images captured by optical light microscopy during IVF. Hum. Reprod. **35**(4), 770–784 (2020)
22. Wang, H., et al.: I2CNET: an intra- and inter-class context information fusion network for blastocyst segmentation. In: Raedt, L.D. (ed.) Proceedings of the Thirty-First International Joint Conference on Artificial Intelligence, IJCAI-22, pp. 1415–1422. International Joint Conferences on Artificial Intelligence Organization (2022). main Track
23. Xia, H., et al.: HRNET: a hierarchical recurrent convolution neural network for retinal vessel segmentation. Multimed. Tools Appl. **81**(28), 39829–39851 (2022). https://doi.org/10.1007/s11042-022-12696-4
24. Yee, D., et al.: An automatic model-based approach for measuring the zona pellucida thickness in day five human blastocysts. In: Proceedings of the International Conference on Image Processing, Computer Vision, and Pattern Recognition (IPCV), p. 1 (2013)
25. Zhao, Y.Y., et al.: Overall blastocyst quality, trophectoderm grade, and inner cell mass grade predict pregnancy outcome in euploid blastocyst transfer cycles. Chin. Med. J. **131**(11), 1261–1267 (2018)

Multivariate-Autoencoder Flow-Analogue Method for Heat Waves Reconstruction

Cosmin M. Marina[1]($\boxtimes$) iD, Eugenio Lorente-Ramos[1] iD,
Rafael Ayllón-Gavilán[2] iD, Pedro Antonio Gutiérrez[3] iD, Jorge Pérez-Aracil[1] iD,
and Sancho Salcedo-Sanz[1] iD

[1] Department of Signal Processing and Communications, Universidad de Alcalá,
Alcalá de Henares, Madrid, Spain
cosmin.marina@uah.es
[2] Department of Clinical-Epidemiological Research in Primary Care, IMIBIC,
Córdoba, Spain
[3] Department of Computer Science and Numerical Analysis, University of Córdoba,
Córdoba, Spain

Abstract. This paper contributes with an alternative to the multivariate Analogue Method (AM) version, using a preprocessing stage carried out by an Autoencoder (AE). The proposed method (MvAE-AM) is applied to reconstruct France's 2003, Balkans' 2007 and Russia 2010 mega heat waves. Using divers such as geopotential height of the 500hPA (Z500), mean sea level pressure (MSL), soil moisture (SM), and potential evaporation (PEva), the AE extracts the most relevant information into a smaller univariate latent space. Then, the classic univariate AM is applied to search for similar situations in the past over the latent space, with a minimum distance to the heat wave under evaluation. We have compared the proposed method's performance with that of a classical multivariate AM (MvAM), showing that the MvAE-AM approach outperforms the MvAM in terms of accuracy (+1.1257C), while reducing the problem's dimensionality.

Keywords: Extreme climate events · Heat waves · Multivariate method · Analogue Method

1 Introduction

In recent years, extreme weather events have become much more frequent [1]. In particular, heat waves have increased in intensity [2] [3] [4] and persistence in an unprecedented manner [5]. Heat waves have a severe impact on the ecosystem [6,7], economy [8], increased mortality [9] and health [10], among others, having regions with greater vulnerability to them [11].

Although the most addressed tasks in heat wave studies are their detection and prediction [12], attribution and causality analysis have also received significant attention in the last years [13]. For these last tasks, the use of the Analogue Method (AM) [14] is widely extended. It is a technique commonly employed

© The Author(s), under exclusive license to Springer Nature Switzerland AG 2024
A. Alonso-Betanzos et al. (Eds.): CAEPIA 2024, LNAI 14640, pp. 223–232, 2024.
https://doi.org/10.1007/978-3-031-62799-6_23

for event reconstruction or down-scaling predictions, which has been applied in the modelling and reconstruction of heat waves [15]. In this work, we focus on enhancing the attribution methods by using Deep Learning (DL) architectures such as *Autoencoders* (AEs) [16]. Specifically, we focus on the AM for multivariable data. For n predictor variables, there are two main ways to handle the multivariate version of an AM: by an n-dimensional search [14], or by an ensemble of the variables [17]. The advantages and drawbacks of both approaches will be discussed at a later stage.

The rest of the paper has been organised as follows: First, in Sect. 2, we describe the employed methodology and datasets and define in detail the AM and how we will use the AEs. Then, in Sect. 3, we present and analyse the experiments performed and the results. Finally, in Sect. 4, we present the conclusions of this work.

2   Methodology

An essential inquiry requiring clarification is the precise definition of a heat wave. We take one of the most classic definitions of heat waves [18], which defines a heat wave as at least 3 consecutive days where the daily maximum temperature, T_{max}, outstrips a threshold based on the climatology, A_d. For a specific climatology period, 1981-2010, with a daily window of 31 days, and $T_{y,i}$ as the temperature T_{max} of day i in the year y, we can define:

$$A_d = \bigcup_{y=1981}^{2010} \bigcup_{i=d-15}^{d+15} T_{y,i}, \tag{1}$$

where the threshold of any day, d, is calculated as the 90th percentile of climatology, $th(d) = P_{90}(A_d)$.

Following this methodology, we have considered one of the most notorious heat waves in the last years, which is related to more than 11000 deaths [18], namely, the **Aug. 2003 mega heat wave in France**. Also, in order to compare the goodness of the model, we selected the **Aug. 2007 in Balkans and Aug. 2010 in Russia mega heat waves**. Table 1 contains all the relevant information about the specification of these heat waves.

Table 1. Summary information of the heat waves considered.

Heat wave	Duration	Max. C	Predictor region	Target region
France 2003	01 Aug. – 19 Aug.	30.7713	32N – 70N	42N – 50N
			28W – 30E	6W – 8E
Balkans 2007	15 Aug. – 28 Aug.	32.3720	32N – 70N	40N – 52N
			8W – 50E	18E – 42E
Russia 2010	16 Jul. – 19 Aug.	35.8202	32N – 70N	38N – 60N
			22E – 80E	40E – 60E

2.1   Data

The used data is obtained from the ERA5 Reanalysis dataset [19] from 1940 to 2022, with a resolution of 2. We have selected different fields as predictor variables based on the most used ones in the literature:

1. The geopotential height of the 500hPA pressure surface (Z500), as it is known to be one of the most suitable drivers for heat waves [20] because of the crucial role of the atmospheric circulation [21].
2. The mean sea level pressure (MSL), as a representative diver of the long-term, synoptic scale information [22].
3. The soil moisture (SM), as a predictor of local information [23].
4. The potential evaporation (PEva), [24] as a driver for summer heat waves.

In Fig. 1, we show an anomaly analysis carried out as the difference between the data throughout the heat wave and the data on the climatology period for each predictor variable. The region within the boxes corresponds to the *predictor region* defined in Table 1. In Fig. 2, we carry out the same analysis for the target temperature. The boxes corresponds to the *target region* from Table 1.

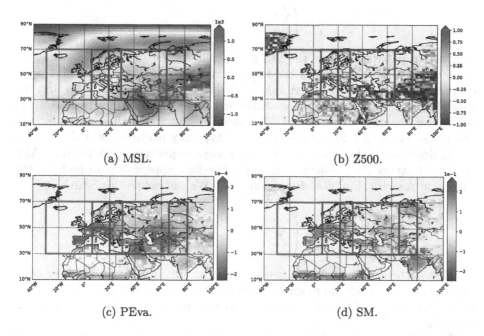

(a) MSL.

(b) Z500.

(c) PEva.

(d) SM.

Fig. 1. Predictors anomaly regarding to climatology. The red region corresponds to France 2003, the green region to Balkans 2007 and the blue region to Russia 2010. (Color figure online)

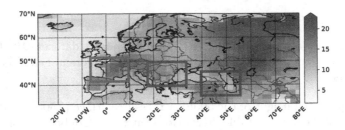

Fig. 2. Temperature anomaly regarding to climatology. The red region corresponds to France 2003, the green region to Balkans 2007 and the blue region to Russia 2010. (Color figure online)

2.2   The Multivariate Analogue Method

The Analogue Method is based on the assumption that local state similarities cause similar effects [25]. Given a dataset of a predictor variable, X, consisting of spatial maps along a period, a target map for a specific time moment, x_{hw}, we can define the Analogue Search as:

$$\min_{t=0}^{T} \left(\sum_{i=1}^{m} |x_{hw,i} - x_{i,t}|^p \right)^{\frac{1}{p}}, \tag{2}$$

in which $x_{i,t}$ is the value of the i-th grid point, of the t-th time, x_{hw},i is the value of the i-th grid point of the target map, m is the amount of grid point on the map, and p is an integer value. The objective of the AM is to find the variable fields with the minimum distance to the target. As can be seen, we define the distance metric as the Minkowski distance, where p stands for the order. Euclidean ($p = 2$) or taxicab ($p = 1$) typically perform the AM.

As described above, there are two main ways to perform a Multivariate AM. Given n features (or predictor variables), the first approach is to perform the Analogue Search (2) in all n dimensions [14]. We can define this Search as:

$$\min_{t=0}^{T} \left(\sum_{j=1}^{n \times m} |x_{hw,j} - x_{j,t}|^p \right)^{\frac{1}{p}} \tag{3}$$

This is the easiest and most used approach, but, in turn, it is a very computationally expensive approach. In addition, the higher the dimensionality, the higher the noise and the more complicated it is to get analogue states close to the target.

The second approach is based on building a search ensemble [17]. Thus, n searches are performed on maps of size m sequentially. Thus, if we have 4 variables ordered arbitrarily, we will perform 4 searches. We will search for the best analogues on the first variable (e.g. 5000 analogues), and use them to perform the next search. For the second variable, we will obtain the nearest analogues, e.g. 1000, from the previous one. This approach has a lower computational cost but a higher time cost. Moreover, it is necessary to set a hierarchy between variables, which produces a bias in the search. For example, it is not the same to find the nearest states in Z500 and search in them for the nearest ones in SM as to do it in the opposite order. For a small number of predictor variables, it is possible to carry out a correlation analysis or to use prior knowledge about which variables are most important for the problem. However, it is difficult to set the hierarchy on a larger scale Even on the small scale, after having set a hierarchy with correlation analysis or prior knowledge, it is not clear that that will be the optimal hierarchy. Therefore, in order to avoid self-introduced bias, we will use the first approach as a reference in this work.

2.3   The MvAE-AM Approach

In addition to the traditional Analogue Method (AM), another approach worth considering is the utilization of Autoencoders (AE) [16]. AEs are a type of Deep Learning architecture consisting of 3 parts: an encoder, latent space (or codification space), and a decoder. In Fig. 3 we can see the general structure of an AE. This model specializes in reducing the dimensionality of the input data. The encoder aims to encode the input received in a smaller dimension, while the decoder aims to reconstruct the input received based on the latent space.

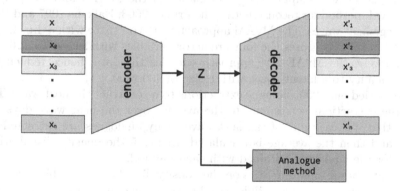

Fig. 3. MvAE-AM structure.

This approach allows transforming a multivariable problem into a univariate one. The Multivariate Autoencoder Analogue Method (MvAE-AM) considers each input predictor variable in a different channel. The encoder applies different convolutional filters to each channel to gather all the information in a single latent space. Thus, the AM uses the latent space as a search space. In this way, there is no need to use any multivariate version of the AM, and we can do the search by using Eq. (2) with $p = 2$ (euclidean). The role of the decoder in this process is only to serve the encoder to train it and to be able to encode the multichannel information in the best possible way.

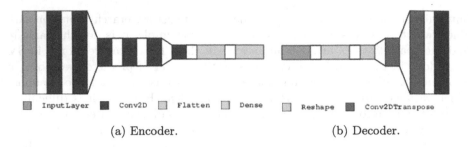

(a) Encoder.   (b) Decoder.

Fig. 4. MvAE-AM architecture.

A detailed scheme of the architecture is shown in Fig. 4. The maps of the different predictor variables, which are at 2 resolution, have a size of (20×30). The encoder consists of six convolutional layers, the first three with 32 filters whilst the others have 26 filters. Meanwhile, the decoder has only two transposed convolutional layers, 16 and 32 filters, respectively.

3   Experiments and Results

In this section, we compare the performance of the MvAM and the proposed MvAE-AM method for reconstructing the France 2003, Balkans 2007 and Russia 2020 mega heat waves. The MvAM approach works on space with a dimension of 2400 (2400×1), as it uses the four predictor variables with size maps (20×30). Alternatively, the MvAE-AM approach encodes the data, hence reducing the dimensionality to a latent space with a size of 400 (400×1).

We carried out 1000 analogue extractions to reconstruct the heat wave. These analogue extractions correspond to the average over the heat wave days. This means that, for each day of the heat wave, daily analogues are extracted 1000 times, and then the average is calculated. In Fig. 5 the density distribution is shown for the analogues obtained with each method.

We can obtain some statistics on the density distributions. Table 2 shows the dimension space, the average difference between analogues and the target in the space of the predictors, the average temperature difference to the target, the average temperature of the analogues, and the standard deviation.

To these results, we can add the time cost of each method. The MvAM method requires 5 min 31 s. for France 2003, 6 min 17 s for Balkans 2007 and 10 min 48 s for Russia 2010 to run. Meanwhile, the MvAE-AM has required for France 2003 2 min 26 s for analogue search and 7 min 32 s for training, for Balkans 2007 4 min 5 s for analogue search and 14 min 40 s for training, and Russia 2010 5 min 52 s for analogue search and 17 min 36 s for training. As the MvAE-AM performs the analogue search in a reduced dimension, this process fasts, but requires a previous step for training the AE. The use of AE to preprocess the data may be computationally expensive. However, several advantages can be derived from their use. There is a reduction of the dimensionality and a simplification

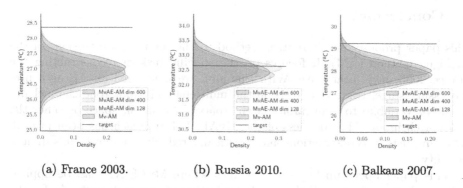

(a) France 2003.   (b) Russia 2010.   (c) Balkans 2007.

Fig. 5. Comparison between MvAM and MvAE-AM distributions.

Table 2. Average MvAE-AM and MvAM results for the studied heat waves.

	Dim.	Avg. Prd. Diff.	Avg. Temp. Diff.	Avg. Temp.	Std. Temp
France 2003					
Target	-	-	-	**28.3582**	-
MvAM	2400	0.0650	1.4455	26.9127	0.3749
MvAE-AM	128	0.0083	1.5942	26.7640	0.3682
MvAE-AM	400	0.0138	1.3198	27.0384	0.3979
MvAE-AM	600	0.0202	1.2363	27.1219	0.3772
Balkans 2007					
Target	-	-	-	**29.2392**	-
MvAM	2400	0.0870	1.3507	27.8885	0.4774
MvAE-AM	128	0.0112	1.4744	27.7648	0.5114
MvAE-AM	400	0.0170	1.2834	27.9558	0.5095
MvAE-AM	600	0.0205	1.2583	27.9809	0.5036
Russia 2010					
Target	-	-	-	**32.6340**	-
MvAM	2400	0.0218	0.2172	32.4168	0.3627
MvAE-AM	128	0.0117	0.2740	32.3600	0.3550
MvAE-AM	400	0.1105	0.1126	32.5214	0.3290
MvAE-AM	600	0.0297	0.1964	32.4376	0.4423

in the analogue search. Instead of working with a Multivariate version of AM, the AE allows transforming the multivariable problem into a univariate one. On the other hand, the reconstruction of the heat wave obtained with MvAE-AM is closer to the target variable field and more precise than the MvAM one. There are two key reasons supporting this result: 1) in a smaller dimensional space, the proximity is better captured, and 2) the AE can obtain and encode the most relevant information of each predictor variable.

4   Conclusions

This paper proposes an alternative method to the multivariate versions of the analogue method (AM). It focuses on the specific task of reconstructing the France 2003 mega heat wave. With this aim, we have used an AE as a pre-processing stage, training it to code the multichannel input (one channel per predictor variable) to a univariate latent space. This latent space becomes the AM search input. The goodness of the MvAE-AM approach has been proved, obtaining better reconstructions and drastically reducing the problem's dimensionality.

This paper opens up two research lines where MvAE-AM can be applied directly: down-scaling predictions and attribution of extreme events. As for the first research line, the AM has been applied as a down-scaling technique for predictions [14]. General Circulation Models (GCMs) are widely used to study climate change. These GCMs are very accurate at large scales, but at smaller resolution scales, they have several issues [26]. This is where our method can be used as a down-scaling technique, looking for analogues to the prediction given by GCMs and reconstructing the event on a local scale. As for the attribution of extreme climate events, the second research line, the MvAE-AM, may have a key role in analysing and assessing climate change [27] and anthropogenic influence. The AM has been used to perform the attribution task, but in a univariate context [28]. MvAE-AM facilitates combining several predictor variables and drivers in the attribution analysis.

Acknowledgements. This research has been partially supported by the European Union, through H2020 Project "CLIMATE INTELLIGENCE Extreme events detection, attribution and adaptation design using machine learning (CLINT)", Ref: 101003876-CLINT. The present study has been partially supported by the "Agencia Estatal de Investigación (España)" (grant ref.: PID2020-115454GB-C21 and PID2020-115454GB-C22 through the projects of the Spanish Ministry of Science and Innovation (MICINN). David Guijo-Rubio has been supported by the "Agencia Estatal de Investigación (España)" MCIU/AEI/10.13039/501100011033 and European Union NextGenerationEU/PRTR (grant ref.: JDC2022-048378-I).

References

1. Salcedo-Sanz, S., et al.: Analysis, characterization, prediction, and attribution of extreme atmospheric events with machine learning and deep learning techniques: a review. Theoret. Appl. Climatol. **155**, 1–44 (2023)
2. Barriopedro, D., Garcia-Herrera, R.A., Ordóñez, C., Miralles, D.G., Salcedo-Sanz, S.: Heat waves: Physical understanding and scientific challenges. Rev. Geophys. **61** (2023)
3. Rousi, E., Kornhuber, K., Beobide-Arsuaga, G., Luo, F., Coumou, D.: Accelerated western European heatwave trends linked to more-persistent double jets over Eurasia. Nat. Commun. **13** (2022)
4. Papari, J.R., Perkins-Kirkpatrick, S.E., Sharples, J.J.: Intensifying Australian heatwave trends and their sensitivity to observational data. Earth's Future **9** (2020)

5. White, R.H., et al.: The unprecedented pacific northwest heatwave of June 2021. Nat. Commun. **14** (2023)
6. He, G.-X., et al.: Assessing the impact of atmospheric heatwaves on intertidal clams. Sci. Total Environ., 156744 (2022)
7. Siboni, N., et al.: Increased abundance of potentially pathogenic vibrio and a marine heatwave co-occur with a pacific oyster summer mortality event. Aquaculture (2024)
8. Materia, S., et al.: Summer temperature response to extreme soil water conditions in the Mediterranean transitional climate regime. Clim. Dyn. **58**, 1943–1963 (2021)
9. López-Bueno, J.A., et al.: Evolution of the threshold temperature definition of a heat wave vs. evolution of the minimum mortality temperature: a case study in Spain during the 1983-2018 period. Environ. Sci. Eur. **33**, 1–10 (2021)
10. Torralba, V., et al.: Nighttime heat waves in the euro-Mediterranean region: definition, characterisation, and seasonal prediction. Environ. Res. Lett. (2024)
11. Adnan, M.S.G., Dewan, A., Botje, D., Shahid, S., Hassan, Q.K.: Vulnerability of Australia to heatwaves: a systematic review on influencing factors, impacts, and mitigation options. Environ. Res., 113703 (2022)
12. Fister, D., Pérez-Aracil, J., Peláez-Rodríguez, C., Ser, J.D., Salcedo-Sanz, S.: Accurate long-term air temperature prediction with a fusion of artificial intelligence and data reduction techniques. ArXiv abs/2209.15424 (2022)
13. Ren, L., Zhou, T., Zhang, W.: Attribution of the record-breaking heat event over northeast Asia in summer 2018: the role of circulation. Environ. Res. Lett. **15** (2020)
14. Zorita, E., von Storch, H.: The analog method as a simple statistical downscaling technique: comparison with more complicated methods. J. Clim. **12**, 2474–2489 (1999)
15. Gao, X., Schlosser, C.A., Morgan, E.: Application of the analogue method to modeling heat waves: a case study with power transformers **16** (2017)
16. Pinaya, W.H.L., Vieira, S., Garcia-Dias, R., Mechelli, A.: Autoencoders. In: Machine Learning, pp. 193–208. Elsevier (2020)
17. Caillouet, L.P., Vidal, J., Sauquet, E., Graff, B., Soubeyroux, J.M.: Scope climate: a 142-year daily high-resolution ensemble meteorological reconstruction dataset over France. Earth Syst. Sci Data (2019)
18. Russo, S., Sillmann, J., Fischer, E M.: Top ten European heatwaves since 1950 and their occurrence in the coming decades. Environ. Res. Lett. **10** (2015)
19. Hersbach, H., et al.: The era5 global reanalysis. Q. J. R. Meteorol. Soc. **146**, 1999–2049 (2020)
20. Demirtaş, M.: The anomalously hot summer of 2021 over the euro-Mediterranean region: underlying atmospheric drivers and heatwaves. Theor. Appl. Climatol. **152**, 861–870 (2023)
21. Jézéquel, A., Yiou, P., Radanovics, S.: Role of circulation in European heatwaves using flow analogues. Clim. Dyn. **50**, 1145–1159 (2018)
22. Salinger, M.J., et al.: The unprecedented coupled ocean-atmosphere summer heatwave in the new Zealand region 2017/18: drivers, mechanisms and impacts. Environ. Res. Lett. **14** (2019)
23. Zeder, J., Fischer, E.M.: Quantifying the statistical dependence of mid-latitude heatwave intensity and likelihood on prevalent physical drivers and climate change. Adv. Stat. Climatol. Meteorol. Oceanograp. (2023)
24. di Capua, G., et al.: Drivers behind the summer 2010 wave train leading to Russian heatwave and Pakistan flooding. NPJ Climate Atmospheric Sci. **4**, 1–14 (2021)

25. Lorenz, E.N.: Atmospheric predictability as revealed by naturally occurring analogues. J. Atmos. Sci. **26**, 636–646 (1969)
26. Grotch, S.L., Maccracken, M.C.: The use of general circulation models to predict regional climatic change. J. Clim. **4**, 286–303 (1991)
27. Hulme, M.: Attributing weather extremes to 'climate change' a review. Prog. Phys. Geogr. **38**(4), 499–511 (2014)
28. Faranda, D., Vrac, M., Yiou, P., Jézéquel, A., Thao, S.: Changes in future synoptic circulation patterns: consequences for extreme event attribution. Geophys. Res. Lett. **47** (2020)

HEX-GNN: Hierarchical EXpanders for Node Classification

Ahmed Begga[✉][iD], Miguel Ángel Lozano[iD], and Francisco Escolano[iD]

University of Alicante, Alicante, Spain
{ahmed.begga,malozano,sco}@ua.es

Abstract. Graph Neural Networks (GNNs) are efficient in learning expressive representations of structured data such as graphs. Recent studies have been focused on addressing heterophily, a common phenomenon in real-world networks, which challenges the homophilic assumption that nodes of the same class are more likely to connect, thus limiting the applicability of conventional GNNs in tasks like node classification. However, existing methods designed for dealing with heterophily still lack effectiveness in some typical heterophilic datasets. Furthermore, finding the optimal combination of node features and graph topology under the heterophilic regime is still an open issue. In this paper, we propose an adaptive GNN architecture for dealing both with homophilic and heterophilic datasets. This architecture leverages the power of expander graphs as a means of effective message propagation (the underlying mechanism of GNNs). In short, we selectively densify the GNN at different hierarchical orders and then find the optimal combination of embeddings. Finally, we test this new approach by performing experiments over different state-of-the-art datasets with a wide range of levels of heterophily and a wide range of sizes.

Keywords: Graph Neural Networks · Node Classification · Semi-supervised learning · Structural Learning · Pattern Recognition

1 Introduction

Graph Neural Networks (GNNs) have found extensive applications in various domains such as social networks [1], traffic networks [2], recommendation systems, and computer vision [3] owing to their robust ability to process graph-structured data. They have been successfully adapted for a range of network analysis tasks, including node classification [4–6], link prediction [7], and graph classification [8].

Node classification, which involves predicting unknown node labels based on node embeddings and graph topology, has been effectively addressed using GNNs and its variants like GCN [4], GAT [5], and GraphSage [9]. These methods demonstrate the effectiveness of leveraging the *principle of aggregation of neighboring nodes*, surpassing Multi-Layer Perceptrons (MLP). However, the efficacy of *blind aggregation* is contingent *under homophily* where the shared features

© The Author(s), under exclusive license to Springer Nature Switzerland AG 2024
A. Alonso-Betanzos et al. (Eds.): CAEPIA 2024, LNAI 14640, pp. 233–242, 2024.
https://doi.org/10.1007/978-3-031-62799-6_24

and/or class labels among neighbors are similar. Real-world networks sometimes exhibit an "opposites attract" behavior, leading to heterophily where nodes with different features and labels tend to be linked [10]. Existing GNNs face limitations in heterophily settings due to the absence of an effective mechanism that leverages graph structure and node similarity [11]. As a result, they are beaten by MLPs in some datasets.

Notable examples of GNN architectures addressing the heterophily issue include CGNN [12], H2GCN [10], and MixHop [13]. Despite these improvements, shortcomings persist in certain heterophilic datasets, primarily due to the inadequate exploitation of graph and node features. This underscores the necessity for more sophisticated methodologies to address these limitations effectively.

Moreover, it is observed that these techniques often encounter challenges in adapting to homophilic datasets, as they predominantly prioritize feature-centric considerations over crucial graph structural information. Furthermore, methods relying on higher powers of the transition matrix [13,14] exhibit increased density in larger graphs, leading to diminished accuracy or memory inefficiencies. Hence, there exists a pressing demand for novel approaches that can reconcile these challenges and provide robust solutions across diverse network configurations.

In addition, it is widely acknowledged that GNNs frequently experience issues related to over-smoothing. This phenomenon occurs when the node representations become excessively similar across multiple layers of the network, leading to a loss of discriminative information. This occurs due to repeated message passing and aggregation steps, leading to the blending of node features and ultimately hindering the model's ability to distinguish between nodes effectively [6,10]. Different works in the literature tackle this issue by proposing different layers that preserve initial node embedding [11], but these techniques are out of the scope of this paper since they focus on limiting information flows instead of selectively leveraging them. Our work addresses the aforementioned limitations in a principled way, which in turn provides a more explainable architecture. We summarize the main contributions of our work as follows:

- We provide insights based on *expander graphs* to mitigate the problems and the struggles of information flow over the heterophilic graphs. Expanders are well suited to improve information flow selectively.
- An effective, sparse, and *principled architecture* that improves the flow of information over the graph and is capable of dealing with homophilic and heterophilic graphs.
- Our proposed method showcases superior performance compared to state-of-the-art techniques, as confirmed by extensive experiments conducted on 12 diverse benchmark datasets.
- When dealing with large graphs, we sparsify the graph attending both to feature similarity and high-order topologic information.

This paper is organized as follows. We commence by reviewing the related works, mostly those focused on Hierarchical or High-Order (HO) GNNs and other significant models in the State-of-the-Art (SoTA), e.g. LINKX for large graph. Then, after some formal preliminaries we present our method and justify its architecture. Finally, we evaluate experimentally the proposed GNN and analyze its results in several regimes (homophilic, heterophilic, large graph). We conclude by summarizing the results and sketching our future work in this field.

2 Related Works

In this section, we address the numerous studies that are actively addressing the heterophily phenomenon, an unsolved problem in GNNs.

H2GCN [10] is a pioneering research on GNNs representational capabilities in the presence of heterophily. This method integrates ego- and neighbor-embedding separation, explores high-order neighborhood structures, and synthesizes intermediate representations. Another innovative architecture is GPR-GNN [15], which integrates an adaptive generalized PageRank approach with GNNs. This integration aims to alleviate feature over-smoothing, leading to enhanced performance, particularly in scenarios with varied node label patterns. Similarly, in GGCN [16] they conducted theoretical analyses on two strategies: degree corrections and signed messages. Based on these analyses, they proposed a generalized model, which aims to tackle both heterophily and over-smoothing issues simultaneously.

The issue of heterophily, which the methods mentioned above primarily address, represents just one aspect requiring meticulous attention. As a result, these methods might not perform well on specific datasets with heterophilic characteristics, underscoring the importance of carefully investigating other aspects of graph datasets that may have been overlooked. Interestingly, simpler models like MLPs and/or LINK [1] demonstrate strong node classification performance on these datasets. MLPs rely solely on node features as input and outperform some general GNNs on heterophilic datasets. Meanwhile, the LINK model, which conducts logistic regression solely on the graph's adjacency matrix, surpasses many existing models on heterophilic datasets. These findings underscore the importance of delving deeper into the relationship between GNN performance and the homophily/heterophily property of graphs. In addition, there is a need to investigate why the exclusive use of node features or network structure can still provide decent performance on specific datasets.

Recent works have emerged addressing this need that combine node features with graph representations. For instance, LINKX [1], which extends node feature MLPs and LINK regression, achieves promising results on heterophilic graphs and mitigates performance degradation in the minibatch setting.

Mixhop [13] and FSGNN [14] are novel approaches that aggregate the features from neighbors from different distances (using powers of the transition matrix). The difference is that FSGNN introduces a novel approach that incorporates softmax as a regularizer and applies L2-Normalization across GNN layers.

Additionally, advancements in graph neural networks come from different angles. For instance, Geom-GNN [6] addresses issues such as the loss of discriminative structures and long-range dependencies in existing GNNs. It accomplishes this by bridging discrete graphs to a continuous geometric space through graph embedding.

3   Preliminaries

In this section, we will introduce the notations used and provide *vanilla* GNNs, offering background information to enhance understanding.

Notations. In this paper, we denote an undirected graph as $\mathcal{G} = (\mathcal{V}, \mathcal{E})$, where $\mathcal{V}$ represents the set of nodes and $|\mathcal{V}|$ denotes the cardinality of $\mathcal{V}$. The edgeset $\mathcal{E} \subseteq \mathcal{V} \times \mathcal{V}$ is described by a symmetric adjacency matrix $A \in \{0, 1\}^{|\mathcal{V}| \times |\mathcal{V}|}$ for unweighted graphs, where $A_{ij} = 1$ signifies the existence of an edge between nodes v_i and v_j. Incorporating self-loops into the graph leads to the formation of the resultant adjacency matrix denoted as $\tilde{A} = A + I$, where I denotes the identity matrix. Nodes features is denoted by a matrix $X \in \mathbb{R}^{|\mathcal{V}|} \times d^{(0)}$ The diagonal degree matrix D of $\mathcal{G}$,characterized by $D_{ii} = d_i = \sum_j A_{ij}$ provides insights unto the degrees of the node. Furthermore, we introduce the normalized transition matrix P, defined as $D^{-\frac{1}{2}} A D^{-\frac{1}{2}}$.

Graph Neural Networks. Graph Neural Networks (GNNs) operate by learning node representations through the aggregation and transformation of information across the graph topology, typically involving three key steps: propagation, aggregation, and updating. In the l-th layer of a GNN, we represent the node representations as $H^{(l)} \in \mathbb{R}^{|\mathcal{V}| \times d^{(l)}}$, where $d^{(l)}$ is the number of features in this layer and the i-th row vector h_i^l encapsulates the embedding of node v_i. The initial representation matrix $H^{(0)}$ corresponds to the matrix X defined previously. Specifically, the node embedding of the l-th layer $h_i^{(l)}$ is obtained as follows: (1) propagation: $\hat{h}_i^{(l)} = \phi^{(l)}(h_i^{(l-1)})$; (2) aggregation: $\hat{h}_i^{(l)} = \square_{v_j \in \mathcal{N}_i}(\hat{h}_j^{(l)})$;(3) updating: $\hat{h}_i^{(l)} = \gamma^{(l)}(\hat{h}_i^{(l)}, \hat{h}_j^{(l)})$. Here, $\square$ represents a differentiable, permutation-invariant operation such as $sum, max, mean$ [9]. Additionally, $\phi^{(l)}$ and $\gamma^{(l)}$ represent differentiable functions commonly implemented using MLPs. A GNN can be formally defined as follows:

$$\hat{h}_i^l = \sigma(A \hat{H}_j^{(l-1)} W_j^{(l)}) . \tag{1}$$

Herein, $W^{(l)}$ is the trainable weight matrix of the l-th layer, and $W_j^{(l)}$ denotes its j-th column. The function σ denotes a nonlinear activation function, such as the ReLU function used in this study. Specifically, we adopt the normalized version of GNNs known as Graph Convolutional Networks (GCN) [4]. GCN is defined similarly to Eq. 1, but with the distinction that instead of using A, we employ $D^{-\frac{1}{2}} A D^{-\frac{1}{2}}$.

Finally, a row-wise softmax operation is applied to the node embedding $\hat{h}^{(L)}$ of the final layer for classification. The loss function $\mathcal{L}$ is formulated as:

$$\mathcal{L} = \frac{1}{|D|} \sum_{(x_i, y_i) \in D} \text{CE}(softmax(MLP(\hat{h}_i^{(L)})), y_i), \tag{2}$$

where D represents the dataset, associating the one-hot encoded label y_i with the feature x_i for node v_i. CE denotes the cross-entropy loss function, evaluating the disparity between the GNN's predictions and the true labels.

4 Method

In this section, we explain the technical details of our proposed framework. We first define what is the high-order component, then we develop the modulated expansion and, we link our insight of expanders concerning heterophily. Finally, we explain the proposed architecture HEX-GNN.

The High-Order component. GNN architectures differ in the way they provide a *template* for effective message passing since the initial network provided by the adjacency matrix A of $\mathcal{G} = (\mathcal{V}, \mathcal{E})$ is (at least) prone to over-smoothing. In the heterophilic regime, a given node (see the red node 3 in Fig. 1) is typically surrounded by nodes of different classes (blue ones in this example). As a result, the levels of its *computational graph* reflect how far its homologs are. High-order (HO) or hierarchical networks skip first-order neighbors and jump towards second (or higher)-order ones to aggregate them directly, thus avoiding over-smoothing.

In practice, HO networks are implemented by leveraging different powers $P, P^2, P^3, \ldots$, of the transition matrix P. P_{ij}^k encodes the probability of reaching node j from i in k hops (or levels in the computational graph). In this regard, HO-GNNs incorporate self-loops $\tilde{A} = A + I$ to the adjacency matrix before computing P to add a bit of flexibility (inclusive diffusion or laziness in the random walks). Doing so, for each P^k with $k \geq 1$, all nodes reached in k hops *or less* are retained thus leading to an inclusive exploration.

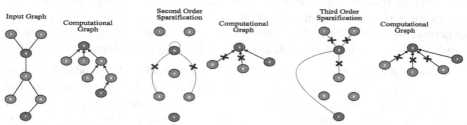

Fig. 1. In the Heterophilic Regime, homologs are far away. (Color figure online)

Modulated Expansion. However, the powers P^k of the transition matrix tend to populate the adjacency matrix in a very dense way as follows: If j is very far from i, then $P_{ij}^k \to 0$ but as *it is not zero*, our experience indicates that this fact often confounds the MLPs within the GNN neurons and those within the classification layer. We address the problem as follows:

Firstly, for any pair of edges $(i, j) \in \mathcal{E}$ we compute the *normalized cosine similarity* $\angle(X_i, X_j)$, where the rows X_i and X_j of the nodes feature matrix X

are the features of nodes i and j (see Fig. 2 where each row is incongruent with the colormap of the corresponding class).

The cosine similarity is used to *sparsify* P^k as follows. We define $\hat{P}_{ij}^k = 1$ if $P_{ij}^k > 0$ and $\angle(X_i, X_j) > \epsilon$, where ϵ is the mean value of all normalized similarities. This filter allows us to integrate homologs with potentially small values of P^{ij}. For instance in Fig. 1, the homolog of node 3 (node 7) can only be reached with a second-order neighborhood P^2 (two levels in the computational graph). Using $\hat{P}^2$ we only discard non-homologs (nodes 5 and 6) but we do not reach node 7 until P^3. Then, $\hat{P}^3$ not only discards non-homologs but fully integrates the features of homolog nodes even when $P_{ij}^k \ll P_{ij}^l$ for $l < k$.

Computing $P_{ij}^k > \epsilon$ does not scale even for $k = 2$ and not-too-large but very dense graphs such as SQUIRREL (see Table 1) which has $198,493$ edges and only $5,201$ nodes. These graphs, as well as the large ones in Table 2, with more than one million edges, require a different treatment. Once we perform the filter $\hat{P}_{ij}^k = 1$ if $P_{ij}^k > 0$ and $\angle(X_i, X_j) > \epsilon$, we retain the $2|\mathcal{E}|$ entries in $\hat{P}^k$ edges with higher similarities, thus preserving the original number of edges. This *second sparsification* is conceptually close to an importance sampling.

Heterophilic Expanders. The above step is called "modulated expansion" because we follow the principles of *expander graphs* (EGs) [17] [18]. EGs are graphs with good information propagation properties. They are specifically designed to break bottlenecks such as the ones emerging from slightly connected communities. The basic idea of an EG is to design a sparse graph that becomes selectively dense at bottlenecks thereby minimizing the graph's diameter (the length of the shortest path) and ensuring that all nodes are reachable within a small number of hops. This concept was recently incorporated into the GNN literature in [19], but the task was exclusively devoted to *graph regression*. When adopting this idea to node classification in the heterophilic regime, we have taken into account that "blind expansion" may usually lead to over-smoothing. This is why we perform a "modulated" or "selective" expansion, thus sparsifying the structural template of the GNN when making it better suited to the task at hand. This idea is close to "graph rewiring" [8] but in the heterophilic regime.

Proposed Architecture. The HEX-GNN (Hierarchical EXpander GNN) is depicted in Fig. 2. We have four GNNs in parallel. The first three ones are fed by $\hat{P}, \hat{P}^2$ and $\hat{P}^3$ diffusing the node features. For the sake of simplicity, we do not display the cosine similarity matrix here. The fourth "branch" is an MLP in the spirit of LINKX. The result of each GNN is an embedding for each node and a linear combination (whose coefficients $\alpha_i \in [0, 1]$ are learned for the sake of explainability) of the four embeddings is forwarded to the classification MLP. In the Heterophilic regime, we naturally have $\alpha_4 \approx 1$).

5   Experimental Settings

In this section, we present the datasets that we use to assess our framework. Additionally, we provide details about the experimental configurations and the baselines for comparison.

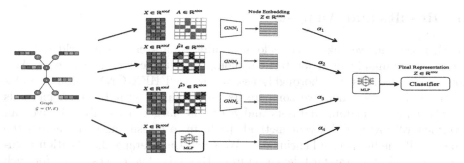

Fig. 2. The HEX-GNN Architecture. The fourth branch (MLP) complements the GNNs and it is quite helpful in the Heterophilic Regime.

5.1 Datasets

We assess the effectiveness of our HEX-GNN framework and various state-of-the-art GNNs on node classification tasks using nine small/medium real-world datasets. These datasets include ACTOR, CHAMELEON, CITESEER, CORA, CORNELL, PUBMED, SQUIRREL, TEXAS, and WISCONSIN, which have been released by [6]. In addition, we test the effectiveness of our method in large real-world datasets, such as PENN94, ARXIV- YEAR, and OGBN-ARXIV, released by [1]. All the descriptions about these datasets are to be found in the first rows of the Tables 1 and 2. Also, we include the edge homophily ratio HOM LEVEL [10], which represents the proportion of intra-class edges in the graph, and the average degree, where $\hat{d} = \frac{1}{|\mathcal{V}|} \sum_{v_i \in \mathcal{V}} d(v_i)$ is determined by summing the in-degree and out-degree of node v_i.

5.2 Settings

Experiments on small, medium, and large-scale datasets are conducted using PyTorch and PyTorch Geometric (PyG) [20], utilizing a single NVIDIA RTX 4090 with a memory capacity of 24 GB. For all benchmark datasets, we employ the feature vectors and class labels supplied by PyG. Regarding the small and medium-scale, we adopt splits (48%/32%/20%) of nodes per class for training, validation, and testing respectively, as in [6]. Meanwhile, for the large-scale datasets, we adopted the same splits (50%/25%/25%) as in [1]. For each dataset, we compute 10000 epochs with an early stopping strategy employed [1]. For more details, all the configurations and code can be found in our github https://github. com/AhmedBegggaUA/HEX-GNN. The performance of node classification is evaluated based on the overall mean accuracy and standard deviation on test sets across the 10 splits for small, medium-scale, and 5 splits for large-scale datasets.

6   Results and Analysis

In this section, we take a close look at nine small-scale real-world datasets that are commonly used for testing, along with three larger-scale ones. Following our analysis, we thoroughly assess how well HEX-GNN classifies nodes in these datasets. Then, we compare its performance with 13 SoTA methods on the smaller/medium datasets and 5 on the larger ones. Table 1 gives an overview of how well different methods perform in classifying nodes across the nine small/medium-scale benchmarks. We show the average classification accuracy alongside the standard deviation from 10 trials. The highest score for each dataset is highlighted in red, the second-best in blue, and the third-best in violet. Similarly, Table 2 summarizes the node classification performance on three large-scale benchmarks. For these datasets, we present the average classification

Table 1. Node-classification accuracies. Top three models are coloured by First, Second, Third.

	Texas	Wisconsin	Cornell	Actor	Squirrel	Chameleon	Citeseer	Pubmed	Cora
Hom level	0.11	0.21	0.30	0.22	0.22	0.23	0.74	0.80	0.81
# Nodes	183	251	183	7,600	5,201	2,277	3,327	19,717	2,708
# Edges	295	466	280	26,752	198,493	31,421	4,676	44,324	5,278
# Features	1,703	1,703	1,703	931	2,089	2,325	3,703	500	1,433
# Classes	5	5	5	5	5	5	7	3	6
MLP	80.81 ± 4.75	85.29 ± 6.40	81.89 ± 6.40	36.53 ± 0.70	28.77 ± 1.56	46.21 ± 2.99	74.02 ± 1.90	75.69 ± 2.00	87.16 ± 0.37
GCN [4]	55.14 ± 5.16	51.76 ± 3.06	60.54 ± 5.30	27.32 ± 1.10	53.43 ± 2.01	64.82 ± 2.24	76.50 ± 1.36	88.42 ± 0.50	86.98 ± 1.27
GAT [5]	52.16 ± 6.63	49.41 ± 4.09	61.89 ± 5.05	27.44 ± 0.89	40.72 ± 1.55	60.26 ± 2.50	76.55 ± 1.23	87.30 ± 1.10	86.33 ± 0.48
GraphSAGE [9]	82.43 ± 6.14	81.18 ± 5.56	75.95 ± 5.01	34.23 ± 0.99	41.61 ± 0.74	58.73 ± 1.68	76.04 ± 1.30	88.45 ± 0.50	86.90 ± 1.04
GPRGNN [15]	78.38 ± 4.36	82.94 ± 4.21	80.27 ± 8.11	34.63 ± 1.22	31.61 ± 1.24	46.58 ± 1.71	77.13 ± 1.67	87.54 ± 0.38	87.95 ± 1.18
H2GCN [10]	84.86 ± 7.23	87.65 ± 4.89	82.70 ± 5.28	35.70 ± 1.00	36.48 ± 1.86	60.11 ± 2.15	77.11 ± 1.57	89.49 ± 0.38	87.87 ± 1.20
GCNII [21]	77.57 ± 3.83	80.39 ± 3.40	77.86 ± 3.79	37.44 ± 1.30	38.47 ± 1.58	63.86 ± 3.04	77.33 ± 1.48	90.15 ± 0.43	88.37 ± 1.25
Geom-GCN [6]	66.76 ± 2.72	64.51 ± 3.66	60.54 ± 3.67	31.59 ± 1.15	38.15 ± 0.92	60.00 ± 2.81	78.02 ± 1.15	89.95 ± 0.47	85.35 ± 1.57
CGNN [12]	71.35 ± 4.05	74.31 ± 7.26	66.22 ± 7.69	35.95 ± 0.86	29.24 ± 1.09	46.89 ± 1.66	76.91 ± 1.81	87.70 ± 0.49	87.10 ± 1.35
GGCN [16]	84.86 ± 4.55	86.86 ± 3.29	85.68 ± 6.63	37.54 ± 1.56	55.17 ± 1.58	71.14 ± 1.84	77.14 ± 1.45	89.15 ± 0.37	87.95 ± 1.05
LINKX [1]	74.60 ± 8.37	75.49 ± 5.72	77.84 ± 5.81	36.10 ± 1.55	61.81 ± 1.80	68.42 ± 1.38	73.19 ± 0.99	87.86 ± 0.77	84.64 ± 1.13
MixHop [13]	77.84 ± 7.73	75.88 ± 4.90	73.51 ± 6.34	32.22 ± 2.34	43.80 ± 1.48	60.50 ± 2.53	76.26 ± 1.33	85.31 ± 0.61	87.61 ± 0.85
FSGNN [14]	87.30 ± 5.29	87.84 ± 3.37	85.13 ± 6.07	35.75 ± 0.96	74.10 ± 1.89	78.27 ± 1.28	77.40 ± 1.90	77.40 ± 1.93	87.93 ± 1.00
HEX-GNN	89.45 ± 4.26	89.60 ± 3.16	87.30 ± 2.11	36.68 ± 0.80	56.74 ± 0.88	71.01 ± 1.18	77.48 ± 1.37	89.66 ± 0.35	88.69 ± 1.12

Table 2. Node-classification accuracies in large graphs. Top three models are coloured by First, Second, Third.

	Penn94	arXiv-year	ogbn-arXiv
Hom level	**0.47**	**0.21**	**0.66**
# Nodes	41,554	169,343	169,343
# Edges	1,362,229	1,166,243	1,166,243
#Features	5	128	128
# Classes	5	5	40
MLP	73.61 ± 0.40	36.70 ± 0.21	55.91 ± 0.15
GCN	82.47 ± 0.27	46.02 ± 0.26	59.61 ± 0.23
GAT	81.53 ± 0.55	46.05 ± 0.51	60.27 ± 0.21
MixHop	83.47 ± 0.71	51.81 ± 0.17	57.23 ± 0.19
LINKX	84.71 ± 0.52	56.00 ± 1.34	55.31 ± 0.81
HEX-GNN	84.73 ± 0.30	48.25 ± 0.30	63.80 ± 0.13

accuracy with standard deviation from 5 trials, highlighting the top performers in the same color scheme. From these experimental results, we can draw several observations and insights.

Homophily Performance. When considering the HOM LEVEL, it is evident that CORA, CITESEER, and PUBMED exhibit the highest levels of homophily. Our proposed method demonstrates competitive performance across these graphs, often outperforming the alternatives. Even when we do not achieve the top spot, our scores are closely trailing the winner, securing second or third place. Notably, Higher-Order techniques such as MixHop or FSGNN show significant disparities from our results.

Heterophily Performance. Considering the level of heterophily, we observe that WISCONSIN, TEXAS, and CORNELL stand out as the most heterophilic datasets. Remarkably, our method surpasses all others on these three datasets. However, on the remaining two datasets, Chameleon and Squirrel, we fall short due to limitations in feature expressiveness [10,12] and the high density of these graphs. Despite these challenges, our method remains competitive and achieves notable results.

Large-scale Performance. When examining the heterophily level in large-scale graphs, we observe significant success with our method on two out of three datasets: PENN94 and OGBN-ARXIV. Our approach demonstrates its scalability and effectiveness in handling large graphs, delivering superior performance in these contexts. Despite the complexities inherent in large-scale datasets, our method proves robust and capable, emphasizing its scalability and adaptability across diverse graph sizes.

7   Conclusion and Future Work

In this paper, we have addressed the issues of node classification (mainly) in the heterophilic regime, by combining high-order mechanism and selective graph sparsification (Expander Graphs). Our results show that this technique is very promising when we deal with heterophilic graphs and it is competitive in some homophilic benchmarks. This suggests that the combination of node features and graph topology with a sparsification strategy can be a good line to work in, particularly in very dense graphs where comprehensive analysis is required. It prompts further exploration into enhancing expressiveness in future works.

Acknowledgement. The authors are funded by the project PID2022-142516OB-I00 of the Spanish Government.

References

1. Lim, D., et al.: Large scale learning on non-homophilous graphs: new benchmarks and strong simple methods. In: Advances in Neural Information Processing Systems (2021)

2. Li, H., et al.: A survey on graph neural networks in intelligent transportation systems. arXiv preprint arXiv:2401.00713 (2024)
3. Chen, C., et al.: A survey on graph neural networks and graph transformers in computer vision: a task-oriented perspective. arXiv preprint arXiv:2209.13232 (2022)
4. Kipf, T.N., Welling, M.: Semi-supervised classification with graph convolutional networks. In: ICLR (2017)
5. Veličković, P., Cucurull, G., Casanova, A., Romero, A., Lio, P., Bengio, Y.: Graph attention networks. Adriana Romero (2017)
6. Pei, H., Wei, B., Chang, K.C.C., Lei, Y., Yang, B.: Geom-GCN: geometric graph convolutional networks (2020)
7. Kipf, T.N., Welling, M.: Variational graph auto-encoders. In: NeurIPS Workshop on Bayesian Deep Learning (2016)
8. Arnaiz-Rodríguez, A., Begga, A., Escolano, F., Oliver, N.: DiffWire: inductive graph rewiring via the lovász bound. In: The First Learning on Graphs Conference. PMLR 2022
9. Hamilton, W., Ying, Z., Leskovec, J.: Inductive representation learning on large graphs. In: Advances in Neural Information Processing Systems (2017)
10. Zhu, J., Yan, Y., Zhao, L., Heimann, M., Akoglu, L., Koutra, D.: Beyond homophily in graph neural networks: current limitations and effective designs. In: International Conference on Neural Information Processing Systems (2020)
11. Song, Y., Zhou, C., Wang, X., Lin, Z.: Ordered GNN: ordering message passing to deal with heterophily and over-smoothing. In: The Eleventh International Conference on Learning Representations (2023)
12. Yamamoto, T.: Crystal graph neural networks for data mining in materials science. Technical report, Research Institute for Mathematical and Computational Sciences, LLC (2019)
13. Abu-El-Haija, S., et al.: Mixhop: Higher-order graph convolutional architectures via sparsified neighborhood mixing. In: ICML (2019)
14. Maurya, S.K., Liu, X., Murata, T.: Improving graph neural networks with simple architecture design (2021)
15. Chien, E., Peng, J., Li, P., Milenkovic, O.: Adaptive universal generalized pagerank graph neural network. In: ICLR 2021
16. Yan, Y., Hashemi, M., Swersky, K., Yang, Y., Koutra, D.: Two sides of the same coin: heterophily and oversmoothing in graph convolutional neural networks. CoRR, abs/2102.06462 (2021)
17. Hoory, S., Linial, N., Wigderson, A.: Expander graphs and their applications. Bull. Amer. Math. Soc. **43**(04), 439–562 (2006)
18. Chung, F.R.K.: Spectral Graph Theory. American Mathematical Society (1997)
19. Deac, A., Lackenby, M., Velickovic, P.: Expander graph propagation. In: Learning on Graphs Conference (2022)
20. Fey, M., Lenssen, J.E.: Fast graph representation learning with PyTorch geometric. In: ICLR Workshop on Representation Learning on Graphs and Manifolds (2019)
21. Chen, M., Wei, Z., Huang, Z., Ding, B., Li, Y.: Simple and deep graph convolutional networks. CoRR, abs/2007.02133 (2020)

The Notion of Bond in the Multi-adjoint Concept Lattice Framework

Roberto G. Aragón[✉] [ID], Jesús Medina[ID], and Samuel Molina-Ruiz[ID]

Department of Mathematics, University of Cádiz, Cádiz, Spain
{roberto.aragon,jesus.medina,samuel.molina}@uca.es

Abstract. The notion of bond in formal concept analysis arose as a mechanism for aggregating contexts, preserving the main information of the original ones. This notion can also be fundamental in the inverse process, that is, in the factorization of contexts, which will allow the computation of the information of a real context from smaller subcontexts (distributed computing). This paper considers the flexible fuzzy multi-adjoint framework in order to introduce the first definition of bond in this setting and presents the first properties and examples of this definition.

Keywords: Formal concept analysis · bonds · multi-adjoint framework

1 Introduction

Ability to efficiently process large amounts of data is essential for extracting useful information from many of the existing real databases. Formal concept analysis (FCA) is a relevant mathematical theory for extracting knowledge from relational databases since its introduction in the eighties [24]. The theory deems databases as formal contexts [13], that is, as a triple interpreted as a relation/table between a set of objects and a set of attributes. FCA tools are capable of manipulating data and extracting relevant information, which is represented using the algebraic structure of a complete lattice [13]. Several extensions of this mathematical theory have been introduced in a fuzzy environment [7,9,15], and theoretical [4,5,20,21] and applied [1,2,22] advances are made on a daily basis. Among the existing fuzzy extensions, the multi-adjoint framework [3,10,11,19] is one of the most flexible and versatile, making it ideal for modeling real-world problems.

Various methods have been developed and utilized in FCA to simplify data processing, such as factoring and aggregating data tables [6,8,12,16,23]. These techniques enable the reduction of large tables into smaller ones, known as factors, from which important information can be extracted. In addition, these factors can be aggregated without modifying the information present in them. In particular, we focus on the notion of bond between formal contexts, which was originally defined in the classical setting [13] and was extended to the fuzzy framework using residuated lattices [14,17,18]. Bonds allow the aggregation of contexts while preserving the information contained in the concepts generated by each individual context. This work aims to extend the aforementioned notion to the multi-adjoint framework and to analyze the conditions that enable obtaining bonds in a simpler manner.

The paper will introduce in Sect. 2 diverse preliminary notions in FCA, including the crisp notion of bond. In Sect. 3, the definition of bond in the multi-adjoint concept lattice framework will be presented based on intents of fuzzy objects and extents of fuzzy attributes of the given context. Furthermore, an illustrative example will be included to display particular cases of bonds and relations that are not bonds. This section will also be focused on two notable fuzzy relations: the constantly top and constantly bottom relations, showing that the first is always a bond and introducing a sufficient condition to ensure that the second is a bond. This result will also be illustrated with examples. The paper will finish with diverse conclusions and prospects of future works.

2   Preliminaries

In this preliminaries section, we introduce foundational notions related to FCA. Throughout this paper, the notation A^B will be employed to denote maps from B to A. Particularly, if $A = \{1, \ldots, n\}$ we may use n^B to denote $\{1, \ldots, n\}^B$. In addition, if a map $f \colon A \to B$ takes only one value, $b \in B$, we may write it as $f \equiv b$.

We now proceed to define what precisely a context is within the setting of FCA.

Definition 1. *A* context *is a tuple* (O, P, R) *such that O and P are non-empty sets (usually interpreted as objects and properties, respectively) and R is a relation in $O \times P$.*

In addition, the derivation operators $\uparrow \colon 2^O \to 2^P$ and $\downarrow \colon 2^P \to 2^O$ are defined, for all $X \subseteq O$ and $A \subseteq P$, as

$$X^\uparrow = \{a \in P \mid (x, a) \in R, \text{ for all } x \in X\}$$
$$A^\downarrow = \{x \in O \mid (x, a) \in R, \text{ for all } a \in A\}$$

A *concept* is a pair $\langle X, A \rangle$ satisfying that $X^\uparrow = A$ and $A^\downarrow = X$, where X is called the *extent* and A is called the *intent*.

From now on, we will consider a family of contexts $\{(O_i, P_i, R_i)\}_{i \in \Gamma}$, with Γ a non-empty set of indices. We will simply denote the derivation operators $\uparrow$ and $\downarrow$ in each context (O_i, P_i, R_i) as $\uparrow_i$ and $\downarrow_i$, respectively. Moreover, if $R_{ij} \subseteq O_i \times P_j$ is a relation, we define the mappings $\uparrow_{ij} \colon 2^{O_i} \to 2^{P_j}$ and $\downarrow_{ij} \colon 2^{P_j} \to 2^{O_i}$ as

$$X^{\uparrow_{ij}} = \{a \in P_j \mid (x, a) \in R_{ij}, \text{ for all } x \in X\}$$
$$A^{\downarrow_{ij}} = \{x \in O_i \mid (x, a) \in R_{ij}, \text{ for all } a \in A\}$$

for all $X \subseteq O_i$ and $A \subseteq P_j$. When we consider $X = \{x\}$ and $A = \{a\}$, we may use the notation $x^{\uparrow ij}$ and $a^{\downarrow ij}$ instead of $\{x\}^{\uparrow ij}$ and $\{a\}^{\downarrow ij}$.

Next, the notion of bond is introduced as a method of aggregating contexts (factors). Bonds allow to construct a new context from factors while preserving the information they contain. In Sect. 3, we will translate this notion into the multi-adjoint framework.

Definition 2. *Given two different contexts (O_i, P_i, R_i) and (O_j, P_j, R_j), a bond from (O_i, P_i, R_i) to (O_j, P_j, R_j) is a relation $R_{ij} \subseteq O_i \times P_j$ such that*

- *$x^{\uparrow ij}$ is an intent of (O_j, P_j, R_j) for every object $x \in O_i$,*
- *$a^{\downarrow ij}$ is an extent of (O_i, P_i, R_i) for every property $a \in P_j$.*

Now, we will examine this definition more closely through a practical example

Example 1. Consider two contexts (O_1, P_1, R_1) and (O_2, P_2, R_2) where

$$O_1 = \{x_1, x_2\}, \qquad P_1 = \{a_1, a_2\}, \qquad R_1 = \{(x_1, a_1), (x_1, a_2), (x_2, a_2)\}$$
$$O_2 = \{x_3, x_4\}, \qquad P_2 = \{a_3, a_4\}, \qquad R_2 = \{(x_3, a_3), (x_4, a_4)\}$$

A bond can be visualized by placing the two contexts diagonally, one beneath the other, and the bond in the top right corner (a bond R_{ji} from (O_j, P_j, R_j) to (O_i, P_i, R_i) would be placed in the bottom left), as observed in Table 1. Since the set of objects and the set of properties are always an extent and an intent of a context, we are guaranteed that the relation $R_{1\,2}^{\top} = O_1 \times P_2$ is a bond. Indeed, for any $x \in O_1$, $x^{\uparrow 12} = P_2$ is an intent of (O_2, P_2, R_2) and, for any $a \in P_2$, $a^{\downarrow 12} = O_1$ is an extent of (O_1, P_1, R_1).

Table 1. Tables showing the relations R_1 and R_2 of Example 1 together with $R_{1\,2}^1$ (left table) and $R_{1\,2}^2$ (right table).

	a_1	a_2	a_3	a_4			a_1	a_2	a_3	a_4	
x_1	×	×	×	×	$R_{1\,2}^1$	x_1	×	×			$R_{1\,2}^2$
x_2		×	×			x_2		×	×		
x_3			×			x_3			×		
x_4				×		x_4				×	

We can usually find other non-trivial bonds, such as

$$R_{1\,2}^1 = \{(x_1, a_3), (x_1, a_4), (x_2, a_3)\}$$

For this relation, $x_1^{\uparrow 12} = \{a_3, a_4\}$ and $x_2^{\uparrow 12} = \{a_3\}$ are intents of (O_2, P_2, R_2). The first one because it is the set of properties P_2 and the second one because

$$a_3^{\downarrow^2 \uparrow^2} = x_3^{\uparrow^2} = \{a_3\}$$

Likewise, $a_3^{\downarrow^{12}} = \{x_1, x_2\}$ and $a_4^{\downarrow^{12}} = \{x_1\}$ are extents of (O_1, P_1, R_1), the first one for being the set of objects O_1 and the second one because

$$x_1^{\uparrow_1 \downarrow^1} = \{a_1, a_2\}^{\downarrow^1} = \{x_1\}$$

However, not all relations in $O_1 \times P_2$ are bonds. Consider for instance the relation $R_{12}^2 = \{(x_2, a_3)\}$. This relation is not a bond because $a_3^{\downarrow^{12}} = \{x_2\}$ is not an extent of (O_1, P_1, R_1), that is,

$$x_2^{\uparrow_1 \downarrow^1} = a_2^{\downarrow^1} = \{x_1, x_2\} \neq \{x_2\}$$

Another interesting case is the empty relation, $R_{12}^\perp = \varnothing$. In this case, the relation $R_{12}^\perp$ is not a bond from (O_1, P_1, R_1) to (O_2, P_2, R_2) due to

$$\varnothing^{\uparrow_1 \downarrow^1} = \{a_1, a_2\}^{\downarrow^1} = \{x_1\} \neq \varnothing$$

This means that the empty set is not an extent of (O_1, P_1, R_1).   □

Remark 1. As Example 1 shows, the empty relation is not always an extent or intent of a context and, therefore, it is not a bond. However, there are cases where it is actually a bond. Given two different contexts (O_i, P_i, R_i) and (O_j, P_j, R_j) satisfying that for every object $x \in O_i$, there exists $a \in P_i$ such that $(x, a) \notin R_i$, and for every property $a' \in P_j$, there exists $x' \in O_j$ such that $(x', a') \notin R_j$, then the empty set is both an extent of (O_i, P_i, R_i) and an intent of (O_j, P_j, R_j). Therefore, these conditions guarantee that the relation $R_{ij}^\perp$ is a bond from (O_i, P_i, R_i) to (O_j, P_j, R_j).

3   Bonds on a Multi-adjoint Framework

In the previous section, we dealt with the classical case, but when considering the fuzzy scenario, we need to work with a more general notion of context, where an object can have a truth degree value about whether it has a given attribute. In particular, we need to recall the fundamentals of the multi-adjoint framework in order to define a bond between contexts associated with a multi-adjoint frame.

First, let us remember what a multi-adjoint framework is.

Definition 3. *A* multi-adjoint framework *is a tuple* $(L_1, L_2, Q, \&_1, \ldots, \&_n)$ *where* $(L_1, \preceq_1, \perp_1, \top_1)$ *and* $(L_2, \preceq_2, \perp_2, \top_2)$ *are complete lattices,* $(Q, \leq)$ *is a poset and* $(\&_k, \swarrow^k, \nwarrow_k)$ *is an adjoint triple with respect to* L_1, L_2 *and* Q, *for all* $k \in \{1, \ldots, n\}$.

Throughout this section, a multi-adjoint framework $(L_1, L_2, Q, \&_1, \ldots, \&_n)$ will be fixed. Once a multi-adjoint frame has been fixed, the notion of a context in that frame is defined in the following way.

Definition 4. *A* context *is a tuple* (O, P, R, σ), *where* O *is the set of objects,* P *is the set of properties,* R *is a* Q-fuzzy relation $R: O \times P \to Q$ *and* $\sigma: O \times P \to \{1, \ldots, n\}$ *is a mapping which associates each element in* $O \times P$ *with a specific adjoint triple.*

The extension of the concept-forming operators are the mappings $\uparrow\colon L_2^O \to L_1^P$ and $\downarrow\colon L_1^P \to L_2^O$ defined as:

$$g^\uparrow(a) = \inf\{R(x,a) \swarrow^{\sigma(x,a)} g(x) \mid x \in O\}$$
$$f^\downarrow(x) = \inf\{R(x,a) \nwarrow_{\sigma(x,a)} f(x) \mid a \in P\}$$

for all $g \in L_2^O$, $f \in L_1^P$ and $a \in P$, $x \in O$. Equivalently, a pair $\langle g, f \rangle$ is called a *multi-adjoint concept* if equalities $g^\uparrow = f$ and $f^\downarrow = g$ hold.

In addition, the following notion is related to a specific family of fuzzy subsets of L_1^P that will play a fundamental role in this work.

Definition 5. *For each $a \in P$, the fuzzy subsets of attributes $\phi_{a,s} \in L_1^P$ defined, for all $s \in L_1$, as*

$$\phi_{a,s}(a') = \begin{cases} s & \text{if } a' = a \\ \bot_1 & \text{if } a' \neq a \end{cases}$$

will be called fuzzy-attributes.

Analogously, the fuzzy-objects are defined in the same way.

Now, we are ready to establish the basis for defining a bond. Hereon, a family of contexts associated with the frame, $\{(O_i, P_i, R_i, \sigma_i)\}_{i \in \Gamma}$, will be considered. Given a Q-fuzzy relation R_{ij} in $O_i \times P_j$ and $\sigma_{ij}\colon O_i \times P_j \to \{1, \ldots, n\}$, we define the mappings $\uparrow_{ij}\colon L_2^{O_i} \to L_1^{P_j}$ and $\downarrow^{ij}\colon L_1^{P_j} \to L_2^{O_i}$ as

$$g^{\uparrow_{ij}}(a) = \inf\{R_{ij}(x,a) \swarrow^{\sigma_{ij}(x,a)} g(x) \mid x \in O_i\}$$
$$f^{\downarrow^{ij}}(x) = \inf\{R_{ij}(x,a) \nwarrow_{\sigma_{ij}(x,a)} f(a) \mid a \in P_j\}$$

for each $g \in L_2^{O_i}$, $f \in L_1^{P_j}$ and $a \in P_j$, $x \in O_i$. Note that when we refer to the context $(O_i, P_i, R_i, \sigma_i)$, we will simply denote the concept-forming operators $\uparrow$ and $\downarrow$ as $\uparrow_i$ and $\downarrow^i$, respectively.

In Definition 2, we described a bond from (O_i, P_i, R_i) to (O_j, P_j, R_j) as a relation R_{ij} in $O_i \times P_j$, which can also be interpreted as a new context (O_i, P_j, R_{ij}). This point of view is fundamental in the following definition of a bond between contexts associated with a multi-adjoint framework.

Definition 6. *Given two different contexts $(O_i, P_i, R_i, \sigma_i)$ and $(O_j, P_j, R_j, \sigma_j)$, a multi-adjoint bond from $(O_i, P_i, R_i, \sigma_i)$ to $(O_j, P_j, R_j, \sigma_j)$ is a context $(O_i, P_j, R_{ij}, \sigma_{ij})$ such that R_{ij} is a Q-fuzzy relation in $O_i \times P_j$ and $\sigma_{ij}\colon O_i \times P_j \to \{1, \ldots, n\}$ satisfying that*

- *$\phi_{x,t}^{\uparrow_{ij}}$ is an intent of $(O_j, P_j, R_j, \sigma_j)$, for every object $x \in O_i$,*

- *$\phi_{a,s}^{\downarrow^{ij}}$ is an extent of $(O_i, P_i, R_i, \sigma_i)$, for every property $a \in P_j$,*

where $s \in L_1$ and $t \in L_2$.

Henceforth, we will assume that Q is bounded by a top element $\top_3$ and a bottom element $\bot_3$. We are particularly interested in studying the contexts whose relations are all $\top_3$ or $\bot_3$, that is, $R_{ij}(x, a) = \top_3$, for all $(x, a) \in O_i \times P_j$, or $R_{ij}(x, a) = \bot_3$, for all $(x, a) \in O_i \times P_j$. We will simply denote these particular relations as $R_{ij}^\top$ and $R_{ij}^\bot$, respectively. Similar to the classical case, the former will always be a multi-adjoint bond, but the latter requires further study. Let us show this fact through an example.

Example 2. Consider the multi-adjoint framework $([0, 1]_4, [0, 1]_4, [0, 1]_4, \&_G^*, \&_L^*)$ where $\&_G^*$ and $\&_L^*$ are the discretization of the Gödel and Łukasiewicz conjunctors, respectively. Also consider the contexts $(O_1, P_1, R_1, \sigma_1)$ and $(O_2, P_2, R_2, \sigma_2)$, where the relations R_1, R_2 and the maps σ_1, σ_2 are defined in Table 2.

Table 2. The relations R_1, R_2 and maps σ_1, σ_2 of the contexts $(O_1, P_1, R_1, \sigma_1)$ and $(O_2, P_2, R_2, \sigma_2)$ in Example 2.

R_1	a_1	a_2	σ_1	a_1	a_2	R_2	a_3	a_4	σ_2	a_3	a_4
x_1	0.5	0.75	x_1	$\&_G^*$	$\&_G^*$	x_3	1	0.75	x_3	$\&_L^*$	$\&_L^*$
x_2	0.25	1	x_2	$\&_G^*$	$\&_G^*$	x_4	0.75	1	x_4	$\&_L^*$	$\&_L^*$

Similar to Example 1, the relation $R_{12}^\top$ together with any map $\sigma_{12} \colon O_1 \times P_2 \to \{\&_G^*, \&_L^*\}$ defines a multi-adjoint bond $(O_1, P_2, R_{12}^\top, \sigma_{12})$ from $(O_1, P_1, R_1, \sigma_1)$ to $(O_2, P_2, R_2, \sigma_2)$. The reason behind this fact is that the maps $g_1^\top \colon O_1 \to [0, 1]_4$ and $f_2^\top \colon P_2 \to [0, 1]_4$ defined as $g_1^\top \equiv 1$ and $f_2^\top \equiv 1$ are respectively an extent of $(O_1, P_1, R_1, \sigma_1)$ and an intent of $(O_2, P_2, R_2, \sigma_2)$, and moreover, we have that

$$\phi_{x,t}{}^{\uparrow_{12}} = f_2^\top \quad \text{and} \quad \phi_{a,s}{}^{\downarrow^{12}} = g_1^\top$$

for every $x \in O_1$, $a \in P_2$ and $s, t \in [0, 1]_4$.

In addition, other multi-adjoint bonds can be defined between these contexts. For instance, $(O_1, P_2, R_{12}, \sigma_{12})$, where $\sigma_{12}(x, a) = \&_G^*$, for all $(x, a) \in O_1 \times P_2$, and R_{12} is represented in Table 3.

In fact, if we change the map σ_{12} but maintain the relation, we obtain other multi-adjoint bonds from $(O_1, P_1, R_1, \sigma_1)$ to $(O_2, P_2, R_2, \sigma_2)$.

Table 3. The relations $R_{12}^\top$ and R_{12} in Example 2.

	a_1	a_2	a_3	a_4			a_1	a_2	a_3	a_4	
x_1	0.5	0.75	1	1	$R_{12}^\top$	x_1	0.5	0.75	1	0.75	R_{12}
x_2	0.25	1	1	1		x_2	0.25	1	1	1	
x_3	1	1	1	0.75		x_3	1	1	1	0.75	
x_4	1	1	0.75	1		x_4	1	1	0.75	1	

On the other hand, if we consider the relation $R_{12}^\bot$ and any map σ_{12}, we are going to show that the context $(O_1, P_2, R_{12}^\bot, \sigma_{12})$, depicted in Table 4, is not a

Table 4. The relation of the context $(O_1, P_2, R_{\bar{1}2}^{\perp}, \sigma_{12})$ of Example 2, which is not a multi-adjoint bond.

	a_1	a_2	a_3	a_4	
x_1	0.5	0.75	0	0	$R_{\bar{1}2}^{\perp}$
x_2	0.25	1	0	0	
x_3	0	0	1	0.75	
x_4	0	0	0.75	1	

multi-adjoint bond from $(O_1, P_1, R_1, \sigma_1)$ to $(O_2, P_2, R_2, \sigma_2)$. Indeed, for $x_1 \in O_1$ and all $a \in P_2$, we have that

$$\phi_{x_1,1}{}^{\uparrow_{12}}(a) = \inf\{R_{\bar{1}2}^{\perp}(x, a) \swarrow^{\sigma_{12}(x,a)} \phi_{x_1,1}(x) \mid x \in O_1\}$$

$$= \{0 \swarrow^{\sigma_{12}(x_1,a)} \phi_{x_1,1}(x_1), \ 0 \swarrow^{\sigma_{12}(x_2,a)} \phi_{x_1,1}(x_2)\}$$

$$= \{0 \swarrow^{\sigma_{12}(x_1,a)} 1, \ 0 \swarrow^{\sigma_{12}(x_2,a)} 0\} = 0$$

The fuzzy set $\phi_{x_1,1}{}^{\uparrow_{12}} \equiv 0$ is not an intent of $(O_2, P_2, R_2, \sigma_2)$, since its closure is

$$\phi_{x_1,1}{}^{\uparrow_{12}\downarrow^2\uparrow_{12}} \equiv 0.75 \neq 0$$

Thus $(O_1, P_2, R_{\bar{1}2}^{\perp}, \sigma_{12})$ is not a multi-adjoint bond.   □

Similarly to the classical case (Remark 1), the relation $R_{ij}^{\perp} \equiv \perp_3$ does not always define a multi-adjoint bond from a context $(O_i, P_i, R_i, \sigma_i)$ to another context $(O_j, P_j, R_j, \sigma_j)$. This was the case with Example 2. In Remark 1, we showed a characterization of when the crisp relation $R_{\bar{1}2}^{\perp}$ was indeed a bond, and a similar property can be determined for multi-adjoint bonds under certain conditions as the following result states.

Theorem 1. *Given a multi-adjoint frame $(L_1, L_2, Q, \&_1, \dots, \&_n)$ and two different contexts $(O_i, P_i, R_i, \sigma_i)$ and $(O_j, P_j, R_j, \sigma_j)$, the context $(O_i, P_j, R_{ij}^{\top}, \sigma_{ij})$ is a multi-adjoint bond from $(O_i, P_i, R_i, \sigma_i)$ to $(O_j, P_j, R_j, \sigma_j)$, for any map $\sigma_{ij} \colon O_i \times P_j \to \{1, \dots, n\}$. Moreover, if the following conditions are satisfied*

- *There exists a non-empty subset $\Lambda \subseteq \{1, \dots, n\}$ such that conjunctors $\&_\lambda$ have no-zero divisors, for all $\lambda \in \Lambda$.*
- *For every row in R_i and column in R_j, there is at least one bottom element.*
- *The equalities $\perp_3 \swarrow^k \top_2 = \perp_1$ and $\perp_3 \diagdown_k \top_1 = \perp_2$ hold, for all $k \in \{1, \dots, n\}$.*

then a context $(O_i, P_j, R_{ij}^{\perp}, \sigma_{ij})$, where $\sigma_{ij}(x, a) \in \Lambda$, for all $(x, a) \in O_i \times P_j$, is a multi-adjoint bond from $(O_i, P_i, R_i, \sigma_i)$ to $(O_j, P_j, R_j, \sigma_j)$.

A particular case of Theorem 1 arises when all conjunctors of the frame have no-zero divisors and the contexts $(O_i, P_i, R_i, \sigma_i)$ and $(O_j, P_j, R_j, \sigma_j)$ are normalized. Recall that a context is normalized if the matrix representation of the fuzzy relation has no rows or columns with all values equal to bottom or with all values different from bottom. The following result outlines this specific case.

Corollary 1. *Given a multi-adjoint frame* $(L_1, L_2, Q, \&_1, \ldots, \&_n)$ *whose conjunctors* $\&_k$ *have no-zero divisors, and two different contexts* $(O_i, P_i, R_i, \sigma_i)$ *and* $(O_j, P_j, R_j, \sigma_j)$ *which are normalized, we have that the context* $(O_i, P_j, R_{ij}^{\perp}, \sigma_{ij})$ *is a multi-adjoint bond from* $(O_i, P_i, R_i, \sigma_i)$ *to* $(O_j, P_j, R_j, \sigma_j)$, *for any* σ_{ij}. *Analogously, the context* $(O_j, P_i, R_{ji}^{\perp}, \sigma_{ji})$ *is a multi-adjoint bond from* $(O_j, P_j, R_j, \sigma_j)$ *to* $(O_i, P_i, R_i, \sigma_i)$, *for any* σ_{ji}.

The above results are illustrated in the following example.

Example 3. Going back to Example 2, we showed that $(O_1, P_2, R_{12}^{\top}, \sigma_{12})$ was a multi-adjoint bond from $(O_1, P_1, R_1, \sigma_1)$ to $(O_2, P_2, R_2, \sigma_2)$, for any σ_{12}. This corresponds to the first part of Theorem 1.

Table 5. The relations R_1, R_2 and maps σ_1, σ_2 of the contexts $(O_1, P_1, R_1, \sigma_1)$ and $(O_2, P_2, R_2, \sigma_2)$ in Example 3.

R_1	a_1	a_2	σ_1	a_1	a_2	R_2	a_3	a_4	σ_2	a_3	a_4
x_1	0.25	0	x_1	$\&_G^*$	$\&_G^*$	x_3	0.25	0	x_3	$\&_L^*$	$\&_L^*$
x_2	0	0.75	x_2	$\&_G^*$	$\&_G^*$	x_4	0	0.25	x_4	$\&_L^*$	$\&_L^*$

Considering the same multi-adjoint frame as in Example 2, let $(O_1, P_1, R_1, \sigma_1)$ and $(O_2, P_2, R_2, \sigma_2)$ be the contexts defined in Table 5. Both the frame and the contexts satisfy the hypotheses of Theorem 1 since, in this case, both adjoint triples satisfy the equalities on the implications, and the conjunctor $\&_G^*$ has no-zero divisors. Additionally, the contexts are normalized, hence every row and column contains a bottom element. Consequently, the context $(O_1, P_2, R_{12}^{\perp}, \sigma_{12})$, where $\sigma_{12}(x, a) = \&_G^*$, for all $(x, a) \in O_1 \times P_2$, is a multi-adjoint bond. Indeed, for any $x_i \in O_1$, $a \in P_2$ and $t \in [0, 1]_4$,

$$\phi_{x_i, t}{}^{\uparrow_{12}}(a) = \inf\{R_{12}^{\perp} \swarrow^{\sigma_{12}(x, a)} \phi_{x_i, t}(x) \mid x \in O_1\}$$
$$= \inf\{0 \swarrow_G^* 0, \, 0 \swarrow_G^* t\} = 0 \swarrow_G^* t$$

When $t = 0$ we have $0 \swarrow_G^* t = 0 \swarrow_G^* 0 = 1$, and hence $\phi_{x_i, t}{}^{\uparrow_{12}} \equiv 1$. Therefore, it is an intent of $(O_2, P_2, R_2, \sigma_2)$. When $t \neq 0$, we obtain that $0 \swarrow_G^* t = 0$, since $\&_G^*$ has no-zero divisors, and therefore, $\phi_{x_i, t}{}^{\uparrow_{12}} \equiv 0$. Let us prove that it is an intent of $(O_2, P_2, R_2, \sigma_2)$. For any $a \in P_2$,

$$\phi_{x_i, t}{}^{\uparrow_{12}\downarrow^2\uparrow_2}(a) = (f_2^{\perp})^{\downarrow^2\uparrow_2}(a) = (g_2^{\top})^{\uparrow_2}(a)$$
$$= \inf\{R_2(x, a) \swarrow^{\sigma_2(x, a)} g_2^{\top}(x) \mid x \in O_2\}$$
$$= \inf\{R_2(x_3, a) \swarrow_L^* 1, \, R_2(x_4, a) \swarrow_L^* 1\}$$

where the maps $g_2^\top : O_2 \to [0,1]_4$ and $f_2^\perp : P_2 \to [0,1]_4$ are defined as $g_2^\top \equiv 1$ and $f_2^\perp \equiv 0$. Considering the values of the relation R_2 and, by hypothesis, $0 \swarrow_L^* 1 = 0$ holds, we obtain that

$$\phi_{x_i,t}^{\uparrow 1\, 2 \downarrow^2 \uparrow 2}(a_3) = \inf\{0.25 \swarrow_L^* 1, 0 \swarrow_L^* 1\} = 0$$

$$\phi_{x_i,t}^{\uparrow 1\, 2 \downarrow^2 \uparrow 2}(a_4) = \inf\{0 \swarrow_L^* 1, 0.25 \swarrow_L^* 1\} = 0$$

Therefore, $\phi_{x_i,t}^{\uparrow 1\, 2 \downarrow^2 \uparrow 2} = \phi_{x_i,t}^{\uparrow 1\, 2} \equiv 0$, i.e., it is an intent of $(O_2, P_2, R_2, \sigma_2)$. Similarly, we can show that $\phi_{a_j,s}^{\downarrow^{1\,2}}$, with $a_j \in P_2$ and $s \in [0,1]_4$, are extents of $(O_1, P_1, R_1, \sigma_1)$.

Now, we will show the importance of the map σ_{12} assigning conjunctors with no-zero divisors, since otherwise we will obtain that $(O_1, P_2, R_{\overline{1}2}^\perp, \sigma_{12})$ is not a multi-adjoint bond. We consider $\sigma_{12}(x_1, a_4) = \&_L^*$ and $\sigma_{12}(x, a) = \&_G^*$ for $(x,a) \neq (x_1, a_4)$, and we focus on the fuzzy-object $\phi_{x_1,0.5}$. It is easy to verify that

$$\phi_{x_1,0.5}^{\uparrow 1\, 2}(a_3) = 0 \swarrow_G^* 0.5 = 0 \quad \text{and} \quad \phi_{x_1,0.5}^{\uparrow 1\, 2}(a_4) = 0 \swarrow_L^* 0.5 = 0.5$$

This is not an intent of $(O_2, P_2, R_2, \sigma_2)$ since $\phi_{x_1,0.5}^{\uparrow 1\, 2 \downarrow^2 \uparrow 2}(a_3) = 0.25 \neq 0.5$.

Lastly, if we consider the frame $([0,1]_4, [0,1]_4, [0,1]_4, \&_G^*, \&_P^*)$ and the same contexts of Table 5, but the map σ_2 associates the product conjunctor $\&_P^*$ instead of Łukasiewicz conjunctor, then we are under the conditions of Corollary 1. Therefore, for any map σ_{12}, the context $(O_1, P_2, R_{\overline{1}2}^\perp, \sigma_{12})$ is a multi-adjoint bond from $(O_1, P_1, R_1, \sigma_1)$ to $(O_2, P_2, R_2, \sigma_2)$. □

4 Conclusions and Future Work

This paper has studied the notion of bond in the multi-adjoint concept lattice framework, showing a new mechanism for merging contexts (relational datasets) without losing relevant information. This definition extends the original one to the considered flexible framework taking into account that the properties of the considered operators in the multi-adjoint frame are fundamental for obtaining a bond. We have studied the two more extreme bonds, the greatest (where the relation is constantly the top element of the poset), which always exists, and the (possible) least bond (where the relation is constantly the bottom element of the poset), whose existence depends on the operators in the given multi-adjoint frame. We have also illustrated the definition and properties in diverse examples.

In the future, more properties will be studied and an in-depth comparison will be made with the residuated framework.

Acknowledgement. Partially supported by the project PID2019-108991GB-I00 funded by MICIU/AEI/10.13039/501100011033, the project PID2022-137620NB-I00 funded by MICIU/AEI/10.13039/501100011033 and FEDER, UE, by the grant TED2021-129748B-I00 funded by MCIN/AEI/10.13039/501100011033 and European Union NextGenerationEU/PRTR, and by the project PR2023-009 funded by the University of Cádiz.

References

1. Alcalde, C., Burusco, A.: reduction of the size of l-fuzzy contexts. A tool for differential diagnoses of diseases. Int. J. Gen Syst **48**(7), 692–712 (2019)
2. Ali, I., Li, Y., Pedrycz, W.: Granular computing approach to evaluate spatiotemporal events in intuitionistic fuzzy sets data through formal concept analysis. Axioms **12**(5), 407 (2023)
3. Antoni, L., Cornejo, M.E., Medina, J., Ramirez, E.: Attribute classification and reduct computation in multi-adjoint concept lattices. IEEE Trans. Fuzzy Syst. **29**, 1121–1132 (2021)
4. Aragón, R.G., Medina, J., Ramírez-Poussa, E.: Identifying non-sublattice equivalence classes induced by an attribute reduction in FCA. Mathematics **9**(5), 565 (2021)
5. Aragón, R.G., Medina, J., Ramírez-Poussa, E.: Impact of local congruences in variable selection from datasets. J. Comput. Appl. Math. **404**, 113416 (2022)
6. Aragón, R.G., Medina, J., Ramírez-Poussa, E.: Factorizing formal contexts from closures of necessity operators. Comp. Appl. Math **43**, 124 (2024)
7. Bělohlávek, R.: Lattices of fixed points of fuzzy Galois connections. Math. Logic Quart. **47**(1), 111–116 (2001)
8. Bělohlávek, R.,, Vychodil, V.: Discovery of optimal factors in binary data via a novel method of matrix decomposition. J. Comput. Syst. Sci. **76**(1), 3–20 (2010). Special Issue on Intelligent Data Analysis
9. Burusco, A., Fuentes-González, R.: Construction of the L-fuzzy concept lattice. Fuzzy Sets Syst. **97**(1), 109–114 (1998)
10. Cornejo, M.E., Medina, J., Ramírez-Poussa, E.: Attribute reduction in multi-adjoint concept lattices. Inf. Sci. **294**, 41–56 (2015)
11. Cornejo, M.E., Medina, J., Ramírez-Poussa, E.: Characterizing reducts in multi-adjoint concept lattices. Inf. Sci. **422**, 364–376 (2018)
12. Dubois, D., Prade, H.: Possibility theory and formal concept analysis: Characterizing independent sub-contexts. Fuzzy Sets Syst. **196**, 4–16 (2012)
13. Ganter, B., Wille, R.: Formal Concept Analysis: Mathematical Foundation. Springer Verlag, Cham (1999)
14. Konecny, J., Ojeda-Aciego, M.: On homogeneous L-bonds and heterogeneous L-bonds. Intl. J. General Syst. **45**(2), 160–186 (2016)
15. Krajči, S.: A generalized concept lattice. Log. J. IGPL **13**(5), 543–550 (2005)
16. Krídlo, O., Antoni, L., Krajči, S.: Selection of appropriate bonds between l-fuzzy formal contexts for recommendation tasks. Inf. Sci. **606**, 21–37 (2022)
17. Kridlo, O., Krajči, S., Ojeda-Aciego, M.: The category of L-Chu correspondences and the structure of L-bonds. Fund. Inform. **115**(4), 297–325 (2012)
18. Krídlo, O., López-Rodríguez, D., Antoni, L., Eliaš, P., Krajči, S., Ojeda-Aciego, M.: Connecting concept lattices with bonds induced by external information. Inf. Sci. **648**, 119498 (2023)
19. Medina, J., Ojeda-Aciego, M., Ruiz-Calviño, J.: Formal concept analysis via multi-adjoint concept lattices. Fuzzy Sets Syst. **160**(2), 130–144 (2009)
20. Ojeda-Hernández, M., Cabrera, I.P., Cordero, P., Muñoz-Velasco, E.: Fuzzy closure structures as formal concepts. Fuzzy Sets Syst. **463**, 108458 (2023)
21. Pérez-Gámez, F., Cordero, P., Enciso, M., Mora, A.: Simplification logic for the management of unknown information. Inf. Sci. **634**, 505–519 (2023)
22. Sokol, P., Antoni, L., Krídlo, O., Marková, E., Kováčová, K., Krajči, S.: Formal concept analysis approach to understand digital evidence relationships. Int. J. Approximate Reasoning **159**, 108940 (2023)

23. Valverde-Albacete, F.J., Peláez-Moreno, C., Cabrera, I.P., Cordero, P., Ojeda-Aciego, M.: Formal independence analysis. In: Medina, J., et al. (eds.) Information Processing and Management of Uncertainty in Knowledge-Based Systems. Theory and Foundations. Communications in Computer and Information Science, vol. 853, pp. 596–608. Springer, Cham (2018). https://doi.org/10.1007/978-3-319-91473-2_51

24. Wille, R.: Restructuring lattice theory: an approach based on hierarchies of concepts. In: Rival, I. (ed.) Ordered Sets, pp. 445–470. Reidel (1982)

Exploring the Use of LLMs for Teaching AI and Robotics Concepts at a Master's Degree

Miguel Á. González-Santamarta(✉)⬤, Francisco Javier Rodríguez-Lera⬤,
Miguel Á. Conde-González⬤, Francisco Rodríguez-Sedano⬤,
and Camino Fernández-Llamas⬤

Robotics Group, University of León, 24006 León, Spain
{mgons,fjrodl,mcong,fjrods,cferll}@unileon.es

Abstract. This article explores the use of Large Language Models (LLM) as transformative tools for teaching Artificial Intelligence (AI) and Robotics concepts at the master's level. LLMs, exemplified by models like ChatGPT, present a unique opportunity to revolutionize the pedagogical landscape by offering advanced capabilities in any service robot. The study investigates the integration of LLMs in the instructional framework, through the llama_ros tool, capable of replacing different classic cognitive functions in a transversal project across different subjects of an official master's degree. The research presents as an example the creation of an LLM-based chatbot on an open hardware platform called Mini Pupper. The reader will find how to emphasize the potential of LLMs to shape their inclusion in bachelor's or master's programs.

Keywords: LLM · robotics · llama_ros · chatbot · ROS 2

1 Introduction

Bachelor's and Master's degrees in computer science span a wide spectrum of courses, encompassing subjects such as Path Planning and Navigation, Robot Perception, and Human-Robot Interaction. Students will also explore the intricacies of Machine Learning for Robotics, delving into algorithms that enable robots to learn from and adapt to their environment. Ethics in AI and Robotics is integrated into the curriculum, encouraging students to critically evaluate the societal implications and ethical considerations associated with these rapidly advancing technologies. The collaboration between Artificial Intelligence (AI) and robotics [6] has played a pivotal role in propelling the progress of robotic systems, granting machines the capability to execute intricate tasks and acclimate to diverse surroundings.

Embarking these concepts in a Master's degree in Robotics and AI represents an exciting journey into the realm of cutting-edge technology, where students dig into the convergence of robotics and AI. The students analyze the realm of

A. Alonso-Betanzos et al. (Eds.): CAEPIA 2024, LNAI 14640, pp. 254–263, 2024.
https://doi.org/10.1007/978-3-031-62799-6_26

classic AI, exploring algorithms, and computer vision techniques. A few years ago, some of these approaches changed for employing machine learning in different components of robot parts, for reaching end-to-end machine learning for robotics. Nowadays, the community is pushing for introducing in almost every part of a robot a component based on Large Language Models (LLM) [7]. Thus, this paper goes through the use of LLMs in a service robot as a part of a traversal project that runs in the Master's Degree of Robotics and AI at the University of León and involves different courses in parallel for two semesters.

1.1 Contribution

This paper provides a comprehensive overview of key AI artifacts utilized in Robotics and AI master's degree programs, emphasizing the substitution of traditional methodologies with LLMs. This exploration aims to shed light on the evolving landscape of educational tools within these programs and the transformative impact brought about by integrating LLMs.

On the technical front, our contributions are twofold. Firstly, it introduced the llama_ros tool[1], a dedicated solution designed to encapsulate the state-of-the-art functionalities of llama.cpp which is publicly available on GitHub[2]. This package serves as a tool for advancing the capabilities and accessibility of the llama.cpp framework in ROS 2 [20] context. Secondly, we present a practical example, showcasing the integration of this package in a project that unifies multiple courses into a cohesive multi-subject proposal. This practical application demonstrates the versatility and practicality of the llama_ros package in real-world, interdisciplinary scenarios.

2 State of the Art

During the last two years, different researchers have been working on using advanced AI-based tools, such as ChatGPT [1], to students, emphasizing their availability for generating original written content to aid academic assessments. The surge in the adoption of LLMs is particularly exemplified by the popularity of OpenAI's ChatGPT [21].

For instance, [3] presents the existing gap in studies examining students' use of LLMs as learning tools leading to the primary objective of the paper: conducting an in-depth case study on the application of ChatGPT in engineering higher education. The objectives encompass investigating whether engineering students can produce high-quality university essays with LLM assistance, evaluating the effectiveness of current LLM identification systems in detecting such essays, and exploring students' perceptions of the usefulness and acceptance of LLMs in learning. In this case, the paper focuses on identifying current parts of a robot and evaluating the integration of LLMs instead of classic AI solutions.

---

[1] https://github.com/mgonzs13/llama_ros.
[2] https://github.com/ggerganov/llama.cpp.

Generative AI tools, notably exemplified by ChatGPT, have witnessed a surge in popularity and widespread utilization across diverse sectors [2]. As presented by Aruleba, ChatGPT is recognized by UNESCO as the fastest-growing app in history [24]. It played a pivotal role in introducing the Generative AI concept to the general public. With its unique features and the ability to engage in discussions on a myriad of topics, ChatGPT stands out as one of the most powerful AI applications, especially for education [8]. Serving as a chatbot capable of persuasive conversations, it is employed for various tasks such as essay writing, literature reviews, paper enhancement, and even computer code generation. Of course, its use for education is out of doubt.

Wensheng et al. work [10] presents a complete vision of all capacities such as learning assistance tools, cross-language communications, or personalized learning experiences among others. However, here it is proposed how to use as a tool for students and teachers to update the current models and state-of-the-art engines such as PDDL (Planning Domain Definition Language) [9] or Behavior Trees, thus, the new changes motivated by the Generative AI should be visited not only by students but also by teachers and their syllabus. The study presented here seeks to fit in educational contexts as in [2], emphasizing the prevalent issues of integrity and loss of knowledge.

3   Materials and Methods

The massive adoption of LLMs has had a significant impact across various subjects in any Master's Degree program devoted to Robotics and AI. In this section, it is presented the Master and the main subjects involved in this first step.

3.1   Courses

The Master's Degree in Robotics and AI is taught at the University of León, Spain. It is organized following a mixed structure of common courses and a set of subjects focused on specific itineraries, with a total duration of one academic year, divided into two semesters. The semester is the basic temporal unit and consists of 30 ECTS credits. Each ECTS credit corresponds to 25 h of student work. To obtain the degree, the student must complete (or have previous studies recognized for) a total of 60 ECTS credits.

The teachings are structured into two modules: Robotics and AI. These two modules contain the subjects presented in Tables 1 and 2. In addition to these courses, the degree has 9 ECTS options for those pupils that seek a more practical perspective and also the Final Project which has 9 ECTS.

3.2   LLMs Impact

This section performs a concise analysis of the primary subjects impacted by the integration of LLMs and its possible negative impact on students. Afterwards, the research transitions into the exploration of practical integration strategies

Table 1. Courses in AI Module

ECTS	Sem.	Course
3	1	Data Preprocessing
4.5	1	Artificial Intelligence
4.5	1	Computer Vision
4.5	1	Machine Learning
4.5	2	Programming in Distributed Data Environments
3	1	Deep Learning
3	2	Object Recognition
3	2	Machine Learning Applications (Opt)
3	2	Reinforcement Learning (Opt)
3	2	Trends in Deep Learning (Opt)

Table 2. Courses in Robotics Module

ECTS	Sem.	Course
4.5	1	Service Robotics
4.5	1	Middleware for Software Design in Robots
3	2	Human-Robot Interaction
3	2	Cognitive Robotics
3	2	Multi-Agent Systems (Opt)
3	2	Trends in Robotics I (Opt)
3	2	Trends in Robotics II (Opt)

- Artificial Intelligence: Incorporating LLMs alongside classical AI methods in an AI course can have both positive and negative effects. Relying solely on LLMs may limit the depth of understanding of traditional AI concepts such as machine learning algorithms, vision and robotics. Students might miss out on foundational knowledge in these areas.
- Computer Vision and Object Recognition: The integration of LLMs in these two courses, specifically Large Visual Models in the Computer Vision course could change the practical process for students. The ability of these models to comprehend linguistic contexts has empowered the interpretation of images and videos, leading to a deeper level of understanding and visual analysis. However, students might lose the in-depth understanding of foundational concepts such as image processing, feature extraction, object detection, and image segmentation, which are crucial for computer vision applications, as well as classy vision-specific frameworks.
- Service Robotics: The adoption of LLMs has transformed human-robot interaction. The robots' ability to understand and generate natural language has elevated the quality of communication in personalized services. Students explore how LLMs can be used to enhance the understanding of commands, questions, and responses, redefining how robots provide adaptive and user-centered services. However, LLMs may not inherently address challenges related to real-world service environments, such as dynamic and unstructured spaces, which may lead to a narrow focus on language-centric applications or hinder their ability to design and deploy fundamental algorithms.
- Cognitive Robotics: This course has undergone a significant shift with the integration of LLMs. Now, robots not only execute tasks but also understand and generate natural language more intelligently. Students explore how LLMs can be applied to improve environmental perception and the ability of robots to interact more contextually and adaptively in complex environments. Relying solely on LLMs may limit students' exploration of dedicated cognitive architectures and models, hindering a comprehensive understanding of cognitive robotics principles, such as classic Deliberative or Reactive approaches, and avoiding state-of-the-art solutions such as BTs or FSMs.

- Trends in Robotics: A course with this title has to overview LLMs. Students analyze how LLMs can forecast and model current trends, providing valuable insights for anticipating and adapting to the dynamic evolution of robotics.

As a result of these courses, we have the Fig. 1. It presents an overview of a simple robot with its Application System Structure with the cognitive functions of a robot, a single presentation of a model employed in the course and the engines applied.

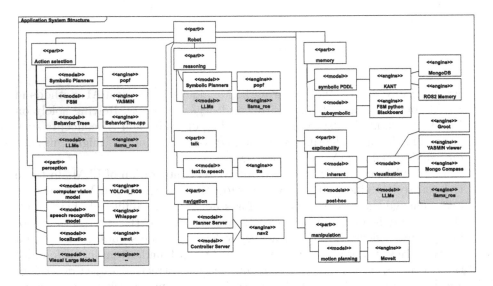

Fig. 1. Application System Structure of a robot with models and engines for a robotics course (it was simplified for the sake of visualization). This structure includes the following cognitive functions: action selection, perception, reasoning, talk, memory, explicability and manipulation.

4   Practical Case

4.1   Project Description

The project takes into account several subjects from both semesters, including Service Robotics, Middleware, and Artificial Intelligence in the first semester, and Trends in Robotics II and Trends in Machine Learning in the second.

During the second semester in the Cognitive Robotics course, Finite State Machines, such as SMACH [4] and YASMIN [15], were used for performing a simple task to provide a service robot that can move between a set of points of interest marked in an apartment. These points of interest are defined a priori in a pre-loaded file.

Behavior trees are also introduced. Deliberative systems, based on PDDL [9], are incorporated to execute tasks in a non-deterministic manner, enabling the capability to overcome issues that may arise during the typical deployment of a robot. Additionally, these systems facilitate interaction with humans with grammar and rule-based NLP is integrated to incorporate dialogue capabilities and reasoning using PDDL.

The proposal is to introduce the use of LLMs in the different components grayed in Fig. 1 where it is possible to change action selection and reasoning as is presented in [14]. Here we describe how to integrate the LLMs in the robot in the shape of a chatbot in order to provide a level of natural interaction to students, opening the door to use the robot as their tutor.

Building a ROS-based chatbot for a robot involves integrating various software components to enable effective communication and interaction. Here are the main software components typically used in a ROS-based chatbot for a robot. First, the Speech Recognition Module processes spoken language and converts it into text. Popular libraries like PocketSphinx or Google's Speech Recognition API were utilized in previous research. Second, the Natural Language Processing (NLP) Engine is essential for understanding and interpreting user input. Common NLP frameworks include Dialogflow, Rasa NLU, or Wit.ai, enabling the chatbot to comprehend and extract meaning from natural language. Third, the Text-to-Speech (TTS) Module converts textual responses generated by the chatbot into spoken words. Popular TTS engines like Google Text-to-Speech or Festival can be integrated. Fourth, the dialogue management component which orchestrates the conversation flow, manages context, user responses, and system actions. This component ensures a coherent and context-aware interaction.

Previous to the use of LLMs, a knowledge base was required to store information that the chatbot could reference during interactions. This may include data about the robot's capabilities, environmental information, or responses to frequently asked questions. At this point, the knowledge base is used for other components in our proposal and is presented as the "memory" part.

4.2 llama.cpp

llama.cpp, as outlined in the GitHub repository [11], constitutes a project dedicated to executing the LLaMA model utilizing integer quantization on hardware-constrained machines. This implementation is rooted in plain C/C++ and operates independently of external dependencies, facilitating the deployment of these models across diverse platforms, including the potential for GPU acceleration.

Engaging with llama.cpp involves a thoughtful approach to prompt engineering. Drawing inspiration from Microsoft's methodology [5], adeptly crafting prompts emerges as a critical aspect in achieving desired outcomes when working with LLM models. This endeavor demands a blend of creativity and precision, involving the careful selection of textual prompts to guide the model toward generating text pertinent to the specified objectives. These prompts are intricately linked with tokens.

Tokens, the elemental units of text or code, serve as the building blocks for language processing and generation within LLM AI. Depending on the chosen tokenization method, these units may encompass characters, words, subwords, or other text/code segments. Tokens are assigned numerical values or identifiers and organized into sequences or vectors, functioning as both inputs and outputs for the model. They represent the foundational elements that convey meaning in language to the model.

Embeddings, in this context, denote the representations or encodings of tokens, ranging from sentences to entire documents. These embeddings capture past event representations generated during the prompting interaction, existing within a high-dimensional vector space where each dimension corresponds to a learned linguistic feature. Embeddings play a central role in preserving and deciphering the meaning and interrelationships within textual data and they act as the mechanism through which the model discerns and distinguishes between various tokens or language components.

4.3   llama_ros

During this research for the right integration of llama.cpp in ROS 2 [20] projects, it is created the tool Llama_ros. The llama_ros tool, detailed in [12], encompasses a suite of ROS 2 packages designed to integrate llama.cpp [11] into the ROS 2 framework to use quantized [19] LLMs locally while operating efficiently within their hardware constraints, leveraging both CPU and GPU. This integration facilitates the utilization of ROS 2 messages for text generation with LLMs, tokenization of text, and the creation of embeddings from textual data.

To illustrate, the UML class diagram of llama_ros is depicted in Fig. 2. The primary class, the Llama, encapsulates all the functionalities of the llama.cpp independently of ROS 2. This class serves as the foundation for the LlamaNode class, a ROS 2 node that exposes ROS 2 interfaces, enabling the invocation of the llama.cpp functions from other ROS 2 nodes.

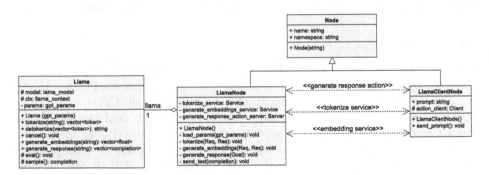

Fig. 2. UML diagram of llama_ros. The diagram includes the Llama class, which wraps llama.cpp, the LlamaNode class, which presents the ROS 2 interfaces; and the LlamaClientNode, which is a node example to use llama_ros.

This tool presents a ROS 2 action server for text generation, alongside two services dedicated to text tokenization and embedding generation. These services prove invaluable when implementing more intricate prompt engineering techniques [16,18]. For example, the embedding service facilitates the conversion of text into vectors, allowing the creation of a vector database. Subsequently, retrieval functions can be employed to search for vectors similar to a given text. This capability enhances the precision of prompt crafting by enabling the retrieval of more accurate prompts based on vector similarity.

4.4 Mini Pupper

Mini Pupper is an economical and open-source quadruped robot inspired by the Stanford Pupper model. Designed for scientific exploration, it enables the assembly of a customizable robotic platform with processing capacity for diverse applications. It has the option of adding lidar or a standard USB camera.

Examining the hardware specifications, Mini Pupper presents the following dimensions: a compact $210 \times 110 \times 165$mm frame, a weight of 509g for optimal portability, a 1000mAh rechargeable battery through micro-USB, a Raspberry Pi 4B processor for computational robustness, a 240×320 ISP LCD screen for interactive displays, a 5V 1A input charger for efficient recharging, and compatibility with Ubuntu and ROS 2, offering a versatile environment for scientific exploration and experimentation. Its unassuming design and technical specifications make it an ideal subject for some practicing course competencies.

4.5 ChatBot Application

The proposed chatbot application is an integrated system within ROS 2, comprising speech recognition for human input, LLMs for generating responses, and text-to-speech for human interaction.

For speech recognition, the chatbot leverages whisper_ros [13], based on whisper.cpp[3]. This implementation utilizes the whisper-large-v3 model [22] from OpenAI, coupled with Silero VAD [23] for voice activity detection. Conversely, llama_ros [12] serves the purpose of response generation. This allows flexibility in selecting LLMs tailored to various domains. Additionally, VITS [17] facilitates text-to-speech conversion, although alternative models can be integrated.

Finally, by integrating into ROS 2 as a distributed system, the chatbot enables the execution of LLMs, the Whisper model, and text-to-speech on dedicated machines, while audio functionalities, such as capturing and playing audio, can be managed on the robot's main computer, for instance inside the Raspberry of the Mini Pupper.

5 Discussion and Conclusions

In incorporating LLMs, in local computers thanks to llama_ros, into our Master's-level courses on AI and Robotics, we have witnessed both positive and challenging aspects. The use of LLMs in teaching has proven beneficial in

---

[3] https://github.com/ggerganov/whisper.cpp

certain domains. In the context of AI, LLMs offer students an insightful exploration into natural language understanding, generation, and their applications, providing a hands-on experience with cutting-edge language models. Additionally, the integration of LLMs in Service Robotics has showcased advancements in human-robot interaction, emphasizing the significance of natural language communication in service-oriented scenarios.

However, the exclusive reliance on LLMs does present limitations, such as the potential neglect of foundational concepts, the overemphasis on language-centric tasks, and the challenges in multi-modal integration, highlighting the need for a balanced approach. Similarly, in Cognitive Robotics, the broader spectrum of cognitive capabilities, including perception and reasoning, requires a more comprehensive approach beyond language-centric tasks. To ensure a comprehensive education in AI and Robotics, it is imperative to supplement LLMs with traditional methods, core algorithms, and practical applications that constitute the holistic landscape of these fields.

As we move forward, we recommend an integrated approach that leverages the strengths of LLMs while addressing their limitations. By combining the advancements offered by LLMs with a well-rounded curriculum encompassing traditional methods and emerging technologies, we can empower students to navigate the dynamic landscape of AI and Robotics with a thorough understanding of both the foundational principles and the latest innovations.

Acknowledgment. This work has been partially funded by an FPU fellowship provided by the Spanish Ministry of Universities (FPU21/01438) and the Grant PID2021-126592OB-C21 funded by MCIN/AEI/10.13039/501100011033 and by ERDF A way of making Europe.

References

1. Achiam, J., et al.: GPT-4 technical report. arXiv preprint: arXiv:2303.08774 (2023)
2. Aruleba, K., Sanusi, I.T., Obaido, G., Ogbuokiri, B.: Integrating ChatGPT in a computer science course: students perceptions and suggestions. arXiv preprint: arXiv:2402.01640 (2023)
3. Bernabei, M., Colabianchi, S., Falegnami, A., Costantino, F.: Students' use of large language models in engineering education: a case study on technology acceptance, perceptions, efficacy, and detection chances. Comput. Educ.: Artif. Intell. **5**, 100172 (2023). https://doi.org/10.1016/j.caeai.2023.100172
4. Bohren, J., Cousins, S.: The SMACH high-level executive. IEEE Robot. Autom. Mag. **17**(4), 18–20 (2011). https://doi.org/10.1109/MRA.2010.938836
5. Bolaños, M., Maeda, J., Buck, A.: Orchestrate your AI with Semantic Kernel. https://learn.microsoft.com/en-us/semantic-kernel/overview/
6. Brady, M.: Artificial intelligence and robotics. Artif. Intell. **26**(1), 79–121 (1985)
7. Chang, Y., et al.: A survey on evaluation of large language models. ACM Trans. Intell. Syst. Technol. **15**, 1–45 (2023)
8. Diego Olite, F.M., Morales Suárez, I.D.R., Vidal Ledo, M.J.: Chat GPT: origen, evolución, retos e impactos en la educación. Educación Médica Superior **37**(2) (2023)

9. Fox, M., Long, D.: PDDL2.1: an extension to PDDL for expressing temporal planning domains. J. Artif. Intell. Res. (JAIR) **20**, 61–124 (2003). https://doi.org/10.1613/jair.1129

10. Gan, W., Qi, Z., Wu, J., Lin, J.C.W.: Large language models in education: vision and opportunities. In: 2023 IEEE International Conference on Big Data (BigData), pp. 4776–4785. IEEE (2023)

11. Gerganov, G.: GitHub - ggerganov/llama.cpp: Port of Facebook's LLaMA model in C/C++ — github.com. https://github.com/ggerganov/llama.cpp (2023)

12. González-Santamarta, M.A.: llama_ros. https://github.com/mgonzs13/llama_ros (2023)

13. González-Santamarta, M.A.: whisper_ros. https://github.com/mgonzs13/whisper_ros (2023)

14. González-Santamarta, M.Á., Rodríguez-Lera, F.J., Guerrero-Higueras, Á.M., Matellán-Olivera, V.: Integration of large language models within cognitive architectures for autonomous robots (2023)

15. González-Santamarta, M.Á., Rodríguez-Lera, F.J., Matellán-Olivera, V., Fernández-Llamas, C.: YASMIN: yet another state machine. In: Tardioli, D., Matellán, V., Heredia, G., Silva, M.F., Marques, L. (eds.) ROBOT2022: Fifth Iberian Robotics Conference, pp. 528–539. Springer International Publishing, Cham (2023). https://doi.org/10.1007/978-3-031-21062-4_43

16. Gupta, U.: GPT-InvestAR: enhancing stock investment strategies through annual report analysis with large language models. arXiv preprint: arXiv:2309.03079 (2023)

17. Kim, J., Kong, J., Son, J.: Conditional variational autoencoder with adversarial learning for end-to-end text-to-speech (2021)

18. Li, N., Kang, B., De Bie, T.: SkillGPT: a RESTful API service for skill extraction and standardization using a large language model. arXiv preprint: arXiv:2304.11060 (2023)

19. Lin, D., Talathi, S., Annapureddy, S.: Fixed point quantization of deep convolutional networks. In: International Conference on Machine Learning, pp. 2849–2858. PMLR (2016)

20. Macenski, S., Foote, T., Gerkey, B., Lalancette, C., Woodall, W.: Robot operating system 2: design, architecture, and uses in the wild. Sci. Robot. **7**(66), eabm6074 (2022). https://doi.org/10.1126/scirobotics.abm6074

21. OpenAI: GPT-4 Technical Report. https://arxiv.org/abs/2303.08774 (2023)

22. Radford, A., Kim, J.W., Xu, T., Brockman, G., McLeavey, C., Sutskever, I.: Robust speech recognition via large-scale weak supervision (2022). https://doi.org/10.48550/ARXIV.2212.04356

23. Team, S.: Silero VAD: pre-trained enterprise-grade Voice Activity Detector (VAD), number detector and language classifier. https://github.com/snakers4/silero-vad (2021)

24. UNESCO: UNESCO: Governments must quickly regulate Generative AI in schools (2023). https://www.unesco.org/en/articles/unesco-governments-must-quickly-regulate-generative-ai-schools

Exploring the Capabilities and Limitations of Neural Methods in the Maximum Cut

Andoni I. Garmendia[✉][ID], Josu Ceberio[ID], and Alexander Mendiburu[ID]

University of the Basque Country (UPV/EHU), Donostia-San Sebastian, Spain
{andoni.irazusta,josu.ceberio,alexander.mendiburu}@ehu.eus

Abstract. The use of Neural Networks (NN) within Combinatorial Optimization (CO) marks a significant shift in the paradigm, moving towards automatically learning heuristic strategies in deterministic and local search frameworks. NNs are capable of learning relevant patterns and symmetries of various CO problems. Despite their potential, the practical application of NNs in both academic and real-world optimization problems has not yet reached the levels of traditional exact solvers or metaheuristic approaches. This study primarily focuses on the Maximum Cut problem to investigate the capabilities and limitations of NN models within the CO domain. We introduce a series of research questions aimed at examining the generalization capabilities, reliability, and computational costs associated with these models. Our findings reveal that: (1) NN models exhibit better modeling capabilities and generalizability when trained on a diverse set of instances, (2) the model's level of uncertainty can act as an indicator of its performance, and (3) employing a unified representation framework, wherein models concurrently learn from diverse tasks or instance types offers a significant training-speedup.

Keywords: Combinatorial Optimization · Deep Learning

1 Introduction

Combinatorial Optimization (CO) encompasses a vast array of problems where the objective is to find the best solution from a finite set of possibilities. These problems are ubiquitous, spanning fields such as logistics [14] and biology [17].

Historically, CO problems have primarily been addressed using *exact methods* or *heuristics* [9]. Exact methods can yield the optimal solution when allowed enough time, yet the time needed can exponentially increase as the problem-complexity grows. Alternatively, heuristics do not ensure the optimal solution but can often deliver reasonably good solutions quickly. Extending this idea, metaheuristics offer a more adaptable idea by introducing higher-level frameworks that guide the search mechanism, positioning them as versatile methods applicable across various problems.

In recent years, the emergence of deep learning and new neural network architectures has led to a novel approach to CO problems, termed Neural Combinatorial Optimization (NCO) [1,8]. This new paradigm leverages the power of

A. Alonso-Betanzos et al. (Eds.): CAEPIA 2024, LNAI 14640, pp. 264–273, 2024.
https://doi.org/10.1007/978-3-031-62799-6_27

neural networks to learn effective heuristics from data, aiming to approximate solutions for CO problems. The interest of NCO lies in its potential to learn complex patterns and exploit symmetries from CO instances.

Despite their potential, the performance of NCO methods has not yet reached the level set by traditional exact solvers, or heuristic and metaheuristic approaches in both academic research and practical applications. This is, in some part, due to the challenges that NCO methods face, such as the limited generalizability across varied problem instances, and the considerable computational resources required for the training of large neural models.

In an effort to investigate these challenges, this study uses the Maximum Cut problem [4] to assess the adaptability and generalization of NCO models when faced with changes in graph connectivity and size. We also explore the uncertainty of these models focusing on those instances where they perform poorly. Finally, we analyse how the training of these models can be accelerated using models previously trained for alternative task as initialization.

2   Background and Limitations

NCO is characterized as the application of NNs for solving CO problems in a standalone, end-to-end fashion. Nonetheless, it's important to recognize that, as recent reviews point out [2], the use of NNs in CO extends beyond this framework, incorporating works where NNs are combined with traditional techniques, such as mixed integer linear programming and genetic algorithms. In the domain of end-to-end NCO methods, we observe two primary methodologies: *Neural Constructive* (NC) and *Neural Improvement* (NI) methods.

NC methods resemble greedy heuristics by starting with an "empty" solution and incrementally adding elements based on a learned policy until the solution reaches completion. In this context, one of the first examples is the work by Vinyals *et al.* [16], which trained a pointer network model to replicate optimal solutions produced by solvers via supervised learning. Bello *et al.* [1] later improved upon this with a reinforcement learning-based model that outperformed the supervised model [16] without requiring pre-computed optimal solutions. More recently, introduction of the transformer model and its attention mechanism [15] have introduced further progress to the field [13], with studies demonstrating significant advances over previous methodologies [1,16] by leveraging attention-based models in NC applications.

NI methods, in contrast, mirror traditional local search algorithms. Starting from an initial, possibly random, solution, these methods iteratively refine this solution based on a learned policy to enhance its quality. The architectural designs used in NC methods have been adapted for NI implementations. For instance, Wu *et al.* [19] designed an attention-based model for routing problems that selects the item-pair in which apply a local operator, e.g. swap, insert or 2-opt. Expanding on this, da Costa *et al.* [5] generalized the prior work to select k-opt operators. Furthermore, Falkner *et al.* [6] introduced a method aimed at the job scheduling problem that learns to modulate the local search process across three dimensions: solution acceptance, neighborhood selection, and solution perturbation strategies.

Despite these advancements, NCO's practical applicability remains behind traditional methods like Genetic Algorithms [3] or solvers such as Gurobi [10], largely due to NCO's novelty [1,2]. Expected advancements in computational power and algorithms in the coming years should enhance NCO's capabilities. However, to realize this potential, we identify certain critical limitations of current NCO methods.

Generalization Challenges. A key limitation of NCO methods is their generalization ability, , particularly for unseen instances that differ in graph size, grade, or density from training data. NCO models are typically trained on fixed-size, randomly generated instances, which may not reflect real-world instance variations. Adapting NCO models to new instances often involves retraining. In contrast, traditional solvers are more flexible, adapting to varied problems with minimal changes.

Training and Computational Costs. The second key limitation pertains to the costs associated with training. Moreover, if online learning, also known as Active Search [11], is also used then the computational effort increases dramatically as it requires the model to be fine tuned (additional training) for each new instance to be solved. The true advantage of NCO systems lies in their ability to be trained once and then deployed multiple times during inference, thereby spreading the initial training costs over multiple uses.

Towards Robust NCO Frameworks. Considering the aspects mentioned above, and acknowledging the *No-Free-Lunch* theorem, which states that no model can excel in all scenarios, the focus is still on developing models that can effectively extract the characteristics of different instances. Such models should be able to transfer the learned heuristics to various situations, rather than overfitting on the training data.

As a preliminary work in this direction, in this paper we analyze these aspects for the Maximum Cut problem, which is described in the following section, together with the model architecture used.

3   Case Study: NCO for the Maximum Cut

3.1   Maximum Cut Problem

The Maximum Cut (MaxCut) [4] is one of the Karp's 21 NP-complete problems [12], which stands out due to its computational complexity and broad applicability in areas such as circuit design and statistical physics [4].

Given a graph G with nodes V and edges E, the objective in MaxCut involves partitioning the nodes into two disjoint subsets V_1 and V_2 such that the number of edges between these subsets is maximized. The objective function can be expressed as:

$$f(\theta) = \sum_{(u,v) \in E} \delta_{[\theta_u \neq \theta_v]} \tag{1}$$

where θ_u and θ_v are binary variables indicating the subset to which nodes u and v belong, and δ is a function which equals to 1 if $\theta_u \neq \theta_v$ and 0 otherwise.

3.2   NCO Model

This study uses a state-of-the-art NCO architecture suitable for both constructive and improvement methods. It consists of an encoder-decoder setup, with the encoder generating latent representations (*embeddings*) of the optimization process and the decoder issuing actions to generate MaxCut solutions.

For a given MaxCut instance represented by a graph G, we express the solution at the current optimization step t as θ_t, a vector of $|V|$ elements. Each element in θ_t can be in one of three states: **0** (first subset), **1** (second subset), or **2** (unassigned), allowing for a unified representation for both NC and NI methods.

The model's encoder is a Graph Neural Network (GNN) [7] that processes the problem instance G and the current solution θ_t via node- and edge-features. For MaxCut, G's edge-features are defined by an adjacency matrix $\mathbf{Y} = [y_{ij}]_{n \times n}$, where $y_{ij} = 1$ if nodes i and j are connected and 0 otherwise. Node features consist of the solution values θ_t.

The GNN processes node- and edge-features across L layers, transforming them into d-dimensional node- and edge-embeddings, $\mathbf{h}$ and $\mathbf{e}$, respectively, through a linear projection. At each layer l, node-embeddings are updated via Eq. 2. Here, $f_{\text{AGGREGATE}}$ is a permutation-invariant function that aggregates features from neighboring ($\mathcal{N}$) nodes and edges, using an attention-based function that computes a weighted average of neighbor embeddings. Additionally, f_{UPDATE} is a two-layer feed-forward network with SwiGLU activation and RMS Normalization, used in recent attention-based architectures [15].

$$h_i^{(l+1)} = h_i^{(l)} + f_{\text{UPDATE}}^{(l)} \left(h_i^{(l)}, f_{\text{AGGREGATE}}^{(l)} \left(\{ (h_j^{(l)}, e_{ij}) : j \in \mathcal{N}(i) \} \right) \right) \qquad (2)$$

The encoder's output, a set of node-embeddings from the last layer (h^L), serves as the input to the decoder. Decoders are designed as two-layer feed-forward networks with SwiGLU activation and RMS Normalization.

We define two decoder types, based on the NCO setting followed: (1) the *constructive decoder* and the *improvement decoder*. Both decoders produce action probabilities using a Softmax function over node-embeddings. The NC decoder generates probabilities for assigning unallocated nodes to one of the sets, while the NI decoder outputs the probabilities for flipping node values.

We train the NCO models using policy-based reinforcement learning [18], with different reward mechanisms for NC and NI models. The NC model receives a reward once completing a solution, based on the obtained objective value, while the NI model is rewarded at each step for any improvement in the objective value.

4   Experiments

This section presents a structured experimental investigation designed to better understand the limitations and strengths of NCO methods. The exploration is structured around four critical Research Questions (RQ), each aimed at exploring different aspects of NCO models' performance and adaptability:

- **RQ1**: How effectively can NCO models acquire representations that are generalizable to graphs with (A) different connectivity and (B) different sizes?
- **RQ2**: What is the level of confidence exhibited by NCO models in their predictions, particularly in instances where their performance is suboptimal?
- **RQ3**: What strategies can be employed to minimize the training costs associated with NCO models?
- **RQ4**: Between Neural Constructive and Neural Improvement methods, which approach holds greater potential for solving CO problems?

We have designed a set of experiments to address these questions. Note that the insights derived from these experiments are specific to the MaxCut problem and the chosen model architecture. Consequently, not all the findings may be applicable to other NCO methodologies or problems. Nonetheless, we endeavor to extract and present conclusions that hold the broadest possible relevance.

4.1   RQ1-A. Generalization to Different Graph Connectivity Levels

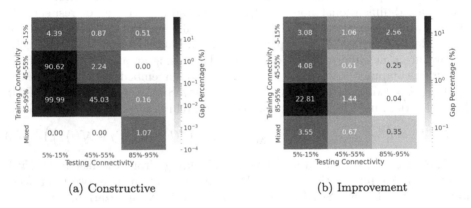

(a) Constructive   (b) Improvement

Fig. 1. Generalization performance in graphs with different connectivity: Gap % over the best testing value for (a) Constructive, and (b) Improvement models.

Our analysis divides test graphs into three categories based on connectivity to assess NCO model adaptability: **sparse graphs** (between **5%** and **15%** connectivity), **balanced graphs** (**45%–55%**) and **dense graphs** (**85%–95%**).

We deployed six models, three models with a constructive decoder and three with an improvement decoder, each trained exclusively on one of the connectivity groups. The training dataset involved 64,000 graphs, each with 100 nodes, distributed across 1,000 episodes with 64 graphs per batch. Furthermore, an additional model, referred to as the **Mixed** model, was trained using a diversified dataset comprising instances from all connectivity ranges, with a training budget identical to that of the connectivity-specific models.

We tested each model with 100 unseen graphs from all three connectivity groups. The results are represented in two heatmaps shown in Fig. 1, with the connectivity used during training (Y-axis) and testing connectivity (X-axis). The color of the cells are based on the performance gap percentage relative to the best-known value for that testing graph category.

Constructive Models. The models trained on sparse graphs exhibited the most robust performance. Notably, models trained on dense graphs demonstrated reduced transferability when tested on sparse graphs. Interestingly, models trained with the mixed dataset obtained the best overall results, performing better that those trained and tested with the same connectivities: $5 - 15\%$ and $45 - 55\%$.

Improvement Models. Improvement models had better overall transferability across different graph connectivity ranges. These models also performed more effectively when trained on sparse graphs. The mixed model obtained competitive results, comparable to those trained with the same connectivity.

4.2 RQ1-B. Generalization to Different Graph Sizes

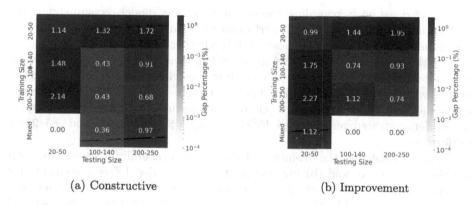

(a) Constructive   (b) Improvement

Fig. 2. Generalization performance across graphs with different size: Gap % over the best testing value for (a) Constructive models, and (b) Improvement models.

In this section, we explore the transferability with varying graph sizes, while maintaining a constant connectivity of 15%, which is a common value used in the MaxCut literature [4]. We categorize the graph instances into three size ranges: **small graphs** (ranging from **20** to **50** nodes), **medium graphs (100–140)** and **large graphs (200–250)**. As done before, we have also trained a model in a mixed dataset with instance sizes from the three groups.

Contrary to the impact of varying connectivity, models demonstrate better adaptability when trained and tested on graphs of different sizes for both constructive and improvement methods (See Fig. 2). This suggests that size variation is less challenging compared to connectivity variation. Moreover, models trained in the mixed dataset obtained the best results, suggesting that training with a varied dataset could help in obtaining better overall models.

4.3   RQ2. Confidence Level of NCO Models

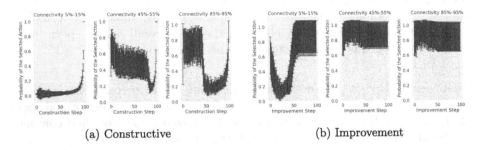

(a) Constructive   (b) Improvement

Fig. 3. Evolution of the selected actions' probability throughout the optimization process of 100 ER graphs of with 100 nodes and different connectivity.

A critical question is regarding the certainty of the model recommendations, mainly in scenarios where their performance is suboptimal. It is essential to understand the uncertainty of these models whether to rely on their decisions or not. In the experimental setup, we focus on the models that exhibited the most varied performance in the preceding evaluations, i.e., those trained on dense graphs with 85%-95% connectivity. The objective is to analyze and compare the confidence levels these models demonstrate across the three connectivity groups, which demonstrated very poor (5–15%), average (45–55%) and good (85–95%) performances.

Figure 3 illustrates the evolution of the action probabilities chosen by both (a) the constructive and (b) improvement models under different connectivity scenarios. Intriguingly, there appears to be a correlation between the model's certainty, as indicated by the action probabilities, and its performance. As Fig. 3 shows, lower probabilities are observed in instances of poor performance, while higher probabilities align with improved performance outcomes. This trend suggests that the model's confidence in its decisions is reflective of its effectiveness in those specific contexts.

4.4   RQ3. Strategies to Minimize Training Costs

A recurrent challenge in NCO is the considerable computational cost involved in training models from scratch for each new task. To address this, we investigate the feasibility and efficiency of reusing encoder weights trained for one task, such as constructing solutions, as a starting point for another task, like improving solutions.

We conduct experiments using ER graphs with 100 nodes with a connectivity probability of 15%. We consider the two decoders presented in Sect. 3 (constructive decoder and improvement decoder), plus two additional decoders: a decoder termed *Action Values*, which predicts the objective value increase when flipping the value of each individual node, and a decoder named *Fitness*, which given a solution, predicts its objective value.

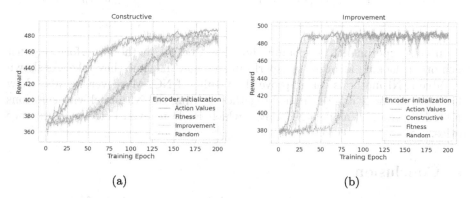

(a)   (b)

Fig. 4. Reward obtained throughout training epochs with different encoder-weights initialization for: (a) Constructive models, and (b) Improvement models.

Our analysis targets the acceleration in training constructive and improvement models through the re-utilization of encoder weights learned from other NCO tasks. Figure 4 illustrates the differences in convergence speeds using various encoder initializations.

For training the *constructive models*, using encoders pre-trained on action-value and improvement tasks demonstrated a 2.2-fold acceleration in convergence speed compared to models with randomly initialized encoders, which serves as our baseline. Intriguingly, encoders pre-trained for predicting the objective value did not exhibit any notable enhancement in training efficiency. In contrast, for training *improvement models*, all three pre-trained encoder initializations resulted in faster convergence. Encoders pre-trained on action-value prediction, constructive tasks, and solution objective value achieved a 5.4, 3.9, and 1.4 times increase in convergence speed, respectively.

These findings give insights about the transferability between distinct NCO tasks, with a notable observation that encoders trained to predict next-step action values significantly boost the training efficiency of improvement models.

4.5   RQ4. NC Vs NI

Few studies have directly compared NC and NI approaches in NCO. To our knowledge, this is the first attempt to develop a flexible framework that can be used as either an NC or an NI method.

Table 1. Performance gap relative to the best-known solution and computation times for different methods applied to the MaxCut problem. Methods were evaluated using 100 ER200 graphs, after training on ER100 graphs.

Method	Gap to Best Known (%) ↓	Time
NC	0.78	0.98 s/instance
NI (Rand. Init., 3|V| steps)	0.12	3.00 s/instance
NI (NC Init., 2|V| steps)	0.07	2.99 s/instance

In this experiment, we examine how NC and NI methods perform against each other, looking at both their performance and the time they take. As shown in Table 1, NI methods can improve the results of NC. Moreover, we also show that both methods can be applied together, feeding the NI model with solutions created by the NC model (NC Init.), which leads to even better performance ratios.

5   Conclusion

In this study, we have explored the capabilities and limitations of NCO models, using the MaxCut as the case study. We studied how these models perform across different graph structures and sizes, their confidence levels and reliability, and how the training times can be reduced. Our analysis highlights the benefit of training NCO models using a diverse set of graphs. Additionally, we have found that combining NC and NI methods appears to be a promising strategy.

Looking forward, we suggest avenues for improvement in this domain: (1) developing varied training datasets or instance generators to improve model adaptability to real-world scenarios, (2) creating uncertainty-aware frameworks that assess when retraining the model is necessary, and (3) designing a unified NC+NI framework that leverages a shared representation, potentially improving knowledge transfer between different decoders.

Acknowledgments. Andoni Irazusta Garmendia acknowledges a predoctoral grant from the Basque Government (ref. PRE_2020_1_0023). This work has been partially supported by the Research Groups 2022–2025 (IT1504-22), the Elkartek Program (KK- 2021/00065, KK-2022/00106) from the Basque Government and the PID2019-106453GA-I00 research project from the Spanish Ministry of Science.

References

1. Bello, I., Pham, H., Le, Q.V., Norouzi, M., Bengio, S.: Neural combinatorial optimization with reinforcement learning. arXiv preprint: arXiv:1611.09940 (2016)
2. Bengio, Y., Lodi, A., Prouvost, A.: Machine learning for combinatorial optimization: a methodological tour d'horizon. Eur. J. Oper. Res. **290**(2), 405–421 (2021)
3. Blum, C., Roli, A.: Metaheuristics in combinatorial optimization: overview and conceptual comparison. ACM Comput. Surv. (CSUR) **35**(3), 268–308 (2003)

4. Commander, C.W.: Maximum cut problem, MAX-cut. Encycl. Optim. **2** (2009)
5. da Costa, P., Rhuggenaath, J., Zhang, Y., Akcay, A., Kaymak, U.: Learning 2-opt heuristics for routing problems via deep reinforcement learning. SN Comput. Sci. **2**, 1–16 (2021)
6. Falkner, J.K., Thyssens, D., Bdeir, A., Schmidt-Thieme, L.: Learning to control local search for combinatorial optimization. In: Joint European Conference on Machine Learning and Knowledge Discovery in Databases, pp. 361–376 (2022)
7. Garmendia, A.I., Ceberio, J., Mendiburu, A.: Neural improvement heuristics for graph combinatorial optimization problems. IEEE Trans. Neural Netw. Learn. Syst. (2023)
8. Garmendia, A.I., Ceberio, J., Mendiburu, A.: Applicability of neural combinatorial optimization: a critical view. ACM Trans. Evol. Learn. (2024)
9. Gonzalez, T.F.: Handbook of Approximation Algorithms and Metaheuristics. CRC Press, Boca Raton (2007)
10. Gurobi Optimization, LLC: Gurobi Optimizer Reference Manual (2023). https://www.gurobi.com
11. Hottung, A., Kwon, Y.D., Tierney, K.: Efficient active search for combinatorial optimization problems. arXiv preprint: arXiv:2106.05126 (2021)
12. Karp, R.M.: Reducibility Among Combinatorial Problems. Springer, Cham (2010)
13. Kool, W., Van Hoof, H., Welling, M.: Attention, learn to solve routing problems! arXiv preprint: arXiv:1803.08475 (2018)
14. Li-Yong, Y., Bing-Yao, J.: Application and research of PBIL algorithm on combinatorial optimization. In: 2010 International Conference on Artificial Intelligence and Computational Intelligence, vol. 2, pp. 562–565. IEEE (2010)
15. Vaswani, A., et al.: Attention is all you need. In: Advances in Neural Information Processing Systems **30** (2017)
16. Vinyals, O., Fortunato, M., Jaitly, N.: Pointer networks. In: Advances in Neural Information Processing Systems **28** (2015)
17. Vrček, L., Bresson, X., Laurent, T., Schmitz, M., Šikić, M.: Learning to untangle genome assembly with graph convolutional networks. arXiv preprint: arXiv:2206.00668 (2022)
18. Williams, R.J.: Simple statistical gradient-following algorithms for connectionist reinforcement learning. Mach. Learn. **8**(3), 229–256 (1992)
19. Wu, Y., Song, W., Cao, Z., Zhang, J., Lim, A.: Learning improvement heuristics for solving routing problems. IEEE Trans. Neural Netw. Learn. Syst. **33**, 5057–5069 (2021)

Author Index

A. Alonso-Betanzos et al. (Eds.): CAEPIA 2024, LNAI 14640, pp. 275–276, 2024.
https://doi.org/10.1007/978-3-031-62799-6

Printed in the United States
by Baker & Taylor Publisher Services